Stories OF Faith
AND Courage from
WORLD WAR II

Battlefields
B L E S S I N G S

Stories OF **Faith**
AND **Courage from**

WORLD WAR II

Battlefields
BLESSINGS

LARKIN SPIVEY

GOD & COUNTRY
PRESS

ISBN 10: 0–89957–040-2
ISBN 13: 978-0-89957040-2
First printing—April 2009
Cover designed by Meyers Design, Houston, Texas
Interior design and typesetting by Reider Publishing Services, West Hollywood,
    California
Edited and Proofread by Jocelyn Green, Dan Penwell, Rick Steele, and Rich Cairnes

Maps by Bowring Cartographic, 258 North Park Dr., Arlington, VA 22203.
www.sitemaps.com

Printed in the United States of America
17 16 15 14 13 12 –W– 9 8 7 6 5 4 3

Dedication

This book is dedicated to the memory of James Arthur Norton Jr. and Edward R. Norton. These young men were pioneers of aviation in my hometown of Conway, South Carolina, and served together in the Army Air Corps during World War II. They were killed in action on May 17, 1943, flying together in a B-26 bomber over Nazi-held Holland. The Norton twins were my mother's younger brothers and my uncles. I was three years old at the time of their death. Their adventurous and heroic lives were legendary in my family, inspiring my brothers to become Air Force pilots and me to pursue a Marine Corps career.

The righteous perish, and no one ponders it in his heart; devout men are taken away, and no one understands that the righteous are taken away to be spared from evil. ~Isaiah 57:1

Contents

List of Maps   viii

Acknowledgments   ix

Introduction   xi

JANUARY—Blitzkrieg in Europe   3

FEBRUARY—Turning the Tide in the Pacific   41

MARCH—Battle of the Atlantic   75

APRIL—War in the Desert   111

MAY—Advance in the Western Pacific   147

JUNE—The Fight for Sicily and Italy   185

JULY—The Air War   221

AUGUST—War on the Homefront   257

SEPTEMBER—The Central Pacific Campaign   293

OCTOBER—The Invasion of France   329

NOVEMBER—Victory in Europe   367

DECEMBER—Victory in the Pacific   403

Bibliography   439

Notes   442

About the Author   460
Topical Index   461

List of Maps

1. German Invasion of the Low Countries and France   2
   May 1940

2. Japanese Expansion in the Pacific July 1942   40

3. The Battle of Midway June 4, 1942   62

4. Operations in North Africa 1942–1943   110

5. Advance in the Western Pacific 1942–1944   146

6. The Fight for Sicily and Italy 1943–1944   184

7. Across the Pacific 1943–1945   292

8. Allied Landings on D-Day June 6, 1944   328

9. Allied Advances in Europe 1944–1945   366

10. Iwo Jima 1945   402

11. Okinawa 1945   402

Acknowledgments

I AM GRATEFUL to Jocelyn Green for her many contributions to this book. Jocelyn is a respected freelance writer, editor, and author of *Faith Deployed: Daily Encouragement for Military Wives.* In addition to her thoroughly professional editing work, she has written a number of daily devotionals in this book herself, each designated on the last line with her initials: (JG).

I wish to express gratitude to my agent, David Sanford, for his encouragement and for creating the opportunity for me to write this book. I am also thankful to Dan Penwell of AMG Publishers for the genius behind the *Battlefields & Blessings* series and for his confidence in me to be a part of it.

I especially acknowledge the great contribution of Catherine-Alexa Rountree, who has been a faithful research assistant throughout this project and is responsible for much of the material from which its stories are derived. In addition to her many amazing qualities, she is also my loving daughter.

I thank the members of the clergy who have provided their expertise and guidance: the Reverends Robert Sturdy, Aubrey Floyd, and Carol Dickerson.

I appreciate the wisdom and advice given daily by my wife, Lani. Her insights have added immeasurably to the spiritual content of this book. She has been my loving partner in this project, as in every other aspect of our marriage.

Finally, I acknowledge my Lord and Savior, Jesus Christ, whom I came to know late in my life, and who changed my life eternally. My career as a writer and speaker has had one goal: to glorify him. While writing this book I have prayed constantly for his guidance and inspiration. Although I can't positively assert that he has always provided these things, I can assure the reader that I could never have completed three hundred and sixty-five daily devotionals on my own.

Introduction

WRITING THIS BOOK has been a privilege and a blessing. I have deep family roots in World War II and have always revered the "Greatest Generation" who endured and won that great conflict. I grew up building models of ships and airplanes from that era and listening to my own father tell of convoy duty in the Battle of the Atlantic.

My previous books have been about God's providential hand in America's past, when the nation's survival was at stake. World War II was clearly one of those times. Victory may seem inevitable now, in retrospect, but history reveals dark days for America and her allies, especially during the early years of that war, when the forces of Germany and Japan were advancing triumphantly around the globe. With obsolete equipment and meager numbers, British and U.S. military forces needed many miracles to survive and slowly turn the tide of the war. God did indeed bless these nations during their darkest hours.

I want to assure the reader that I am not suggesting that God causes or even looks favorably on war. I emphasize my belief that this in not the case. Human nature seems to be the completely adequate explanation for conflict between individuals and nations. I believe that God is disappointed when wars occur and does not take sides in such conflicts. I do believe, however, that God has an agenda and can use any human event or condition to further it. I believe that one of his important agendas for mankind has been human freedom, and that this was the basis for his favor of the American and Allied cause during World War II.

As a Christian and one who has fought in war, I condemn it. However, as a wise man said, *"They are dead who have seen the end of war."* I have to believe that there are things worth fighting for, and that there are times when God blesses those who do. I admit that my attitudes are colored by my own career in military service. One of my reference works as a young officer made the following statement that I believe is true today:

> *One may abhor war fully, despise militarism absolutely, deplore all the impulses in human nature which make armed force necessary, and still*

agree that for the world as we know it, the main hope is that "peace loving nations can be made obviously capable of defeating nations which are willing to wage aggressive war."[1]

These words come not from a warrior, but from the great intellectual and pacifist Bertrand Russell.

This book is a daily devotional based on inspirational stories from World War II. Some of these stories reflect God's miraculous intervention in the larger course of the war, but most deal with the faith and courage of individual soldiers, sailors, and citizens. These stories may reflect to some extent a universal tendency to turn to God in perilous times, however, I believe they more consistently reveal a widespread spirituality among the American and British populace and the leaders of that era. We can only pray that our nation continues to seek God's favor and to fulfill God's purpose now and in the future.

As a daily devotional, this book is centered on the stories contained in the readings for each day of the year. There is also information intended to provide the historical context of these stories and to inform the reader about the course of the war at important stages. Each month presents a separate campaign of the war with an historical overview at the beginning of that month. Daily devotionals during the month pertain to that campaign. My selection of this material reflects my own understanding and interests. This book is not a complete history, and many important events could not be included.

The most inspiring image of World War II.
Raising the Flag on Mount Suribachi, Iwo Jima (see pages 403–404)
(National Archives, Joe Rosenthal, Associated Press)

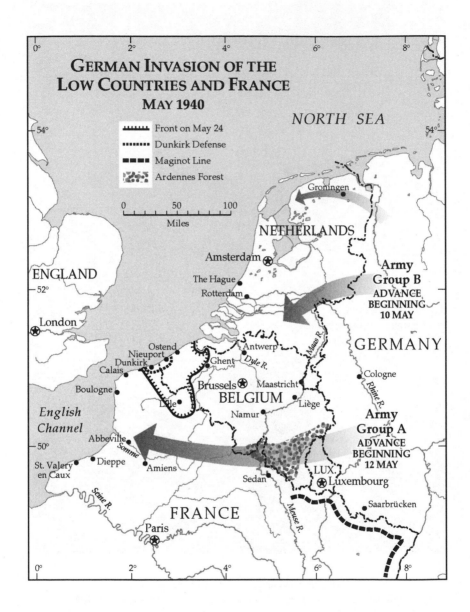

GERMAN INVASION OF THE
LOW COUNTRIES AND FRANCE
MAY 1940

NORTH SEA

Front on May 24
Dunkirk Defense
Maginot Line
Ardennes Forest

0   50   100
Miles

NETHERLANDS

Amsterdam

ENGLAND

The Hague
Rotterdam

Army
Group B
ADVANCE
BEGINNING
10 MAY

London

GERMANY

Antwerp
Ostend
Nieuport
Dunkirk
Calais
Ghent
Dyle R.
Maas R.

Cologne

Boulogne
Brussels
Maastricht
Lille
BELGIUM
Liège
Rhine R.

English
Channel
Namur

Army
Group A
ADVANCE
BEGINNING
12 MAY

Abbeville
Somme
St. Valery
en Caux
Dieppe
Amiens
Sedan
LUX.
Luxembourg

Saarbrücken

Seine R.

FRANCE
Meuse R.

Paris

JANUARY
Blitzkrieg in Europe

IN EARLY MAY 1940 almost two million French and English soldiers waited anxiously for the long-expected invasion of France. Allied strategists were convinced the German attack would come through Holland and Belgium in a sweeping movement similar to the opening of World War I. These expectations were fulfilled on May 10 when massive German forces poured across the Dutch border. French and British units advanced immediately northward to the Dyle River where the opposing forces met in the opening clashes of the war.

Unknown to the Allies, however, the German main attack came as Army Group A, under Gen. Col. Gerd von Rundstedt, penetrated the supposedly impenetrable Ardennes Forest, crossed the River Meuse on May 12–13, and broke into open country. This force of more than eighteen hundred panzer tanks and three hundred Stuka dive-bombers knifed through the French 2nd and 9th Armies, reaching the English Channel on May 19. This bewildering success left large French units and the entire British Expeditionary Force cut off and surrounded, with their backs to the sea. This vast pocket centered more or less on the little port town of Dunkirk.

As the German advance from north and south rapidly reduced the size of the Allied pocket, Lt. Gen. Allan Brooke, commander of the British II Corps, succinctly summed up the situation on May 23: *"Nothing but a miracle can save the BEF."*[2] On May 24 the first installment on that miracle came. Hitler ordered his panzer divisions to halt in place and to regroup. His generals persuaded him that the tanks were needed elsewhere and that the Luftwaffe and infantry units could finish the job of annihilating the remaining Allied forces in the pocket.

To meet this crisis Great Britain mustered every seagoing vessel that could reach Dunkirk, assembling an armada of ships, ferries, tenders, yachts, and small boats to rescue its army. Between May 26 and June 4, more than three hundred thirty-eight thousand British and French troops were rescued despite bitter opposition from German aircraft, artillery, infantry, and patrol boats. Even though this was in effect a "retreat" from France, spirits soared in England at the sight of these returning troops.

The new prime minister, Winston Churchill, called the dramatic rescue a *"miracle of deliverance."*[3] On June 22 France fell to the advancing German forces, but, with a large portion of her army on home soil, Great Britain survived to fight on.

The fight did continue, but the scene shifted to a new battlefield: the airspace over England. By now Britain stood alone, and only the Royal Air Force (RAF) stood between Germany and complete domination of the continent. The Battle of Britain began in late June 1940. Aerial combat was unremitting as German bombers raided British airfields day after day, with the Spitfires and Hurricanes of the RAF rising to meet them.

Encountering unexpected resistance and losses, the Germans changed strategy in early September. Turning away from Fighter Command bases, they focused instead on England's cities. These attacks became known as the 'Blitz,' and would continue for much of the war. Although many cities were devastated, these attacks did not help the Luftwaffe achieve air superiority. The RAF fought on, with increasing effectiveness. On September 15, two massive raids were turned back and fifty-six German aircraft shot down during the Luftwaffe's worst day. Two days later, Hitler canceled plans for the invasion of Great Britain.

New Year's Day

MYRON MAYCOCK was a British soldier who spent much of World War II as a prisoner of war. During his many trials he was comforted by a short poem:

New Year's Day

I see not a step before me
As I tread on another year,
But I've left the past in God's keeping
The future his mercy shall clear,
And what looks dark in the distance
May brighten as I draw near.[4]

"*Through the difficult days of captivity this verse was constantly before me, suggesting, as it did, a brighter path in the distance, to which the course of time—with faith—must ultimately lead me,*" Maycock said. "*The full beauty of these words came to me at the close of my last hour of freedom.*"[5]

This poem is appropriate for any day, but is especially perfect for this day. This is the time to look forward and not back. The past cannot be changed no matter how hard we try and is truly in God's hands. Neither do we know what lies ahead, and it is just as useless to worry about that. Jesus' instruction on this point is crystal clear: "*Do not worry about tomorrow, for tomorrow will worry about itself.*"[6] What we can do is concentrate on our actions in the present and look forward to the future with a joyful hope. Even though we have problems looming ahead, we don't have to face them alone. Our Savior walks with us and guarantees us the strength to endure and to overcome. There is no darkness that will stand against the light of his presence.

> This is the message we have heard from him and declare to you: God is light; in him there is no darkness at all . . . if we walk in the light, as he is in the light, we have fellowship with one another, and the blood of Jesus, his Son, purifies us from all sin. ~1 John 1:5–7

5

Into Darkness

CHRISTMAS 1939 came in the dark winter of fear for much of the world. Britain and France had declared war on Germany after Germany's invasion of Poland. An eerie calm settled over Europe as armed conflict drew inexorably closer. To provide a word of encouragement to his subjects, King George VI made a radio broadcast heard by millions. Not usually an eloquent speaker, his words on that day resound for all time:

King George VI. (Franklin D. Roosevelt Presidential Library)

I believe from my heart that the cause which binds together my peoples and our gallant and faithful allies is the cause of Christian civilization. On no other basis can a true civilization be built.

Let us remember this through the dark times ahead of us and when we are making the peace for which all men pray.

. . . I feel that we may all find a message of encouragement in the lines which, in my closing words, I would to say to you: "I said to the man who stood at the Gate of the Year, 'Give me a light that I may tread safely into the unknown.' And he replied, 'Go out into the darkness, and put your hand into the Hand of God. That shall be to you better than light, and safer than a known way.'"

May the Almighty Hand guide and uphold us all.[7]

What more can any leader do in a time of crisis than to show his own belief in the source of ultimate safety in this world? By articulating this faith to your soldiers, your employees, or your own children you give them a source of strength and comfort that can be found nowhere else. However dark the situation God's hand is always our light.

For you were once in darkness, but now you are light in the Lord. Live as children of light (for the fruit of the light consists in all goodness, righteousness and truth) and find out what pleases the Lord . . . Everything exposed by the light becomes visible, for it is light that makes everything visible. ~Ephesians 5:8–10, 13–14

Tears and Sweat

ON THE DAY GERMANY invaded Holland, Neville Chamberlain realized he could not continue as prime minister of Great Britain. At 5:00 p.m. on that day he went to Buckingham Palace, tendered his resignation, and advised the king to send for Winston Churchill. An hour later, Churchill was prime minister.

At that moment the new leader was a controversial figure. Many doubted his ability to hold together a coalition government and to lead the nation in a time of such crisis. He clearly came into office in the most perilous circumstances ever faced by a new prime minister. Riding back to his office after his appointment, he commented: *"I hope it is not too late. I am very much afraid it is."*[8]

His first speech as prime minister was delivered to the House of Commons on May 13, 1940. Though he was received coolly at first, his words carried great weight:

> *I would say to the House, as I said to those who have joined this Government, I have **nothing to offer but blood, toil, tears and sweat**. We have before us an ordeal of the most grievous kind. We have before us many long months of toil and struggle.*
>
> *You ask what is our policy. I will say, it is to wage war with all our might, with all the strength that God can give us, to wage war against a monstrous tyranny never surpassed in the dark, lamentable catalogue of human crime.*
>
> *You ask what is our aim? I can answer in one word: Victory. Victory at all cost. Victory in spite of all terror. Victory however long and hard the road may be. For without victory there is no survival.*[9]

Winston Churchill began to build his authority through his words. He didn't sound like a politician. In a time of great uncertainty he did not consult opinion polls or use vague language. Jesus Christ demonstrated who he was in many ways, but his authority was evident from the beginning of his ministry by the nature of his amazing words. When the crowds heard his Sermon on the Mount, they knew that he was no ordinary teacher.

When Jesus had finished saying these things, the crowds were amazed at his teaching, because he taught as one who had authority, and not as their teachers of the law. ~Matthew 7:28–29

Men of Valor

WINSTON CHURCHILL'S first radio broadcast as prime minister came on May 19, 1940, the day the German advance in France reached the English Channel. The military situation in Europe was deteriorating rapidly. Fear and uncertainty were growing at home. Churchill spoke to the British people and adapted a quotation from 1 Maccabees 3:58–60, a book of the Protestant Apocrypha.

Winston Churchill making a radio broadcast.
(Franklin D. Roosevelt Presidential Library)

*Today is Trinity Sunday. Centuries ago words were written to be a call and a spur to the faithful servants of Truth and Justice: "Arm yourselves, and be ye **men of valour**, and be in readiness for the conflict; for it is better for us to perish in battle than to look upon the outrage of our nation and our altar. As the will of God is in Heaven, even so let it be."[10]*

With a biblical reference Churchill called his people to be courageous in the face of great danger. Throughout the Bible we find examples of men and women who faced danger and found their ultimate source of courage in God. Peter and John were arrested and brought before the Sanhedrin for openly proclaiming the message of Jesus Christ. They refused to recant their public witness and told their accusers, "It is by the name of Jesus Christ of Nazareth, whom you crucified but whom God raised from the dead, that this man stands before you healed" (Acts 4:10).

When they saw the courage of Peter and John and realized that they were unschooled, ordinary men, they were astonished and they took note that these men had been with Jesus . . . Then they called them in again and commanded them not to speak or teach at all in the name of Jesus. But Peter and John replied, "Judge for yourselves whether it is right in God's sight to obey you rather than God." ~Acts 4:13, 18–19

Unit Integrity

AS BRITISH AND FRENCH troops began pouring onto the beaches and areas surrounding Dunkirk, some units were amazing examples of good order and discipline. The Queen's Own Worcestershire Yeomanry marched smartly into the perimeter singing "Tipperary" to the accompaniment of a mouth organ.[11] The commander of the 8th King's Own Royal Regiment reminded his men that they wore the badge of one of the oldest regiments of the line and that it was up to them to set an example for the rest. They marched to the beach with arms swinging in unison and weapons slung properly, in perfect formation.[12] The 2nd Grenadier Guards marched in as if changing the guard at Buckingham Palace, erect, clean-shaven, and boots echoing on the cobblestone streets.[13] The 1st Queen's Own Cameron Highlanders wore their kilts.[14]

It is easy to see the benefits of belonging to a strong, closely knit military unit. Each member can depend on the other and draw strength from those around him. For Christians, unit integrity is found in the body of Christ, his church. There we find the support that we so urgently need to persevere in our beliefs and actions. We have safety in numbers and strength to do his work, as we are called by the old hymn, "Onward Christian Soldiers":

> *Like a mighty army moves the church of God;*
> *Brothers we are treading where the saints have trod.*
> *We are not divided, all one body we,*
> *One in hope and doctrine, one in charity.*

Our churches may not be perfect, but they are functioning the way Christ intended when we support and complement each other and move as one body toward the ultimate goal: reflecting the glory of God.

The body is a unit, though it is made up of many parts; and though all its parts are many, they form one body. So it is with Christ . . . God has arranged the parts in the body, every one of them, just as he wanted them to be . . . Now you are the body of Christ, and each one of you is a part of it. ~1 Corinthians 12:12, 18, 27

Close-Order Drill

MANY UNITS DID NOT arrive intact on the beaches at Dunkirk. Countless men were separated from their units during days and nights of rear-guard fighting. Many units seemed to dissolve as they were drawn piecemeal out of the front lines, usually under cover of darkness, with vague instructions to move toward the beaches. Crowds of disorganized troops began to appear on the beaches, adding to the growing confusion.

At one point an old Irish Guards captain, Tom Gimson, restored order in his area by commanding all present to *"Fall In!"* Amazingly, all within earshot complied with the familiar and age-old command known to every military man and woman. Everyone lined up as on parade. The captain then exercised them in close order drill. The familiar orders seemed to instill a calm confidence in the men. Order was restored and the embarkation was able to continue.[15]

The men on the Dunkirk beaches recognized a voice of authority. They responded accordingly to the benefit of all. Our challenge is to recognize God's voice, our ultimate authority. For his own reasons he seldom commands us directly or issues orders in an overt manner. He expects us to seek him and to make the effort to discern his guidance. In answer to our prayers, he speaks quietly. He works subtly through our conscience and through our Christian friends. Most often we hear him in Scripture. When we have a measure of familiarity with the Bible, we will hear God's calming voice whenever we need it, even in times of strife.

> Even though I walk through the valley of the shadow of death,
> I will fear no evil, for you are with me;
> Your rod and your staff, they comfort me. ~Psalm 23:4

Surf Conditions

CONTEMPORARY OBSERVERS were amazed at the fortuitous turns of the weather during the Dunkirk evacuation. Surf conditions were critical to the boarding and movement of small craft along the beaches. Offshore winds kept the waters amazingly calm for all but one day, a very unusual occurrence in the English Channel. On the day after the evacuation, the wind shifted to the north and great breakers came rolling in along the Dunkirk coast.[16] One noted weather expert commented, *"By a twist of fate, or better yet a meander of the jet stream . . . the one set of conditions that most favored the Allied evacuation persisted for days."*[17]

Most of us read about biblical miracles and don't question God's ability to perform such great acts. Still, I have heard Christians wonder why God did these amazing things only in the ancient past. It is my belief that there are many examples of his miraculous intervention in much more modern times. In the details of our wars we can see evidence of God's providential hand moving to change the odds in crucial situations. Dunkirk was clearly a very critical episode to the survival of the Allied cause. The "Miracle of Dunkirk" was real and much more than a catchy phrase.

Great is the LORD and most worthy of praise; his greatness no one can fathom.
One generation will commend your works to another; they will tell of your mighty acts.
They will speak of the glorious splendor of your majesty,
And I will meditate on your wonderful works. ~Psalm 145:3–5

Cloud Cover

THE LUFTWAFFE STAGED numerous devastating raids on the port, beaches, and areas around Dunkirk. However, their effectiveness was mercifully limited by frequent low clouds, rain, fog, and smoke. Even though the sun shone brightly at the Luftwaffe bases, flying conditions were impossible over Dunkirk on May 28 and 30, and for parts of May 27, 29, and 31.

Henry Bond was an engineer with the 700th Construction Company. His unit reached the outskirts of Dunkirk on May 27, and for two days they waited anxiously for instructions to embark, all the while under frequent artillery and air attack. When the call finally came, no vehicles were available, so the move had to be on foot, the slow and dangerous way. Bond wrote:

> *Rain commenced falling heavily and in answer to our fervent prayers it increased and continued for the whole of our 4 mile trek along the wide promenade of Malo-les-Bains to the jetty at Dunkerque. Thanks to the providential rain and I feel that only, we were spared a bombing and machine gun attack along the prom where there was little or no cover.*[18]

In addition to the beneficial changes in surf conditions, the "providential" rain over Dunkirk was an equally amazing manifestation of God's miraculous intervention. During biblical times there were many examples of God bringing changes in the weather. On the catastrophic level he brought the Flood, ultimately to give mankind a new beginning. On another occasion, he brought drought to Israel under the misguided reign of Ahab. He has often intervened in history, just as he does in our lives, to fulfill his own plans for mankind and for us individually.

I am going to bring floodwaters on the earth to destroy all life under the heavens. ~Genesis 6:17

Now Elijah . . . said to Ahab, "As the LORD, the God of Israel, lives, whom I serve, there will be neither dew nor rain in the next few years except at my word." ~1 Kings 17:1

Captured British soldiers at Dunkirk.
(National Archives)

Soldiers wait to be evacuated.
(Imperial War Museum, HU 1135,
Collection of Major H. E. N. Bredin)

Troops lined up on the Dunkirk beaches.
(Imperial War Museum, NYP 68075)

To Volunteer

NINETEEN-YEAR-OLD Bill Towey was a medic with the 11th Casualty Clearing Station whose unit treated casualties throughout the campaign in Belgium and during the long retreat toward Dunkirk. Early on May 31 his commander announced that the time had come to pull back to the beaches. However, five volunteers were needed to stay behind with the wounded. The command was given, *"Volunteers, one step forward, march!"* More than half the unit responded. The process was repeated until, on the third try, Bill Towey found himself standing with four other men. They remained to care for the wounded until the end.[19] Their thoughts are not recorded as they watched their comrades depart for the beaches and safety.

Every modern recruit hears the age-old barracks advice, *"Don't volunteer for anything!"* I have heard great Marines and selfless leaders repeat this advice. In military service you face inevitable risks. Why expose yourself to ones you can avoid? Everyone understands this logic and even pays lip service to it. However, in times of need, I have seen many unlikely men step forward in response to the call. God has given each of us gifts, and he expects us to put them to good use. However, he seldom commands. He waits patiently for us to volunteer. We each have to carefully discern our own call to action and take our own "step forward."

Then I heard the voice of the Lord saying, "Whom shall I send? And who will go for us?" And I said, "Here am I. Send me!" ~Isaiah 6:8

Unexpected Inspiration

ON JUNE 1, Bill Towey was still caring for his wounded comrades. He was now with the last British forces defending the shrinking beachhead at Dunkirk. To honor fallen comrades, an officer in his unit held a hurried and informal funeral service for a score of soldiers laid out in rows in the darkness of the night. With no hope of conducting a proper Christian service, the officer gave his best effort, reading by flashlight. He chose a reassuring passage from Revelation:

> *And God shall wipe away all tears from their eyes; and there shall be no more death, neither sorrow, nor crying, neither shall there be any more pain: for the former things are passed away.* ~Revelation 21:4 (KJV)

At this point in the long and harrowing campaign, these men had begun to feel as if hope was gone. Weeks of pain, sorrow, and death had begun to eat into their souls. John's vision of a New Jerusalem brought hope and a spiritual uplift to those gathered in the darkness. In Towey's words: *"It would be difficult to convey the great impact of those words, in those special circumstances, made upon a very impressionable and religious 19 year old lad, but the scene has remained indelibly impressed on my memory in the 63 years and more since it happened and, no doubt, will continue to do so until my dying day."*[20]

God doesn't promise to shield us from trouble. He does promise that he will be with us through every trial. There is always comfort and hope to be found in his Word, *no matter* how dire our crisis might be.

Luck of the Draw

AFTER THE 2:00 a.m. funeral service, Bill Towey waited through another long, dark night of uncertainty. He and his comrades continued to seek out the wounded and to get them to their makeshift aid station. Just before first light on June 1, an officer called the remaining medics together and told them that the Germans were just down the road and would soon overrun their position. He didn't want them all to be killed or captured, but, again, they couldn't abandon the wounded. To make a terrible decision, he put twenty pieces of paper in his hat. Eight had numbers, representing those who would stay behind. The men drew their lots. Towey drew a blank lot and was immediately dispatched with the others to the beach. He made it off the beach with the last of the survivors.[21]

I believe that God blessed this officer's attempt to be fair to all his men under the extreme conditions of the Dunkirk beaches. There are even biblical examples of the Israelites resorting to the casting of lots for certain decisions. In normal circumstances, however, God would not be pleased if we made our decisions by drawing lots or flipping coins. He expects us to go to great lengths to discern his will, including prayer, Bible study, and consultation with other Christians. We need to incorporate this thoughtful approach into our decision making and make every effort to hear God's voice and his guidance for choices that we have to make.

> The lot is cast into the lap, but its every decision is from the LORD. ~Proverbs 16:33

Leave It Behind

ONLY THE MEN could be rescued at Dunkirk. Everything else had to be abandoned and, to the extent possible, destroyed. Thousands of vehicles were drained of oil and left running until the engines seized. Mountains of uniforms, blankets, and equipment of every description went up in flames in the fields around the beaches. The voluminous smoke actually was a blessing as it helped screen activity on the beaches from air attack. One officer was observed trying to board the *Brighton Belle,* an old paddle steamer, with his golf clubs. A bearded sailor remedied this situation by dispatching the clubs into the surf. Arthur May suffered with the destruction of his battery's howitzers. He was with the 3rd Medium Regiment, the same unit his father served with during World War I. As bad as times were then the 3rd never had to destroy its own guns. May's conscience plagued him that he had *"let the old man down."*[22]

If the port facilities at Dunkirk had permitted evacuation of equipment perhaps the decision would have been different. We will never know. As it was, only the men could be saved. In a well-known Bible story, Jesus once healed a sick man at the expense of a herd of pigs. The townspeople were incensed over the loss of their property, ignoring the value of a human life. If we think about it, we have a choice in our lives that is even starker. We often have to choose between our spiritual condition and our possessions. Jesus clearly taught us where to put our priorities. If anything gets in the way of our relationship to God, we need to "leave it behind."

But store up for yourselves treasures in heaven, where moth and rust do not destroy, and where thieves do not break in and steal. For where your treasure is, there your heart will be also. ~Matthew 6:20–21

One More Kick

PILOT OFFICER G. W. SPIERS was flying patrol over Dunkirk in a twin engine Blenheim IV light bomber when his aircraft was attacked and fatally damaged by a formation of German Messerschmitt 109 fighters. He knew he had to ditch the aircraft and struggled to keep it level as the water came up to meet him. After a violent impact, water rushed into the cockpit as a dam bursting. Spiers tried to get to the escape hatch over his head but his feet were slipping and he could make no progress toward it. He found himself underwater. *"I had never prayed to God with such agony or earnestness . . . as I realized that I would not escape,"* Spiers said. *"I tried to suck water into my lungs to hasten the end, but I was unsuccessful and only swallowed it. My lungs were bursting and my pulse pounded in my eardrums, brilliant flashes and yellow spots appeared in front of my eyes."*

Starting to drift downward, Spiers somehow found the reserve to give one more kick with his right leg: *"I had sufficient consciousness to realize my right leg was straight and not in contact with what I thought was the floor of the aircraft. Thinking this may be a way out, I drew my left leg up to it and paddled my way down . . . after I had descended several feet I slowly backed away and then swam to the surface."*[23]

A friendly trawler picked up the brave airman and delivered him back to safety in England where he was hospitalized for a broken ankle and other injuries.

Fortunately, few of us are taken to the absolute limit of either our endurance or our patience. However, we all experience situations where "one more kick" might make the difference between success and failure. We sometimes call it "going the extra mile," often so important in business and sports. We sometimes forget that such effort is also needed many times with friends and family. Meeting someone more than halfway can save a relationship. God is always there to provide that extra reserve when we need it and call on him for it.

When my spirit grows faint within me, it is you who know my way. ~Psalm 142:3

Nerve Tonic

ARTHUR DAVEY was an ambulance driver in the evacuation to Dunkirk. Air raids interrupted several attempts to bring his convoy to the port, and he endured two days of anxious waiting outside the town, as the bombs seemed to fall ever closer. Finally, late in the afternoon of the second day, an officer came with instructions to move to the port, one ambulance at a time, in three-minute intervals. The officer promised that this time, there would be air cover for the embarkation. Davey described what happened next:

> When we reached the quay, and drove onto the huge concrete jetty, now holed with craters, and jagged at the sides, where bombs had torn away sections of the concrete, no ship was waiting. We turned off our motors, and proceeded to wait –for the ship or the bombers. After about 20 minutes, it seemed hours, had passed, about 30 planes appeared high in the sky, from seaward –we thought they were our own at first, then, when they dived, we knew that the promised air protection was merely a 'nerve tonic.'[24]

The British soldiers apparently used the term "nerve tonic" to describe lies told in tense times to calm them down. I doubt that the practice was widespread, because such a breach of honesty would destroy a regular unit over time. Soldiers have to trust their officers and vice versa. The same is true in all organizations, including our families. It's easy to make promises that we fail to follow up on later. We all are tempted to downplay the negative and to give hope for something good to come. However, false hope is good for no one. Sooner or later, reality must prevail. We can all deal with reality better than a loss of trust in a parent, friend, or employer.

Therefore each of you must put off falsehood and speak truthfully to his neighbor, for we are all members of one body. ~Ephesians 4:25

Never Surrender

THE EVACUATION of the army from Dunkirk offered hope and a brief respite for the British people. However, the Germans continued their drive through France, and the fate of Great Britain hung in the balance. Many British politicians were beginning to consider accommodations with Hitler that would allow the nation to avoid complete catastrophe. They wondered what would happen when the country stood alone against a Europe dominated by the Nazis. In this hour of fear and uncertainty, Winston Churchill addressed the nation to illuminate the difficult, but clear path ahead:

> We shall not flag or fail. We shall go on to the end. We shall fight in France, we shall fight on the seas and oceans, we shall fight with growing confidence and growing strength in the air. We shall defend our island, whatever the cost may be. We shall fight on the beaches, we shall fight on the landing-grounds, we shall fight in the fields and in the streets, we shall fight in the hills. **We shall never surrender!**[25]

Looking back we can now appreciate these bold words as heroic and inspiring—but how easy it is to forget the uncertainty prevailing at the time they were spoken. It must have been tempting for Churchill to hedge his bets. He could have alluded to the possibility of some accommodation with Hitler that would have guaranteed Britain's continued existence. He knew, however, that there was only one difficult path to long-term survival.

The apostle Paul also painted a clear picture of our spiritual path and the urgency required to successfully pursue it. He left no room for half-hearted efforts.

Do you not know that in a race all the runners run, but only one gets the prize? Run in such a way as to get the prize. Therefore, I do not run like a man running aimlessly; I do not fight like a man beating the air. ~1 Corinthians 9:24, 26

A New Spirit

FROM THE OPENING of the war to the evacuation at Dunkirk, the British Army suffered one traumatic setback after another. It became a soldier's battle at every point as the "fog of war" descended over the vast battlefield. Coordination was difficult, reliable information scarce, and rumors were rampant. The junior officers, sergeants, and individual soldiers saved the army from disintegration by taking the initiative to keep their units together in the confusion of retreat. It was not pretty, but it worked. Instead of the greatest military disaster in British history, the army's successful retreat and miraculous escape from Dunkirk became a source of national inspiration and hope. As one historian noted:

> Dunkirk had started something. The spirit of Britain was roused, a vast flame of self-sacrifice and endeavour which swept the country and kept it going through the next dark eighteen months. In this campaign there had been no differentiation by rank. Everybody, from the commanding general downwards, had faced the same conditions, the same dangers and the same hardships. All the privileges of peacetime had disappeared and there grew from it not only inter-service co-operation but also that tremendous comradeship that carried the forces through Alamein and Normandy.[26]

Across the Atlantic, sensing this new spirit of defiance in the people and government of Great Britain, *The New York Times* proclaimed:

> So long as the English tongue survives, the word Dunkirk will be spoken with reverence. In that harbour . . . at the end of a lost battle, the rags and blemishes that had hidden the soul of democracy fell away. There, beaten but unconquered, in shining splendour, she faced the enemy, this shining thing in the souls of free men which Hitler cannot command . . . It is the future. It is victory.[27]

But I call to God, and the LORD saves me. Evening, morning and noon I cry out in distress, and he hears my voice. He ransoms me unharmed from the battle waged against me. ~Psalm 55:16–18

We Had Winnie

AN AMERICAN BISHOP asked an Englishman after the war, "How did you British survive that period during World War II between Dunkirk and the coming of the American personnel and supplies?" John Marsh, the principal of Mansfield College in Oxford, replied:

> *We had Winnie [Winston Churchill]. Those speeches of his in the House of Commons were worth a million men to us. What he said compelled us by his persuasion to believe. He said that no matter what happened, we were going to win. He said, we were on the side that was going to prevail . . . we were going to win. There was no doubt about that.*[28]

It may be difficult to quantify Winston Churchill's contribution to the war effort, but there is no doubt that his moral leadership was pivotal. There was an Old Testament leader who also had to help his nation overcome seemingly insurmountable odds. King Asa was the third king of Judah and was known as a man of great integrity. During his reign he instituted a moral revival and a renewal in purity of worship to God. When his country was invaded by a vast Ethiopian army, he was also able to inspire his troops by ensuring them that they were on the "right side." He placed himself and his kingdom under God's providential care and, through his faithfulness, led his nation to a great victory.

Then Asa called to the LORD his God and said, "LORD, there is no one like you to help the powerless against the mighty. Help us, O LORD our God, for we rely on you, and in your name we have come against this vast army. O LORD, you are our God; do not let man prevail against you." ~2 Chronicles 14:11

Prayer on the Beach

A S THE BRITISH EXPEDITIONARY FORCE retreated toward Dunkirk, the Green Howards Regiment was part of the rear guard fighting to delay the German advance. This unit, like many others, had endured days and nights of constant action, and every man was bone tired, hungry, and anxious. On May 29 orders finally came for withdrawal to the evacuation beaches. A Green Howards rifleman described what he saw:

> We looked a sorry sight, covered with dirt and grime with hunger gnawing at our bellies. The going was hard, the sand being so soft and deep. Thousands of men were forming queues leading down to the sea and were in the water up to their shoulders, doing their utmost to get onto one of the small boats, which very often capsized. Beachmasters had a very difficult task keeping some semblance of order, but by and large the lads just waited patiently for their turn to come until the planes came over. Those in the water just ignored the bombs—where could they run? I saw some poor lads crying and others, on their knees, praying. In the prevailing mood of many of the men it was common to see groups of soldiers being led by a Padre, in prayer.[29]

Many men were reassured and comforted on the beaches of Dunkirk as they turned to God both individually and in small groups. In the midst of this chaotic and dangerous ordeal these soldiers were able to go to a quiet place inside, where God always waits. We don't know how each prayer was answered, but we do know that each man was touched in some way and strengthened by God's presence. This is God's promise to each of us: if we call out to him, he will listen, and he will be there for us in every crisis.

Let us then approach the throne of grace with confidence, so that we may receive mercy and find grace to help us in our time of need. ~Hebrews 4:16

Calm in the Storm

TWENTY-ONE-YEAR-OLD Pilot Officer John Beard was flying his Hurricane fighter at 15,000 feet, waiting for an attacking formation of enemy bombers and fighters to appear. Suddenly, his flight leader called out that he had them in sight. From a distance the other aircraft seemed like an unusual cloud formation, at first quite beautiful. Then, as they drew closer, the details began to stand out:

I could see the bright yellow noses of Messerschmitt fighters sandwiching the bombers, and could even pick out some of the types. The sky seemed full of them, packed in layers thousands of feet deep. They came on steadily, wavering up and down along the horizon. "Oh, golly," I thought, "golly, golly . . ."

And then any tension I had felt on the way suddenly left me. I was elated but very calm. I leaned over and switched on my reflector sight, flicked the catch on the gun button from "Safe" to "Fire," and lowered my seat till the circle and dot on the reflector sight shone darkly red in front of my eyes.

The squadron leader's voice came through the earphones, giving tactical orders. We swung round in a great circle to attack on their beam - into the thick of them. Then, on the order, down we went. I took my hand from the throttle lever so as to get both hands on the stick, and my thumb played neatly across the gun button. You have to steady a fighter just as you have to steady a rifle before you fire it.[30]

I doubt that all pilots were so calm going into combat. But it is surely a priceless ability to be able to quiet oneself in the midst of chaos. Some are able to accomplish this through the force of their own will power. Whether you and I have that capability is an interesting question. Fortunately, we know that we don't have to rely on our own resources in times of trouble. Christians are blessed with knowledge of the sure path to inner tranquility in all situations. When we place our trust in Jesus Christ, we are assured of the most lasting and perfect peace possible to human beings.

And the peace of God, which transcends all understanding, will guard your hearts and your minds in Christ Jesus. ~Philippians 4:7

Instinct

JOHN BEARD FOUND himself in the midst of a swirling melee of fighters and bombers. At one point a German Dornier 17 flew across his path followed by a pursuing Hurricane. Behind the Hurricane came two Messerschmitts. With a kick of his rudder he lined up on the German fighters, thumbed his gun button, and opened fire.

> The first burst was placed just the right distance ahead of the leading Messerschmitt. He ran slap into it and he simply came to pieces in the air. His companion, with one of the speediest and most brilliant 'get outs' I have ever seen, went right away in a half Immelmann turn. I missed him completely.
>
> At that moment some instinct made me glance up at my rear-view mirror and spot two Messerschmitts closing in on my tail. Instantly I hauled back on the stick and streaked upward. And just in time. For as I flicked into the climb, I saw, the tracer streaks pass beneath me.[31]

Checking his cockpit, Beard saw that his fuel supply and ammunition were low. He knew that he couldn't take on two enemy fighters. At that point, however, the Messerschmitts broke off their attack and turned for home. A flood of relief washed over him as he put his nose down and did the same thing.

A religious person might attribute this flash of "instinct" to God's saving grace. A skeptic would undoubtedly chalk it up to good luck. As a former skeptic I can understand the latter attitude. In thinking about my experiences in combat, I have wondered about the amazing extent of my own good luck. Did God intervene on my behalf? I can't prove it to a skeptic, but I believe earnestly that he did. I thank God daily for watching over me in the past and for keeping my family and me safe through all the dangers we face now. The question for me is no longer *Has God saved me?* but *Why has he done so?* And what should I be doing in response to this amazing grace?

Enter his gates with thanksgiving and his courts with praise; give thanks to him and praise his name. For the LORD is good and his love endures forever.
~Psalm 100:4–5

Trust Your Instruments

HUGH GODEFROY was one of my great heroes: a Spitfire pilot during World War II. In 1940 he was an engineering student at Toronto University. He left school to volunteer for the Royal Canadian Air Force and to join the air battle in defense of England. Early in his training he encountered the difficulty of flying in clouds with no horizon or other outside reference points.

> *One day I spent doing nothing but cloud flying. We had to master the technique of fighting the vertigo which plagues pilots flying on instruments. In the early days often I found myself sweating. I felt as though I were spinning in a spiral dive. One had to say to himself, 'The instruments are right, and I am wrong.' Finally I would break cloud, and find to my great relief that I was flying straight and level. We never worried in England at that time over what else might be flying in the same cloud. We never gave it a thought.*[32]

In the early days of aviation, pilots had to fly "by the seat their pants." There were no instruments to guide them. Now there are myriad devices that enable flight in darkness or clouds without visual references. Like most pilots I have experienced the overwhelming sensation while flying on instruments that the aircraft was doing something totally different from what the instruments were telling me. It became a struggle between my feelings and my knowledge of what was correct.

In our daily lives, our "instruments" are God's words as revealed in the Bible. Sometimes biblical instructions are also counterintuitive. Jesus' entire Sermon on the Mount is a departure from what then was considered 'conventional' wisdom. Even when our hearts attempt to steer us in the wrong direction, we must instead move in the direction God provides in his Word.

You have heard that it was said, "Love your neighbor and hate your enemy." But I tell you: Love your enemies and pray for those who persecute you, that you may be sons of your Father in heaven. ~Matthew 5:43

British Spitfire fighter.
(Imperial War Museum, E(MOS) 1348)

Children in London after bombing.
(National Archives)

Superstition

AS A SPITFIRE PILOT with combat experience, Hugh Godefroy took some pride in his lack of superstition. He summed up his own attitude: *"I was not superstitious, and finding someone who was, had always made me want to prove them wrong."* One day he was preparing for a patrol over enemy territory. One of his fellow pilots pointed out that it was the 13th of the month, also reminding him that he had been hit several times before on that day. In spite of his disdain for such thinking, he was suddenly struck with a mortal fear that he had never before experienced. For the entire mission he flew with a sense of dread. He unaccountably kept repeating the only prayer that he could remember: *"Now I lay me down to sleep, I pray the Lord my soul to keep."*

When a group of enemy fighters attacked, he suddenly found himself flying and fighting for his life. He fatalistically resolved to sell himself dearly. Finally, grey with strain, nauseated, and out of ammunition, he sensed the end. With a Focke-Wulf 190 still on his tail, he turned for England, straightened out, and closed his eyes. After waiting for what seemed an eternity, he opened his eyes to see the enemy aircraft beside him, the other pilot looking over. After a few seconds the German broke off and headed back to France. Alone, on the ground, sitting in his cockpit, Hugh surveyed the holes in his damaged Spitfire and contemplated the folly of his own emotions. He resolved never again to let a superstitious reaction take over in the cockpit.[33]

While in combat I have also fought off dark thoughts about my chances of surviving and of my "luck" running out. Unfortunately for me, I was a spiritual skeptic at that time and can attest to the fact that such thoughts can be overpowering without a strong faith in God and a sure knowledge of a place in his kingdom.

> He will swallow up death forever. The Sovereign LORD will wipe away the tears from all faces; he will remove the disgrace of his people from all the earth.
> ~Isaiah 25:8

Teamwork

IN SEPTEMBER 1940 Kathleen Rainer was working in the fields near Ewhurst, Sussex, with her mother and brother. That day she observed an unforgettable incident in the sky above. As a dogfight between Allied and enemy fighters was raging overhead she saw a parachute appear. She realized it must be an Allied pilot when, to her horror, German fighters began to make passes, firing their machine guns at the helpless aviator. Then she saw an amazing sight:

> We were so proud of our pilots for what they did next...the other Spitfires began to circle the parachute, protecting the pilot from the German attack. As the pilot descended down, the rest of his squadron would spiral down with him, guiding him to the ground and protecting him. We were so proud of them, risking their lives to save that one pilot who was otherwise totally defenceless against the German fighters.[34]

A big part of Great Britain's success during the Battle of Britain is attributed to the survival rate of her invaluable pilots. The great advantage of fighting over home soil was the fact that so many of these young men were able to make it safely back to base, even if their aircraft were lost. For this to happen, however, it took teamwork and a strong belief in the value of each pilot's life. Again, we see how important it was then to have strong, close-knit units in the face of danger.

We need the same sense of urgency now in supporting and protecting each other within our own spiritual units of the body of Christ. The dangers may not be as obvious as those of actual combat, but the battle for our hearts and souls is just as real. We need each other—our brothers and sisters in Christ—if we hope to come through unscathed.

Speaking the truth in love, we will in all things grow up into him who is the Head, that is, Christ. From him the whole body, joined and held together by every supporting ligament, grows and builds itself up in love, as each part does its work. ~Ephesians 4:15–16

Thoughts of Death

FIGHTER PILOTS had to live with their own thoughts of death. Most, such as Squadron Leader Peter Townsend, were able to keep such thoughts at a distance:

> *Some of us would die within the next few days. That was inevitable. But you did not believe that it would be you. Death was always present, and we knew it for what it was. If we had to die, we would be alone, smashed to pieces, burnt alive, or drowned. Some strange, protecting veil kept the nightmare thought from our minds, as did the loss of our friends. Their disappearance struck us as less a solid blow than a dark shadow which chilled our hearts and passed on.*[35]

As a religious skeptic during wartime, my thought process was similar to this. In moments of panic, I prayed to God, even though I didn't know him and didn't really expect an answer. When the crisis of the moment was over, I never gave him credit for the result. During the lulls in action I fought off the same dark realizations expressed by this British pilot. A lonely death could come at any time. I had a good enough imagination to know that it could happen to me. Still, I tried not to dwell on that fact.

When you only expect a void after death, the best you can do is to avoid thinking about it. What amazing peace is available to us in any crisis when we are confident in our relationship with God and in the knowledge of where we are ultimately going. The apostle Paul gave us the classic statement of reassurance:

For I am convinced that neither death nor life, neither angels nor demons, neither the present nor the future, nor any powers, neither height nor depth, nor anything else in all creation, will be able to separate us from the love of God that is in Christ Jesus our Lord. ~Romans 8:38–39

The Face of God

DURING THE BATTLE OF BRITAIN hundreds of Americans went to Canada to enlist with the Royal Canadian Air Force (RCAF) and to join the fight against Nazi Germany. Eighteen year-old John Magee was one of these daring young men. After training he was sent to England where he joined No. 412 Fighter Squadron, RCAF. Flying his Spitfire in fighter sweeps over France and England he achieved the rank of pilot officer.

One day while flying at the extremely high altitude of 30,000 feet, he was struck with inspiration for a poem. On the ground he finished his poem and put it on the back of a letter to his parents. The words of the young airman continue to paint a vivid picture:

> Up, up the long, delirious burning blue
> I've topped the wind-swept heights with easy grace
> Where never lark, or ever eagle flew—
> And, while with silent, lifting mind I've trod
> The high untrespassed sanctity of space,
> Put out my hand, and touched the face of God.[36]

Unfortunately John Magee was killed three months after writing this poem. His majestic words have been quoted often, most notably by Ronald Reagan, eulogizing the Challenger 7 crew after their tragic loss in 1986: *"They waved goodbye and slipped the surly bonds of Earth to touch the face of God."*[37]

To say that you have 'touched the face of God' may sound presumptuous. However, I believe that we all desire to come closer to God, and that there are moments when we feel his presence. The beauty of a sunset, a storm, many natural vistas, all evoke thoughts of God and his majesty. In quiet moments of prayer we often sense his presence and tender mercy. These moments are real and open to us daily as a sure way for each to *"touch the face of God."*

The heavens declare the glory of God;
The skies proclaim the work of his hands. ~ Psalm 19:1

Miraculous Escape

IT WAS SHEILA DELANEY'S eleventh birthday, but after school, sadly, there was no party. In the fall of 1940 the usual routine for her family was to move to the bomb shelter at about 6:00 p.m. Soon after that the air raids started. The bombers were heard droning overhead searching out their targets. This night it was Sheila's town, Birmingham. They were comfortable enough in the shelter with their flask of tea, flashlights, and extra clothing for a long night. They could hear bombs exploding all around, but tried to keep occupied with singing and talking. Lying on a bunk, Sheila eventually drifted off to sleep, peacefully unaware of the bomb that was about to destroy her shelter. Later, she said:

> *I remember nothing more until I recovered consciousness to find myself being carried to a first-aid post, where they bandaged my cut head. Our shelter had had a direct hit and the shelter and bunks had become a tangled, twisted mess. We had all been thrown out onto the ground outside but survived with cuts and bruises.*
>
> *In the daylight the adults surveyed the devastation. Shrapnel had shattered all the windows and blown the roof off our house along with a couple of houses on either side. The bomb crater measured 24 feet across and in it were the remains of our air-raid shelter. We had a truly miraculous escape.*[38]

What could be more random than the path of a falling bomb? Imagine life in an air raid shelter. Where is the next bomb going to fall? Undoubtedly, thousands of prayers went up to God during the Blitz, and many survivors could claim God's protection. However, we know that many who prayed did not survive. Did God answer some and not others? No one can answer such a question. We know that death and destruction do occur in this world, and God doesn't promise to protect us from all earthly harm. He does hear each of our prayers, and he does promise to be with us always.

O LORD, you are my God; I will exalt you and praise your name, for in perfect faithfulness you have done marvelous things, things planned long ago.
~Isaiah 25:1

New Value System

FIGHTING FOR YOUR life has to change your outlook on life. Dennis Robinson was nearing his home base after a long mission. Even though he knew better, his guard was down.

> *The first thing I felt was the thud of bullets hitting my aircraft and a long line of tracer bullets streaming out ahead of my Spitfire. In a reflex action I slammed the stick forward as far as it would go. For a brief second my Spitfire stood on its nose and I was looking down at Mother Earth, thousands of feet below . . . I felt fear mounting. Sweating, mouth dry and near panic. No ammo and an attacker right on my tail. Suddenly the engine stopped.*[39]

At this point Robinson's aircraft was without power, defenseless, and gliding down. He began frantically searching for signs of the enemy fighter. Miraculously, he found himself alone in the sky. He managed to crash land his Spitfire in a field near Wareham and walk away with only a bullet graze on his leg. He felt strangely elated:

> *The release of tension as I realized my good fortune is something that cannot be described. You only know what it is like to be given back your life if you have been through that experience. I experienced this feeling several times during the Battle and it had a profound effect on me, which remains with me to this day. It somehow changed my value system, so that things that had seemed important before never had the same degree of importance again.*[40]

This young pilot's combat experience is a good reminder for us living in comfortable surroundings. We need to periodically and intentionally reappraise our own value systems. The problems and crises in our lives often take our attention away from what is truly critical: our relationship to God the Father. We realize what is unimportant only when we grasp what is ultimately important.

> By faith we eagerly await through the Spirit the righteousness for which we hope. For in Christ Jesus neither circumcision nor uncircumcision has any value. The only thing that counts is faith expressing itself through love. ~Galatians 5:5–6

Children

NORMAN ENGLISH was seven years old in August 1940 and lived adjacent to an RAF base. Bombs fell on and around the base often as the anti-aircraft guns returned fire. To a child it was very exciting:

> We used to sit on the fence for a grandstand view of the action! Until the adults came on the scene and sent us down to the shelter. I remember vividly, the vapour trails in the sky and watching dogfights in the sunny clear skies during the Battle of Britain. During the war living where we did, we were bombed, parachute land mined, aerial torpedoed, doodle bugged, and finally V2 rockets. Some of my school chums and their parents were killed.
>
> One aircraft machine gunned our road then dropped a bomb which blew up the gas main, and destroyed Banfields the greengrocers on the corner, and smash(ed) the water main — with the huge fire of the gas main and with the water filling both sides of the road and flooding the gutters.
>
> It was not long after the all clear was sounded that all the children in the road were paddling along the gutters and towing their toy boats behind them! All this within 20 minutes or so of being bombed and machine gunned.[41]

God bless the little children. I am sure that the parents of these were gratified to see them acting their age even under the direst of circumstances. Jesus also admired the openness and honesty of children, and, in fact, stated that only those like children would be able to enter his kingdom. By this he meant that we all should cultivate a childlike wonder at the world and ability to accept simple truths. Jesus' message is the ultimate in simplicity. Most children understand it immediately. We can't work our way to God. God's grace is a gift.

I tell you the truth, unless you change and become like little children, you will never enter the kingdom of heaven. Therefore, whoever humbles himself like this child is the greatest in the kingdom of heaven. ~Matthew 18:3–4

Watching dogfights high in the sky.
(Harry S. Truman Library)

Fighting fires during the London blitz.
(National Archives)

A Nation Prays

FORTY DAYS AFTER the German invasion of France and Holland it began to appear that all was lost. The French army was largely routed. The noose was tightening at Dunkirk. Panic was beginning to ripple through Great Britain at the specter of her army being annihilated on the beaches of France. In utter desperation the church leaders of England, with the support of King George, many political leaders, and much of the nation's press, called for a National Day of Prayer on May 26. On that Sunday church attendance mushroomed as thousands flocked to the altar, turning to God in the hour of their greatest trial.

As we know in retrospect, these prayers did not go unanswered. Hitler's panzer divisions continued to hold back from an assault on the beaches at Dunkirk. Amazingly, the weather on the French coast and English Channel seemed to be finely tuned to benefit the desperate soldiers on the beaches. Somehow the Royal Air Force stemmed the tide of the Luftwaffe. Many years later the Reverend Clive Duncan of St. Mary's Church delivered a sermon about these events:

> There were two phases to the Battle of Britain. One was the Military side and the other was the Spiritual phase . . . the Germans initiated the Battle of Britain in order to clean the RAF out of the air. However, they lost the battle not only because of the RAF's defence of the skies over London but also because they could not break down the courage and resolve of the civilian population. It took Christian courage in both phases to face the battle and to win.[42]

If there ever were a time for people to quake with fear, this would have been it. But regardless of how they may have felt, the people of Great Britain found the strength to behave courageously. Their faith sustained them during their darkest hour. In the same way, whenever we feel daunted by circumstances beyond our control, we should call upon God and move forward courageously in the power of the Holy Spirit.

Call upon me in the day of trouble;
I will deliver you, and you will honor me. ~Psalm 50:15

Faith of a Child

ELIZABETH BATTEN was five years old when World War II started and had vivid recollections that she shared with her daughter, Ellen. She saw the sky light up over Liverpool during the bombings and heard the sounds of aerial combat overhead. She spent hours and sometimes all night in a shelter under the stairs. She cried a lot and forever after had an aversion to small spaces. She consoled herself by sticking Bible verses and Sunday school pictures on the walls of the shelter. She took special comfort in a picture of Jesus as the Good Shepherd and the image of him watching over her and her family.

In recent years Ellen Batten was leafing through her mother's Bible and found a picture of her grandfather with an inscription on the back, *"To Betty, lots of love, Daddy."* She thought about her mother's prayers and how they were eventually answered when her father came home from the war. Her mother's faith had sustained her through many difficult years. Ellen realized that her mother's faith had also profoundly influenced her own spiritual life:

> *Today in a world ravaged by war and human rights abuse, many question the existence of God. However, I have come to share my mother's quiet faith. Faith turned to constructive prayer and action, faith placed in a God of love and compassion surely can give strength in dark times.*[43]

The key to Ellen's faith, modeled after the faith of her mother, was that it was based not on what men do, but on who God is. It is a lesson that would serve all of us well to remember in every trial we face. The character and power of God is unchanging.

My message and my preaching were not with wise and persuasive words, but with a demonstration of the Spirit's power, so that your faith might not rest on men's wisdom, but on God's power. ~1 Corinthians 2:4–5

The Few

THE BATTLE OF BRITAIN was raging. Every resource of Fighter Command was engaged in defense against the attacking Luftwaffe. On August 20 Winston Churchill went before the House of Commons once more to inform and reassure his countrymen. In this speech he coined the phrase "the few" to refer to the fighter pilots of the RAF. The phrase would stick.

> *The great air battle which has been in progress over this Island for the last few weeks has recently attained a high intensity. It is too soon to attempt to assign limits either to its scale or to its duration. We must certainly expect that greater efforts will be made by the enemy than any he has so far put forth.*
>
> *The gratitude of every home in our Island, in our Empire, and indeed throughout the world, except in the abodes of the guilty, goes out to the British airmen who, undaunted by odds, unwearied in their constant challenge and mortal danger, are turning the tide of the world war by their prowess and by their devotion. Never in the field of human conflict was so much owed by so many to so few.*[44]

We know from the outcome of this great struggle the effectiveness of a few good men. There are other examples of this phenomenon from previous wars. In biblical times, Gideon faced the army of Midian with thirty thousand of his own troops. God told him that he had too many men. Twenty thousand were dismissed, and, still, God told Gideon that he had too many men. Finally, three hundred were selected to battle the powerful Midianites. God did this to ensure that Israel would know that he had saved them, and not their military might. God also knew that a few good men could be more effective than a nervous horde.

> The LORD said to Gideon, "You have too many men for me to deliver Midian into their hands. In order that Israel may not boast against me that her own strength has saved her, announce now to the people, 'Anyone who trembles with fear may turn back and leave Mount Gilead.'" ~Judges 7:2–3

A British air raid shelter.
(National Archives)

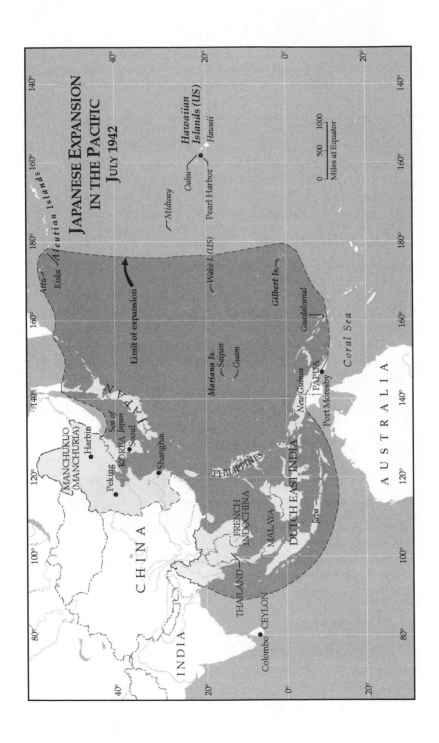

JAPANESE EXPANSION
IN THE PACIFIC
JULY 1942

Aleutian Islands

Attu
Kisha

Limit of expansion

Midway

Wake I. (US)

Hawaiian
Islands (US)

Oahu
Pearl Harbor
Hawaii

0   500   1000
Miles at Equator

Gilbert Is.

Mariana Is.
Saipan
Guam

Guadalcanal

Coral Sea

New Guinea
PAPUA
Port Moresby

PHILIPPINES

FRENCH
INDOCHINA

MALAYA

DUTCH EAST INDIA

Java

THAILAND

CEYLON
Colombo

INDIA

CHINA

MANCHUKUO
(MANCHURIA)
Harbin

Peking

KOREA
Seoul

Shanghai

Sea of
Japan

JAPAN

AUSTRALIA

FEBRUARY
Turning the Tide in the Pacific

ON DECEMBER 7, 1941, six Japanese aircraft carriers launched a massive air strike against the United States Pacific Fleet at Pearl Harbor. All eight American battleships were moored in port and were caught totally unprepared. Four were sunk and four were severely damaged. More than three hundred aircraft were destroyed, mostly on the ground. There were thousands of American casualties. By crippling the U.S. Pacific Fleet with one stroke, Japan hoped to achieve clear dominance in the Pacific for years to come. They came tantalizingly close to total success. Unfortunately for them, all three American aircraft carriers were away from Pearl Harbor on the day of the attack.

On December 8th the United States declared war on Japan. Japan's allies, Germany and Italy, immediately declared war on the United States. America found herself facing adversaries with powerful and effective military forces, victorious so far on all fronts. In the Pacific the Japanese Fleet was superior in every category. Three American aircraft carriers faced an overwhelming naval force of ten carriers, well-trained veteran aircrews, and superior aircraft. The United States Army, numbering only one hundred ninety thousand in 1939, was frantically expanding for war.

Almost simultaneously with the Pearl Harbor strike, Japanese attacks were launched against Wake Island, Guam, the Philippines, Thailand, Malaya, and the Gilbert Islands. All fell before the onslaught. In early March 1942 the conquest of Java and the Dutch East Indies was complete. Japan had accomplished all her immediate war aims in half the planned time and with virtually no naval losses.

Desperate for some success, the U.S. Navy carried out a daring strike of its own on April 18. The carrier *Hornet* took sixteen B-25 bombers into Japanese waters. Led by Jimmy Doolittle, the American airmen bombed Tokyo and other Japanese cities. The minimal damage inflicted caused a furor within the Japanese high command, which was disgraced for allowing such a strike against the homeland. Strategically, the Japanese had to face the need for defense of their home waters for the first time.

In June a vast Japanese armada of more than two hundred ships and seven hundred aircraft returned to the central Pacific to finish the job started at Pearl Harbor. The objective was destruction of America's three remaining aircraft carriers, the last vestige of U.S. naval power in the Pacific. The stark contrast in forces made victory in this engagement as close to a sure thing as it is possible to achieve in war. The Japanese again came very close to achieving their aim.

On the morning of June 4 the opposing forces came within striking distance of each other north of Midway Island. Both sides employed heightened air search efforts to find the other side, but the Americans got the earliest sighting and launched their attacks. After an amazing sequence of events, U.S. dive-bombers found the Japanese carrier strike group and delivered fatal blows to four enemy carriers. Even though he still had superior forces on the scene, the Japanese commander ordered a full retirement. Japanese expansion in the Pacific had reached its limit.

The President Speaks

IN HIS FIRST INAUGURAL ADDRESS, President Franklin D. Roosevelt tried to provide reassurance and spiritual comfort to a troubled nation facing economic depression at home and military conflict abroad:

President Franklin D. Roosevelt
(Franklin D. Roosevelt Presidential Library)

We face the arduous days that lie before us in the warm courage of national unity; with the clear consciousness of seeking old and precious moral values; with the clean satisfaction that comes from the stern performance of duty by old and young alike. We aim at the assurance of a rounded, a permanent national life.

We do not distrust the future of essential democracy. The people of the United States have not failed. In their need they have registered a mandate that they want direct, vigorous action. They have asked for discipline and direction under leadership. They have made me the present instrument of their wishes. In the spirit of the gift I take it.

In this dedication of a Nation we humbly ask the blessing of God. May He protect each and every one of us. May He guide me in the days to come.[45]

Roosevelt was a lifelong Episcopalian, baptized in St. James Church at Hyde Park, New York. He served as a vestryman and senior warden. Like many Episcopalians he was very personal in his faith. He once said, *"I can do almost anything in the 'Goldfish Bowl' of the president's life, but I'll be hanged if I can say my prayers in it . . ."*[46] Nevertheless, in crucial times he turned the focus of the nation toward God, his own ultimate source of guidance and protection. While none of us may ever confront the weight of responsibility carried by Franklin Roosevelt, we have equal access to God and the same source of strength that sustained the president and America during the dark days before and during World War II.

I lift up my eyes to the hills—where does my help come from? My help comes from the LORD, The Maker of heaven and earth. ~Psalm 121:1–2

Public Reaction

WAR CAME SUDDENLY and unexpectedly in the Pacific. Pearl Harbor was an attack without warning launched even before war had been declared. The first public reaction was utter outrage. All the leaders and politicians called for unity. In its December 15, 1941, issue, *Time* magazine tried to capture the public mood. What was happening in America? Behind the initial outburst of emotion there seemed to be evidence of an underlying calmness and determination:

> *At the docks in San Diego, as the afternoon wore on, a crowd slowly grew. There were a few people, then more, then a throng, looking intently west across the harbor, beyond Point Loma, out to the Pacific where the enemy was. There was no visible excitement, no hysteria, and no release in words for the emotions behind the grim, determined faces.*
>
> *In every part of the U.S. the terse, inadequate words gave outward and visible signs of the unfinished emotions within. Many just said, "Well, it's here." Sometimes they had nothing at all to say.*
>
> *Thus the U.S. met the first days of war. It met them with incredulity and outrage, with a quick, harsh, nationwide outburst that swelled like the catalogue of some profane Whitman. It met them with a deepening sense of gravity and a slow, mounting anger. But there were still no words to express emotions pent up in silent people listening to radios, reading papers, taking trains. But the U.S. knew that its first words were not enough.* [47]

Quiet determination reveals a depth of character and commitment not usually revealed by outward displays of emotion. Americans have always identified with the phrase, "Actions speak louder than words." In December 1941 this trait began to show itself among the American people. This national characteristic has specific biblical roots. Scripture enjoins us to pay more attention to what we do than what we say.

> If anyone has material possessions and sees his brother in need but has no pity on him, how can the love of God be in him? Dear children, let us not love with words or tongue but with actions and in truth. ~1 John 3:17–18

I Joined to See the World

JOE MORGAN didn't expect to be in a war when he joined the Navy as a teenager. *"I joined up to see the world, not fight a war,"* he said. *"When the attack started I was scared and looked for a place to hide."*[48] Morgan was at the airfield on Ford Island when the Japanese struck. Inside a hangar he found an I-beam to hide beneath. From his position of relative safety, he began to observe others outside the hanger firing back at the enemy airplanes: *"Here I was, a trained gunner hiding in an I-beam and I began to feel ashamed of myself. The shame overpowered my fear. I went into the armory and grabbed a machine gun to fight back."*[49]

Fear is an understandable reaction to confusion and danger. However, this sailor and many others rose above it to do their duty, often courageously. In our daily lives we usually do not have to be heroes. However, it does take courage to admit our mistakes and to ask for forgiveness. It often takes courage to commit to a relationship, and to stick with it. It may even take courage for some to get up in the morning. An article in my Bible gives this insight: *"Courage isn't only for heroes . . . Because we have Jesus Christ behind us—all his love, power, and wisdom—we can afford to be brave. For Christians, this life is about living in God's strength."*[50]

"But Lord," Gideon asked, "how can I save Israel? My clan is the weakest in Manasseh, and I am the least in my family." The LORD answered, "I will be with you, and you will strike down all the Midianites together." ~Judges 6:15–16

Readiness

THE MAIN STORY of Pearl Harbor was the woeful lack of readiness on the part of political and military leaders who should have known better. Any degree of alertness, coupled with minimal dispersal of ships and aircraft could have saved countless lives and invaluable equipment. *Pearl Harbor*, the movie, was released in 2001. In a thoughtful review of the movie Ken James compared the state of military forces then to our spiritual condition now:

> *Being reminded of the true story behind Pearl Harbor I can't help but think about the spiritual parallels. While the majority of people live their lives in relative peace, thinking everything is just fine, how many of us will be blindsided when death comes? And yes, I'm talking to church-goers too. What have you done to ensure you are ready when the end comes? There's a statistic that says death is 100% fatal. Sooner or later it'll happen. I hope you have put your trust in Jesus Christ. He's the only way to a bright eternity. Trusting in your own good works will get you nowhere. The USS* Arizona *and other members of the fleet at Pearl Harbor weren't ready, and they sadly found that out too late.*[51]

As we live our daily lives, often marked by ordinary routines, it may be difficult to grasp the inevitability of death and the importance of being ready for it. Even so, we must realize that when our time comes, we may not have the luxury of even a moment to prepare ourselves. Even without a clear and present danger to focus our attention, we need to make sure our souls are prepared for the eternal future. (JG)

> Therefore keep watch, because you do not know the day or the hour. . . .
> Then the King will say to those on his right, "Come, you who are blessed by my Father; take your inheritance, the kingdom prepared for you since the creation of the world." ~Matthew 25:13, 34

Japanese aircraft launch for attack on Pearl Harbor.
(National Archives)

USS *Shaw* explodes during Pearl Harbor attack.
(National Archives)

Attacking the Hinges

ON A SHIP, the worst disaster imaginable is capsizing. Plunged into darkness and turned upside down, the crew has no way to escape. The hull sits on top of them, a barrier to the outside world. At Pearl Harbor, this happened quickly to the *Oklahoma,* and the *West Virginia* was in danger of the same fate. Ripped by repeated torpedo hits on the port side, her compartments were flooding rapidly, and the ship was at a twenty-eight-degree list. Capsizing seemed inevitable.

Below deck, there was a group of sailors called Shipfitters who knew what needed to be done. The ship had to be counter-flooded so she could rest squarely on the mud beneath. This required opening a series of valves to let in seawater. The Shipfitters, however, were stymied because the special valve handles they needed were locked in a chest. They gathered around the chest, frantically beating at the lock with whatever was at hand, but it wouldn't budge. In the midst of the panic and confusion, one of the sailors, Sylvester Puccio, barked for everyone to step aside. He came forward with his tools and started attacking the hinges on the locker. He soon had the doors removed. Within minutes, the little group was opening valves, and the West Virginia started settling on an even keel.

There were many heroes at Pearl Harbor who were recognized for their service. However, it was not until many years later that the son of another survivor pieced together the details of this unheralded incident. He learned that he owed his life and his children's lives to this man who had saved his father, thousands of others, and a battleship. He was forever thankful that Sylvester Puccio stepped forward on that day, able to think for himself, and able to calmly solve a problem in the midst of chaos. He called him, *"An Angel Sent by History."*[52]

We may not often have the opportunity to prove our own heroism in a dramatic way, but if we are willing and available, we can be as angels to those around us by recognizing a need and rising to the occasion to meet it.

In all their distress he too was distressed, and the angel of his presence saved them. ~Isaiah 63:9

Rumors

HENRY LACHENMAYER was a twenty-two-year-old crewmember of the USS *Pennsylvania* at Pearl Harbor. During the attack he did his best to perform his battle duties as a medic. He was eyewitness to the destruction wrought on the *Pennsylvania* and surrounding ships. After recounting the events of the day in his diary, he summarized the rumors that were swirling in the aftershock of the attack:

> *Here are some of the rumors passing amongst us, none of us having real solid information. Some of the enemy planes were piloted by German fliers. The enemy tried to land troops at Nanakuh and Waikiki beaches, but were repulsed. We sank two enemy aircraft carriers some distance from the islands. Wake and Midway islands are in Japanese hands. Saboteurs land in great numbers on the island. We had two more alarms . . . but these proved to be only scares.*[53]

We always hear rumors, especially in times of uncertainty. When the facts are unknown, there always seems to be someone willing to supply them out of his own imagination. Jesus was aware of this all-too human tendency and tried to prepare his disciples to deal with it. When they asked him to explain what would happen at the time of his return, Jesus warned them, "You will hear of wars and rumors of wars, but see to it that you are not alarmed" (Matthew 24:6). He then told them to ignore the rumors. He told them, in fact, that they could ignore all human sources of news. They would directly and personally know when the Son of Man returned to Earth.

> For as lightning that comes from the east is visible even in the west, so will be the coming of the Son of Man. . . . They will see the Son of Man coming on the clouds of the sky, with power and great glory. ~Matthew 24:27, 30

More Rumors

AFTER PEARL HARBOR had been attacked, news spread like wild-fire throughout the nation. As you would expect, every question could not be answered immediately. Where will the Japanese strike next? Is the rest of the nation safe? Rumors began to circulate to "answer" these questions. People heard that bombs were hitting American cities, that American ships were being sunk at sea, that the Panama Canal was blocked. Word spread that Japanese forces had established beachheads at San Francisco and Long Beach. Widespread anxiety was reported:

> It was a rough Sunday night on the West Coast, where a follow-up Japanese attack seemed more likely than anywhere else. Around San Francisco Bay, fire sirens sounded falsely three times to warn residents of possible air attacks. Unpracticed civilian defense volunteers darted around neighborhoods yelling "Lights Out!" Police ordered drivers to turn out their headlamps and proceed using only their parking lights. Japanese planes never did appear that night to inflict any damage, but all that driving in darkness caused a lot of damaging accidents.[54]

There are times when we must react to crisis situations to protect our loved ones and ourselves. However, in times of great uncertainty we know that rumors are inevitable and often cause our plight to seem worse than it is. Christians should feel less cause for panic at such times because we have the assurance that God is in charge. We know that he wants us to do what needs to be done calmly, without unreasonable fear of the uncertainties that lie ahead. This quiet strength can be found only in God and the certain knowledge that he is in control.

Who of you by worrying can add a single hour to his life? ~Matthew 6:27

Tapping on the Hull

RICHARD FISKE was a Marine on the USS *West Virginia*. On December 8, the day after the ship was sunk at her Pearl Harbor berth, he and other crew members heard a desperate, insistent tapping sound from inside the hull. An urgent search began of the accessible compartments, but, despite their best efforts, they were unsuccessful in finding the trapped crewmen. Fiske described with difficulty the events that followed:

> *That tapping went on all week long. They sent divers down 14 times to find those guys. They did the best they could, but they just couldn't find them. We didn't know who was down there, but the tapping continued until December 24ᵗʰ. When we went into dry-dock on June 18, 1942, we found them. They were in the last watertight compartment we opened. We found a calendar and a clock with them. I often wonder what they were thinking about. Their lives were cut so short and they never had a chance to realize their dreams.*[55]

This incident deeply affected Fiske for the rest of his life. He could never forget what happened and could only state that, *"I pray every day because the good Lord was with us."*[56] Today, we also hope and pray with this survivor that the Lord was with all the crew on the *West Virginia* that day, including those men trapped below. We pray that they were sustained by the strength that can come only from God to calmly face such a hopeless situation. We need to remind ourselves today that God is the source of our own strength. He promises to be beside us, no matter the time, place, or crisis.

"Am I only a God nearby," declares the LORD, "and not a God far away? Can anyone hide in secret places so that I cannot see him?" declares the LORD. "Do I not fill heaven and earth?" declares the LORD. ~Jeremiah 23:23–24

Saved from Drowning

THE USS *ARIZONA* and other battleships moored along "Battleship Row" were the primary targets of the first Japanese attack. Within ten minutes a bomb crashed through the Arizona's armored decks to ignite the magazine. The ship's sides were ripped out and fire engulfed almost the entire ship. Within minutes the great vessel sank with a loss of thirteen hundred crewmen. Marine Cpl. E. C. Nightingale was preparing to abandon ship:

> *Charred bodies were everywhere. I made my way to the quay and started to remove my shoes when I suddenly found myself in the water. I think the concussion of a bomb threw me in. I started swimming for the pipe line which was about one hundred and fifty feet away. I was about half way when my strength gave out entirely. My clothes and shocked condition sapped my strength, and I was about to go under when Major Shapley started to swim by, and seeing my distress, grasped my shirt and told me to hang on to his shoulders while he swam in.*
>
> *We were perhaps twenty-five feet from the pipeline when the major's strength gave out and I saw he was floundering, so I loosened my grip on him and told him to make it alone. He stopped and grabbed me by the shirt and refused to let go. I would have drowned but for the Major. We finally reached the beach.*[57]

The major undoubtedly knew that continuing to help Nightingale might result in death for them both. He also knew that letting go of him would mean certain drowning for the corporal. Shapley considered the risk to his own life and counted the attempt worth the effort. How often are we faced with situations in which helping someone else poses a risk to ourselves, either in terms of physical health, monetary loss, social status, or reputation? And how often do we consider that risk worth it for the chance to aid someone else in need? (JG)

> Greater love has no one than this, that he lay down his life for his friends.
> ~John 15:13

Will Whiskey Do?

FOR A FEW MINUTES, Lee Soucy, a pharmacist's mate aboard the USS *Utah*, and his shipmates thought some kind of crazy bombing practice was going on over the harbor. Then "General Quarters" sounded, sending them to their battle stations. Within minutes the ship was shaken by a series of violent jolts and began to list badly. Over the ship's PA system, Soucy heard a bugle call followed by the boatswain's shout, *"Abandon ship!"* He was soon in the water swimming for Ford Island.

Ashore, he helped treat the wounded at an emergency first-aid station set up in a nearby Bachelor Officers' Quarters building. The wounded flooded in, and it did not take long to exhaust the medical supplies on hand. Someone called for more alcohol and heard the reply, *"Alcohol? Will Whiskey do?"* In a few minutes a case of scotch and other assorted bottles of liquor appeared. These served the purpose of washing off the sticky oil and providing antiseptic for the wounds. There were other uses as well:

> At one point, an exhausted swimmer, covered with a gooey film of black oil, saw me walking around with a washcloth in one hand and a bottle of booze in the other. He hollered, "Hey Doc, could I have a shot of that medicine?" He took a hefty swig . . . then he spewed it out along with black mucoidal globs of oil. He lay back a minute after he stopped vomiting, then said, "Doc, I lost that medicine. How about another dose?"[58]

One of the hallmarks of American military men and women has always been the ability to see humor in tense situations. This probably reflects a degree of optimism in the American culture not seen in many others. We also have biblical encouragement for a light heart in the secure hope of a joyful future, reunited eternally with our Savior.

He will yet fill your mouth with laughter and your lips with shouts of joy. ~Job 8:21

Encouraging a Mother

THE END OF THE Doolittle raid came a little after midnight for Billy Farrow and the other four members of his crew. They had flown their B-25 off the carrier *Hornet*, bombed Japan, and continued until they were near Nanchang, China. As the fuel ran out and the engines started to cough, they had no option left except to bail out of their aircraft into the inky darkness. They were captured the next day. A few months later Farrow and two others were put on trial for unspecified charges, found guilty, and sentenced to death.

B-25 takes off from the USS *Hornet*. (National Archives)

A day before his execution, Farrow composed a letter to his mother at home in Darlington, South Carolina. He himself was unshaken and unbowed in his hour of trial, but he knew how devastating his death would be to his mother. He sought to comfort her by reassuring her of his own faith. The final lines of his letter were: *"Don't let this get you down. Just remember God will make everything right and that I'll see you all again in the hereafter. Read 'Thanatopsis' by Bryant if you want to know how I am taking this. My faith in God is complete, so I am unafraid."*[59]

Farrow's letter home was found in the files of the Japanese War Ministry after the war was over. It was given wide circulation in the United States and became the basis for countless sermons and editorials. His concern for his mother and his spiritual strength in the darkest possible circumstance were a witness to the world of the power of his faith. His words brought comfort and encouragement to millions.

Now faith is being sure of what we hope for and certain of what we do not see. ~Hebrews 11:1

Thanatopsis

WILLIAM CULLEN BRYANT published "Thanatopsis" in 1817 when he was a twenty-three-year-old lawyer. *Thanatos* is the Greek word for death, and the poem is a meditation on the subject. As he faced his own certain death, Billy Farrow wrote to his mother: *"Read 'Thanatopsis' . . . if you want to know how I am taking this."*[60] The following is the most well-known excerpt:

As the long train
Of ages glides away, the sons of men—
The youth in life's fresh spring, and he who goes
In the full strength of years, matron and maid,
The speechless babe, and the gray-headed man—
Shall one by one be gathered to thy side,
By those, who in their turn, shall follow them.

So live, that when thy summons comes to join
The innumerable caravan, which moves
To that mysterious realm, where each shall take
His chamber in the silent halls of death,
Thou go not, like the quarry-slave at night,
Scourged to his dungeon, but sustained and soothed
By an unfaltering trust, approach thy grave
Like one who wraps the drapery of his couch
About him, and lies down to pleasant dreams.

Under the tutelage of my high school English teacher, I studied this poem and memorized large portions of it when I was fifteen. I should not have been surprised to learn that a young airman in World War II found comfort in its thought-provoking lines. Bryant, unfortunately, didn't elaborate on where his *"unfaltering trust"* lay. However, Billy Farrow did elaborate by clearly stating that, *"My faith in God is complete."*[61] With a secure faith in the right place he was able to face the worst possible fate with tranquility, bearing witness to the power of his own unfaltering trust.

O LORD, see how my enemies persecute me! Have mercy and lift me up from the gates of death, that I may declare your praises. ~Psalm 9:13–14

Prisoner of War

JAKE DESHAZER was the bombardier on the last of Doolittle's B-25's to launch from the *Hornet*. His aircraft crashed in China where he and others of his crew were captured by the Japanese. He was beaten, half-starved, and subjected to solitary confinement. Three of his buddies were executed by firing squad. He said that at that time, *"The bitterness of my heart against my captors seemed more than I could bear."*[62] He eventually was taken to Tokyo where he remained imprisoned throughout the war.

In May 1944 he was given a copy of the Bible, which he began to read feverishly for the first time. The more he read, the more he became convinced that what he was reading was true and relevant to him. He said, *"On 8 June 1944, the words in Romans 10:9 stood out boldly before my eyes: 'If thou shalt confess with thy mouth the Lord Jesus, and shalt believe in thine heart that God hath raised Him from the dead, thou shalt be saved.' In that very moment God gave me grace to confess my sins to Him, and He forgave me all my sins and saved me for Jesus' sake."*[63]

This amazing story is a witness to the power of Scripture to change lives. God's Word alone penetrated this man's miserable circumstances to convict him of the true way to salvation. By reading and hearing the Word, he was able to take this step of faith and become a new man. Even though still in prison, his heart changed toward his captors. His bitter hatred became "loving pity" when he realized that the people who were so cruel to him had not even heard of Jesus Christ.

> If we confess our sins, he is faithful and just and will forgive us our sins and purify us from all unrighteousness. ~1 John 1:9

Evangelist

AFTER GIVING HIS life to Christ, Jake DeShazer's physical circumstances as a prisoner of war did not change. In fact, sickness brought him close to death, and his suffering grew worse. Spiritually, however, he began to grow stronger. His attitude toward his captors changed in a profound way:

> *I realized that these Japanese did not know anything about my Saviour and that if Christ is not in your heart, it is natural to be cruel. I read in my Bible that while those who crucified Jesus on the cross had beaten Him and spit upon Him before He was nailed to the cross, He tenderly prayed in His moment of excruciating suffering, "Father, forgive them for they know not what they do." And now from the depths of my heart, I too prayed for God to forgive my torturers, and I determined by the aid of Christ to do my best to acquaint the Japanese people with the message of salvation that they might become as other believing Christians.*[64]

Freedom came at last to Jake DeShazer on August 20, 1945, when American troops parachuted into his compound to ensure that he and the other prisoners were protected. After returning to the States and recovering his strength, he heard God's call to take Christ's message to the Japanese people. He attended a Christian college and returned to Japan a missionary, starting churches throughout the country. Of the many that he influenced, one of the most notable was Mitsuo Fuchida, the lead pilot in the attack on Pearl Harbor and the subject of another story. Jake DeShazer's life became a testament to the fact that his heart was truly changed by Christ's message. Love, as defined in 1 Corinthians, became the foundation of his work and his relationships.

> Love is patient, love is kind. It does not envy, it does not boast, it is not proud. It is not rude, it is not self-seeking, it is not easily angered, it keeps no record of wrongs. Love does not delight in evil but rejoices with the truth. It always protects, always trusts, always hopes, always perseveres. ~1 Corinthians 13:4–7

Fuchida

EARLY ON DECEMBER 7, 1941, Cdr. Mitsuo Fuchida looked down on the ships of the U.S. fleet peacefully moored at their Pearl Harbor berths. As air group commander and leader of the first attack wave he wanted to make sure that the battleships were there. They were neatly lined up alongside Ford Island as expected. Excitedly he shouted over his radio the codeword to attack, *"Tora! Tora! Tora!"* and then led the Japanese aircraft to their target. He later described this moment as "the most thrilling exploit of my career."

Fuchida was severely injured at the battle of Midway in 1942 and served for the remainder of the war as a high-level staff officer. As the end of the war neared he did not want to surrender, but favored fighting to the last man. He did as the emperor directed, however, and left the service a bitter and disillusioned man.

After the war Fuchida became a farmer so that he could feed his family. Living a life of isolation and poverty, he went through an intense period of introspection and questioning. Before, he had not been a religious man. Now he began to see God in his surroundings and in the working of the seasons. He said, *"There on my farm, God began to come into my heart . . . I began to realize slowly that all things were dependent upon a divine Creator, and that I was living under the grace of God. I could sow the seeds; I could plant the saplings; I could draw water with my hands. But they all came from the benevolence of a kind and far-seeing Creator."*[65] Mitsuo Fuchida's long spiritual journey began with a sense of wonder about the natural beauty of the world around him.

Ascribe to the LORD the glory due his name; worship the LORD in the splendor of his holiness. ~Psalm 29:2

16

Forgiveness

THE WAR CRIMES trials after the war were a source of bitterness and frustration for Mitsuo Fuchida. Although he himself was not accused, he could not understand the moral basis for the victors putting the defeated on trial. The Japanese military code allowed for no mercy toward a fallen foe and abhorred the idea of any form of surrender. He was convinced that atrocities toward prisoners must have been committed on both sides. He eagerly sought out returning Japanese prisoners to confirm his feelings.

In the spring of 1947 he met an old acquaintance, Sublieutenant Kazuo Kanegasaki, who had been a survivor of the aircraft carrier *Hiryu's* sinking during the Battle of Midway. Kanegasaki had eventually been held in a Colorado POW camp. He told Fuchida the remarkable story of an eighteen-year-old American girl named Margaret Covell who came to the camp as a volunteer worker.

Over time, Covell's unusual compassion aroused the curiosity of the prisoners. One of them asked her, *"Why are you so kind to us?"* She answered, *"Because Japanese soldiers killed my parents."*[66] As the prisoners stared at her in astonishment, she explained that her parents were missionaries before the war at a mission school in Yokohama. When she learned they had been arrested and beheaded, she was choked with hatred at first. But gradually, she became convinced in her heart that her parents would have forgiven her captors. Could she do less? As a sign of her sincerity, she volunteered to serve the Japanese prisoners.

On hearing this story, Fuchida was thunderstruck. The concept of forgiveness was foreign to his "code." A teenaged American girl seemed to have an answer to the problem of hatred and suspicion in the world. Fuchida knew that such towering goodness could not have a human source. He wondered, *"Where did this great love come from—this love that could forgive enemies their cruelest deeds?"*[67]

Be kind and compassionate to one another, forgiving each other, just as in Christ God forgave you. ~Ephesians 4:32

The Second Day to Remember

AS HE WAS PASSING through a train station in early October 1948, a stranger handed Mitsuo Fuchida a pamphlet entitled "I Was a Prisoner of Japan," by Jacob DeShazer. The story of the American airman's ordeal and life-changing experience greatly affected the Japanese airman. The parallel between DeShazer's experience and that of Margaret Covell was amazing. Here was another story of love overcoming hatred, only from a more convincing source. DeShazer was a fellow warrior who had suffered even more than he had because of war. Fuchida purchased a Bible, not to pursue Christianity, but to better understand someone like DeShazer. Fuchida reflected:

> *His story . . . was something I could not explain. Neither could I forget it. The peaceful motivation I had read about was exactly what I was seeking. Since the American had found it in the Bible, I decided to purchase one myself, despite my traditionally Buddhist heritage. I read this book eagerly. I came to the climactic drama—the Crucifixion. I read in Luke 23:34 the prayer of Jesus Christ at His death . . . I was impressed that I was certainly one of those for whom He had prayed. Right at that moment I seemed to meet Jesus for the first time. That date, April 14, 1950—became the second "day to remember" of my life. On that day, I became a new person.*[68]

Fuchida's life did not become easier because of his conversion. Many of his countrymen accused him of currying favor with the occupation forces. Despite such criticism he joined a Christian evangelical group dedicated to spreading the gospel. Instead of growing bitter and resigned to the cynical attitudes of his fellow countrymen, he spoke boldly before large audiences in Japan and America and, through his faithful service, influenced countless others to meet Jesus for the first time.

Father, forgive them, for they do not know what they are doing. ~Luke 23:34

Forgive as the Lord forgave you. ~Colossians 3:13

The Miracle before the Battle

IN MAY 1942 the USS *Yorktown* represented one-third of American combat power in the Pacific. Unfortunately, she was severely damaged early in May at the Battle of the Coral Sea. Two bombs had ruptured fuel tanks and damaged the hull. Worse still, an eight-hundred-pound bomb had penetrated three decks and exploded deep within the ship. In addition to massive casualties, whole compartments were wiped out, bulkheads were warped, and large areas were charred by fire. Many of the casualties were incurred fighting the widespread fires and keeping the ship afloat.

On May 27 the crippled *Yorktown* arrived in Pearl Harbor and slid into Dry Dock Number 1. One admiral estimated the time needed for repairs as ninety days. The Navy Yard inspectors thought it possible to get her back to sea in two weeks. Admiral Nimitz, aware of the impending showdown at Midway, had the final say. He wanted the Yorktown ready to fight in three days! One historian notes:

> *Overnight, more than 1400 workers swarmed aboard the stricken ship. Civilian contractors and Navy technicians dragged miles of electrical cable. Other men on scaffolds patched the hull. Steel plates were dropped over the holes in the deck...acetylene torches burned everywhere. The work on the Yorktown had become one of the most intensive repair jobs the Navy had undertaken. The requirement for electricity alone became so great that districts in Honolulu endured shortages so that the yard could get the extra power it needed.[69]*

Over the next three days the "impossible" was accomplished. The *Yorktown* put to sea on May 30 to play her vital role in the Battle of Midway. This story inspires us to raise our expectations of what dedicated people with a mission can accomplish. We can expect the "impossible" in God's service. The saying goes, "God doesn't call the qualified. He qualifies those he calls." All we need are willing hearts and unlimited expectations.

Then Jesus came to them and said, "All authority in heaven and on earth has been given to me. Therefore go and make disciples of all nations, baptizing them in the name of the Father and of the Son and of the Holy Spirit, and teaching them to obey everything I have commanded you. ~Matthew 28:18–20

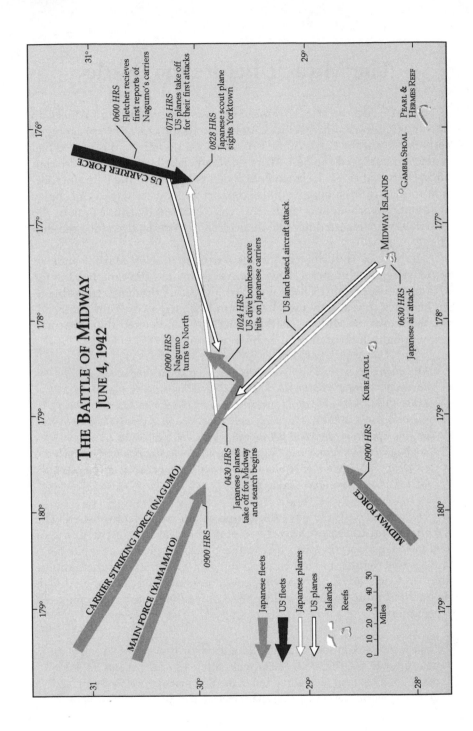

THE BATTLE OF MIDWAY
JUNE 4, 1942

0600 HRS
Fletcher recieves
first reports of
Nagumo's carriers

0715 HRS
US planes take off
for their first attacks

0828 HRS
Japanese scout plane
sights Yorktown

US CARRIER FORCE

0900 HRS
Nagumo turns to North

1024 HRS
US dive bombers score
hits on Japanese carriers

US land based aircraft attack

MIDWAY ISLANDS

0630 HRS
Japanese air attack

KURE ATOLL

GAMBIA SHOAL

PEARL &
HERMES REEF

0430 HRS
Japanese planes
take off for Midway
and search begins

CARRIER STRIKING FORCE (NAGUMO)

MAIN FORCE (YAMAMATO)

0900 HRS

0900 HRS

MIDWAY FORCE

Japanese fleets
US fleets
Japanese planes
US planes
Islands
Reefs

Miles
0 10 20 30 40 50

31°   176°   177°   178°   179°   180°   179°   178°   177°   179°
31°   29°   30°   29°   28°

This War Is Over

BEFORE THE START of World War II Cdr. John Ford organized the Field Photographic Branch of the Office of Strategic Services. Sent to Pearl Harbor in January 1942, he later found himself on Midway Island to record events during the looming battle. He was assigned to the top of one of the prominent buildings on the island to report on enemy aircraft and to take pictures. He was later cited for his actions during the battle. Commander Ford had an insightful observation about the young men who had been around him:

> The Marines with me—I took one look at them and I said, "Well this war was won." They were kids, oh, I would say from 18 to 22, none of them were older. They were the calmest people I have ever seen. I have never seen a greater exhibition of courage and coolness under fire in my life and I have seen some in my day. Those kids were really remarkable, and as I said before, I figured "Well, this war is over, at least we are going to win it if we have kids like that."[70]

Young people are often associated with a lack of life experience and a corresponding lack of wisdom. Yet youth also goes hand in hand with idealism and courage in every arena, as evidenced by the young Marines whom this officer observed on Midway Island. The apostle Paul charged Timothy to ignore any criticism of his youth and to set an example for all generations in the way he lived his life for the Lord. No matter our age, we are never too young or too old to make a difference in the world around us, and to bring glory to Christ in so doing. (JG)

Don't let anyone look down on you because you are young, but set an example for the believers in speech, in life, in love, in faith and in purity.
~1 Timothy 4:12

Jack Waldron

L T. CDR. JACK WALDRON was the only experienced pilot in his squadron. He had graduated from the Naval Academy in 1924 to become a naval aviator. At Midway he commanded Torpedo Squadron 8 aboard the USS *Hornet*. Early on June 4 he knew that their first combat action was imminent. He briefed his aircrew with prophetic words: *"I want each of us to do his utmost to destroy our enemies. If there is only one plane left to make a final run, I want that man to go in and get a hit. May God be with us all."*[71]

He knew that his men were piloting obsolete aircraft. Top speed for his fifteen TBD Devastators was two hundred miles per hour, compared with three hundred fifty for the Japanese Zeros. Not a man in his squadron had ever carried a torpedo in his aircraft, much less flown off a carrier with one. Their training had consisted mainly of "chalkboard" exercises. Even with all these disadvantages, however, Waldron knew that he and his men faced one of those grave, historic moments that found a few men in a desperate but vital role. They had to do whatever was humanly possible. One hit on an enemy carrier might make all the difference.

Jack Waldron exemplified great leadership in a crisis situation. One of his pilots said of him later: *"I know that if I had it all to do over again, even knowing that the odds were going to be like they were, knowing him like I did know him, I'd follow him again through exactly the same thing because I trusted him . . ."*[72] This kind of trust is built over time by a leader who puts the needs of those under him ahead of his own. The model of this servant attitude was Jesus Christ.

> The greatest among you should be like the youngest, and the one who rules like the one who serves. ~Luke 22:26

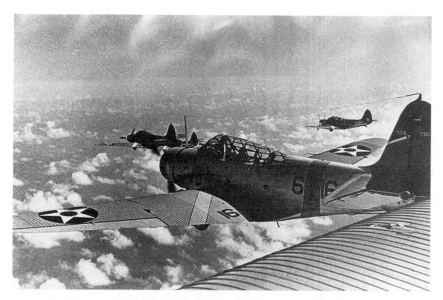

TBD Devastator torpedo bombers in formation.
(U.S. Naval Historical Center)

SBD Dauntless dive bomber.
(U.S. Dept. of Defense) (public domain photo from militaryfactory.com)

Torpedo 8

NAVAL AVIATION tactics in World War II called for coordinated attacks on enemy ships. The torpedo planes were to come in low, dive bombers would strike from high altitude, and fighters would provide air cover against enemy fighters. During the Battle of Midway there was no such coordination. The various types of squadrons arrived on the scene piecemeal and disorganized. Low on fuel and knowing that any opportunity might be fleeting, leaders had to make split-second decisions.

The fifteen slow-moving TBD Devastators of Torpedo 8 found the Japanese carriers first at 9:20 a.m. on June 4. Sighting the enemy ships on the horizon at a distance of about four miles, Jack Waldron waggled his wings, signaling, "Follow me," dropped down in altitude and bore in on the *Soryu*, one of the four enemy carriers. Suddenly, anti-aircraft fire began exploding among his aircraft. Japanese Zeros appeared and began riddling the formation. One by one Waldron's aircraft plunged into the sea. The rest continued the attack. Within eight minutes only three were left. Then two more went down. The last TBD, piloted by Ens. George Gay, was able to drop a torpedo, passed over the *Soryu*, and crashed into the sea.

Twenty-nine airmen died in this attack. Ensign Gay was the only survivor. The individual courage of every one of these pilots is almost unfathomable. During the agonizingly slow, low-altitude run, every pilot witnessed the destruction of his fellow airmen and his own leader. Any pilot could have rightly concluded that this was a futile effort. Anyone could have turned back. Not one did.

> Because the hand of the LORD my God was on me, I took courage. ~Ezra 7:28

Apparent Futility

THE SACRIFICE OF Torpedo 8 in its attack on the Japanese strike force might seem like a gallant, but useless, gesture. The "Charge of the Light Brigade" comes to mind:

> *Theirs not to make reply,*
> *Theirs not to reason why,*
> *Theirs but to do and die:*
> *Into the valley of Death*
> *Rode the six hundred.*[73]

Only in retrospect do we know that Torpedo 8's attack was indeed not futile. In fact there are few instances in any war when such an apparently futile effort accomplished so much. As the Japanese carriers maneuvered to avoid these attacks, they could not launch their own aircraft. The American carriers may have been saved because of this delay. Of equal importance, the Zeros that shot down the aircraft of Torpedo 8 at low altitude found themselves hopelessly out of position minutes later at the climax of the battle. The skies high above the Japanese carrier fleet were undefended when the American dive-bombers appeared.

My father used to quote Robert E. Lee: *"Duty is the sublimest word in the English language."* These intrepid young pilots individually demonstrated the full meaning of this sentence. Fortunately, most of us do not face such life-and-death situations. However, we are all called to do the right thing every day. Sometimes it isn't easy, and often we don't see the immediate benefit. But we know what we should do.

Now all has been heard; here is the conclusion of the matter: Fear God and keep his commandments, for this is the whole duty of man. ~Ecclesiastes 12:13

Ensign Gay

WATCHING HIS FELLOW pilots go down around him, Ens. George Gay pressed his attack on the Japanese carrier *Soryu*. He stayed in the air long enough to successfully launch his torpedo and was the sole survivor of Torpedo Squadron 8. He recalled:

> *Everything was shooting at me. I flew right down the gun barrel on one of those big pom poms up forward . . . I figured the only way that I could evade all that anti-aircraft fire was not to throw my belly up in a turn away from the ship, but was just to go right straight to her and offer as small a target as I could. So I flew right down the gun barrels, pulled up on the port side, did a flipper turn right by the island, I could see the little Jap captain up there jumping up and down raising hell. Just a little bit after that . . . the Zeros jumped on me and . . . shot my rudder control and ailerons out and I pancaked into the ocean.*[74]

After struggling from his sinking aircraft, Gay found a cushion floating nearby. He hid himself as best he could from the Japanese fleet, which passed by him several times that day. He was witness to the destruction of three of the enemy carriers. Gay was rescued the next day and returned to duty for other operations in the Pacific war. He eventually returned to the States, where he made frequent public appearances in support of the war effort and continued speaking as a civilian.

In 1980 Gay came to Charleston, South Carolina, to talk to naval science cadets at The Citadel and to deliver a message calling for military preparedness. I heard him say, "I was lucky. I've never understood why I was the only one that came back." He felt that his mission in life since that day was to ensure that American boys not be sent again into a conflict without the best equipment and training that their nation could provide.

While Ensign Gay attributed his survival to luck, as Christians we can be sure that God has numbered our days for a specific reason (Psalm 139:16). It is our responsibility to be ready for the tasks that he has determined we should accomplish.

Get ready; be prepared, you and all the hordes gathered about you, and take command of them. After many days you will be called to arms. ~Ezekiel 38:7–8

The horse is made ready for the day of battle, but victory rests with the LORD. ~Proverbs 21:31

Suicide

ENSIGN GAY FOUGHT to control his Devastator during his long, tortuous torpedo run on the *Soryu*. Through every burst of enemy gunfire he kept the nose of his aircraft pointed at his target. He witnessed his fellow pilots going down and was very aware that his own life could be measured in seconds. Every detail seemed to stand out as he focused his eyes on the looming enemy carrier. The flight deck was full of aircraft and scrambling figures. For an instant, a strange thought flashed through his mind: *"I had a thought right in a split second there to crash into those planes . . . because I could have started a beautiful fire."* However, his thought process then changed course rapidly: *"The plane was still flying and I felt pretty good and I didn't see any sense in crashing into those planes. I thought maybe I'd get a chance to go back and hit them again someday and as long as there's life there's hope. So I pulled up and went over them."*[75]

For some reason America seems to face foes who glorify suicide. The Japanese in World War II sent countless young kamikaze pilots on one-way missions. Terrorists of today kill themselves and innocent victims for their own "higher" cause. American values, thankfully, do not permit this approach. In the beginning, our Founding Fathers acted on the firm belief that the value and dignity of every human being comes from God and that every citizen is "endowed by his Creator with certain unalienable rights." In wartime our leaders sometimes have to send men on dangerous missions. However, every effort is made to provide for their safe return. Every American soldier knows that he will never be considered "expendable."

> So God created man in his own image, in the image of God he created him; male and female he created them. ~Genesis 1:27

Prepare to Abandon Ship

LT. JOSEPH POLLARD went aboard the USS *Yorktown* on May 27 and sailed with her three days later. As one of the ship's medical officers, he prepared his men and equipment for the action ahead. On June 4, the Japanese task force was finally sighted. The *Yorktown's* aircraft were armed, fueled, and launched late that morning. An eerie lull ensued. Finally, at about 2:00 p.m. the aircraft began returning, many with battle damage. In the midst of recovery operations, the general quarters alarm was sounded, alerting the crew to an enemy attack. Suddenly two sickening thuds shook the ship, resulting in an immediate hard list to port.

Pollard remembered: *"Just then word came over the speaker, 'Prepare to abandon ship!' I was dumbfounded. It was uncomprehensible. A man lying beside me with one foot shot away and a severe chest wound turned his head towards me and asked, 'What does this mean for us?' and turned his head away. He knew that he would have no chance in the water."*[76]

We have sympathy for anyone like this who is suddenly jolted from calm conditions to utter chaos. How would you or I react? We hope we would be cool and confident in a crisis, but we never know until it happens. We can only pray for courage under fire and the ability to think clearly. Confidence in God and in our relationship to him is a big advantage at such a time. Jesus promised, *"The peace of God, which transcends all understanding"* (Philippians 4:7). This peace pertains not only to our long-term spiritual well-being, but also helps us find confidence and a calm mind in an emergency.

> When they saw the courage of Peter and John and realized that they were unschooled, ordinary men, they were astonished and they took note that these men had been with Jesus. ~Acts 4:13

Wade McClusky

EARLY ON JUNE 4 Lt. Cdr. Wade McClusky led a squadron of Dauntless dive-bombers from the USS *Enterprise* in search of the Japanese carriers. Arriving at the designated point, he found the sea empty. Unknown to him or anyone else, the Japanese task force had changed course. The search then became a guessing game. Having climbed to high altitude with heavy bomb loads, fuel and time were running out.

As he was calculating his next move, McClusky looked down to see a lone Japanese ship far below:

> *Call it fate, luck or what you may, because at 1155 (0955 local time) I spied a lone Jap cruiser[77] scurrying under full power to the northeast. Concluding that she possibly was a liaison ship between the occupation forces and the striking force, I altered my Group's course to that of the cruiser. At 1205 (1005) that decision paid dividends. Peering through my binoculars which were practically glued to my eyes, I saw dead ahead about 35 miles distant the welcome sight of the Jap carrier striking force.[78]*

This decision not only "paid dividends" in the Battle of Midway, it was one of the most pivotal decisions ever made in any war. Twenty minutes later McClusky's dive-bombers delivered fatal blows to the Japanese carriers *Kaga* and *Akagi*, ensuring one of the most improbable yet decisive defeats ever inflicted in naval warfare. McClusky's decision was one of many "lucky" events contributing to this amazing and miraculous victory.

> Suddenly the fingers of a human hand appeared and wrote on the plaster of the wall, near the lampstand in the royal palace. The king watched the hand as it wrote. His face turned pale. ~Daniel 5:5–6

Another Stroke of Luck

THE AIR GROUP from the USS *Enterprise* was amazingly successful in finding the Japanese carrier force on June 4. The Americans were also astounded to find no fighter opposition to their attack. As Lieutenant Commander McClusky bore in on his bombing run, he discovered one more surprise:

> *As we neared the bomb-dropping point, another stroke of luck met our eyes. Both enemy carriers had their decks full of planes that had just returned from the attack on Midway. Later it was learned about the time we had discovered the Jap force, an enemy seaplane had detected our forces. Apparently then, the planes on deck were being refueled and rearmed for an attack on our carriers. Supposing then we, Air Group Six, had turned southward toward Midway, as the* Hornet *group did, I can vividly imagine the* Enterprise *and* Hornet *at the bottom of the sea as the* Yorktown *was some three days later.* [79]

The condition of the flight decks on the Japanese carriers at this decisive moment was critical to the outcome. There was great confusion because the aircraft were being rearmed for a strike on the American carriers, instead of a second attack on Midway. The flight decks were filled with fuel lines and aviation ordnance. The bomb hits of McClusky's dive-bombers would probably not have been fatal in themselves. However, they were devastating due to what McClusky termed *"another stroke of luck."* In this case the "luck" was confusion on the part of the Japanese and the sacrifice of Torpedo 8. Human planning could not have orchestrated the sequence of these improbable circumstances.

The LORD our God has shown us his glory and his majesty, and we have heard his voice from the fire. ~Deuteronomy 5:24

Spruance

AFTER THE WAR, Mitsuo Fuchida, the leader of the attack on Pearl Harbor, coauthored a book about the Battle of Midway. The book contains a foreword written by Adm. Raymond Spruance, the officer most responsible for the success of the U.S. forces during the battle. In the foreword Admiral Spruance makes this comment:

> *In reading the account of what happened on June 4th, I am more than ever impressed with the part that good or bad fortune sometimes plays in tactical engagements. The authors give us credit, where no credit is due, for being able to choose the exact time for our attack on the Japanese carriers when they were at their greatest disadvantage—flight decks full of aircraft fueled, armed, and ready to go.*[80]

Admiral Spruance displays a sense of humility unique to a military hero. He makes an unusual concession that the actions of the leaders involved were not the determining factor in this great victory. He attributes the amazing timing of his own attack to "good fortune," which, for a nonreligious person, would be a perfectly adequate explanation. It is my belief, however, that, instead of a series of "lucky" incidents at Midway we have seen a pattern of events that shows evidence of God's hand acting on behalf of the American forces at this crucial moment of the war. It is difficult to imagine the long-range consequence of a different outcome to this battle. If the Japanese had achieved mastery of the Pacific, America would have been forced to drastically alter its commitment to the war in Europe. The shape of Europe and the world after the war would not have been the same.

When the trumpets sounded, the people shouted, and at the sound of the trumpet, when the people gave a loud shout, the wall collapsed; so every man charged straight in, and they took the city. ~Joshua 6:20

Big guns firing from U.S. warship. (National Archives)

MARCH
Battle of the Atlantic

DURING THE 1930s, isolationist sentiment against involvement in the growing European conflict was strong. Negative public opinion and budget restrictions resulted in a meager allocation of resources to the U.S. military establishment. Up until 1940, the comfortable assumption prevailed that the army of France and the navy of Great Britain could successfully contain Nazi Germany in Europe. When this illusion was shattered, the United States, while continuing to profess "neutrality," adopted a more open role designed to "keep England in the war" and to prepare herself for war.

Walking a political tightrope, President Roosevelt entered into base-sharing agreements with Canada and Great Britain, and pushed a "Lend-Lease" program through Congress to provide ships and materiel to the beleaguered British. On the day that Paris fell, the president signed a naval expansion bill that had been in debate for months, in effect doubling the size of the U.S. Navy.[81] Unfortunately, it would take two years to bring this expansion on line. In September 1940 the Selective Training and Service Act was passed creating the military draft.

From the beginning, the German submarine (U-boat) threat to U.S. and British shipping had been serious. With the fall of France, however, the Germans were able to establish bases on the French coast, almost doubling the effective range of their submarines. Admiral Donitz, the German commander of U-boat operations, initiated a new concept called *Rudeltaktik*, or "wolf-pack" tactics, enabling groups of submarines to force their way through escort screens to effectively attack merchant convoys. The toll on Allied shipping began to rise ominously. During late 1940, 217 merchant vessels were sunk, representing more than a million tons of shipping. Britain's survival became ever more tenuous. Winston Churchill declared, *"The only thing that ever really frightened me during the war was the U-boat peril."*[82]

The Battle of the Atlantic continued furiously for the duration of the war. Allied losses continued to be heavy during 1942 and 1943. Upon America's official entry into the war, German operations also moved into American waters, inflicting heavy losses on coastal shipping and commerce in the Western Hemisphere. Progress countering this threat was painfully slow. Escorted convoys were the preferred countermeasure against submarines. There just weren't enough escorts. Slowly, more destroyers became available, as Britain, Canada, and the United States were able to commit more resources to this theater of the war. Land-based air coverage was gradually extended, and the final gap eventually filled by escort carriers after 1943.

The climax of the Battle of the Atlantic came in late April 1943 when a forty-two-ship Allied convoy came against a U-boat picket line of fifty-one submarines off Iceland. Cdr. P. W. Gretton, RN, fought a decisive action over nine days in the worst possible weather. With nine ships he sank five U-boats, while aircraft disposed of two more.[83] The German high command had to reappraise strategy. After this battle, most submarine activity was directed toward less defended, and less strategic, shipping lanes.

Sink the Bismarck

REVENGE WAS THE order of the day. The German battleship *Bismarck* had destroyed HMS *Hood* in the Denmark Strait. The British battle cruiser was the pride of the Royal Navy, and her sudden loss was one of the most shocking events of World War II. The British high command devoted every available resource to find and sink the *Bismarck*. The battle was joined on May 26, 1941, when a squadron of Swordfish aircraft from HMS *Ark Royal* found the enemy battleship and made a torpedo strike that damaged her steering. The next morning a group of British warships closed in with a withering surface attack that sank the *Bismarck* in less than two hours.

Lt. Ludovic Kennedy was on the bridge of HMS *Tartar* and watched the final moments of the great warship. His thoughts were conflicted:

> *It was not a pretty sight.* Bismarck *was a menace that had to be destroyed, a dragon that would have severed the arteries that kept Britain alive. And yet to see her now, this beautiful ship, surrounded by enemies on all sides, hopelessly outgunned and out maneuvered, being slowly battered to a wreck, filled one with awe and pity . . . George Whaley, our Canadian lieutenant, wrote, "What that ship was like inside did not bear thinking of; her guns smashed, the ship full of fire, her people hurt; and surely all men are much the same when hurt." It was a thought shared by many British sailors that day.*[84]

It is somehow comforting to hear these conflicting emotions in a moment of triumph. The climax of this battle was surely satisfying to every British seaman. At the same time, there were pangs of conscience at the suffering of enemy counterparts. It is reassuring to know that such humanity existed then and that it is there within each one of us now. Jesus said, *"I desire mercy, not sacrifice"* (Matthew 9:13). In our moments of success we must open our hearts to him and let ourselves be the vessels of his mercy. This kind of loving humility is only possible through our Lord, Jesus Christ.

> Yet when they were ill, I put on sackcloth and humbled myself with fasting. . . . I went about mourning as though for my friend or brother. I bowed my head in grief. ~Psalm 35:13, 14

At Sea on a Corvette

CORVETTES WERE small naval vessels built early in the war to fill the urgent need for convoy escorts. Even smaller than destroyers, they were a violent ride in heavy seas. Actually designed for coastal duty, they were often pressed into the service of ocean-going convoys. Frank Curry spent much of the war on the HMCS *Kamsack*, a Canadian Navy corvette operating out of Newfoundland and Nova Scotia. Unending days at sea aboard these little ships was a true test of human endurance. From Curry's diary:

> *Now I know something of the meaning of rough seas. Mountainous seas are breaking completely over the ship, and it is turning into massive coatings of ice as it hits. We are sheathed in sixteen inches of ice and I do not know what keeps us from going to the bottom of the Atlantic as we pitch, toss, roll and everything else imaginable.*
>
> *Just as we were about to head back to Sydney, we received urgent orders to proceed to the rescue of a torpedoed ship in the Gulf. So off we went into the very teeth of terrific seas. Boy, are they ever huge green ones. Going on watch at 10:00 p.m., I stood for a few minutes by the wheelhouse which is all of 20 feet above the water line, and looked straight up at mountainous seas that made our little corvette seem very insignificant indeed—I hung on for dear life as I made my way in pitch dark with the roaring gales tearing at me every foot of the way, up to the bridge. How can anyone know what a night like this is at sea who has never actually experienced it.*[85]

Sometimes when we study history we focus on the big picture of military campaigns and strategy, and lose sight of the "little" picture: the toll on each man and woman who has to implement those strategies. The life of the corvette sailor is a reminder of the individual sacrifice and hardship endured for years by thousands during the Battle of the Atlantic. Their struggle gives special meaning to the words of the "Navy Hymn":

> *Eternal Father, strong to save, whose arm hath bound the restless wave,*
> *Who bidd'st the mighty ocean deep its own appointed limits keep;*
> *Oh, hear us when we cry to Thee, for those in peril on the sea!*[86]

They saw the works of the Lord, his wonderful deeds in the deep. For he spoke and stirred up a tempest that lifted high the waves. ~Psalm 107:24–25

The Old Sailing Rule

FRANK CURRY continued his harrowing account of rescuing a torpedoed ship in the Gulf of St. Lawrence during a winter storm:

> Terrible seas still running as we pounded our way into them. We are bouncing all over creation. Somehow we found the merchant ship at 0200 of the wildest darkest night imaginable, and got a line aboard her. Headed slowly back to Sydney from close to St. Paul's Island. It is rougher than I ever dreamt the ocean could be. Our mess decks are knee-deep in bitterly cold sea water, everything possible is afloat from spilled tins of jam to best uniforms, hats, sea-biscuits, letters and books. No one gives it a second thought—for it seems all-important to think of survival. Arms and legs and joints are screaming for even a moment's relaxation from the jarring and pitching and beating. One has to go back to the old sailing rule of one hand for the ship, one hand for yourself, particularly on the upper deck where one false move means the end.[87]

The "old sailing rule" originated with an old salt who wisely realized that aboard ship the best intentions are useless if you get injured or lost at sea because you neglected the violent movements of the ship itself. No matter the importance of the task at hand, you have to first make sure that you are physically secure in your surroundings. This is a great analogy for our spiritual lives. Our spiritual anchor point is our Savior, Jesus Christ. We always have to have one hand out for him, to support us and guide us as we tackle the vexing problems of our daily lives. Without him, we will be battered by our problems and lost in our spiritual journey.

He said to his disciples, "Why are you so afraid? Do you still have no faith?" They were terrified and asked each other, "Who is this? Even the wind and the waves obey him!" ~Mark 4:40–41

A Child's Perspective

IN MARCH 1943 eleven-year-old Joan Corbin wrote to her uncle, Walter Kellogg, serving aboard ship in the North Atlantic:

Dear Uncle Joe:

Is it fun on your boat? I hope so. I am in Maryland but am going home very soon. It's very warm; 70 degrees today! We waded in the woods even! I have made lips here. Mine! I have kissed them. You kiss them too. The love will carry. I hope you will come home safely. I am telling God to keep you in His grace. Please remember me. I won't forget you, or the job you are doing for your country.

Love, Joanie[88]

I'm sure it was best that little Joanie didn't know the details of her uncle's service at sea. In fact, this is one of the main objectives of all servicemen in war, to protect their loved ones, especially the children, at home. It is also refreshing to hear a child's perspective on some things that we take so seriously as adults.

During my time in Vietnam, we received many letters from grade school children. Their honesty and naîveté were always uplifting. It is wonderful to catch glimpses of their perspective on the world, especially the innocence and wonder that we too often lose as adults. We know that Jesus honored the children and that he exhorts us to maintain a childlike attitude. This doesn't mean that we stop thinking or reasoning. It does mean that our faith has to be simple and complete, as a child's love of a parent or an uncle at sea.

> Let the little children come to me, and do not hinder them, for the kingdom of God belongs to such as these. ~Mark 10:14

Armed Guard

IN 1941 MY thirty-six-year-old father was a businessman in Conway, South Carolina. He wanted to join the war effort and went to great lengths to go on active duty with some military service. Finally successful in obtaining a commission in the Naval Reserve, he was assigned to the newly organized Armed Guard of the Navy where he took detachments of Navy sailors aboard merchant vessels as gun crews for submarine and air defense. He saw sea duty with convoys to England, North Africa, and South America.

Early in the war the merchant seamen viewed these detachments suspiciously. The merchantmen were professionals at their business and rightfully considered these sailors as out of their element. They especially resented young Armed Guard officers who tried to throw their weight around by dictating to the ship's crew. It was soon found that a special type of officer was needed for this type of duty:

> *Emphasis soon shifted away from the procurement of the very young officer and especially of the person who knew or thought he knew too much about running merchant ships. The ideal Armed guard officer was a tactful person who could look after the interests of his men and at the same time keep relations smooth between the Navy complement and master, officers and crew of the merchant ship. He was a man who could get along with people who were under great mental strain and who could win their confidence. His relations with his gunners was close. He was a kind of doctor, chaplain and commanding officer at the same time. The highly nervous individual did not last in the Armed Guard.[89]*

I must admit to a feeling of pride in reading these qualities of an Armed Guard officer, which I feel are very descriptive of my father. He was a Citadel graduate with military experience and a broad range of civic, business, and family responsibilities. He was an active man and able to get any job done while taking care of those under him. In later life he often repeated his favorite advice on leadership, which he said was "straight out of the Bible." I learned later that these were actually the words of our Lord and Savior, Jesus Christ:

Whoever wants to become great among you must be your servant, and whoever wants to be first must be your slave—just as the Son of Man did not come to be served, but to serve, and to give his life as a ransom for many. ~Matthew 20:26–28

Sighted Sub

EARLY IN THE WAR, an affectionate epithet for the Armed Guard circulated in Navy circles: *"Sighted Sub—Glub Glub."* This uncomplimentary perception changed as the war wore on and these units proved their effectiveness. The phrase itself was a takeoff from one of the most famous phrases in U.S. naval history.

On January 28, 1942, Donald Mason was piloting a Lockheed Hudson twin-engine aircraft on antisubmarine patrol out of Argentia, Newfoundland. After hours of boredom staring at an empty sea, an alert crewman spotted the thin, characteristic wake of a submarine periscope breaking the surface. Mason attacked at once, dropping two bombs from an altitude of about 25 feet, straddling the periscope. With the detonation of the bombs the submarine was seen to lift out of the water and then to sink vertically. Minutes later an oil slick was observed bubbling to the surface.[90] Shortly thereafter Mason radioed an historic four-word message back to base: *"Sighted sub, sank same."*[91]

Donald Mason was probably following protocol to keep radio traffic to a minimum. However, he gives us a lesson in effective word power. Fewer is usually better. The apostle John was able to communicate the complete Christian gospel in only twenty-six words, showing the beauty and simplicity of Christ's message in a way that makes it easy for us to succinctly share the good news with others:

> For God so loved the world that he gave his one and only Son, that whoever believes in him shall not perish but have eternal life. ~John 3:16

Attack of the Minesweepers

HMS *HARRIER* was one of four minesweepers in Kola Inlet when a radio message came in that the cruiser HMS *Edinburgh* had been torpedoed and was trying to reach Murmansk. The *Harrier* and other minesweepers quickly got under way to help. The little minesweepers just had time to deploy around the *Edinburgh* when three German destroyers opened fire from a distance. Cdr. Eric Hinton immediately turned *Harrier* toward the enemy, put on maximum speed, and opened fire with his single four-inch gun. Two British destroyers soon joined him, and, together, they caused the Germans to break off the attack. One of Hinton's subordinates later wrote:

> *Seeing gun flashes from five separate directions, the Germans probably imagined that they were confronting a superior force. Each of these heavy destroyers was armed with five 5.9 inch guns in addition to torpedoes, so had they pressed in they might easily have sunk every ship in our force. However, Harrier and the other 'fleet' minesweepers looked not unlike destroyers when seen end-on, so probably the Captain's action in heading straight for the enemy had saved our lives.[92]*

Commander Hinton's attack saved his own ship and the others at the scene of this battle. He showed what a small force could accomplish with determination and decisive action, even against great odds. This story is an encouragement to all who follow Jesus Christ. Our numbers are often few in the midst of a culture apparently going in a different direction. However, we know the power of a "small force" that is on God's side. We need to take action with confidence when we have opportunities to serve him, even when we have doubts that we can make a difference.

The race is not to the swift or the battle to the strong. ~Ecclesiastes 9:11

Murmansk Run

IN MAY 1942 the cargo ship SS *Atlantic*, laden with aircraft and explosives, was sailing above the Arctic Circle, bound for Murmansk, Russia. Arctic ice forced *Atlantic* and the other thirty-five ships in this convoy close to the north coast of Norway and German airbases located there. May 27 brought clear weather and almost continuous air attacks for ten hours. Seven ships were lost, and three badly damaged. One of the officers assessed the toll:

> *Taking stock, ships were being sunk at the rate of one every two hours. We still had at least 60 hours sailing to get to Murmansk with 29 merchant ships left. Moreover, our ship had used up more than half its ammunition, and presumably the others were in similar straits.*
>
> *If the pace of the attacks was kept up, the arithmetic seemed to add up to the possibility of all our ships being sunk . . . Everything depended on where the bomb or torpedo would strike. No. 3 hold was full of explosives. If that were hit, we would all disappear in a flash of light and a cloud of smoke—one ship had already done so.*[93]

These sailors on the Murmansk Run were pushed to the limit of human endurance by arctic storms, ice, deadly cold water, volatile cargoes, and the constant threat of attack by enemy aircraft and submarines. They understood the overwhelming odds against their own survival and still found the courage to do their duty as sailors and to fight every battle as soldiers. Thanks to their valiant effort a tenuous but absolutely critical lifeline between the Allied nations was kept open throughout World War II.

In the same way, many great heroes of the faith have achieved much while doubting their own ability to succeed or survive. There are times when we too feel that God is asking us to do more than we are capable of doing. In times like these, remember that if God asks us to accomplish something, he will not forsake us on the way.

> Be strong and courageous. Do not be afraid or terrified because of them, for the LORD your God goes with you; he will never leave you nor forsake you.
> ~Deuteronomy 31:6

New Life

IN MARCH 1942, the Esso tanker *T. C. McCobb* was sunk by a German submarine four hundred miles off the northern coast of Brazil. Michael Wajda suffered a severe head wound while trying to abandon ship, and found himself on a raft with two of his shipmates. By the thirty-fifth day both of his shipmates had succumbed to the elements, leaving Wajda alone. On the forty-fifth day he saw the first muddy streaks in the water and knew land was near. He was picked up the next day and taken to a hospital in Georgetown, British Guiana.

Meanwhile, Wajda had been presumed dead for weeks since many of his other shipmates had already been rescued. His family was in mourning when the news of his survival arrived:

> *"Sea Gives Back Sailor to Jersey Mother," was the headline in the New York Herald-Tribune on May 21. And that is how Michael Wajda's mother, in nearby New Jersey, learned that the son she had given up for dead had been returned to life. She abandoned the mourning garments she had worn for a month and joyously awaited the return of her son— whom the news article said she would not recognize in "the red-bearded, sun-blackened young man, gaunt from hunger, who was picked up from a life raft that drifted toward the shore of British Guiana after forty-six days at sea."*[94]

This is a wonderful story of rebirth. We share the joy of this mother, who was able to abandon her mourning garments after reaching the depths of despair. Christians experience a similar spiritual journey each spring. After a Lenten season of reflection and the shared agony of the Stations of the Cross, we come to the Easter season with a fuller appreciation for the depths of despair. From this perspective, the resurrection of our Savior takes on its full meaning and gives us the ultimate cause for joyful celebration.

"Don't be alarmed," he said. "You are looking for Jesus the Nazarene, who was crucified. He has risen! He is not here. See the place where they laid him." ~Mark 16:6

Hard Choices

THERE WERE MANY times during the Battle of the Atlantic when destroyer commanders faced a painful dilemma. When enemy submarines attacked their convoys, there were inevitably survivors in the water at the same time that other attacks were in progress. Obviously, the destroyer's mission was to pursue all submarine contacts to protect the other ships in the convoy. However, survivors could not be expected to last long in the North Atlantic. One such episode, with a happy ending, was reported by Capt. Donald MacIntyre of the HMS *Walker*.

On a wild night in March 1941, five cargo ships in his convoy were torpedoed. The *Walker* raced about the convoy and made several depth charge runs on sonar contacts with uncertain results. At one point confusing sonar echoes from all the explosions necessitated a lull in the action. MacIntyre recalled:

> *I had for some time past noticed in the distance the bobbing lights from the lifeboats of one of our sunken ships, but with an enemy to engage there was nothing for it but to harden my heart and hope that the time might come later when I could rescue the crews. This lull seemed a good opportunity and perhaps if we left the area temporarily the U-boat commander might think he had shaken us off and be tempted into some indiscretion. So . . . we stopped and picked up the master and thirty-seven of the crew of the SS J. B. White.*[95]

Our choices may not be as stark as those of a destroyer commander in wartime, but they are nevertheless often difficult. We need to understand that God intends for us to face hard choices in our lives. He gives us the capacity to make decisions, and he holds us accountable for them. The Old Testament gives us repeated admonitions to choose obedience to God's laws, which is of course what we should always try to do. But Jesus brought a new perspective and a new choice. When we choose Jesus Christ, we are choosing life over death. He explained this to Martha by telling her that the physical preparations for his visit were not as important as understanding this message.

"Martha, Martha," the Lord answered, "you are worried and upset about many things, but only one thing is needed. Mary has chosen what is better, and it will not be taken away from her." ~Luke 10:41–42

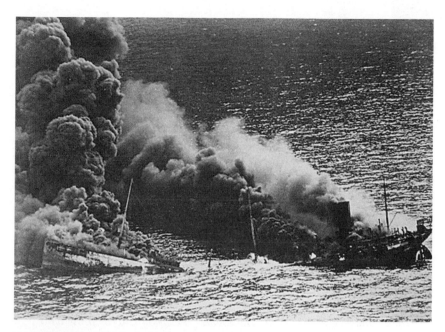

Torpedoed ship sinks in the Atlantic.
(National Archives)

Depth-charge attack on a Nazi U-boat.
(National Archives)

The Four Chaplains

THE SS *DORCHESTER* almost made it to safety. On the evening of February 2, 1943, the troopship broke away from its convoy and headed into Narsarsuaq, Greenland, the destination for this trip. At about 1:00 a.m. a violent explosion lifted the ship. As the lights went out, nine hundred men scrambled for the upper decks and lifeboats. Those that made it topside found the ship listing to starboard and sinking fast. Men were frantically trying to break the ice off the tackle holding the boats. Only a few were launched. Those with life jackets started jumping clear of the ship. Many did not have one. Amid this confusion four chaplains from the embarked units manned the storage locker where extra life jackets were kept. They handed these out as fast as they could. When the supply was exhausted, each chaplain took off his own jacket and gave it to an astonished soldier.

> In the midst of the chaos around them, time stood still for those who watched as four men on a sinking ship gave away their life jackets. Those who witnessed the act were momentarily stunned. Said one survivor, "It was the finest thing I've seen, or hope to see, this side of heaven." The chaplains, now without life jackets, continued to minister to men, calming those who were crying in fear, praying with others, helping the men prepare themselves for what was about to happen. As the lifeboats rowed away from the ship, some of the men in the boats said they could see the chaplains standing on deck, arms linked together and heads bowed, when the Dorchester *finally succumbed.*[96]

The four chaplains were George Fox (Methodist), Clark Poling (Dutch Reformed), Alex Goode (Jewish), and John Washington (Catholic). They were each awarded the Distinguished Service Cross posthumously for their heroism. Together they have left us one of the finest examples of Christian service ever recorded.

Taking the very nature of a servant . . . He humbled himself and became obedient to death—even death on a cross! ~Philippians 2:7–8

Reading the Bible

RABBI ALEXANDER GOODE enlisted in the Army in 1942 and was thirty-two years old when he completed Chaplain School at Harvard University. In January 1943 he said goodbye to his wife, Theresa, and their four-year-old daughter, Rosalie Bea. He boarded the troopship, SS *Dorchester*, for the fateful voyage that would see him and his fellow chaplains heroically sacrifice their lives for the sake of countless others.

Before the war, as a rabbinical student, Alex wrote a letter to Theresa, then his sweetheart. He shared some thoughts about his favorite poets at that time and then expressed some heartfelt thoughts about the most important book of his life:

> *Speaking of the Bible I might mention that by this time in my preparation for the career of a Rabbi I have read most of the Bible, and when I say read I really mean studied carefully, at least three times, so that I am more familiar with this great library of our people than I am with any other volume I have ever studied or read. In it is stored such a mine of information and beauty that I am tempted to think with our ancestors who absolutely believed that everything in the Bible was true and that all things that man can experience under the sun are contained therein. So much is treasured up that I could not begin to describe its contents. It really is heartbreaking that more people do not seek out its treasures.[97]*

No doubt many passages of Scripture were in Goode's mind as he ministered to others amid the chaos of a sinking ship. When we study God's Word and hide it in our hearts (Psalm 119:11) we build a resource of incalculable value to help us face difficult times. In a moment of decision, Scripture will guide our choice if we have been diligent in our efforts to not only read it, but to understand and remember it.

> You have known the holy Scriptures, which are able to make you wise for salvation through faith in Christ Jesus. All scripture is God-breathed and is useful for teaching, rebuking, correcting and training in righteousness, so that the man of God may be thoroughly equipped for every good work. ~2 Timothy 3:15–17

Where to Sleep

LIFE ABOARD A merchant ship in convoy across the Atlantic was a mixture of boredom and fear. Long days and nights passed without incident. However, when something happened, it usually happened suddenly. Life jackets and precious valuables were kept close at hand. There was also the issue of where to sleep:

> *The civilian Merchant Marines who manned the ships grimly calculated where they slept aboard ship by the cargo they carried. If you were hauling a load of iron ore, you slept on deck for you had only a few seconds to clear the ship once a torpedo hit. If you carried general cargo, you could sleep below decks but kept your clothes on because your survival time was calculated in minutes. If, however, your ship carried a load of aviation fuel, you were free to sleep naked below decks, with the door closed since you would never have the time to escape the certain and sudden oblivion of a torpedo attack.*[98]

When there is real danger, it is human nature to be more careful. Our senses are heightened, and we take extra precautions. We don't want to be caught unprepared. Vigilance is even more important in our spiritual lives. We may think that we have unlimited time and therefore feel no need for urgency. Jesus tried to emphasize the foolishness of this stance with the parable of the ten virgins waiting at night for the bridegroom. Not knowing how long it would be before he arrived, five of the virgins took extra oil for their lamps. They were prepared when the time came. The door to the wedding banquet was shut to the others who failed to keep the vigil.

"Sir! Sir!" They said. "Open the door for us!" But he replied, "I tell you the truth, I don't know you." Therefore keep watch, because you do not know the day or the hour. ~Matthew 25:11–13

Hope to Go On

PAUL HIRSCH was forcefully thrown into the water by an exploding shell that totally destroyed the bridge of the SS *Hurley*. He remembered every horrendous detail: *"My life jacket slowly raised me to the surface where I saw a scene from hell. The heat was intense and the sounds were unreal. Flames danced on the waves slick with burning oil, the ship was cracking to pieces, men were screaming."*[99]

With his ship destroyed by a German submarine, Hirsch began a twenty-one-day ordeal with twenty-three other seamen in a lifeboat designed for ten. Stranded in the mid-Atlantic outside normal shipping lanes, their chances of rescue seemed slim. As they grew weaker, the seamen seemed to sense that they were nearing the limit of their endurance.

At this stage, they began to pray. They prayed for the wounded and for each other. As they continued these prayers they came closer together and found hope to go on. Hirsch later recalled that they managed to keep their civility, their self-respect, and their courage. Above all, these men nurtured the hope that they would survive. Their faith was rewarded on the twenty-first day when a British freighter came over the horizon to end their ordeal.

God wants us to be hopeful in Him. Finding hope in all circumstances is a recurring biblical theme reflected throughout the Psalms; *"Be strong and take heart, all you who hope in the LORD"* (Psalm 31:24). *"But now, Lord, what do I look for? My hope is in you"* (Psalm 39:7). *"For you have been my hope, O Sovereign LORD, my confidence since my youth"* (Psalms 71:5). Our heavenly Father also sent his Son into the world to bring us an even greater and ultimate hope: that through him, we have a place in his everlasting kingdom.

> We also rejoice in our sufferings, because we know that suffering produces perseverance; perseverance, character; and character, hope. And hope does not disappoint us. ~Romans 5:3–5

Navy Shower

WHEN THE FRESH water supply runs low on a Navy ship, the inevitable and dreaded recourse is "water hours," limiting the time available for showers. To prevent this and to educate the new crew members, the following article was run in a ship's newsletter on New Year's Day 1942:

> *The way most so-called sailors waste water, it is little wonder the ship may be required to establish washroom hours.*
>
> *If some of you have no regard for engineering efficiency or ship's spirit, most of you should still realize that fresh water aboard ship at sea is precious, and that the evaporators can't make enough water for you to waste any!*
>
> *So, for the benefit of first, second, third and fourth cruise "boots," we shall endeavor to explain the proper way for a sailor to take a shower; in four easy lessons. 1. Wet yourself down. 2. Turn-off the water while soaping yourself. 3. Rinse. 4. Turn off the water and scram. P.S. If you want to linger longer than that under a shower, wait until you hit the "Y". If all hands can learn to take a shower on board as outlined above, washroom hours may be extended, to the better comfort of all of us. Be a shipmate! Be a sailor!!!*[100]

Fresh water is always a precious commodity aboard a Navy ship, requiring careful conservation by every man on board. It is also a precious commodity in many arid regions of the world. In the Middle East, a gallon of water used to cost more than a gallon of gasoline.

Water was an especially critical resource during biblical times, and for that reason, was an important source of imagery. The psalmist described longing for God as a deer panting for *"streams of water"* (Psalm 42:1). Jesus told us that they are blessed who *"thirst for righteousness"* (Matthew 5:6). The culmination of this imagery is found in Jesus' encounter with a Samaritan woman. After asking her for a drink of water from a well, Jesus offered her another kind of drink that would forever replenish itself. This image of "living water" presents a powerful picture of eternal life with Jesus and our Father in heaven.

> Everyone who drinks this water will be thirsty again, but whoever drinks the water I give him will never thirst. Indeed, the water I give him will become in him a spring of water welling up to eternal life. ~John 4:13–14

I Couldn't Die

ON JUNE 9, 1940, the British aircraft carrier HMS *Glorious* was intercepted returning from Norway by two German battle cruisers. The *Glorious* and her two escort destroyers were sunk, with more than fifteen hundred sailors lost. Ronald Healiss, a Royal Marine, was one of the few survivors. Sighting a lifeboat in the distance, he began the longest swim of his life. After what seemed like hours, every muscle was cramped and his stomach was in a knot. He thought his time had come.

> *It's true that when you see death approaching your past life passes before your eyes. I remembered my boyhood, the day I joined the Royal Marines. I could see my mother clearly. And the girl who would have been my wife in a few short days. In my trouser- pocket there had been a little leather case in which I always carried a picture of my parents and my girl. I felt about me with a frozen hand. The case was still there. I took it out while I floated, intent on bidding them goodbye. But I couldn't. The faces were too real. The sodden photographs smiled up at me and I knew I couldn't die without seeing those three people again. I thrust the wallet back in my pocket and struck out again with fresh strength.[101]*

A friend once told me a similar story of survival in a Vietnamese rice paddy. He decided that in spite of his wounds and "hopeless" situation, he was just *not* going to die in that place. He reached down within himself for the strength to keep going and somehow got to a safe place. These stories are a reminder of how precious life is and how strong we can be once we make the decision to move ahead. God stands ready to reach out to us when we choose to go forward in spite of our difficulties and when we turn to him for help. In him there is truly no hopeless situation.

But you, O LORD, be not far off; O my Strength, come quickly to help me.
~Psalm 22:19

One More Round

" GENTLEMAN JIM" Corbett became heavyweight boxing champion by defeating the great John L. Sullivan in 1892. One of his famous remarks was quoted to give the crew of an American battleship inspiration to perform their duties under the difficult conditions of wartime:

> *Fight one more round. When your feet are so tired that you have to shuffle back to the ring, fight one more round. When your arms are so tired that you can hardly lift your hands to come on guard, fight one more round. When your nose is bleeding and your eyes are black and you are so tired that you wish your opponent would crack you one on the jaw and put you to sleep, fight one more round—remembering that the man who always fights one more round is never whipped.*[102]

It may be difficult for many to identify with boxing as a metaphor for living. These days our struggles are usually not of such an intensely physical nature. However, even our everyday problems relating to work and family often require great patience and at times even a degree of dogged determination. Then there are our spiritual struggles, which are on a different plane altogether. Our efforts in this sphere have eternal consequences and are worthy of our utmost perseverance. Scripture exhorts us to, *"Fight the good fight"* (1 Timothy 6:12) and *"Stand firm in the faith; be men of courage; be strong"* (1 Corinthians 16:13). When we are discouraged or tempted to give up, standing up in faith to fight 'one more round' may make all the difference.

> Brothers, as an example of patience in the face of suffering, take the prophets who spoke in the name of the Lord. As you know, we consider blessed those who have persevered. You have heard of Job's perseverance and have seen what the Lord finally brought about. ~James 5:10–11

Staring at a Bomb

THE BATTLE OFF the coast of Norway went on for twenty hours. Seaman Robert Case was firing his anti-aircraft gun at real targets for the first time. He quickly became a veteran. His ship, the SS *Steel Worker*, had several near-misses as enemy aircraft darted over and through the convoy. Suddenly, two Messerschmitts bore in from an altitude of about 2,000 feet, their wings thin black lines in the distance. As Case stared through his sights, those wings grew thicker and flames began to erupt from them. Keeping his eyes to the sights and hand on the trigger he opened fire. The empty shell casings started clattering over the deck under his feet. Then, time seemed to stand still:

> *The aftermost plane peeled off . . . The other kept on, right into our fire, smack for us. Then he dropped it, a 550–pounder. He was gone, away from our fire, and . . . all we could do was look up at that bomb. It fell, slanting with the pull of the plane's speed. It whirled, screaming and howling in the air directly over-head. We could very clearly see the cylindrical khaki shape, the fins, even the white blur that was the serial markings on the side. This was for us, we thought. This was death . . . the .sound of it seemed to possess all sound*[103]

Then, according to Case, the bomb *"veered a bit."* It struck the sea twenty feet astern of the *Steel Worker*, lifting the ship in the water and splitting deck plates. Case and his shipmates were water-soaked from the blast, but alive.

No one would ever fault a man for looking death in the face and fighting to survive, as Case and his shipmates did. When Christ looked death in the face, however, he didn't fight. He allowed himself to be crucified, even though he knew the anguish that horrible death would bring. His resurrection spelled victory both for him and for all of us who accept the gift of salvation he offers to us. (JG)

Where, O death, is your victory?
Where, O death, is your sting? ~1 Corinthians 15:55

Evacuated to America

WHEN WAR CAME to England, families faced difficult decisions. Concerned about the safety of their children during the bombing, many parents in industrial areas chose to send them to rural towns to keep them from harm. Marion Hunt's father went to even greater lengths. After considerable effort he was able to arrange for his two children and his wife to go to America to live with relatives in Boston for an indefinite period. They left England in 1940 on a hazardous journey. While crossing the Atlantic in a large convoy, they watched two ships go down after being attacked by U-boats. Eventually, they made their way to Boston and a new life.

George Hunt, Marion's father, had been a merchant marine since the last days of World War I and had spent most of his life at sea. He knew that in this war he had a very uncertain future. Above all else, he wanted his family to be safe. Marion's last memory of him was haunting. *"I will always remember his leaving, watching him walking down the road and out of sight, and we never saw him again."*[104] He was killed when his ship, the SS *Congolian*, was sunk in 1944. Her story is another poignant illustration of the tragedy and sacrifice endured by so many families touched by this war. Her father gave up everything, his wife, his children, and his life, trying to do his best for his country and his family.

> You do not delight in sacrifice, or I would bring it; you do not take pleasure in burnt offerings. The sacrifices of God are a broken spirit; a broken and contrite heart. ~Psalm 51:16–17

Nearer to Thee

AFTER YEARS OF declining health, Franklin Roosevelt died on April 12, 1945, of a massive cerebral hemorrhage, tragically ending his unprecedented fourth term of office as president. He was buried with full military honors at his home in Hyde Park, New York, with his long-time pastor, the Reverend George Anthony, officiating. After gun salutes, aircraft flyovers, and the final bugle call, the burial ceremony started promptly at 10:30 a.m. The words came from the *Episcopal Book of Common Prayer*, "*All that the Father giveth me shall come to me; and him that cometh to me I will in no wise cast out.*" There were no words of eulogy. The Reverend Anthony quoted an old hymn:[105]

> *Now the laborer's task is o'er; now the battle day is past;*
> *Now upon the farther shore lands the voyager at last.*
> *Father, in Thy gracious keeping, leave we now Thy servant sleeping.*

Also prominent in the event was another old and familiar hymn, "Nearer My God to Thee," played at the funeral of President James Garfield and quoted by William McKinley on his deathbed:

> *Nearer, my God, to Thee, nearer to Thee!*
> *E'en though it be a cross that raiseth me,*
> *Still all my song shall be, nearer, my God, to Thee.*
>
> *There let the way appear, steps unto Heav'n;*
> *All that Thou sendest me, in mercy giv'n;*
> *Angels to beckon me nearer, my God, to Thee.*
>
> *There in my Father's home, safe and at rest,*
> *There in my Savior's love, perfectly blest;*
> *Age after age to be, nearer my God to Thee.*[106]

And this is the will of him who sent me, that I shall lose none of all that he has given me, but raise them up at the last day. For my Father's will is that everyone who looks to the Son and believes in him shall have eternal life. ~John 6:39–40

Picking Friends

ANYONE WHO HAS served in the military has learned some hard lessons. Associating with the wrong people has led to the downfall of many well-intentioned young soldiers and sailors. One wizened veteran wrote to his son, who had recently been assigned to the USS *Washington*, with some strong advice on this subject:

> *You will no doubt find a few things not to your liking. Everything will be new and strange; you will get homesick—that is natural. You will also become lonesome and disgusted and you will want for sympathy. There are always a few fellows who expect to get the world for nothing, and they are chronic kickers. So my advice to you is, to cultivate the acquaintance of the boys who are satisfied with the Navy and who appreciate what the Navy is doing for them, who are trying to make themselves better, physically, morally, and mentally, so they will be fitted to step into a position in civilian life. So try and make the Navy and incidentally yourself better for having been a part of it.*[107]

Suggesting that someone associate with others who focus on the positive aspects of life is good advice for a person of any age or position. It is especially important for us as Christians to seek out a few close friends who will be positive influences during the ups and downs of our spiritual journey. These friends should share our desire to grow constantly closer to God. True Christian friends of this kind will feel empowered to hold us accountable and will want us to hold them accountable as well. Such friendships don't just happen. It takes time and energy to build relationships of this depth, and such effort is notoriously difficult for men. Small groups have been a great answer to this need for many. Prayer and Bible study with a small circle of Christian friends is a sure path over time to a stronger relationship with those friends and, even more importantly, to God.

He who walks with the wise grows wise, but a companion of fools suffers harm. ~Proverbs 13:20

Eric's Knife

WOODEN BOATS made good minesweepers because they were invulnerable to magnetic mines. HMS *Cloughton Wyke* was a deep sea fishing trawler converted to this use early in the war. The little ship also came with her civilian crew. One of the members was a young man named Eric, noted for his large blue eyes and baby face. Eric's pride and joy was a standard issue pocketknife, which he spent hours honing to a fine edge. He got a lot of ribbing over this little ritual, but kept to his self-appointed task every day.

In early 1942 the *Cloughton Wyke* was working with a group of other minesweepers in the English Channel on a rough winter day. Suddenly, out of the clouds a German bomber bore in on the small ship. One of several bombs exploded beneath the hull, breaking the ship in two and sending the crew scrambling for the lifeboat. Eric made it, but was knocked unconscious. The other crewmen realized they were in great danger when they found the lifeboat still lashed to the sinking ship. As they tried frantically to loosen the ropes, someone remembered Eric's knife. Digging through the unconscious man's pockets, a sailor found the knife and was able to slice through the large ropes as if they were butter. The lifeboat was free, thanks to Eric and his diligence in keeping a sharp blade.[108]

A long time ago, there was a mother who was diligent in taking care of her duty. When her son went off for the day, she packed him a lunch of five small barley loaves and two small fish. This was her simple, self-appointed task that she performed joyfully and with no expectation of reward. Little did she know that her small offering would be used by the Son of God in performing one of his greatest miracles. Jesus would take those loaves and fishes and make them into a feast to feed five thousand hungry followers. We never know how God will use our efforts to glorify him. It is up to us to faithfully and diligently perform the tasks, no matter how simple, that he puts before us.

> For we are God's workmanship, created in Christ Jesus to do good works, which God prepared in advance for us to do. ~Ephesians 2:10

Survivors of torpedoed ship being rescued.
(National Archives)

Arctic ice coats ship.
(U. S. Naval Historical Center)

Quarter Inch of Steel

SAM HAKAM was radio operator on the SS *Lehigh* when she was torpedoed off the coast of Africa in October 1941. He vividly recalled a shipmate running around the deck shouting, *"They can't do this to us!"* due to the fact that the United States was not then at war. Fortunately, most of the crew made it to one of the four lifeboats before the ship went under. Within a few days conditions on Hakam's boat worsened due to the extreme tropical conditions. Water was scarce and the days were hot. Dehydration set in as parched throats and swollen tongues plagued each man.

One night a storm came up, promising rain and blessed relief. All that came, however, were high winds and crashing waves. Hakam later described his thoughts: *"Our small boat was tossed about wildly. Good seamanship kept us afloat. It finally passed. I lay exhausted on the bottom of the boat and reflected there was only about one quarter inch of steel thickness between myself and hell."*[109]

Hopefully, each of us can comprehend the fragile nature of life without being in a lifeboat at night threatened by stormy seas. Sam Hakam's experience only dramatizes the obvious. Since we are not guaranteed any specific amount of time on this earth, we should use the time we have wisely. We do this when we focus daily on the purpose of our lives: finding and nourishing a relationship with God. The Westminster Shorter Catechism asks the question: *"What is the chief end of man?"* Every day we should meditate on the answer: *"Man's chief end is to glorify God, and to enjoy him forever."*[110]

Then the man and his wife heard the sound of the LORD God as he was walking in the garden in the cool of the day, and they hid from the LORD God among the trees of the garden. But the LORD God called to the man, "Where are you?"
~Genesis 3:8–9

A Sharp Tongue

LIFE IS NEVER easy aboard a navy ship. The quarters are cramped, the days and nights are long, and wartime deployments can seem unending. In addition to regular duties, everyone stands watches at ever-changing hours, interrupting any sense of a normal routine. Fear, frustration, fatigue, and the virtual absence of alone time make friction among crew members inevitable. One sailor's advice to his shipmates was published in his ship's newsletter to remind everyone to: *"Be kind! It's so easy to make a sarcastic remark that may hurt a shipmate. Besides, sometimes a man is not being so brilliant as he thinks."*[111]

There are times when every one of us gets frustrated with other people. I am especially guilty of voicing displeasure at clerks and service workers who don't seem to be as conscientious as I think they should be. There is very specific biblical instruction in both the Old and New Testaments advising us to be careful of what we say. Proverbs tells us, *"Reckless words pierce like a sword, but the tongue of the wise brings healing"* (Proverbs 12:18), and *"He who guards his mouth and his tongue keeps himself from calamity"* (Proverbs 21:23). These are words to remember when feeling impatient toward others.

My dear brothers, take note of this: Everyone should be quick to listen, slow to speak and slow to become angry. ~James 1:19

The Gear That Saved His Life

THE ARCTIC WEATHER was at its worst. The air temperature was thirty degrees below zero, and the entire ship was caked with ice. Gale force winds had dispersed the convoy after leaving Murmansk, leaving the SS *Puerto Rican* steaming alone, under radio silence. At 10:00 p.m. on March 9, 1943, a violent explosion rocked the ship.

August Wallenhaupt was awakened in his bunk and knew immediately what had happened. He had experienced being torpedoed before. He didn't panic. He had the gear on hand for this disaster, and he knew how to use it. One journalist recounted his actions: *"Wallenhaupt took time to dress warmly; he slipped on his rubber lifesaving suit, put on his life jacket over the suit and then put on a knee-length woolen seaman's coat with a hood to protect his head. This is the gear that saved his life."*[112]

Due to the heavy ice, the *Puerto Rican*'s lifeboats couldn't be launched. Wallenhaupt found himself in the water and, unable to swim, managed to stay afloat just long enough to find a small doughnut shaped raft. After getting into the raft, he helped seven others aboard. On the morning of the third day a destroyer discovered the tiny raft. All were frozen to death except August Wallenhaupt. The young seaman survived because he was able, in the chaos of a sinking ship, to calmly prepare for the worst. By doing the right thing first, all his subsequent actions paid off in his survival.

This story dramatically illustrates the importance of taking care of life's most important tasks first. Our relationship to God should be at the top of the list. When this relationship is solid, every other part of our lives will make sense. This spiritual preparation will ensure our ultimate and eternal survival and should be our first priority in normal times, before we come face to face with a crisis.

> He is like a man building a house, who dug down deep and laid the foundation on rock. When a flood came, the torrent struck that house but could not shake it, because it was well built. ~Luke 6:48

Prolonged Suffering

AUGUST WALLENHAUPT made it into his tiny raft missing only one important item: his heavy fur-lined gloves. His hands were numb in minutes. Even though he was fully clothed in his survival gear, he also lost feeling in his legs. He did a lot of praying during the three days he was exposed to the brutal Arctic elements. By the time he was rescued he was in a semiconscious state.

Safe at last, the real pain began for the young seaman. His hands were swollen to three times normal size and were white with frostbite. He was kept alive by injections of blood plasma, intravenous feeding, and morphine. Wallenhaupt unfortunately lost both legs below the knee and most of his fingers, but miraculously survived. He not only survived physically, but he became a legend at the Staten Island Marine Hospital for his perpetual good humor. He even courted a clerk at the hospital whom he later married.

A fellow seaman paid tribute to this brave young sailor: *"August Wallenhaupt symbolizes the sufferings that hundreds of other seamen have had to endure during torpedoings and he also expresses the same courage and cheerfulness that are indicative of the seamen who have been within reaching distance of death."*[113]

A close brush with death may cause fleeting feelings of euphoria. However, to maintain a positive outlook through prolonged suffering requires another level of courage. This seaman's optimistic attitude was amazing—and rare. Few of us can count on having such strength within ourselves. The only reliable source of this kind of courage is the same source that sustained the apostles through their suffering: the amazing love of our living Savior, Jesus Christ.

Dear friends, do not be surprised at the painful trial you are suffering, as though something strange were happening to you. But rejoice that you participate in the sufferings of Christ, so that you may be overjoyed when his glory is revealed. ~1 Peter 4:12–13

A Jubilant Mood

THE CANADIAN SHIP *Kamsack* had been through a rough deployment. Days of mountainous seas and freezing rain had sapped the crew's strength and spirit. Sent to rescue a torpedoed ship under the worst possible conditions, they had labored and suffered at their duty stations aboard the small corvette. Frank Curry described his feelings as this ordeal came to an end on Christmas Eve:

> We staggered into Sydney harbour this Christmas Eve, feeling pretty good about accomplishing our mission. What a feeling to tie up securely to a jetty where everything is still—the crew in a jubilant mood, and I am no exception. Make and mend in the afternoon and we spent it cleaning our mess decks. Duty watch for me—on Quartermaster from 2000–2400, and I saw Christmas Day come in from the frozen gangway. Celebrated by taking a hot shower and climbing into my hammock at 0100.[114]

There are few satisfactions like that of successfully completing a difficult job. This wartime sailor ushered in Christmas Day in pretty miserable conditions on a small and battered ship, but he nevertheless knew that he was safe and warm—and that he and his fellow crewmen had accomplished a difficult task under almost impossible conditions.

One of my mother's favorite sayings was, *"Happiness is a byproduct of duty well performed."* Her point was that happiness is not found as an end in itself. It finds us when we do what we're supposed to do. This was certainly the case with these sailors of the *Kamsack*. In Colossians Paul exhorts us to work at our duties with all our hearts, recognizing two things: first, that this kind of effort will be rewarded by the Lord, and second, that we are really serving Jesus Christ with our work (Colossians 3:23–24). If we can remember this as we diligently do our jobs, happiness will indeed be the wonderful byproduct of our work!

Whatever you do, work at it with all your heart, as working for the Lord, not for men, since you know that you will receive an inheritance from the Lord as a reward. It is the Lord Christ you are serving. ~Colossians 3:23–24

Was God There?

IN 1943 GEORGE HURLEY wrote a poetic description of the physical, mental, and spiritual hardships of shipboard life in the Arctic. There are seventy-eight verses in this work, and several touch on the issue of God's presence in this remote corner of the world.

> *Rosary beads are my frozen tears / Will they thaw in future years?*
> *Valor so common not recorded in history / Ships just vanish, a Russian*
>   *mystery.*
> *Dear friend, Jesus, to You I call / Help your lambs before we fall*
> *I can't promise I'll be good tomorrow / But the Bible says you watch the*
>   *sparrow.*
> *No one is talking, I hear no voices / Am I spared? Has God made his*
>   *choices?*
> *Why did he leave me, I'll never know / But it looks to me like the end of*
>   *the show.*
> *Drink a toast to the bastardly sons / Don't mention the battle we surely*
>   *won*
> *God took a vacation, left us alone / Out in the ocean, so white with*
>   *foam.*
> *Oh we cursed you, old ship, you were so slow / But you took us there,*
>   *where no one would go*
> *Brought us back to the American shore / No one could ask for anything*
>   *more.*[115]

It's ironic and very human that the seaman would credit his ship for a safe return home, but accuse God of abandoning him. As an unbeliever, I have done the same thing in times of stress. I wondered where God was, even while marveling at the selflessness of young Marines helping each other. Since becoming a Christian I have asked God to forgive this lack of faith and appreciation. One solid pillar of my faith is that God did indeed protect me many times in the past. I try to make amends for my blindness every day by thanking him for watching over me then and now.

Remember the wonders he has done, his miracles, and the judgments he pronounced. ~Psalm 105:5

The Arctic Is Neutral

GEORGE HURLEY, the young sailor-poet, wrote of his despair at the death that he witnessed:

No life boat for me, I die where I stand / Like an icicle, shiny and grand
The arctic is neutral, it takes no side / All dressed in white, waiting for
its bride.

So much suffering, so many dying / So many shipmates died just for trying
All of their labor, all of the toil / all of the bodies covered with oil.[116]

In combat I have experienced my own despair in the midst of violence and death. I was unfortunately not a Christian at that time. I anguished at the apparent randomness that took some and not others, and felt that God could not be involved in any of what I was seeing on a daily basis. I am not qualified even now to comment on God's attitude toward war or those involved in the fighting. There have obviously been good men and women on all sides in every war praying fervently for deliverance. Many believe that their prayers were answered. What about those whose prayers were not answered?

There is no definitive answer to such a question. We don't know the spiritual condition of those who have fallen, and we don't know God's plan for their eternal futures. We do know that everyone must die eventually and that the span of our lives, whether twenty-five years or eighty-five, is nothing from God's perspective. God never promised to shield us from hardship or harm. He only promises to be with us in every situation, if we faithfully turn to him. We also have the same dilemma as the apostle Paul, not knowing who gets the better deal: the person called to heaven or the person left to face the challenges of this world.

For to me, to live is Christ and to die is gain . . . I am torn between the two: I desire to depart and be with Christ, which is better by far; but it is more necessary for you that I remain in the body. ~Philippians 1:21, 23–24

The Best Solvent

AN UNKNOWN SAILOR was concerned that so many of his friends were wasting time worrying. He wrote an article that appeared in his ship's weekly newsletter in June 1942 with timely advice for any era:

> *Have you ever stopped to realize that the best solvent for worry is work? Throw yourself into your job, master its details and in addition to serving your ship and country better, you will be rewarded by contentment.*
>
> *Work is healthy! You can hardly put more on a man than he can bear. But worry is rust upon the blade. It is not movement that destroys the machinery, but friction . . . many deaths are provoked chiefly by worry over matters which never repay the time wasted on them, and which breed a race of brooders prone to disease and death . . .*
>
> *Be matter of fact: first get to the bridge, then cross it.*
>
> *And meanwhile, don't worry whether you get to the bridge or not.*
>
> *What does your anxiety do? It does not empty tomorrow of its sorrow; but it does empty today of its strength.*[117]

Jesus proclaimed the same message during his Sermon on the Mount. He asked, *"Who of you by worrying can add a single hour to his life?"* (Matthew 6:27; Luke 12:25). The point is clear: worrying accomplishes nothing. It is a pointless mental activity that only distracts us from what we should be doing. With Jesus in our lives we can focus on the truly important things that can actually be accomplished, while lifting those other concerns to him.

But seek first his kingdom and his righteousness, and all these things will be given to you as well. Therefore do not worry about tomorrow, for tomorrow will worry about itself. ~Matthew 6:33–34

An Act of Faith

STEAMING IN CONVOY at night was an exhausting experience in seamanship. To reduce the risk of submarine attack every ship had to make sure that no lights were showing. This made keeping station with the rest of the convoy an unremitting task of intense focus and eyestrain. If an escort ship were to lose position there was more than embarrassment involved. A dangerous gap could open in the defensive screen around the convoy that could let a submarine through. As if this was not challenging enough, the escorts often were required to follow a zigzag course to further thwart submarine attacks. In his classic, *The Cruel Sea*, Nicholas Monsarrat describes one young corvette officer's experience with this maneuver:

> *A zigzag on a pitch-black night, with thirty ships in close contact adding the risk of collision to the difficulty of hanging on to the convoy, was something more than a few lines in a Fleet Order. Lockhart . . . evolved his own method. He took* Compass Rose *out obliquely from the convoy, for a set number of minutes: very soon, of course, he could not see the other ships, and might have had the whole Atlantic to himself, but that was part of the manoeuvre. Then he turned, and ran back the same number of minutes on the corresponding course inwards: at the end, he should be in touch with the convoy again, and in the same relative position.*
>
> *It was an act of faith that continued to justify itself, but it was sometimes a little hard on the nerves.*[118]

We live our lives with faith that the things we rely on every day will continue to work properly: a shipboard procedure, the automobile brakes, our relationships. Such faith is a matter of trust based on experience. The most vital part of our lives is of course our relationship with God, which we have entirely through faith. This faith is also based on experience and grows as we actively practice it. The more we seek him by praying and listening, the more we will feel his presence and grow in confidence that we are "on station," even in the darkest and most uncertain waters.

Now faith is being sure of what we hope for and certain of what we do not see. ~Hebrews 11:1

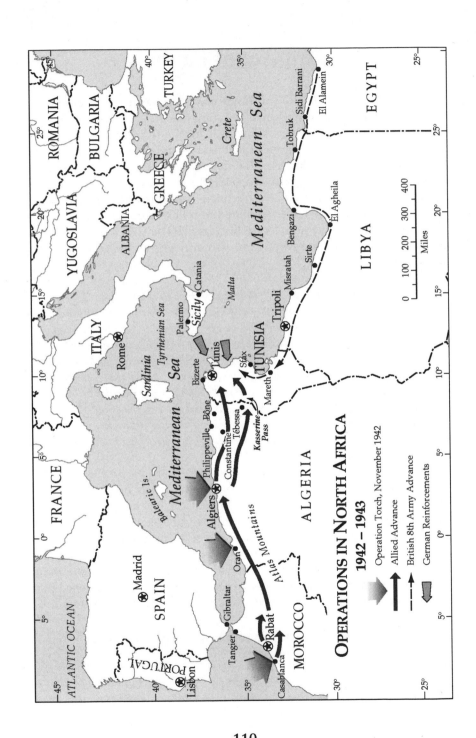

OPERATIONS IN NORTH AFRICA
1942–1943

Operation Torch, November 1942
Allied Advance
British 8th Army Advance
German Reinforcements

APRIL

War in the Desert

THE SHIPPING LANES of the Mediterranean Sea have historically been vital to France and England in support of their commerce with the Middle East and Asia. In 1939, even though war was imminent in Europe, the Mediterranean seemed secure, with strong British and French naval and ground forces in place and an ostensibly neutral Italy. This picture changed dramatically with the defeat of France. On June 10, 1940, the day after the fall of Paris, Italy declared war on the Allies. With an Italian army and navy opposing them and a French fleet potentially in enemy hands, Britain suddenly faced a crisis on another front.

With visions of a new Roman Empire, Mussolini ordered his forces in Libya to begin a land offensive on September 13 to seize Egypt and the Suez Canal. Marshal Graziani, with two hundred fifty thousand troops available in Libya, ordered the Italian 10th Army to advance into Egypt. They were opposed by thirty thousand British, Indian, and Australian troops under Gen. Archibald Wavell. After advancing about one hundred kilometers, the Italian advance was stopped at Sidi Barrani and was then routed by a counterattack that advanced five hundred miles back into Libya.

To shore up his faltering ally, Hitler deployed Luftwaffe units to Italy in December 1940 to interdict British shipping and to keep supply lines open to North Africa. The Afrika Korps was organized under Gen. Erwin Rommel and began moving to Africa in early 1941. It consisted initially of one light division and one panzer division, and was later expanded into the Panzer Army Africa. Rommel soon earned the nickname, "Desert Fox," and began to make his presence felt.

Disregarding instructions from Italian authorities and his own superiors, the German general quickly launched an offensive that penetrated almost to Egypt. He finally had to stop in late May to resupply and reorganize his forces. From this point on, for over a year, the war in North Africa became a back-and-forth struggle along a narrow one-thousand-mile strip of Libyan and Egyptian coastline. Each side sought to build up strength for the next offensive while seeking some way to outflank or outguess the enemy.

During this period the supply lines of the opposing forces became the key to victory or defeat in North Africa. The British Navy and air units stationed on Malta gradually began to turn the tide, making resupply of the Afrika Korps increasingly difficult. Finally, in September 1942 the British 8th Army, under Gen. Bernard Montgomery, launched a major offensive that decisively penetrated the German line at El Alamein. Rommel did not have the resources to stop this advance and was forced back across Libya and into Tunisia.

Throughout 1942, the United States prepared for its role in the widening war. The site of America's entry into the European theater was hotly debated by the Allies. Even though American military leaders favored a direct strike at Germany, President Roosevelt finally succumbed to Churchill's insistence on an invasion of North Africa. Operation Torch commenced on November 8, 1942, with more than one hundred thousand British and American troops, commanded by Gen. Dwight Eisenhower, landing at three widely separated objectives: Casablanca, Oran, and Algiers. Ironically, these landings were initially opposed by French forces occupying these areas under the control of the Vichy French government. The Operation Torch forces ultimately met the British 8th Army in Tunisia, successfully driving the Axis out of North Africa in May 1943.

Submitting to the Desert

AT TIMES DESERT warfare had many similarities to war at sea. The lines were fluid and ever changing. There were no forts and seldom even fixed positions, as there were few noteworthy terrain features to be held. The mission was usually to find and engage enemy units wherever found, with little regard to the land being fought over. A correspondent eloquently described the relationship of the army to the environment surrounding it:

> As a ship submits to the sea by the nature of its design and the way it sails, so these new mechanized soldiers were submitting to the desert. They used the desert. They never sought to control it. Always the desert set the pace, made the direction and planned the design. The desert offered colours in browns, yellows, and greys. The army accordingly took these colours for its camouflage. The sandstorm blew, and the tanks, profiting by it, went into action under the cover of the storm. We made no roads. We built no houses. We did not try to make the desert livable, nor did we seek to subdue it. We found the life of the desert primitive and nomadic, and primitively and nomadically the army lived and went to war.[119]

We don't usually think of "submitting" to our environment. Part of our nature as human beings is to try to shape events and overcome obstacles, as we plan and work toward a better future. Theoretically, we know that we are supposed to submit ourselves to God's plan, but this is not practically possible unless we know what he wants us to do. We need to remember the biblical wisdom that there is *"A time to be silent and a time to speak"* (Ecclesiastes 3:7). We submit to God's will when we take time to pray, to listen, and to seek help in discerning his guidance. He will give us direction if we seek it. Our striving then takes on a new character. Only when we submit our efforts to his plan will we ever be able to fulfill our true purpose and find lasting peace.

Whether the cloud stayed over the tabernacle for two days or a month or a year, the Israelites would remain in camp and not set out; but when it lifted, they would set out. At the LORD's command they encamped, and at the LORD's command they set out. ~Numbers 9:22–23

To Shave

BRIG. JAMES HARGEST, a New Zealander, was captured in North Africa in July 1941. He reported an interesting meeting with Gen. Erwin Rommel:

He stood looking at me coldly. Through his interpreter he expressed displeasure that I had not saluted him. I replied that I intended no discourtesy, but was in the habit of saluting only my seniors in our own or allied armies . . . It did not prevent him from congratulating me on the fighting quality of my men.

"They fight well," he said.

"Yes, they fight well," I replied, "but your tanks were too powerful for us."

"Perhaps my men are superior to yours."

"You know that is not correct."

Although he had been fighting for over a week and was traveling in a tank, he was neat and clean, and I noticed that he had shaved before entering the battle that morning.[120]

My battalion commander in Vietnam, Lt. Col. Gary Wilder, enforced a strict policy of daily shaving, whether in rear areas or in the field. When water was scarce the men did as they were told but with great complaint. For a while it seemed like a waste of time and water to me as well. In time, however, I began to appreciate the benefits of such discipline. I learned that in combat, when men are tired, afraid, and frustrated, there can be a thin line between human and animal behavior. The disciplines of personal hygiene helped keep that line in clear focus.

Sometimes our spiritual vision can also get blurry when we allow ourselves to drift apart from God. We need certain spiritual disciplines to keep this from happening. Regular prayer and Bible study are vital to our spiritual health, but unfortunately, are easy to neglect. The simple discipline of attending to these regularly will pay great dividends in sharpening our vision of what is most important in our lives: a continuing personal relationship with our Father in heaven.

Naaman's servants went to him and said, "My father, if the prophet had told you to do some great thing, would you not have done it? How much more, then, when he tells you, 'Wash and be cleansed'!" ~2 Kings 5:13

Responsibility

IN EARLY 1942 Winston Churchill faced unprecedented burdens. The home islands remained under threat of invasion. British and Axis forces were clashing in the Atlantic, Far East, and North Africa, with setbacks on every front. A steady stream of decisions had to be made on the priority of effort and the allocation of scarce resources. Churchill had to deal with all of this as well as a constant barrage of criticism from his own Parliament and press. At one point he lamented, *"I must confess to feeling the weight of the war upon me even more than in the tremendous summer days of 1940."*[121] As criticism peaked over losses in Asia and North Africa, he went before the House of Commons to address the issue of blame:

> *I take the fullest personal responsibility. If we have handled our resources wrongly, no one is so much to blame as me. If we have not got large modern air forces and tanks in Burma and Malaya tonight, no one is more accountable than I am. Why then should I be called upon to pick out scapegoats, to throw the blame on generals or airmen or sailors? Why then should I be called upon to drive away loyal and trusted colleagues and friends to appease the clamour of certain sections of the British and Australian press . . . ?*[122]

We can only imagine Churchill's temptation to shift the blame for these catastrophes. Many of his ministers and generals certainly contributed to his plight. The Bible relates how the very first man and woman succumbed to this urge. When confronted by God about the forbidden fruit, Adam responded, *"The woman you put here with me—she gave me some fruit from the tree, and I ate it."* [Eve responded,] *"The serpent deceived me, and I ate"* (Genesis 3:12–13). Thanks to our Savior, we no longer have to play the "blame game." We know that through Jesus Christ we will be forgiven the wrong things we do or things we leave undone, once we fully accept responsibility and ask for forgiveness in his name.

Then I acknowledged my sin to you and did not cover up my iniquity. I said, "I will confess my transgressions to the LORD"—and you forgave the guilt of my sin. ~Psalm 32:5

A Strong Bulkhead

IN JUNE 1942 the British garrison at Tobruk fell to Rommel's advancing forces. More than thirty thousand troops and mountains of stores and equipment were lost. Winston Churchill received the devastating news by telegram during a meeting with President Roosevelt in the White House. Soon, the newspapers began to blare alarming headlines: *"Anger in England," "Tobruk Fall May Bring Change of Government," "Churchill to Be Censured."* Churchill did indeed face a debate in the House of Commons over a vote of censure soon after returning to England. After listening to several days of criticism, he finally stood before the House to respond. One of his remarks contained an element of universal truth:

> *I cannot pretend to form a judgment upon what has happened in this battle. I like commanders on land and sea and in the air to feel that between them and all forms of public criticism the Government stands like a strong bulkhead. They ought to have a fair chance, and more than one chance. Men make mistakes and learn from their mistakes . . . you will not get generals to run risks unless they feel they have behind them a strong government.*[123]

I find special meaning in these words as they point logically to another, ultimate authority. Our Savior, Jesus Christ, is our strong bulkhead. With him in our hearts we have the freedom to be ourselves and are no longer subject to fear and anxiety. When our relationship is on sound footing we are able to live bold lives in his service. If he calls us to a task, we know that he will equip us for it and that he will remain faithful to us. We can risk being ridiculed or rejected and always know that our ultimate authority accepts us. Our strong bulkhead will not be moved.

So if the Son sets you free, you will be free indeed. ~John 8:36

Gen. Erwin Rommel, "The Desert Fox."
(National Archives)

Gen. Bernard "Monty" Montgomery
(National Archives)

A   P   R   I   L

Monty's Prayer

O N AUGUST 13, 1942, Lt. Gen. Bernard Montgomery, known to most as "Monty," took command of the British 8th Army. Rommel had pushed the British across North Africa into Egypt, to within less than one hundred miles of Alexandria. Montgomery knew that a new attack was coming soon and positioned his forces to defend a key ridgeline at Alam El Halfa. From August 31 to September 2 another great tank battle was fought that proved to be Rommel's last major offensive to threaten Egypt. Monty did a masterful job of simplifying the defensive plan and orchestrating the battle.

Afterward, General Montgomery posted a prayer in his command vehicle that would remain for the duration of the war:[124]

Prayer of Sir Francis Drake
on the Morning of the Attack on Cadiz
1587

O Lord God
When thou givest to thy servants
To endeavour any great matter
Grant us also to know that it is not the beginning,
But the continuing of the same unto the end
Until it be thoroughly finished, which yieldest the true glory;
Through Him that for the finishing of Thy work
Laid down his life.[125]

Montgomery knew that in the fog of war it is easy to become cautious and to overestimate the enemy's strength. He put this reminder before him that victory always requires a final push, that there is a point where a supreme effort is necessary to win the battle, as exemplified by Jesus Christ. The apostle Paul exhorts us to the same supreme effort to finish the race and to complete our work for the Lord.

I consider my life worth nothing to me, if only I may finish the race and complete the task the Lord Jesus has given me. ~Acts 20:24

The Führer

IN NOVEMBER 1942 Field Marshal Erwin Rommel knew that the end was near for Germany's forces in North Africa. The British 8th Army had broken his line at El Alamein and was pushing relentlessly westward across Libya. A large American and British force had landed in Morocco and Algeria, and was advancing eastward toward Tunisia. Supplies of fuel and ammunition to his own army had been reduced to a trickle by Allied interdiction. Rommel returned to Germany for a meeting with Adolf Hitler on November 28. In a tense atmosphere the field marshal went over the details of the recent campaign. When he tried to point out the inevitable, he was astounded at the reaction:

> *Unfortunately, I then came too abruptly to the point and said that, since experience indicated that no improvement in the shipping situation could now be expected, the abandonment of the African theatre of war should be accepted as a long-term policy. If the army remained in North Africa, it would be destroyed . . . the mere mention of the strategic question worked like a spark in a powder barrel. The Fuehrer flew into a fury and directed a stream of completely unfounded attacks upon us.*
>
> *There was no attempt at discussion. I began to realize that Adolf Hitler simply did not want to see the situation as it was, and that he reacted emotionally against what his intelligence must have told him was right.*[126]

In many ways Adolf Hitler was a genius. He was a charismatic leader and master motivator. He had at his disposal one of the great military machines in history, led by a corps of supremely capable general officers. Fortunately for the Allies, he sometimes overruled these officers during his fits of rage. Anyone who becomes so obsessed with his own ego that he can't listen to others is doomed to failure. This fatal flaw was a manifestation of evil in Adolf Hitler that played a large role in his and Germany's eventual destruction.

They are free from the burdens common to man; they are not plagued by human ills. Therefore pride is their necklace; they clothe themselves with violence. From their callous hearts comes iniquity; the evil conceits of their minds know no limits. ~Psalm 73:5–7

7

God of the Free

STEPHEN VINCENT BENET received the Pulitzer Prize in 1929 for his long narrative poem, "John Brown's Body." He is most famous, however, for his short story, "The Devil and Daniel Webster," which appeared in the *Saturday Evening Post* in 1938 and was made into a movie in 1941. The story is about a New England farmer who, despairing over his bad luck, made a pact with the devil. When the final payment came due, Daniel Webster defended him before a jury of famous evildoers. Even though these jurors were under the devil's jurisdiction, Webster won the case by appealing to their innately American trait of independence. Benet's feelings for American patriotism and freedom are major themes of the story. In 1942 he wrote a prayer for President Roosevelt reflecting these same themes. The president recited the prayer before the nation on Flag Day of that year:

> *God of the free, we pledge our hearts and lives today to the cause of all free mankind. Grant us victory over the tyrants who would enslave all free men and nations. Grant us faith and understanding to cherish all those who fight for freedom as if they were our brothers. Grant us brotherhood in hope and union, not only for the space of this bitter war, but for the days to come which shall and must unite all the children of earth . . . We are all children of earth—grant us that simple knowledge. If our brothers are oppressed, then we are oppressed. If they hunger, we hunger. If their freedom is taken away, our freedom is not secure. Grant us a common faith that man shall know bread and peace—that he shall know justice and righteousness, freedom and security, an equal opportunity and an equal chance to do his best, not only in our own lands, but throughout the world. And in that faith let us march, toward the clean world our hands can make. Amen.*[127]

It is for freedom that Christ has set us free. Stand firm, then, and do not let yourselves be burdened again by a yoke of slavery. ~Galatians 5:1

Ike

Gen. Dwight
Eisenhower
(Eisenhower
Presidential
Library)

DWIGHT D. EISENHOWER's rise to major command can legitimately be described as meteoric. In 1940 "Ike" was a lieutenant colonel and had never commanded any sized unit in combat. By 1942, after four promotions, he was a lieutenant general in command of Operation Torch and all forces landing in North Africa. Even though most Army officers knew of his organizational talents, some considered his success extremely fortunate and some even thought it providential. George Patton privately claimed Eisenhower's initials stood for "Divine Destiny."

On November 5, 1942, Eisenhower arrived in British-held Gibraltar to establish his headquarters for Operation Torch. As one historian noted, the British began to take his measure:

> *He was a true believer in Allied righteousness: "If (the Axis) should win we would really learn something about slavery, forced labor, and loss of individual freedom." He took pride in being apolitical, as required of American Army officers, and he impressed others—as one British admiral later noted—as "completely sincere, straightforward, and very modest." There was that incandescent grin, of course, said to be "worth an army corps in any campaign." Both his face and his hands moved perpetually, and he exuded a magnetic amiability that made most men want to please him. Perhaps that was because, as one admirer asserted, they intuited he was "good and right in the moral sense," or perhaps it was because, as a British air marshal concluded, "Ike has the qualities of a little boy which make you love him."*[128]

General Eisenhower was a complicated and uniquely gifted man. His open and sincere nature disguised a keen intellect, a broad range of knowledge, and an amazing capacity for hard work. I believe, however, that one of the greatest keys to his success was his essential "goodness" as a human being, which others sensed in his presence. This quality ensured the loyalty of many strong personalities under his command in spite of many contentious disagreements over strategy.

So he sent and had him brought in. He was ruddy, with a fine appearance and handsome features. Then the LORD said, "Rise and anoint him; he is the one." So Samuel took the horn of oil and anointed him in the presence of his brothers, and from that day on the Spirit of the LORD came upon David in power. ~1 Samuel 16:12–13

An Orgy of Disorder

THE OPERATION TORCH landings were the first large-scale amphibious operations conducted at night. The confusion and resulting disarray were beyond anyone's expectations. Gen. George Patton went ashore at Red Beach 1, near Fedala, to a scene of complete chaos. Instead of a four-mile beachhead, troops and equipment were scattered over forty miles of Moroccan coastline. Only five of seventy tanks had reached shore. To direct naval gunfire, nine fire control parties had landed, but only two were able to communicate with the ships providing support. Local civilians were out on the beaches pilfering supplies and discarded equipment.

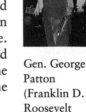

Gen. George Patton (Franklin D. Roosevelt Presidential Library)

Patton had once described combat as *"an orgy of disorder."*[129] What he found in his first actual exposure fully confirmed this view. Once ashore he had little information on what was happening anywhere other than on his own beach. He said, *"My theory is that an army commander does what is necessary to accomplish his mission and that nearly 80 percent of his mission is to arouse morale in his men."*[130] He did motivate those around him as he worked through the confusion to gain control of his units and to coordinate the advance.

George Patton had many great qualities as a military leader. Demonstrated here is the ability to live with ambiguity, or "the fog of war," as it is called, and to function in spite of it. This is the norm in combat. In our daily lives we also experience confusing situations where the way ahead is not clear. Our best strategy is to constantly strive to deepen our relationship with the One who cares most for us. As we become more intimate with God, we will be better able to discern the difference between our own thoughts and his voice. When we understand and act on his will, the ambiguity in our lives will disappear.

For now we see through a glass, darkly; but then face to face: now I know in part; but then shall I know even as also I am known. ~1 Corinthians 13:12 (KJV)

Grand Entrance

ON THE SECOND DAY of the Allied landings in North Africa, the British flagship HMS *Bulolo* steamed into Algiers harbor. A group of French citizens waited on the jetty to greet the ship. Unknown to the captain on the bridge or the crew in the engine room, the engine order telegraph had been damaged earlier by a German bomb's near miss. Since the telegraph transmits orders to the engine room from the bridge, a routine docking order for full steam astern went unheard. The result was almost catastrophic.

The French welcoming committee on the jetty watched with mounting alarm as the ship loomed nearer at twelve knots. Officers on the bridge debated whether Bulolo's *masts would likely shear off forward or backward upon impact. Shrieking bysanders scattered; the captain yelled, "Everyone lie down!" to his crew; and the great bow heaved up onto a fortuitous mudbank, demolishing the seawall and nicking a waterfront house before settling back into the harbor, intact. Applauding spectators recovered their wits and agreed that the Royal Navy knew how to make an entrance.*[131]

In 1981 Ronald Reagan was about to have surgery for a gunshot wound inflicted by a would-be assassin. He looked around at the surgical team and commented, *"I hope you're all Republicans."*[132] We're always thankful for someone who can see some humor in an otherwise dire situation. This kind of humor can relieve the tension that tends to compound the problem. It also reflects an ability to live in the present moment and a faith that all will be well in the end. Such faith can be contagious, especially when it comes from an authority figure. We should always look for ways to lighten the burden of those around us with humor.

Our mouths were filled with laughter, our tongues with songs of joy. ~Psalm 126:2

Vital Lessons

MAJ. ROBERT MOORE was second-in-command of 2nd Battalion, 168th Infantry, landing near Algiers during Operation Torch. He came ashore eight miles from his assigned beach to find his troops scattered and disorganized. Although resistance from French forces was sporadic, his unit took casualties in their advance. The first time he came under fire, he ducked for cover and then looked up cautiously to try to see what was ahead. He suddenly found himself on his back, stunned and confused. A soldier beside him was bleeding. Taking off his helmet he found a deep black groove cut across the side of it. An inch lower and the war would have been over for him.

In these first hours of the war, Moore learned some vital lessons:

> *Some lessons were fundamental: stay low; take a few extra moments to study the map before setting off. But others involved the nature of combat and leadership: a realization that battlefields were inherently chaotic; that improvisation was a necessary virtue; that speed and stealth and firepower won small skirmishes as well as big battles; that every moment held risk and every man was mortal.*[133]

Some people have a distinct spiritual advantage in life. Firemen, doctors, soldiers, and others close to life-and-death situations are never able to overlook the fact that they are indeed mortal. When someone faces frequent danger or sees the results of others doing so, they know how fragile life is. The poet who wrote, *"Death hath a thousand doors to let out life,"*[134] seemed to understand this reality as well. For those of us leading more tranquil lives, we need constant reminders of our mortality to help focus our attention on matters of eternal significance.

You sympathized with those in prison and joyfully accepted the confiscation of your property, because you knew that you yourselves had better and lasting possessions. ~Hebrews 10:34

An Old Ally

ON NOVEMBER 11, 1942, the French forces in North Africa agreed to a cease-fire on all fronts. In three days of fighting, U.S. forces had sustained more than 1,100 casualties, including 337 killed. In spite of these losses, the Americans set about restoring what to them was the natural order—friendly relations with an old ally, France. Historian Rick Atkinson described the reconciliation:

> *The bloodletting of the past three days, if neither forgotten nor quite forgiven, was set aside, just as a marital indiscretion might be glossed over for the sake of the children.*
>
> *Just past noon on November 11, Patton and Hewitt hosted a luncheon at a Fedala brasserie for their French counterparts, lubricating the pleasantries with Bordeaux and cognac.*
>
> *At the Miramar later that afternoon, Nogues, Michelier, and other French commanders drove past the coconut palms and banana trees lining the driveway to find that Patton had posted a welcoming honor guard. In the smoking room he complimented his adversaries on their gallantry and proposed a gentlemen's agreement under which French troops could keep their arms. Patton sealed the deal with a toast to "our future victory over a common enemy."*[135]

We can learn a lesson from General Patton in "getting over" an argument. If we really want to mend a fence we can start by honoring our former antagonist and acknowledging the validity of their motives. As one of my good friends says, this may require some amount of "eating crow," or something that looks like it to others, but this is a small price to pay for a new and stronger relationship. We have the assurance always that peacemakers *"will be called sons of God"* (Matthew 5:9).

> Therefore, if you are offering your gift at the altar and there remember that your brother has something against you, leave your gift there in front of the altar. First go and be reconciled to your brother; then come and offer your gift.
> ~Matthew 5:23–24

The Hand of God

AFTER THE ALLIED landings in North Africa, Lt. Gen. Kenneth Anderson took command of the British 1st Army advancing to the east to capture Tunisia. With a mixture of British and American units, coordination was difficult and the logistics network chaotic. Anderson himself was a good soldier with a reputation for personal valor.[136] However, his approach to the campaign was to carefully marshal his forces before advancing, and this unfortunately served to give the off-balance German defenders time to regroup. As German reinforcements poured into Tunis and winter weather turned the roads into quagmires, it became apparent that there would be no quick victory.

On Christmas Day 1942 Anderson wrote a lengthy letter to Alan Brooke explaining his actions and revealing a deep religious conviction. He said in part:

> *Things have not gone well and all my plans have had to be scrapped. . . . This is the hand of God . . . I feel deflated and disappointed, but it is no use getting depressed. It would be too easy if we all attempted everything and succeeded. The Almighty is much too wise to spoil us mortals that way.*[137]

In my earlier life as a skeptic I would have looked on these statements as a rationalization for lack of success. Now, as a Christian, I look at the general's thoughts as a simple acknowledgment that human beings are not in complete control of any situation. We are always confronted with unforeseen acts of nature, especially *human* nature. God does not always act to smooth our way or to ensure our success. He acts in accordance with his own plans and purpose, which we often do not understand. We can only pray constantly that our actions are in accordance with *his* will.

Why, O LORD, do you stand far off? Why do you hide yourself in times of trouble? . . . You, O God, do see trouble and grief; you consider it to take it in hand. ~Psalm 10:1, 14

A Prayer

GENERAL EISENHOWER arrived at the command post near Sidi bou Zid in central Tunisia well after midnight. In the cramped confines of a personnel carrier General McQuillan briefed him on the dispositions of Combat Command A units and German activity in the sector. Other than a discussion about minefields, the commanding general had little to say. Finally, Eisenhower stepped out of the personnel carrier into a still, moonlit night. Nearby a group of men were gathered. As he approached he heard an infantry captain leading his men in prayer:

> We do not pray for victory, not even for our individual safety. But we pray for help that none of us may let a comrade down—that each of us may do his duty to himself, his comrades, and his country, and so be worthy of our American heritage.[138]

The general silently wept on hearing these words. It is hard not to be moved by such simple eloquence. This young officer's prayer was genuine and heartfelt, and it reflected a great truth about combat. Men don't fight as much for a higher cause as they do for each other. It's hard to imagine a more meaningful prayer for a soldier than, "God, help me to not let a buddy down."

Greater love has no one than this, that he lay down his life for his friends.
~John 15:13

Father, Forgive Them

DURING THE DARKEST days of World War II, Dean Willard Sperry of Harvard University compiled a book of prayers for wartime devotionals. Even though the nation's enemies were victorious on all fronts and feelings against the Axis powers were running high, he included a special prayer calling the nation back to its Christian values:

> O Peaceful Light, Redeemer of the universe, whose love embraces the whole world, we hear thy prayer from the Cross: "Father, forgive them." In the name of the universal pardon, we dare to beseech the heavenly Father to give eternal peace to his enemies and ours . . . O Lord, do not condemn those who have persecuted us with their calumnies and their perfidy; be merciful toward all those whom we Christians have hardened without knowing it; may our holy prayer be for them a mystery of reconciliation. Amen.[139]

Dean Sperry was not a pacifist. He apparently saw no contradiction between fighting our enemies and asking God to forgive them. I believe that in our own lesser conflicts we can do the same and more. We can ask God to forgive those who have wronged us, and we can also forgive them ourselves. Even when we have to stand up against wrong behavior, we should be not be motivated by hate or anger. Such a forgiving attitude will often be beyond our capacity as human beings. We have to have a resource far greater than ourselves to act with love in the face of injustice. The only resource powerful enough to give us this kind of strength is the love of Jesus Christ within our hearts.

If you love those who love you, what credit is that to you? Even 'sinners' love those who love them. And if you do good to those who are good to you, what credit is that to you? ~Luke 6:32

He's Our Guy

CAPT. ALBERT HOFFMAN was a chaplain with the 34th Infantry
Division during the North African campaign. As one of the first
Americans in the war, he began to redefine the traditional role of the com-
bat chaplain. He didn't neglect religious services when appropriate, but
he felt that his primary duty was in the front line with his men. Historian
Patrick Skelly wrote:

> He held (that) the unaided wounded lying out in the field had the high-
> est call on the chaplain's services. Then front-line troops would fight
> from greater moral motivation from knowing that their accredited rep-
> resentative of religion was with them personally.
>
> Hoffman, although a quiet nonbelligerent man, simply had a front-
> line temperament. And the front line troops throughout the regiment
> would tell one another, "He's our guy." They thought of him as a per-
> sonal possession, the way they did a good combat officer.[140]

Albert Hoffman provided an example to his men and to us of the
most effective form of evangelism. Assigned to a combat unit, he concluded that he would be most effective if he shared the same risks as those
he hoped to influence. He didn't try to be a "holy man" or to stand apart
from his soldiers. By sharing everything with them, he became one of
them. From this position he was able to influence these men spiritually to
an extent that would have been impossible otherwise. The apostle Paul
first described this approach to ministry. It is the approach best used by
all Christians, whether ordained or not, in bringing others to Christ.

Though I am free and belong to no man, I make myself a slave to everyone, to
win as many as possible.... I have become all things to all men so that by all
possible means I might save some. ~1 Corinthians 9:19, 22

Innovations

PVT. JEFFERSON WHITE landed at Safi with 2nd Armored Division shortly after midnight on November 8. His tank platoon cleared mines on the way to Casablanca and then saw action in Algeria and Tunisia. Based on his experiences, he had some interesting observations on American and German soldiers:

> The Germans I saw were good soldiers. But they needed somebody to tell 'em what to do, how to do it—and when. The Americans—we were mostly farm boys. If we couldn't whip you one way, we'd whip you another. We had guys inventing things and coming up with practical ideas. One soldier invented a gadget that mounted on the front of tanks to clear mines. One of our machine-gunners switched out the rounds in the belts of .50 cal. ammunition so that one round was standard ball, the next was armor piercing, then a tracer. That way we could shoot by eyesight, not by gunsight. Those kinds of innovations kept a lot of American soldiers alive.[141]

American soldiers, past and present, have been credited for their ingenuity. In fact, innovation and "out of the box" thinking are hallmarks of Americans in general. Freedom and independence seem to foster a mindset that is uncomfortable with doing anything simply because it's the way it has been done before. Even though this attitude can be misdirected, it can and has contributed to the greatest achievements. I believe that this trait has specific biblical roots.

In his parable of the talents, Jesus praised the two servants who did something with the talents given them. Even though they started on unequal footing and achieved unequal results, both were declared *"good and faithful servants."* The servant who hid his talent lost what little he had.

Take the talent from him and give it to the one who has the ten talents. For everyone who has will be given more, and he will have an abundance.
~Matthew 25:28–29

Roosevelt and Churchill at Casablanca.
(Franklin D. Roosevelt Presidential Library)

American Generals
(Eisenhower Presidential Library)

Unconditional Surrender

IN JANUARY 1943, as the battle for Tunisia was still in progress, Franklin Roosevelt and Winston Churchill met in Casablanca. Speaking to journalists, Roosevelt made a bold statement: *"The elimination of German, Japanese, and Italian war power means the unconditional surrender of Germany, Italy, and Japan."*[142] Churchill nodded and then voiced his agreement. This "unconditional surrender" position, taken with relatively little deliberation, had long-range and controversial consequences. Many voiced criticism that the war would be prolonged, as the Axis dictators would be forced to fight on to the bitter end. Winston Churchill disagreed with this objection:

> We . . . demand from the Nazi, Fascist, and Japanese tyrannies unconditional surrender. By this we mean that their will power to resist must be completely broken, and that they must yield themselves absolutely to our justice and mercy. It does not mean, and it never can mean, that we are to stain our victorious arms by inhumanity or by mere lust of vengeance, or that we do not plan a world in which all branches of the human family may look forward to what the American Declaration of Independence finely calls "life, liberty, and the pursuit of happiness."[143]

With this statement Churchill articulated a higher vision of the Allied purpose in the war. The war had first to be won, but the peace would be characterized by mercy. This vision was ultimately borne out by the actions of the victorious nations. The defeated countries were not subjugated or pillaged. Instead they were rebuilt and reintegrated into the free world.

Mankind has been blessed that our infinitely powerful and righteous Creator is also amazingly merciful. Rather than giving us what we deserve in judgment, he has given us redemption through his only son, Jesus Christ. It is only through God's mercy that we have any hope of a secure place in his kingdom. When we display compassion toward others we are reflecting this mercy and doing his will.

Speak and act as those who are going to be judged by the law that gives freedom, because judgment without mercy will be shown to anyone who has not been merciful. Mercy triumphs over judgment! ~James 2:12–13

Lost Friends

BILL CHEALL was a member of the Green Howards Regiment and part of General Montgomery's 8th Army advancing into Tunisia in 1943. Jumping off early in an attack on a place called Wadi Akarit, Cheall's company covered about four miles under bright moonlight before coming under heavy artillery, mortar, and machine-gun fire. Under the eerie illumination of flares the Green Howards struggled up the hill toward their objective in intense close-range fighting. By 8:00 a.m. the hill was taken with heavy casualties on each side.

Shortly after, Cheall and another soldier were detailed to bury a member of their unit who was killed nearby. He was appalled at having to gather horribly disfigured body parts, likely caused by an exploding artillery shell. As he went about his gruesome job, he found the dead man's identity tags. He learned that he was about to bury one of his closest friends in the company. There was nothing to do but carry on with the task at hand. He later said, *"I don't know how I contained my emotions at that moment."* The next day he learned that another close friend in another unit died in the same attack. He lamented:

> I was now devastated once again. That was two grand lads only nineteen years of age—dead—and when I had last seen them only a matter of days ago they were laughing and cracking jokes. What a tragedy war is. No, I will never forget the 6th of April 1943, but life had to go on.[144]

In wartime soldiers often have little time to mourn lost comrades. This is a big part of the psychological stress that they have to endure during and after combat. Thankfully, the grieving process can be more deliberate for most of us. We can find comfort for ourselves and confidence in the fate of our lost loved ones through our faith and in the promises of God revealed in his Word:

Never again will they hunger; never again will they thirst. The sun will not beat upon them, nor any scorching heat. For the Lamb at the center of the throne will be their shepherd; he will lead them to springs of living water. And God will wipe away every tear from their eyes. ~Revelation 7:16–17

Purple Heart Box

DURING A LULL in the North African campaign, Gen. George Patton escorted a British general on a tour of his frontline units. He was not slow to brag on his men and equipment. At one point the generals came up to a crew working on a vehicle known as a half-track. Sgt. Bob Bishop was underneath the vehicle, making repairs.

He and the other men present heard General Patton explain the vehicle's superb mobility, great firepower, and armor that could stop almost anything.

> *"Isn't that right, Sergeant?" asked General Patton.*
>
> *"No, sir," said Sergeant Bishop, getting up. He walked around to the other side of the half-track, the generals following him, and he pointed up.*
>
> *"You see this hole? One bullet from a strafer. One bullet, pierced the armor here, rattled around inside, and killed Private Torgerson. The men call it the 'Purple Heart Box,' sir."*
>
> *General Patton turned pale and quickly escorted General Alexander somewhere else.[145]*

The truth sometimes hurts. It was certainly dismaying to the general to have it thrown in his face. Most of us would probably have been a little more tactful or even supportive of the views of such an exalted leader. This tendency is one of the great problems of anyone in authority, whether in the military, business, church, or family. When approaching the boss, many tend to cushion the bad news or paint a rosier picture than is warranted. Worse still, many leaders consciously or unconsciously promote this kind of behavior. The truth does sometimes hurt. But the truth is necessary for any group to effectively deal with its problems. Facing the truth is even more vital to our individual spiritual health.

> But whoever lives by the truth comes into the light, so that it may be seen plainly that what he has done has been done through God. ~John 3:21

Red Oak

BY EARLY 1943 the United States had been at war for just over a year. So far on the home front the war was remote and felt mainly as a void, with the absence of many friends, family members, and consumer goods. Little was known about the details of early setbacks in North Africa. The battle for control of the Kasserine Pass in Tunisia was fought in late February and proved disastrous for the Allied forces. There was no inkling of this at home until the Western Union telegrams began to arrive. Particularly hard hit was the little Iowa town of Red Oak, population 5,600. On March 6 more than two dozen telegrams arrived, almost at the same time, with the dreaded words: *"The Secretary of the Army desires me to express his regret that your son . . ."* A historian described the effect on this small town:

> On March 11, the Express *printed a headline no one could dispute: "SW Iowa Is Hit Hard." The photographs of missing boys just from Red Oak filled four rows above the fold on page one. "War consciousness mounted hourly in Red Oak, stunned by the flood of telegrams this week," the article began. The busiest man in town was a boy, sixteen-year-old Billie Smaha, who delivered wires for Western Union. "They kind of dreaded me," Billie later told the* Saturday Evening Post. *A* New York Herald-Tribune *reporter calculated that "if New York City were to suffer losses in the same proportion . . . its casualty list would include more than 17,000 names."*[146]

Red Oak was a microcosm of what was happening across the nation. Instead of an abstraction, war had finally become real. Instead of newsreels of ships and tanks and newspapers with maps and arrows, war had become a matter of dead, wounded, and missing boys. War was finally experienced by the American public for the human disaster that it was then and will always continue to be.

He makes wars cease to the ends of the earth; he breaks the bow and shatters the spear, he burns the shields with fire. "Be still, and know that I am God."~Psalm 46:9–10

Rite of Purification

MAJ. GEN. TERRY ALLEN was a division commander during the North African campaign. He was third generation Army and raised by his father to be a soldier. The young Allen was *"Saddle-hardened before he was ten,"* and learned *"to ride, smoke, chew, cuss and fight at the earliest possible age."*[147] Later on, hard drinking became another characteristic, and this got him into trouble. It came to the attention of Generals Marshall and Eisenhower that the attitude toward alcohol was somewhat loose within Allen's division and that Allen himself was drinking too much. Allen was warned about the problem and had an encounter with General Patton, who didn't care for Allen's rather loose interpretation of uniform regulations.

As Allen was about to go into battle, he tried to prepare himself by purging some of these stains. He described this in a letter to his wife explaining how he burned various personal records, including the letter in which Marshall had warned him about excessive drinking. By incinerating *"all that stuff,"* Allen told his wife, he hoped to purge all *"rancor or ill-will in my mind or in my heart."* The little fire was like a rite of purification to give himself a clean slate going into combat.[148]

This story reminds me of a little ceremony that I once experienced during a regular church service. Each person was asked to write down the one thing that he or she most regretted having done. Later in the service we were invited forward to give these little pieces of paper to God and to throw them into a fire beneath the cross, where they were consumed. This act was to dramatize how God will remove any stain if, through his Son, we confess it and ask for his forgiveness. It was a powerful reminder of God's grace and of our standing as adopted children in his family. Through Jesus Christ, and him alone, we always have the opportunity to gain a clean slate.

He forgave us all our sins, having canceled the written code, with its regulations, that was against us and that stood opposed to us; he took it away, nailing it to the cross. ~Colossians 2:13–14

May I Fulfill My Duty

GEN. TERRY ALLEN had remarkable success leading two different divisions during World War II. British Field Marshal Sir Harold R. L. G. Alexander called him the *"finest divisional commander he had seen in two wars."*[149] When asked about the qualities of leadership that won such devotion from his troops, one of his officers replied: *"It's just because he's so . . . honest."*[150] He was honest about his affection for his men and his desire to keep casualties at a minimum. He knew that the combat infantrymen represented 20 percent of U.S. forces overseas, but suffered 70 percent of the casualties. He was a fierce combat leader, but was ever conscious of his responsibility to the men under him.

Terry Allen was also devoutly religious and prayed strenuously for his troops before every battle. He contributed the following prayer to the *Soldiers' and Sailors' Prayer Book*:

May I Fulfill My Duty

O Jesus, Prince of soldiers, through many terrible days thou hast protected me. For this I thank thee with all my heart but, all the while, I am thinking of the soldiers who fought valiantly with me and fell bravely at my side. Give them rest and peace and the rewards thou hast reserved for the brave. Comfort their loved ones by the sweetness of thy Grace.

But there are other battles ahead and I feel more than ever the need of being close to thee. However rigorous the task that awaits me, may I fulfill my duty faithfully. Give me strength to lead and inspire my soldiers with daring and courage.

May our tears and sweat and blood, in this struggle, be acceptable in thine eyes unto the remission of our sins, for the glory of thy Name and for the preservation of our beloved Country. Amen.[151]

Now all has been heard; here is the conclusion of the matter: Fear God and keep his commandments, for this is the whole duty of man. ~Ecclesiastes 12:13

Seventeen Minutes

THERE ARE MOMENTS when time slows down. Capt. Robert Crisp of the British 3rd Royal Tank Regiment led his squadron of tanks into action near Tobruk in November 1941. The order to advance came at exactly 1:00 p.m., sending his unit into an attack against a German formation about one thousand yards away. After penetrating the enemy position, Crisp had to halt his tank on the edge of a steep embankment where he continued firing.

Suddenly he was showered with water and realized that the water cans stored on the back of his turret had been hit. Looking back he saw a German anti-tank gun only fifty yards away loading for another shot. He could only stare in amazement as the gun ejected a puff of smoke, and he felt his tank shudder from the hit. He looked down in his turret to see a gaping hole and a wounded gunner. With only seconds before the anti-tank gun could reload, he frantically ordered his driver over the precipice. The tank dropped out of the line of fire and continued down a dry wadi until eventually emerging at a point away from the battle. Crisp recalled later:

> We followed the wadi southwards as it grew shallower, eventually disgorging us unobtrusively on to the plateau over which we had charged so bravely . . . when? An hour ago? Today? Yesterday? And how many lives ago? My wrist watch was staring me in the face as we paused on the rim of the depression. The hands pointed to 17 minutes past one. 17 minutes.[152]

I have seen men age years after being under fire for minutes. Time is relative from our human perspective, passing faster or slower in different situations. But what about God's perspective? We know that God created time itself and is not constrained by it. He lives outside it. The old hymn says it well: *"A thousand ages in Thy sight are like an evening gone."*[153] If we can keep God's perspective in mind, the significance of our time on Earth will shrink in comparison with our eternal future.

He has also set eternity in the hearts of men; yet they cannot fathom what God has done from beginning to end. ~Ecclesiastes 3:11

It Might Have Come Off

FROM HIS NEW vantage point Captain Crisp looked over a scene of destruction not more than five hundred yards distant. Columns of smoke billowed up from four of his disabled tanks. Three others were immobile and abandoned. A line of German anti-tank guns and their crews lined the drop-off that he had just gone over. Men were running about among the vehicles. He saw groups of his own men herded together by gesticulating Germans. It all made him sick at heart:

> *Was there nothing I could do? My mind moved round the prospect of a sudden charge into that line of anti-tank guns, over-running them before they could get their sights on me. If I had had a gunner to fire the Browning, perhaps I might have. As it was I was grateful for the opportunity of rejecting it as impossible, and so prolonging my life and those of my crew. But who knows? It might have come off.[154]*

I will always remember one notable occasion when I had to make a somewhat similar decision in the heat of combat. Could I take the hill or not? I decided not, undoubtedly saving many lives, not to mention my own. Through the years I have wrestled with my conscience over that decision. I have to admit that I was also grateful for the opportunity of rejecting an action that seemed impossible. I strongly identify with the doubts of this British officer in another war. Since becoming a Christian I have come to believe strongly that God protected me on that day and during many dangerous times when I was not a Christian. This is an essential element of my faith. My spiritual life is motivated by gratitude for his faithfulness in blessing me even while I was blind to him.

This is love: not that we loved God, but that he loved us and sent his Son as an atoning sacrifice for our sins. ~1 John 4:10

Straightforward Job

THROUGHOUT THE WAR General Eisenhower would be challenged to select and direct the men best suited for command. Having to contend with disparate personalities like Patton, Bradley, Fredenhall, Clark, and Montgomery, his abilities were tested repeatedly. This was especially true in the early stages of the North African campaign when many of these subordinates were unknown quantities. Eisenhower gradually developed his own approach to evaluating those under him. In March 1943 he wrote his son at West Point: *"I have observed very frequently that it is not the man who is so brilliant (who) delivers in time of stress and strain, but rather the man who can keep on going indefinitely, doing a good straightforward job."*[155]

This statement is revealing in that it also describes Eisenhower's own qualities as commander in chief. Early in the war, even though many of his deficiencies were exposed, he was honest with himself and worked methodically to improve. He became more and more effective as he honed his own uncomplicated style and began to focus on simple themes: Allied unity and the certainty of victory.

Fortunately, God does not always require brilliance from us in service to his kingdom. When we humbly seek to determine his will, we may find times when we are called to great tasks. More often, however, it is the simple work in support of our family, friends, and church that needs to be done with patience and consistency. A dependable, straightforward job is usually the key to pleasing God.

His work will be shown for what it is, because the Day will bring it to light. It will be revealed with fire, and the fire will test the quality of each man's work.
~1 Corinthians 3:13

The Desert

ALAN MOOREHEAD was a renowned war correspondent for the London *Daily Express* and one of the most successful British writers of World War II. He eloquently described the setting of the war in North Africa:

> *Yellow rocks, saltbush, grey earth and this perfect beach was the eternal background wherever you looked in the north of the Western Desert. Except at spots along the coast and far inland it never even achieved those picturesque rolling sandhills which Europeans seem always to associate with deserts. It had fresh colours in the morning, and immense sunsets. One clear hot cloudless day followed another in endless progression. A breeze stirred sometimes in the early morning, and again at night when one lay on a camp bed in the open, gazing up into a vaster and more brilliant sky than one could ever have conceived in Europe . . . there was a sense of rest and relaxation in the tremendous silence, especially at night, and now the silence is still the best thing I remember of the desert, the silence, the cool nights, the clear hot days and the eternal flatness of everything.*[156]

When I first read this description, I was impressed with its almost biblical quality. On reflection, this is no accident. The historical events presented in the Bible take place over practically the same desert as the one described here. The desert was not only the scene of many biblical events, it was also a powerful metaphor. Practically surrounding Israel, it was a place of hardship, punishment, and testing. God's salvation was likened to the gift of water and new life to a parched earth. The desert was a place of special significance to Jesus, where he found respite and a place of blessed solitude. Just like each one of us, he needed alone time, to reflect and to pray, and to renew his relationship with the Father. We should each seek out our own 'desert time' in contemplative prayer.

And he said unto them, Come ye yourselves apart into a desert place, and rest a while: for there were many coming and going, and they had no leisure so much as to eat. ~Mark 6:31 (KJV)

Greatest Cathedrals

CHAPLAINS SERVING in war zones seldom saw the inside of church buildings. A lot of ingenuity was required to get their special work done. One combat chaplain described his places of worship:

Outdoor Cathedral
(National Archives)

> *During these months I held services in every conceivable location—on the open deck, in the men's mess hall, aboard ship, on the cargo hatch of a sunken Liberty ship, aboard a floating pier, ashore, in the open, in the rain, and under tarpaulined shelter . . . These services were in many ways far more real than those held in the greatest cathedrals.*[157]

During my military career I marched in countless ceremonies. The ultimate in pageantry was an evening parade under spotlights on the White House lawn. I also vividly recall another parade of the same military format, but devoid of pageantry. On Okinawa, where my Marine ancestors fought during World War II, I marched in a combat review with other Marines about to deploy for combat. This parade featured helmets, packs, weapons, and camouflage. Even though the audience was small, it was one of my most moving experiences.

The common denominator of these stories is found in the attitude of the participants. When soldiers or saints face the urgency of their mission and realize their vulnerability, their ceremonies become intensely meaningful. At the same time, the outward form loses significance. When we know what we have to do, and we realize that the capacity to do it can only come from God, worship becomes urgent and real. This is the attitude we need every time we come before his altar. It makes no difference whether that altar is in a tent or a cathedral.

> Yet a time is coming and has now come when the true worshipers will worship the Father in spirit and truth, for they are the kind of worshipers the Father seeks. ~John 4:23

Ernie Pyle

FROM 1935 until his death on Okinawa in 1945, Ernie Pyle was a roving correspondent for the Scripps Howard newspaper chain. He was never a "big picture" kind of guy. Before the war his stories focused on out-of-the-way places and the people who lived in them. His style had the flavor of personal letters home. During the war he traveled with U.S. forces in just about every theater, and he never changed his approach. Early in the war, United Press writer Reynolds Packard, who considered himself a "more serious" war correspondent, gave him some advice:

> *"You're on the wrong track. Nobody cares about these GI stories you write from the line. You've got to learn how to analyze the communiqués that come out of Eisenhower's headquarters. That's the secret of being a war correspondent. Figuring out from all that what is really going on."*
>
> *"You're right, Pack, absolutely right," said Ernie Pyle miserably. "I'm a lousy correspondent. I know it. I'm trying. Believe me. I'm trying. But I just can't seem to get that stuff straight."*
>
> *"I know," said Packard heroically. "It takes a lot of experience."*[158]

Pyle may have made a conscientious effort to better understand the "big picture" of politics and strategy, but, fortunately, he continued to focus his stories on the ordinary soldiers fighting the war. He said, *"I love the infantry because they are the underdogs . . . they have no comforts . . . and in the end they are the guys that wars can't be won without."*[159]

When he was killed on Okinawa, the soldiers erected a simple plaque: *"At this spot, the 77th Infantry Division lost a buddy, Ernie Pyle, 18 April 1945."*[160] Ernie Pyle's personal humility and empathy toward others made him a beloved figure to the soldiers he wrote about and to readers in four hundred daily newspapers.

For whoever exalts himself will be humbled, and whoever humbles himself will be exalted. ~Matthew 23:12

Down to Bed Rock

NO ONE ON EARTH complains like a soldier in combat—or has more reason to. He suffers from hunger, thirst, exhaustion, fear, and the perceived incompetence of those "above" him. And he doesn't suffer in silence. Expressing himself effectively with a mixture of profanity and humor is a matter of professional pride. Sgt. Ray Salisbury was with the U.S. forces in North Africa in 1943 and had his own observations on this trait of the American soldier:

> We can complain to ourselves, grouse about conditions and yell about anything or everything but when something comes up that needs everyone's cooperation the Americans are there to do it. Then they go back to their complaining . . . Just to witness the ingenuity of soldiers who aren't provided with the comforts of home, to see them make crystals for their watches out of a turret canopy—to watch them repair their shoes with nails made from carpet tacks. There are countless other things they do. They do not complain because they are without facilities—they make their own . . . Here is where you get down to bed rock. Here is where you discover that you have pools of energy that have never been tapped.[161]

It is the same now as it was then: our soldiers are a product of the society they come from. They are used to thinking for themselves and don't usually hesitate to state their opinions, even when they irritate those "above" them. The smart officer (as well as employer or parent) doesn't fight this ingrained trait. They do better to facilitate it. You will have a better military unit, business, or family if those under your supervision have a regular way to express their opinions. When you insist on positive suggestions along with the complaints, you tap into the "bed rock" mentioned above: the creative potential and energy of people molded in the spirit of freedom.

I run in the path of your commands, for you have set my heart free. ~Psalm 119:32

Soldiers landing on North African beaches
(National Archives)

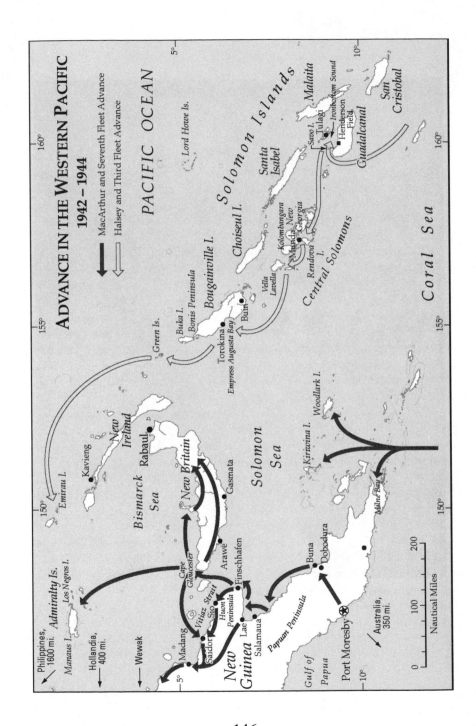

ADVANCE IN THE WESTERN PACIFIC
1942–1944

MacArthur and Seventh Fleet Advance

Halsey and Third Fleet Advance

PACIFIC OCEAN

Solomon Islands

Lord Howe Is.

Malaita

San Cristobal

Ironbottom Sound

Tulagi
Savo I.
Henderson Field
Guadalcanal

Santa Isabel

Choiseul I.

Kolombangara
Munda
New Georgia
Rendova I.
Central Solomons

Vella Lavella

Bougainville I.

Buka I.
Bonis Peninsula
Torokina
Empress Augusta Bay
Buin

Green Is.

Coral Sea

New Ireland

Kavieng

Emirau I.

Bismarck Sea

Rabaul
New Britain

Gasmata

Solomon Sea

Woodlark I.

Kiriwina I.

Milne Bay

Admiralty Is.
Manaus I.
Los Negros I.

Philippines, 1600 mi.

Hollandia, 400 mi.

Wewak

Madang
Saidor
Sio
Cape Gloucester
Vitiaz Strait
Huon Peninsula
Arawe
Finschhafen
Lae
Salamaua

Buna
Dobodura

New Guinea

Papuan Peninsula

Gulf of Papua

Port Moresby

Australia, 350 mi.

Nautical Miles
0   100   200

146

MAY

Advance in the Western Pacific

AFTER THE Battle of Midway, the strategic focus of Japan and the United States shifted to an obscure and remote corner of the Western Pacific known as the Solomon Islands. On August 7, 1942, the 1st Marine Division, commanded by Maj. Gen. Alexander Vandegrift, landed on Guadalcanal and quickly took control of a partially finished airstrip, which the Marines renamed Henderson Field. Work on the runway was rushed to completion, and, in little over a week, Marine dive-bombers and fighter aircraft were landing to add airpower to the defense of the new base.

Contrary to the ease of its capture, the defense of Guadalcanal became a long, drawn-out nightmare for the Marines ashore and the sailors at sea. On the night of the second day, a strong Japanese naval force arrived and decimated the U.S. covering force. In the night Battle of Savo Island the Allies lost four cruisers and one thousand seamen. The Japanese fleet turned away before finishing the fleet of transport ships still off-loading cargo across the beaches, miraculously saving the invasion from ruin.

The desperate struggle for Guadalcanal continued for four months. Both sides were forced to resupply and reinforce at night due to the threat of air strikes during daylight hours. The Japanese were able to bring in a constant stream of new troops and, by early November, outnumbered the Marines. They launched attack after attack against the positions around Henderson Field. The Marines held on in spite of hunger, malaria, and severe shortages of equipment and supplies. At this point in the war, the North African landings and supply convoys to England and Russia were competing for every item of logistical support.

As the Marines held on ashore the Navy fought a series of battles at sea that would prove critical to the final outcome. Fortunately, the determined and aggressive Adm. William F. "Bull" Halsey took command of the naval forces conducting the Solomons campaign. On the night of November 14–15 a battleship engagement was fought off Guadalcanal. The Japanese lost one of their largest ships, and another major resupply effort was thwarted. After this, the Japanese did not launch another significant offensive against the island. The Marines were relieved on

December 9, at which time General Vandegrift told his men: "*It may well be that this modest operation begun four months ago today has, through your efforts, been successful in thwarting the large aims of our enemy in the Pacific.*"[162]

As the Marines were securing Guadalcanal, American and Australian forces under Gen. Douglas MacArthur were defeating Japanese forces defending the Papuan Peninsula on the southern end of New Guinea. In early 1943, both forces went on the offensive, advancing toward the Japanese stronghold of Rabaul on the eastern end of New Britain. MacArthur's units leapfrogged up the coast of New Guinea as Halsey's force, spearheaded by the Marines, attacked through the central Solomons and Bougainville.

By early 1944 both forces converged on the Admiralty Islands. When Manus was taken and forward naval and air bases established, Rabaul was effectively bypassed, isolating and neutralizing more than ninety thousand Japanese troops in strong defensive positions. At this point, MacArthur was ready to continue his advance along the coast of New Guinea toward the Philippines as the bulk of Navy and Marine units turned their attention to the Central Pacific.

Hearing God

AS THE JAPANESE moved relentlessly through Southeast Asia, a group of Christian missionaries assembled on the Netherlands East Indies island of Celebes to anxiously await developments. In late January 1942 the Dutch police came to Dr. Robert Jaffrey, the mission chairman, to inform him that a ship was lying at anchor to evacuate the last of the foreigners from the island. Dr. Jaffrey called a meeting to share this information and to determine who was going to leave and who was going to stay. He gave them challenging instructions:

> I want to counsel you not to discuss this decision that must be made with each other—not even husband and wife. Go to your knees and say, 'Lord, what do You want me to do? Shall I go or shall I stay?' This is extremely vital, because then no matter what happens in the months or possibly years ahead, you will know that you are exactly where God wants you to be. If He leads you to leave, you'll never feel that you were a coward and fled. If you are led to stay, no matter what happens you can look up and say, 'Lord, you intended for me to be right here.'[163]

Later, when the trucks arrived to pick up the missionaries, not one stepped forward to leave. All knew with certainty that God had called them to stay. Dr. Jaffrey said, "*God does not work in confusion, a wife against her husband or vice versa, in a matter that concerns both of you. This is but a confirmation to your hearts of His directive.*"[164]

Three days later it was reported that their assigned ship had been torpedoed and sunk with no known survivors. God had obviously spoken to these missionaries, and, amazingly, they were able individually to discern his guidance. We have to be inspired by the example of these spiritual people. Like them, we should seek to grow constantly in our ability to distinguish God's voice amid the clutter and distractions of our lives. This is no less a matter of life and death for us than for a group of missionaries long ago in the Pacific.

He calls his own sheep by name and leads them out. When he has brought out all his own, he goes on ahead of them, and his sheep follow him because they know his voice. ~John 10:3–4

106 Miles through the Valley

SEVENTEEN-YEAR-OLD Glenn Frazier was captured on the Bataan Peninsula in April 1942 and spent three and a half years in Japanese prisoner camps. His worst ordeal was the first six days and seven nights. Glenn surrendered with seventy-eight thousand other U.S. and Philippine troops who found themselves at the mercy of an enemy who held the act of surrender in the greatest contempt. The Japanese forced their already exhausted and disease-ridden captives to march overland with practically no food or water to distant prison camps. Those who fell out along the way were killed. Thousands died along this grim trail in a tragedy that the survivors would never forget. Throughout the infamous Bataan Death March, Glenn Frazier turned to God for the strength to keep going and, because of his powerful faith, ultimately survived the brutal trial of endurance. He later described his ordeal and his salvation in a paraphrase of the 23rd Psalm:

> *Yea though I walked 106 miles through the valley and in the shadow of death, I feared the evil of the imperial Japanese soldier. They had the guns and bayonets to use against me. All I had was the love and faith that God would comfort me. I knew the Lord was my shepherd. They forbid me to lay down in green pastures for six days and seven nights. I was marched by running water but was forbidden a drink. The Japanese prepared their tables before me but I was forbidden food. They maketh me march without mercy. But only God could restoreth my soul. He leadeth me step by step along the way in the face of my enemies. He promised to anoint my head with love and understanding and, even though my cup was empty, I knew it would be filled in his name's sake. I knew that goodness and mercy would follow me. My life would be spared in his name. I knew that even though the path was long and hard, it was the path of righteousness for his name sake.[165]*

Praise be to the Lord, to God our Savior, who daily bears our burdens. . . . Our God is a God who saves; from the Sovereign LORD comes escape from death.
~Psalm 68:19–20

3

The Fighting Chaplain

CHAPLAIN GEORGE RENTZ was liked and admired by all aboard the USS *Houston*. Fifty-nine years old and a veteran of World War I, he was probably the oldest man on the ship. He was most often found walking among the men, helping where he could and giving words of encouragement. He often brought ice water and cookies to those on watch, and was even known to give out a few unauthorized drinks of harder stuff when conditions called for it.[166] Even when the ship was under air attack, Chaplain Rentz remained topside to be with the anti-aircraft gun crews. An officer noted that when the gunners *"saw this man of God walking fearlessly among them, they no longer felt alone."*[167]

On February 28, 1942, the *Houston* was fatally wounded during the Battle of the Java Sea and had to be abandoned. In the darkness of night Chaplain Rentz entered the water with his life jacket and hundreds of other survivors. He found a spot of relative safety with others on an over-crowded floatplane pontoon, and seeing that there wasn't room for everyone, he said to the men around him, *"You men are young, I have lived the major part of my life and I am willing to go."*[168] He let go the pontoon and tried to drift away, but the men brought him back several times. Finally, he said a prayer, took off his life jacket, placed it near a sailor without one, and silently slipped below the surface. For this extraordinary act of heroism, George Rentz was posthumously awarded the Navy Cross—the only Navy chaplain to be so honored during World War II.

> *He had followed the law of the Apostles' Creed,*
> *His life the price of a noble deed.*
> *He went to his Lord with no regret*
> *Our Fighting Chaplain we'll never forget.*[169]

The wicked man flees though no one pursues, but the righteous are as bold as a lion. ~Proverbs 28:1

Boot Camp

WILLIAM MANCHESTER (1922–2004) was the best-selling author of eighteen books and deemed by the *Washington Post* as one of the greatest popular historians of the twentieth century.[170] His books focused on the lives of military and political leaders such as Douglas MacArthur, Winston Churchill, and John Kennedy.

Not quite so well known is the fact that Manchester was also a Marine during World War II. He joined the Corps in 1942 while still in college. His first experience was boot camp at Parris Island, South Carolina, where his head was shaved and he was given a number. He met a new god-like figure, the Drill Instructor, and learned the three ways of doing things: the right way, the wrong way, and the Marine Corps way. Discipline was harsh and corporal punishment was common. In spite of the shock, Manchester somehow concluded that he adored Parris Island.

> *How could I enjoy this? Parts of it, of course, I loathed. But the basic concept fascinated me. I wanted to surrender my individuality, curbing my neck beneath the yoke of petty tyranny. Since my father's death I had yearned for stern discipline, and Parris Island, where he himself had learned discipline a quarter-century earlier, gave it to me in spades. Physically I was delicate, even fragile, but I had limitless reservoirs of energy, and I could feel myself toughening almost hourly. Everything I saw seemed exquisitely defined—every leaf, every pebble looked as sharp as a drawing in a book. I knew I was merely becoming a tiny cog in the vast machine which would confront fascism, but that was precisely why I had volunteered.[171]*

William Manchester brought a great writer's discernment to a brutal process. He saw through his own personal agony to the higher purpose of this experience. To win a war, many good men had to subject themselves to the severest discipline. There are times in our lives when God's discipline can also be difficult to endure and to understand. God disciplines us mainly through our hardships and setbacks, and, when we allow these experiences to bring us closer to him, we grow that much "tougher" for our service in his kingdom.

Know then in your heart that as a man disciplines his son, so the LORD your God disciplines you. ~Deuteronomy 8:5

The Code

ABRAHAM FELBER landed at Red Beach on Guadalcanal with the first wave of Marines on August 7, 1942. He was a thirty-six-year-old sergeant and grizzled veteran of the old Corps. As 1st Sergeant of Headquarters Battery, 11th Marines, it was up to him to pass on the time-honored traditions of the Corps to the younger men. Some of those traditions were contained in an unwritten code that distinguished the Old Breed. According to Felber, the "Code" required certain things of every Marine:

> *You don't hold a grudge against your fellow Marine, and you don't let anyone hold a grudge against you. You settle matters here and now. If words don't work, then with fists.*
>
> *You take the responsibility, and you take the blame, even if it's not yours.*
>
> *When war comes, you fight, because that's what you owe your country.*
>
> *In war, you depend for your life on your fellow Marine, and he depends for his life on you.*
>
> *You respect your own sailors and airmen doing battle for you. They are fighting and dying in the skies and on the seas to protect you. That's a service you can't return to them.*
>
> *You respect your enemy. They are husbands, fathers, and sons who fight and die just as bravely as you do.*
>
> *And when the warrior's day is done, and your nation seems quick to forget your sacrifice and your honor, you remain ever faithful, ever loyal.*[172]

The "Code" was an unusual blend of toughness and compassion that probably had its roots centuries ago among the knights of England. It was harsh and unyielding in war and chivalrous in peace, calling each man to a higher level of personal responsibility for his actions. In the end, it reflects the motto of the Marine Corps: *Semper Fidelis*. This is a standard that we should all attain to: being always faithful to the cause, even when our efforts are not understood or appreciated. We know that our cause in service to God and his kingdom is ultimately important and worthy of this dedication. We also know that no matter what God is faithful to us.

His master replied, "Well done, good and faithful servant! You have been faithful with a few things; I will put you in charge of many things. Come and share your master's happiness!" ~Matthew 25:23

White Linen

A S THE 1ST MARINE DIVISION hit the beaches on Guadalcanal, two battalions made simultaneous landings less than twenty miles away on the little island of Tulagi. Here the Marines got a taste of the fanatical resistance they would face for the rest of the war. It took three days of bitter fighting to secure the little island.

Lt. Paul Moore was a platoon commander in the Tulagi invasion force. Within just a year he had graduated from Yale, joined the Marine Corps, trained as an infantry officer, and sailed half way around the world to this remote spot. He now found himself in a place that he had never even heard of a few weeks before. It was a challenge just to exist in the jungle with almost constant rain and the sickening stench of decaying vegetation. He was shocked at his first sight of dead Japanese, and affected even more by the sight of wounded and dead fellow Marines. A few days after the island was secured he attended a religious service that left a lasting impression:

> *Sunday came several days after Tulagi had been secured. It may even have been the third day, when we were still very dirty and still terribly upset by our first experience with death. The whole outfit, those who were not on duty, came down to the cricket field, and the chaplain celebrated mass. The only clean thing on that entire island was the white linen, which he had salvaged to put over the makeshift altar, and perhaps his vestments. I remember having—it sounds sentimental—but a feeling, you know, about the world being broken, sinful, full of horror, terror, filth, but God being still pure. I had a real sense of reassurance.*[173]

Every Episcopal church has an altar guild of church people who voluntarily serve to maintain the altar linens and priestly vestments in an immaculate condition. I will never again take this service lightly after hearing the testimony of this Marine lieutenant on Tulagi. What a glorious mission: to give a hint of God's purity by this attention to detail in the physical elements of worship. These physical symbols of God's holiness are just as meaningful in our Sunday church services today as they were on a jungle island in wartime.

Such a high priest meets our need—one who is holy, blameless, pure, set apart from sinners, exalted above the heavens. ~Hebrews 7:26

Inbeat

THE MARINES WERE pinned down by an enemy machine gun and were taking casualties. Lt. Paul Moore raised himself up to throw a grenade and was struck in the chest by an enemy bullet. Looking down at the wound, his mind raced:

> *The air was going in and out of a hole in my lungs. That didn't mean I was finished, but I thought I was dead, going to die right then, because I thought if that happened you were gone. I wasn't breathing through my mouth but through this hole. It felt like a balloon going in and out, going pshhh. I was thinking to myself, Now I'm going to die.*

While undergoing treatment for his wound, he later learned:

> *The bullet . . . came through my chest between two ribs, slightly shattering them, went past my heart, as the doctors later told me, when it must have been on an inbeat instead of an outbeat, and then missed my backbone as it went through the other side of my body about an inch. So it was a very close shave.*[174]

What would life be like knowing that a bullet had missed your heart by less than an inch? Perhaps you would feel that it was no coincidence, and that God had spared your life for a purpose: your work on this earth was not yet complete.

The apostle Paul told the Corinthians all about his own "close shaves." Five times he received from the Jews the forty lashes minus one (forty lashes were thought to be lethal, so they stopped short at thirty-nine). He was beaten with rods three times, stoned once, shipwrecked three times, and the list goes on (2 Corinthians 11:24–27). Instead of these brushes with death stopping him from his work, he carried on by God's strength. God has numbered each of our days as well, from the moment we were born (Psalm 139:16). The Lord will call us home when the time is right, whether we die from a car accident, a heart attack, or an act of war. But in the meantime, he has work for us to do; we should not think our contributions to the kingdom of God are over as long as we are alive. (JG)

> For we are God's workmanship, created in Christ Jesus to do good works, which God prepared in advance for us to do. ~Ephesians 2:10

Hearing the Call

THE MISSION CAME from Col. "Chesty" Puller himself. Lt. Paul Moore was to assault a Japanese position on the other side of the Matanikau River with his platoon of Marines. Four other units had been repulsed in the same effort. It seemed like suicide, but he didn't hesitate.

Expecting to wade across, he and his men found themselves swimming instead. As he neared the opposite bank, he described an incredible scene: "*mortars and hand grenades going over our heads and into the water as if it were raining, with bullets striking all around us.*" As casualties mounted the Marines could not continue to advance. Moore finally called for his platoon to fall back. As he was trying to help one of his men to safety across the open beach under fire, an amazing thought passed through his mind:

> I remember when I was leaning over trying to bring one of my men to safety seeing bullet marks in the sand around my feet and thinking, you know, it I get out of this, maybe it means I should do something special. There was a feeling—I don't know if it's good theology, whether it's superstition or what, but certainly I felt that I had been extremely fortunate, and that I was, in a sense, living on borrowed time, and that this was another good reason to give my life to the Lord, and it seemed that being a priest was the way.[175]

Paul Moore did become an Episcopal priest and bishop after the war. I doubt that many discern their call to the priesthood in such dramatic fashion, but in every case it is a powerful calling. We are blessed that good men and women have heard and responded to this call in the past and continue to do so today. The body of Christ is made up mostly of lay people trying to do his work. Our "commissioned officers" are our priests and ministers. We need them to teach and lead us spiritually. They need our support and loyalty in return.

Then I heard the voice of the Lord saying, "Whom shall I send? And who will go for us?" And I said, "Here I am. Send me!" ~Isaiah 6:8

Chesty

LEWIS B. "CHESTY" PULLER arrived at Guadalcanal on September 18, 1942. He was forty-four years old and had already spent more than half his life as a Marine. Just promoted to lieutenant colonel, he commanded 1st Battalion, 7th Marines. When another famous Marine, Mike Edson, saw Puller land, he commented to someone nearby, "*There comes the greatest fighting man in the Marine Corps.*"[176]

Lewis B. "Chesty" Puller. (U.S. Marine Corps)

With two Navy Crosses already to his name, Puller was destined to earn three more before his career was over. His units were called on for the toughest assignments, and Puller put himself in the most dangerous places to best direct the action. In training and in combat he demanded every ounce of effort from every man and was unrelenting in his drive to successfully complete every mission. He was hard on his men, but he was also hard on himself.

Chesty Puller was undoubtedly a natural soldier and a great fighter. His men respected and feared him, but amazingly, they also loved him. This is because he looked after them like a father. He was ruthless with junior officers who took advantage of their "privileges." He was often seen standing in chow line with the men and eating with them. He pushed them to the limit on forced marches, but was usually seen helping carry machine guns and mortars to give those men some respite. Of commanders on Guadalcanal, he alone wrote personal letters to the wounded who had been evacuated. Sharing every danger and privation, he made his men feel like he was one of them.

Puller made a lasting contribution to the unique style of leadership that became firmly imbedded in Marine Corps tradition. It was not a "rank has its privilege" model. It was fundamentally a "servant" model. Every Marine officer learns, almost as a religious principle, that the needs of his men come before his own. The true prototype of this model is of course Jesus Christ. Service and sacrifice were the hallmarks of his life and ministry on Earth.

Your attitude should be the same as that of Christ Jesus: Who, being in very nature God, did not consider equality with God something to be grasped, but made himself nothing, taking the very nature of a servant. ~Philippians 2:5–7

Chaplain Controversy

CHESTY PULLER was not known as an outwardly religious man. Nevertheless, he took an active interest in the religious welfare of his men and made sure frequent services were held, especially for his troops in the front lines. He wanted the chaplains to do their jobs and to be with their men. He became incensed when his Protestant chaplain remained in a rear area during an extensive patrol into enemy-held areas. The chaplain protested that he thought he could do more working in a medical station caring for the wounded. Puller shouted, *"You weren't up where the fighting was. I think I'll prefer charges against you for being absent from your regiment. Your place was with the fighting men—your battalion."*[177]

Due to this incident and others not known, Puller formed some strong opinions about chaplains and their denominations. He complained that, *"In all our fighting I've known only a few Protestant chaplains worth their rations."* After the war, he made another pointed comment to his Episcopal bishop in Virginia: *"I can't understand why our Church sends such poorly prepared men as chaplains when fighting breaks out. The Catholics pick the very best, young, virile, active and patriotic. The troops look up to them."*[178]

Chesty Puller's opinions on clergy reflect his own experience, and I don't know how generally true they were. I cite his comments only to point out that his priorities were in the right place, for himself, his officers, and his chaplains. We can't effectively lead our families, employees, or congregations from a distance. We need to be "in the trenches" where the problems and frustrations can be understood and dealt with.

> Be shepherds of God's flock that is under your care, serving as overseers—not because you must, but because you are willing, as God wants you to be; not greedy for money, but eager to serve; not lording it over those entrusted to you, but being examples to the flock. ~1 Peter 5:2–3

Marines man a machine gun in the jungle.
(National Archives)

Worshiping in a jungle chapel.
(National Archives)

Manila John

SGT. JOHN BASILONE is a Marine Corps legend. Nicknamed "Manila John" by his men, he single-handedly held a key position defending the line on Guadalcanal against an all-out Japanese assault on October 24, 1942. Noticing one of his machine-gun positions silenced during the battle, he carried another gun and tripod, weighing about ninety pounds, across two hundred yards of fire-swept terrain and took up the fight by himself. During the night he retraced his steps to get more ammunition, holding his position all night under repeated attacks. For these feats he was awarded the Congressional Medal of Honor. He was awarded the Navy Cross for heroism on Iwo Jima, where he was tragically killed in action on February 19, 1945.

In between these battles Basilone returned to the United States, where he traveled the country, speaking on behalf of the war effort. The Marine Corps offered to commission him an officer and to assign him to stateside duty. His response, *"I ain't no officer, and I ain't no museum piece. I belong back with my outfit."*[179]

Before returning to duty in the Pacific, he found time to pen a thoughtful prayer for publication in the *Soldiers' and Sailors' Prayer Book*:

Prayer by a Marine Corps Sergeant

O God, I confess that I did not really appreciate the value of religious freedom until I was wholly certain of the righteousness of our course. Born of humble parentage I was not endowed with a spiritual expressiveness. Since my exploits I was uplifted by the power of Christ. It was He who watched over me with an unmistakable sign of divine guidance. How I ever was spared from the Great Beyond only the Lord knows. I pray each night for my comrades who paid the Supreme Sacrifice and I know that they are triumphant inhabitants of heaven—white flowers of a blameless life. I now carry the riches of God in my heart—something that I shall forever be thankful for. Almighty God, I ask for your continued guidance. Please redeem and purify humanity, for thine is the power forever and ever. Amen.[180]

Man born of woman is of few days and full of trouble. He springs up like a flower and withers away; like a fleeting shadow, he does not endure. ~Job 14:1–2

Munro

COAST GUARD PERSONNEL were an important part of the amphibious forces assembled for the Guadalcanal operation. Many of them came from lifeguard stations and their experience with small boats in rough seas was invaluable. They proved to be seasoned coxswains for the all-important landing craft moving men and supplies from ship to shore.

Douglas Munro was one of these Coast Guard sailors. He distinguished the Coast Guard and himself by heroically rescuing a group of Marines in trouble on Guadalcanal. The Higgins boats used by Munro in this action were thirty-four foot plywood craft with no protection for the crews. The story is best told in Munro's Medal of Honor citation:

> *For extraordinary heroism and conspicuous gallantry in action above and beyond the call of duty as Officer-in-Charge of a group of Higgins boats, engaged in the evacuation of a Battalion of Marines trapped by enemy Japanese forces at Point Cruz, Guadalcanal, on September 27, 1942 . . . Munro, under constant risk of his life, daringly led five of his small craft toward the shore. As he closed the beach, he signaled the others to land, and then placed his craft with its two small guns as a shield between the beachhead and the Japanese. When the perilous task of evacuation was nearly completed, Munro was killed by enemy fire . . . By his outstanding leadership, expert planning, and dauntless devotion to duty, he and his courageous comrades undoubtedly saved the lives of many who otherwise would have perished. He gallantly gave up his life in defense of his country.*[181]

Douglas Munro grew up in the small town of Cle Elum, Washington. He showed an early aptitude for music and was a leader in his high school and college bands. In 1939 he was twenty years old when he felt the call to serve his country. He picked the Coast Guard because *"it was dedicated to saving lives."*[182] By putting this mission before his own life, he became the only member of the U.S. Coast Guard to receive the Medal of Honor.

I tell you the truth, unless a kernel of wheat falls to the ground and dies, it remains only a single seed. But if it dies, it produces many seeds. ~John 12:24

Why?

O N THE NIGHT OF October 13, 1942, a group of Marines on Guadalcanal had a special celebration for a young private who they affectionately called "The Kid." That afternoon a rare delivery of mail had brought news that the Kid's wife had finally had her baby.

Sgt. Jim O'Leary, one of the toughest noncommissioned officers in the unit, was especially excited, as he had taken a special interest in the expectant father over the weeks of anxious waiting for this news. He organized a party and led the celebration on a night seemingly blessed by the absence of the usual air attacks.

Later that night, however, the Japanese launched a frenzied all-out attack on the Marine lines. During a lull in the fighting a Navy chaplain went forward to help with the wounded. In the darkness, he found Jim O'Leary wandering in a daze, his face streaked with tears. When O'Leary recognized the chaplain, he yelled:

"The Kid's dead . . . he's gone. What the h___ good are your prayers and your religion? Did they stop the shrapnel that tore half his head off? Why wasn't it me instead of him? If there is really a God and He had to have a human sacrifice, why couldn't He have been satisfied with O'Leary, instead of taking a kid with a young wife and a brand new baby who'll never see his father? Why should anyone believe and trust in Jesus or Mary when they've allowed a crime like this to happen? Why did it happen, Padre? Why? Why?"[183]

Knowing it wouldn't help much at the moment, the chaplain softly replied, *"We must take God on faith."*[184]

Books have been written attempting to answer this apparent riddle. If God is good and all-powerful, how can he let such bad things happen? The answer lies in how God created human beings and the universe. It was his plan that humans have the freedom to do good and bad, and that nature should create and destroy according to properties that he established. He doesn't cause our pain, but he knows that we will be blessed by it if it brings us closer to him.

> I am still confident of this: I will see the goodness of the LORD in the land of the living. Wait for the LORD; be strong and take heart and wait for the LORD.
> ~Psalm 27:13–14

Looking for a Divine Hand

THE NIGHTTIME bombardment of Henderson Field was more intense that night than usual. The naval gunfire shells from the Japanese ships streaked red as they rained in and around the Marines' positions. Each blast was a violent upheaval of shrapnel, dirt, and acrid smoke. An ammunition truck was hit, causing an enormous explosion that shook the island and hurled thousands of fragments through the air. A Navy chaplain huddled in his trench, sharing the terror with those around him:

> *Alongside me, head bowed, there were Catholic boys reciting their rosaries, Protestants murmuring prayers, and Jewish boys, with closed eyes, fingering the holy mezuzahs they wore around their necks. The adage that there are no atheists in foxholes was already familiar to me. In moments of deadly peril, the human hand reaches out for help from above. Even those who hadn't uttered a word of prayer or been inside a house of worship for years before the war, were looking now for a Divine hand to shield them.*[185]

In times of real danger our superficial concerns are stripped away, and we are brought back to an elemental reality. There is a God, and we need him desperately. The universal need to pray at such times is proof of this point. Unfortunately, these prayers are often not remembered after the crisis passes. On this score I have been the worst offender. My bargains made with God while in physical danger were soon forgotten. I didn't give him credit or thanks that I survived a war and was able to live a blessed life with my family. One of my foremost tasks as a new Christian has been trying to make up for all those years of ingratitude. I have a long way to go.

O Lord, I say to you, "You are my God." Hear, O Lord, my cry for mercy. O Sovereign Lord, my strong deliverer, who shields my head in the day of battle.
~Psalm 140:6–7

Tokyo Rose

DURING THE WAR, a dozen women of American descent made daily broadcasts on Radio Tokyo designed to demoralize U.S. servicemen deployed in the Pacific. These women combined "soft" propaganda with popular music, and became known collectively by the GIs as "Tokyo Rose."[186] As the war progressed, the troops enjoyed the music and generally laughed off the obvious attempts to undermine their morale.

During the Guadalcanal campaign, however, it was not so easy for the Marines to laugh off Tokyo Rose's insidious effort to make them feel isolated and abandoned. The Marines could see for themselves that they were undersupplied and, at times, seemingly forgotten in their prolonged struggle. A Navy chaplain explained:

> *The Mata Hari of the airwaves had no competition for our attention or our interest. Though we naturally discounted most of what she told us, some of it couldn't help sinking in. There was a gnawing fear among us that the home front was incapable of giving us the help we desperately needed. "You are forgotten like the men of Bataan and Corregidor were forgotten," Tokyo Rose would purr at us. I was worried about the spirit of valorous men who were beginning to feel that they, too, were expendable.*[187]

Discerning the truth in what we hear is often difficult. Unfortunately, Satan's voice can be very soothing and plausible, with just enough "truth" to deceive us. As we filter what we hear, our own self-serving inner voice can also override our objectivity. We have to remember that God normally speaks to us in a quiet voice that we must diligently seek to hear and to understand through our prayers, Scripture, and Christian friends.

My sheep listen to my voice; I know them, and they follow me. ~John 10:27

Jungle Fighting

FIGHTING A DETERMINED and fanatical enemy should have been challenge enough. However, the jungles of New Guinea added unimaginable suffering to the ordeal. The equatorial climate inflicted torrential rains, high humidity, and insufferable heat on those unfortunates who had to live and fight in it. Wet clothing, rusting equipment, omnivorous insects, and an endless variety of tropical maladies were the constant companions of every soldier.

As the battles raged on and around Guadalcanal in late 1942, U.S. Army forces were committed on the north coast of the Papuan Peninsula to take the port of Buna and to relieve another threat against Australia. As the campaign wore on, the Japanese defenders and the jungle took their toll:

> The track is now knee deep in thick, black mud. For the last ten days no man's clothing has been dry and they have slept—when sleep was possible—in pouring rain under sodden blankets . . . Every hour is a nightmare.[188]
>
> . . . The troops were riddled with malaria, dengue fever, tropical dysentery, and were covered with jungle ulcers.[189]
>
> . . . It was a sly and sneaky kind of combat which never resembled the massive and thunderous operations in Europe . . . In New Guinea, when the rains came, wounded men might drown before the litter bearers found them. Many did. No war is a good war, and death ignores geography. But out here I was convinced, as were my soldiers, that death was pleasanter in the Temperate Zone.[190]

There truly has never been a good place for a war. However, these heroes of the early days of World War II in the Pacific endured more hardship than most. With tenuous supply lines and great uncertainty about the outcome, they fought on for interminable months. During the darkest days of the war, they not only survived—they also turned the tide of battle and gave a glimmer of hope to an Allied cause that had up until then seen only defeat.

Endure hardship with us like a good soldier of Christ Jesus. . . . If we died with him, we will also live with him; if we endure, we will also reign with him.
~2 Timothy 2:3, 11–12

Battleships and cruisers in formation.
(National Archives)

Savo Island

By the evening of the second day the invasion of Guadalcanal was progressing successfully. More than ten thousand Marines had landed and were in the process of securing their major objectives. Nineteen cargo vessels were beginning to move their stores of food, ammunition, and equipment ashore.

Although taken by surprise, the Japanese responded aggressively to this challenge. Within hours Vice Adm. Gunichi Mikawa launched a naval counterstrike from Rabaul, six hundred miles away. He personally led a task force of five heavy cruisers, two light cruisers, and one destroyer south to destroy the invasion force off the beaches. Unfortunately, this threat was not detected by air search as it approached.

At 1:42 a.m. on August 8, 1942, Mikawa's fleet passed Savo Island and made contact with the U.S. screening force, deployed about thirty miles north of the invasion beaches. In half an hour the U.S. Navy suffered one of the worse defeats in its history. Surprised and outmatched in night gunnery tactics, the U.S. force lost four heavy cruisers and more than one thousand men. At 2:20 a.m. Mikawa reassembled his largely unscathed but scattered ships, and pondered briefly what to do next. The now undefended transport fleet lay exposed only miles away.

At this moment, Admiral Mikawa made one of the most fateful decisions of the war. Considering his "victory" and the possibility of air attacks after daybreak, he turned north, away from the invasion beaches. The transport fleet and the 1st Marine Division that it sustained were spared. The most perilous moment of the Guadalcanal campaign had passed.

This decision, made in darkness and under the stress of combat, saved America's first offensive effort in the Pacific. This is another moment when we can see evidence of God's providential hand moving to change the odds in a desperate struggle.

Daniel answered, "O king, live forever! My God sent his angel, and he shut the mouths of the lions. They have not hurt me, because I was found innocent in his sight." ~Daniel 6:21–22

The Parson

R ADM. ROBERT MILLS tells the story of an unnamed Kansas divinity student who enlisted in the Navy in 1941. Seeing an opportunity to serve his country and the Lord, the young man brought one hundred miniature Bibles with him when he reported aboard his first ship, the destroyer USS *Ralph Talbot*. Since storage on the ship was extremely limited, the Bibles had to go in his own locker. Also, no chaplains were assigned to destroyers, so he started holding worship services himself. The rough-talking crew attended sparingly and showed little interest in the Bibles. They did start calling the young man "Parson."

In August 1942 the *Ralph Talbot* was assigned to support the landings on Guadalcanal. The Parson's battle station was the Number 4 five-inch gun mount on the main deck. This mount was unshielded and ammunition had to be passed hand-to-hand across the deck from the ammunition hoist. The Parson was the last man in the chain and had to hand the sixty-pound shells up to the ever-moving gun mount.

During the night Battle of Savo Island the *Ralph Talbot* was heavily engaged, attracting the fire of at least three enemy cruisers. One of several shells hit the crew living compartment, flooding it with a mixture of seawater and oil. Another shell struck the main deck, as the admiral described while telling his story:

> *Of more instant concern, one incoming shell hit the underside of #4 five inch gun, bursting just behind the large brass and steel fuse setter, not three feet from where the Parson was busy at his battle station. The explosion and shrapnel killed the man on the Parson's right, the man on the Parson's left, and killed or injured nearly every other man in that gun crew. The Parson was untouched.*[191]

After this incident, the crew regarded the Parson with a sense of awe. His church services on the fantail soon became overcrowded. The hottest items on the ship were salt-water-soaked, fuel-oil-stained miniature Bibles.[192] Surely the hand of God was on this man dutifully trying to do God's work in a difficult place.

But you, O LORD, be not far off; O my Strength, come quickly to help me. Deliver my life from the sword, my precious life from the power of the dogs. ~Psalm 22:19–20

Personal Responsibility

DURING THE NAVAL battle of Savo Island, the USS *Astoria* was the first Allied cruiser to engage the Japanese fleet, suffering severe damage from accurate Japanese gunfire. At about 2:00 a.m. Signalman 3rd Class Elgin Staples was hurled overboard when an 8-inch gun turret exploded. In the water, he was able to stay afloat thanks to the life belt around his waist that he managed to inflate in the darkness.[193]

Four hours later, Staples was rescued by a passing destroyer and returned to the *Astoria*. The captain was trying to save the fatally wounded ship by grounding her on the beach. When this effort failed, Staples again found himself in the water. He was one of five hundred survivors rescued again later. Once safely aboard a transport ship, he examined the life belt that had saved his life. It had been made by the Firestone Tire and Rubber Company of Akron, Ohio, and had a serial number inscribed on the label.

Later in the war, Staples was able to return home to Ohio on leave. Since his mother worked for Firestone, he asked her about the number on his life belt. She told him that numbers were assigned to each inspector, so that one individual would be responsible for each piece of equipment sent to the war. Since everything about that life belt was indelibly imprinted on his mind, he told his mother the number. Astonished, she told him that that was her personal code affixed to every item that she was responsible for approving.[194]

Very few people in any walk of life have ever been so directly rewarded for faithfulness in doing their job.

Whatever you do, work at it with all your heart, as working for the Lord, not for men, since you know that you will receive an inheritance from the Lord as a reward. ~Colossians 3:23–24

Thanksgiving

IN NOVEMBER 1942 the USS *San Francisco* was part of an American fleet engaged in one of several bitterly fought night actions in the waters off Guadalcanal. Lt. Cdr. Herbert Schonland was performing his duties as Damage Control Officer at his battle station below decks when the ship received a series of devastating hits. Holes were ripped in the hull causing flooding and fires in the boiler and engine rooms. One shell demolished the bridge, killing the admiral, captain, executive officer, and many others.

Schonland was soon informed that he was senior officer aboard and in command of the ship. Deciding that his most important duty was keeping the ship afloat, he remained below decks, systematically making repairs and extinguishing fires. Communicating with the bridge by messenger, he steered the ship and operated the engines from below. His night-long struggle succeeded in saving the *San Francisco* and her crew. For his *"extreme heroism and courage above and beyond the call of duty"* he was awarded the Congressional Medal of Honor by President Roosevelt.[195]

Commander Schonland later wrote a prayer for the *Soldiers' and Sailors' Prayer Book*, which he described in this way: *"I addressed the crew after engaging superior enemy Japanese forces on November 12–13, 1942, and I consider this a prayer of thanksgiving for all of us who came through"*:

> *Most merciful Father, our humble and gracious thanks for the safe deliverance through the raging inferno of battle when mere boys turned veterans, hard and sturdy, in brief moments. Our hearts are heavy with grief for those who have fallen during the "Call of Duty;" shipmates and friends whose loss can never be replaced. Our sympathy is extended to the loved ones whose suffering can only be relieved with the thought that: "He could do no more than give his life for his country in a cause that is just." They, forever, shall be an inspiration to all fighting men and their spirit and deeds shall never die. We who have come through can say: Thank God for the U.S.S. San Francisco and the crew that made her great. Amen.*[196]

Offer unto God thanksgiving; and pay thy vows unto the most High: And call upon me in the day of trouble: I will deliver thee, and thou shalt glorify me.
~Psalm 50:14–15 (KJV)

Love Your Enemy

ENEMY RESISTANCE on Guadalcanal ended when the last Japanese troops left the island on February 9, 1943, during a nighttime evacuation. A few days later Father Frederic Gehring accompanied a patrol to Cape Esperance, the sight of the last Japanese withdrawal. During their search for maps and documents the group was surprised by the appearance of four ragged, half-starved Japanese soldiers. Under the watchful eyes of the Americans, three of them raised their hands, submitting themselves to capture. The fourth collapsed on the beach.

Gehring moved to help the man up, but someone said, "Let him die there, Padre. Who needs him?" The chaplain had a different agenda:

> I shook my head, bent over and picked him up. Then I carried him gingerly to the boat. Lieutenant Merson smiled thoughtfully at me. "For six months, the Japs have soaked this island in blood," he said. "Not only did they kill so many of your boys, but they massacred missionaries, women, and harmless natives, and nearly massacred your little Patsy Li (an orphan girl rescued by the chaplain). Yet when one of their poor devils falls on his face in front of you, you pick him up—lice and all—and tote him like a baby. I salute you, Padre. You really do love your enemies!"[197]

We might expect this kind of tender mercy from a "man of God." However, few of us have experienced the trauma of Guadalcanal. What we see in Chaplain Gehring surely is not of human origin. An attitude and action such as this flow from one source: the indwelling spirit of Jesus Christ. From this inexhaustible fountain we see mercy pour out of a man exposed to months of fear, despair, and anger. There has to be a divine origin for this kind of love.

Do not be overcome by evil, but overcome evil with good. ~Romans 12:21

Nails in a Sure Place

DAN SNADDON spent most of World War II as a prisoner of war doing forced labor in Japanese work camps. Throughout his ordeal he was sustained by a powerful faith in Jesus Christ that had been an integral part of his life since childhood. He grew up in the small village of Tillicoultry, Scotland, where godly parents and a warm church profoundly influenced his life. He described the process of spiritual awakening in simple terms:

> My conversion was unspectacular. There were no emotional experiences, no blinding lights, but looking back over my life one can see God's hand leading in definite steps toward conversion. I believe that my Sunday School teachers played a big part . . . Gospel texts were greatly used in gently leading me to Christ; they were as nails in a sure place.[198]

A day eventually came when someone in his church that he knew and respected asked him, *"What will you do with Jesus, Dan?"* His friend quoted John 3:16 to him.

> I was expecting this: somehow I knew it would happen. I knew those words by heart, but somehow they were different that night, the meaning was clear—and from the depth of my young heart I said, "I will take Christ as my Savior now." Immediately a great peace filled my heart, my joy knew no bounds. I had to tell my dad and mom, my grandparents, everybody. As I look back on that day I consider it the greatest in my life.[199]

Dan Snaddon ended his story with a comment meant for all of us privileged to read it: *"Dear reader, as you eagerly press on into the contents of this book, may I urge you to pause for a moment's reflection? Do you know Jesus Christ as your personal Savior? Before another minute passes, why not trust Him and be saved."*

For God so loved the world that he gave his one and only Son, that whoever believes in him shall not perish but have eternal life. ~John 3:16

To Die Is Gain

DAN SNADDON was taken prisoner when Singapore fell to the Japanese early in the war. Cruel guards, scarce food, and hard labor made his life one of total misery. It somehow got even worse when he was sent deep into the jungle of Thailand to build the so-called "Railway of Death." There, dejected and broken men labored in tropical heat in spite of being naked, sick, and crazed by hunger and thirst. The guards were quick to become enraged over any apparent rule violation.

Snaddon became the focus of the guards' attention after being caught giving aid to a Chinese prisoner. He was beaten into unconsciousness, revived, and beaten again. At this point he could only lean on his child-hood faith:

> *Being brought back to consciousness for the second time, I felt that I was living my last few moments on earth. Strange as it may seem I was not loathe to let go the strings of life. The words of Paul were my constant inspiration, "To die is gain." Lifting my heart to the Lord I prayed, "Dear Father I am ready to go or stay at your command." The presence of my precious Savior was so real, His love in which He had enclosed me was impregnable and impervious to the threats of my barbaric assailants. Thus fortified, the inner peace and radiance burst through the filth, the scars and the coagulated blood, and formed a smile—the onlookers said that it was a heavenly smile. The furious Japanese soldiers stared in disbelief; there was some Power here which they had never encountered before and could not understand.*[200]

From this point the guards seemed powerless to continue with the beatings. Dan was left alone to be cared for by his comrades, who were deeply impressed by this incident. He heard them say: "*This is a faith worth having,*" and "*This is a God worth trusting.*" As Snaddon himself said, "*Eternity alone will reveal the work of God that was done in the hearts of many of these men.*"[201]

Be strong and courageous. Do not be afraid or terrified because of them, for the Lord your God goes with you; he will never leave you nor forsake you.
~Deuteronomy 31:6

Shipboard Communion

DURING THE PACIFIC campaign the Marines became very familiar with troopships, or attack transports as they were designated by the Navy. The *President Adams* was typical of the class, converted from civilian cargo use in 1941. Capt. Felix Johnson took command in early 1943 in time to move troops to Guadalcanal and Bougainville. His crew of sixty-five officers and six hundred enlisted contained only one career Navy man: himself. His executive officer was a New York broker, the 1st lieutenant was a Sears Roebuck salesman, the engineer was a power plant worker from California, and the navigator was an ROTC graduate from Yale.

In darkness on November 1, 1943, the *President Adams* entered Empress Augusta Bay on Bougainville with twelve other attack transports and eleven destroyers. Her troops were to go ashore at 7:30 a.m. the next day with the rest of the 3rd Marine Division. Knowing the island was heavily defended there was a lot of apprehension among the Marines. Captain Johnson described the actions of the Navy chaplain during the night:

> *I had a wonderful young Baptist chaplain from Texas on board, a junior lieutenant. Before the men landed he had something like twelve hundred men to give communion to, so he was up the whole night before they debarked. I remember that he came up on the bridge about four o'clock saying, "Captain, would you like to have communion? I can give you four minutes' worth." That was the most impressive communion I ever had.[202]*

We know that the purpose of communion is to strengthen our union with Jesus Christ. Bread and wine are taken as symbols of his body and blood, in accordance with the tradition established by Jesus himself at the "Last Supper" with his disciples. Countless young Marines on this night received this reassurance through a Navy chaplain. For some, it would be their own "last supper." We should all approach this sacrament with the same sense of urgent necessity.

> Jesus took bread, gave thanks and broke it, and gave it to his disciples, saying, "Take it; this is my body." Then he took the cup, gave thanks and offered it to them, and they all drank from it. "This is my blood of the covenant, which is poured out for many." ~Mark 14:22–24

Marine jungle fighters on Bougainville.
(National Archives)

Up to God

LOUIS ZAMPERINI was one of the war's most interesting characters. After some troubled teenage years he became a well-known distance runner and made the 1936 Olympic team. During the games he so impressed Adolf Hitler that he was summoned for an audience. In 1941 he volunteered for the Army Air Corps and earned his wings as a navigator on B-24 bombers. His squadron deployed to the Pacific and flew long-range missions out of different island bases.

On May 27, 1943, he was with his crew on a search-and-rescue mission looking for a lost B-25. Flying low due to cloud cover, his B-24 suddenly lost power to one engine. When an inexperienced engineer shut down the other good engine on that wing, the aircraft went out of control. Zamperini described the feeling:

The most frightening experience in life is going down in a plane. Those moments when you fall through the air, waiting for the inevitable impact, are like riding a roller coaster—with one important difference. In a plummeting plane there's only sheer horror, and the idea of your very imminent death is incomprehensible. You think, this is it. It's over. I'm going to die. You know with 100 per cent of your being that the end is unavoidable. Yet a part of you still believes you can fight and survive no matter what your mind knows. It's not so strange. Where there's still life, there's still hope. What happens is up to God.[203]

After sinking with the aircraft, tangled in severed control cables and seemingly trapped, Zamperini lost consciousness. He woke suddenly to find himself free of the aircraft and swimming more than seventy feet back to the surface. He and two others survived the crash to begin a separate ordeal adrift in a life raft. He was convinced that God was looking out for him throughout this experience.

There is no god besides me. I put to death and I bring to life, I have wounded and I will heal, and no one can deliver out of my hand. ~Deuteronomy 32:39

I Looked Up

LOUIS ZAMPERINI and two other crewmen amazingly survived the crash of their B-24 in a remote part of the Pacific Ocean. With two small life rafts, six bars of chocolate, and eight half-pints of water, they started one of the longest survival ordeals ever recorded.

For forty-seven days they faced hunger, thirst, storms, and attack by an enemy aircraft. Sharks were with them constantly, often bumping the raft. A constant lack of water seemed to be the most trying part of their ordeal. They were often tantalized by showers that passed by just too far away, as they exhausted themselves trying to row toward them. Trying to fight dehydration, one would tread water beside the raft while the other two fought off the sharks with paddles. They came to a point of crisis after seven days without water. They were ready to try anything, as Zamperini related:

> *In the end, we resorted to prayer.*
>
> *When I prayed, I meant it. I didn't understand it, but I meant it. I knew from church that there was a God and that he'd made the heavens and the earth, but beyond that I wasn't familiar with the Bible because in those days we Catholics, unlike Protestants, weren't encouraged to read it carefully—at least in my church we weren't. Yet on the raft, I was like anybody else, from the native who lived thousands of years ago on a remote island to the atheist in a foxhole: when I got to the end of my rope, I looked up.*[204]

The three men prayed specifically for water. Within an hour a squall was heading for them, and this time did not veer away. They drank until they could drink no more. They didn't know if they had received a miracle or not, but they decided not to take any chances. Their prayers became a daily and serious matter.

I lift up my eyes to the hills—where does my help come from? My help comes from the LORD, the Maker of heaven and earth. ~Psalm 121:1–2

Another Kind of Race

LOU ZAMPERINI was "saved" from his liferaft ordeal by a Japanese patrol boat. He spent the rest of the war in prison camps where he endured even worse deprivations, losing the faith that he had found on the life raft. As he put it, *"I believed that my date with death was set."*[205] He lived, but without hope. His day-to-day existence was filled with fear and hatred.

Zamperini returned home after the war to a welcoming family and a certain amount of fame. He was soon married and seemed on his way back to a normal life, at least on the surface. All the while, however, he had recurring nightmares of his prison experiences. He tried to drown his bitterness in alcohol. Excessive drinking, business failures, and marital problems led to an inevitable downward spiral. He occasionally thought of God in his hopelessness, but he now blamed God for deserting him.

On a September day in 1949, Zamperini's wife insisted he go with her to a meeting in a tent on the corner of Washington and Hill Streets in downtown Los Angeles. The speaker was a little-known preacher named Billy Graham. Under great protest, he went, and, with great antipathy, listened. Little by little, he was convicted by Graham's patient and persistent presentation of the gospel of Jesus Christ. Earlier in his life he had been an Olympic runner. He now realized that he was in another kind of race, a race for his life:

> *I dropped to my knees and for the first time in my life truly humbled myself before the Lord. I asked Him to forgive me for not having kept the promises I'd made during the war, and for my sinful life. I made no excuses. I did not rationalize, I did not blame. He had said, "Whosoever shall call upon the name of the Lord shall be saved," so I took Him at His word, begged for His pardon, and asked Jesus to come into my life.*[206]

Let us run with perseverance the race marked out for us. Let us fix our eyes on Jesus, the author and perfecter of our faith. ~Hebrews 12:1–2

Patsy Li

ONE NIGHT THREE natives came through the Marine lines on Guadalcanal, asking for the "priest-man." They were taken to Father Frederic Gehring's tent, where they presented the chaplain with a badly wounded child. He was horrified to see a five- or six-year-old girl who had been bayoneted, smashed in the head with a rifle butt, and consumed now with fever. A corpsman applied bandages to stop the bleeding. A doctor arrived later and was even more shocked at the state of the young girl. She had yet to respond in any way and seemed to be very close to death. The doctor told the chaplain to, *"Pray hard for her. She needs the Great Physician. Only a miracle can keep her alive."*[207]

Through the next day and night the chaplain and a group of Marines maintained a vigil, praying for the girl as her life hung in the balance. Finally, on the second day, the girl began to whimper, as her fever seemed to subside ever so slightly. The doctor was called again. After another examination, he proclaimed, *"I'm either a genius doctor, or you're a genius priest, but in any case, by golly, I think our girl is going to make it."*[208]

Since evacuation was impossible at the time, Father Gehring became the girl's unofficial guardian. Thinking that she was probably of Chinese origin, he made up a suitably Chinese name: Patsy Li. News spread quickly through the ten thousand Marines on Guadalcanal that they had a "miracle girl" in their midst. They began to come in droves to see the girl and to bring gifts. They brought fruit, flowers, chocolate, handmade dolls, and parachute silk sarongs. Patsy Li seemed to become a symbol of love and hope in an otherwise God-forsaken place.[209]

> He has delivered us from such a deadly peril, and he will deliver us. On him we have set our hope that he will continue to deliver us. ~2 Corinthians 1:10

Miracle Child

B Y LATE NOVEMBER 1942, Chaplain Gehring was finally able to arrange for the evacuation of Patsy Li from Guadalcanal. Through a French priest on Espiritu Santo he had her admitted to an orphanage run by French Sisters on the little island of Efate. He delivered her there himself and, while on this mission, met Foster Hailey, a correspondent for the *New York Times*. Hailey took an immediate interest in the fantastic story of the girl, and sent a series of articles home about Patsy Li and the "Padre of Guadalcanal."

Years later, Frederic Gehring began receiving letters from a Chinese woman in Singapore named Ruth Li. The *New York Times* articles had finally come to her attention, and Mrs. Li felt strongly that this must be her daughter (also named Patsy Li), who had been lost at sea in February 1942. The only problem was, she was lost in waters off the coast of Malaysia, four thousand miles from Guadalcanal, when the Lis' ship was bombed fleeing the Japanese invasion of Singapore. Gehring also knew that his Patsy's name was a pure fabrication on his part.

Even though Chaplain Gehring discouraged her, Mrs. Li felt compelled to make the costly journey to Efate, via Australia, to see for herself. She finally reached the orphanage in July 1946 to find an awkward, ten-year-old child that she did not recognize at first. Due to the psychological trauma of her early life, young Patsy could remember practically nothing before her years on Efate. Her mother found a scar on her eye and peculiarities of her handwriting that convinced her that this was her child. Within days, Gehring received a telegram: "You have been the architect of a miracle, for I have found my Patsy Li."[210] The priest went to the altar and prayed:

> *Thank you . . . for having given Ruth Li the strength to ignore the words of fools like me who would have stopped her from completing her mission of faith. Thank you for teaching me that there is no power greater than mother love—that mother love can still flatten mountains, turn the earth upside down, and make the wildest dreams of mortals come true.*[211]

Honor your father and your mother, so that you may live long in the land the LORD your God is giving you. ~Exodus 20:12

An Act of Love

PATSY LI'S LIFE with her newfound mother did not go well. Ruth Li had been raised in a strict household where much was expected of the children. She felt it her duty to impose the same kind of discipline on her daughter. Since Patsy had only spoken French for years, there was also a language barrier that made intimate conversations impossible. Back in Singapore, Mrs. Li became estranged and then divorced from her husband, causing more tension and insecurity for Patsy. The young girl became increasingly rebellious.

In 1949 a desperate Ruth Li turned again for help to Father Frederic Gehring, now living in Pennsylvania. At her and Patsy's request, Father Gehring arranged for a guardian and admission to a private school in Williamsburg, Virginia. Patsy seemed to flourish in America, making friends and excelling in academics. She successfully graduated from Catholic University and entered training to become a nurse.

Throughout these years Father Gehring tried unsuccessfully to bridge the gulf between Patsy and her mother. Patsy, however, could not get past her feelings of abandonment. After a lot of prayer and conversation focused on this problem, the story of Moses' mother finally occurred to the priest. This Hebrew woman had also been forced to abandon her baby to save it. He told Patsy:

> You see, there can be times when a mother deserts a child—or seems to desert it—for very good reason. Moses' mother left her youngster in an act of love. Your mother's 'desertion' of you was an act of love, too. Your mother has never lost her love for you, Patsy. She has told me that many times, and even though she finds it hard to get this across to you, I have never doubted her.[212]

Father Gehring's patient and biblically based counseling led to the final miracle in Patsy Li's story, reconciliation between a long-estranged mother and daughter.

When the child grew older, she took him to Pharaoh's daughter and he became her son. She named him Moses, saying, "I drew him out of the water." ~Exodus 2:10

Moral Power

In war moral power is to physical as three parts out of four (Napoleon).[213]

MAO TSE-TUNG was a founding member and leader of the Chinese Communist Party from 1921 until his death in 1976. During World War II he interrupted a bitter civil war against the ruling Chinese government to fight their common and external enemy, the Japanese. He ultimately resumed the civil war and established the Communist People's Republic of China in 1949. Mao was not only a politician and soldier, but a philosopher as well. More than 900 million copies of his *Little Red Book* were printed as required reading for every citizen of China. Concerning what is important in war, he wrote:

> *Weapons are an important factor in war, but not the decisive factor; it is people not things, that are decisive. The contest of strength is not only a contest of military and economic power, but also a contest of human power and morale. Military and economic power is necessarily wielded by the people.*[214]

Mao Tse-Tung focused on simple principles. He was a great revolutionary leader because he devoted himself to educating and motivating his followers. He knew that great achievements spring from great ideas, not things.

This principle is important in our own lives and, I believe, especially applicable to children. My wife, Lani, made sure our children were never "spoiled" with possessions. She concluded early in our marriage that our kids' experiences and education were more important than things. As latecoming Christians, we came to realize the even greater importance of experiences contributing to spiritual growth. With children, as in all else, we need to keep our priorities straight. There is no possession that equals the importance of one life or the status of that life in the eternal future.

Wisdom is supreme; therefore get wisdom. Though it cost all you have, get understanding. ~Proverbs 4:7

A Navy F6F fighter preparing to launch. (National Archives)

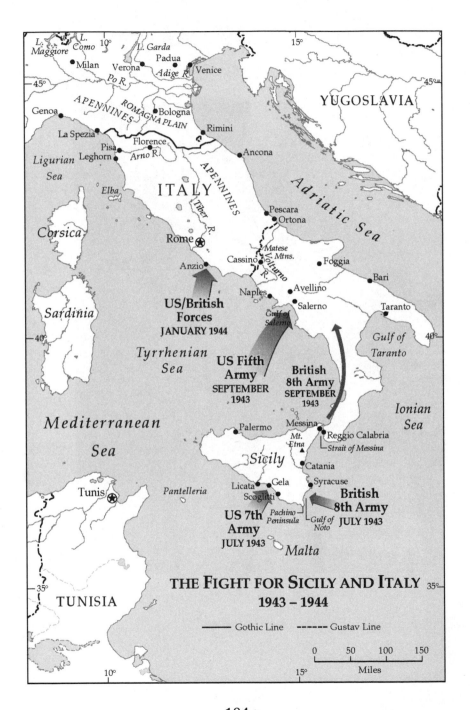

THE FIGHT FOR SICILY AND ITALY
1943 – 1944

Gothic Line ----- Gustav Line

0   50   100   150
Miles

JUNE
The Fight for Sicily and Italy

IN JANUARY 1943 President Roosevelt and Prime Minister Churchill met in Casablanca to discuss future strategy. By this time, American success on Guadalcanal was assured, and it was agreed that enough resources would be allocated to the Pacific to retain the initiative in that theater. In Europe, the Americans favored an early attack across the English Channel, but Churchill and his staff felt that the Allies were not yet ready. After a lengthy debate, it was decided that Sicily and Italy presented the best opportunity for continuing the offensive in 1943.

Operation Husky, the invasion of Sicily, began soon after midnight on July 10, 1943. The American 82nd and British 1st airborne divisions dropped into landing zones inland to block enemy movements toward the invasion beaches. Meanwhile a naval armada of more than two thousand ships and craft staging out of North African bases converged on Sicily from the south and east. Under cover of darkness the assault waves of Patton's 7th Army landed on the southern coast to seize the small ports of Gela, Licata, and Scoglitti. The British 8th Army under Montgomery landed on the Pachino Peninsula and Gulf of Noto to the east to seize the port at Syracuse. In all, more than four hundred seventy thousand troops went ashore across a beachhead extending nearly one hundred miles.

The overriding Allied objective on Sicily was to converge all forces on Messina in a large pincer movement, to trap the Axis defenders before they could evacuate the island. Characteristically, Patton drove his troops forward with all possible speed, capturing Palermo on July 22. He then turned eastward along the north coast, leapfrogging enemy defenses in a rapid series of amphibious landings. Montgomery decided to bypass the stiff coastal defenses in his sector and moved his forces inland over the rugged terrain around Mount Etna. Falling back along interior lines, the German and Italian forces were able to buy enough time to evacuate more than one hundred thousand troops and their equipment to the mainland, to oppose the next advance.

The next Allied move came with the September 1943 invasion of Italy. Montgomery's 8th Army crossed the Straits of Messina on September 3 with no opposition. On September 9 the main attack came at Salerno by the newly formed 5th Army under General Mark Clark. There, the Germans waited in strength behind well-prepared defensive positions. Bitter fighting to gain and hold the beachhead reached a climax on September 13–14 when a massive German counterattack with six hundred tanks and mobile guns was beaten back. On October 1 Allied forces entered Naples, as the Germans fell back to a new defensive line along the Volturno River.

From this point the Italian campaign became a slugfest as the American and British forces tried to surmount a series of bitterly contested German defensive positions. By year-end, fighting was stalled on the Gustav Line, seventy miles south of Rome. Anchored on the mountaintop abbey of Monte Casino, this German position proved to be almost impregnable. In an effort to break the stalemate, the Allies launched a major amphibious attack on January 22, 1944, at Anzio, thirty miles from Rome. This effort also stalled against determined and effective German resistance. It was not until May that the Monte Casino position fell to Allied assaults, precipitating a German retreat to new positions in the northern part of Italy. On June 4, 1944, Mark Clark's 5th Army entered Rome unopposed, two days before the focus of the war would shift to the beaches of Normandy.

The Mosta Dome

THE ROTUNDA of the Church of St. Marija Assunta on the island of Malta has a fascinating history. The Mosta Dome, as it is called, is one of the largest freestanding rotundas in the world, spanning a diameter of 122 feet. It was the architectural masterpiece of Grognet de Vasse, completed in 1860. Built over a church on the same site, the older structure was used as scaffolding for the new. The high spherical vault was painted blue, with various heavenly scenes depicted to represent paradise.

In 1942 two German Luftwaffe pilots attacked the nearby Ta' Qali airfield. One dropped a bomb that scored a direct hit on the Mosta Dome. That pilot was downed by anti-aircraft fire and died in the crash. The second pilot, Felix Sauer, witnessed the bombing of the Dome before he too was shot down. Sauer was a Catholic and lived thirty-three years with remorse, thinking he had helped destroy the unique and historic Malta church. When he returned as a tourist in 1975 he found what he first thought was a completely restored structure. Only then did he learn of the "Miracle."

On April 9, 1942, church services were being held in the Church of St. Marija Assunta with three hundred people gathered under the great dome. An aircraft was heard overhead, and suddenly there was a crash in the ceiling as a falling bomb penetrated the dome. The bomb struck the floor of the church and skidded across it until finally coming to rest. It missed the entire congregation and failed to explode. This incident became famous in church lore as a great modern demonstration of God's providential hand protecting his people and his church. Today a replica of the bomb can be seen there commemorating the Miracle of the Mosta Dome.[215]

> When the people of Ashdod rose early the next day, there was Dagon, fallen on his face on the ground before the ark of the LORD! . . . His head and hands had been broken off and were lying on the threshold; only his body remained.
> ~1 Samuel 5:3–4

Do What You Can

CAPT. EDWIN SAYRE was a company commander with the 505th Parachute Infantry Regiment. As night fell on July 9, 1943, his unit boarded C-47 transports in Tunisia for the airborne assault of Sicily. His flight of aircraft drifted off course and had to make a second run for the drop zone, delaying their arrival. Instead of a moonlit jump the paratroopers faced total darkness. High winds then wrought havoc, scattering them over a wide area. Unable to see the hand in front of his face, Sayre was able to collect only a handful of his men by dawn.

Shortly after daylight, Sayre and his men were taken under fire by an enemy machine gun. Moving forward, they found not one machine gun but a series of pillboxes. This was not the primary objective, but General Gavin had told the paratroopers, *"If you land somewhere and don't know where you are, just find the nearest enemy and attack."*[216]

Well, here was Sayre's nearest enemy. He was able to contact some of his unit by radio, and, by firing a series of shots, gave them a signal to find him. He gradually assembled enough men and weapons to organize an assault of the enemy emplacements. In close fighting with small arms and grenades they eliminated the pillboxes and captured about fifty prisoners.

General Gavin's instruction to his paratroopers is often the kind of direction that is appropriate for us as Christians. As we try to do the right thing in our service to God's kingdom, we sometimes face uncertainty or lack a clear direction. At such times, we simply have to do what we can do. Even if a bigger mission is unclear, we can lovingly tend to the everyday tasks that present themselves in our families and churches. A child or a friend with a problem is an opportunity for each of us to do God's work on a personal level, possibly the most important level of all.

His master replied, "Well done, good and faithful servant! You have been faithful with a few things; I will put you in charge of many things." ~Matthew 25:23

Every Private Was a General

SGT. TIMOTHY DYAS was knocked unconscious when he hit the ground near Gela, Sicily. Jumping from three hundred feet, there was barely time for his parachute to open before he made a hard landing. When he regained consciousness, he started gathering scattered soldiers together. He knew his mission was to keep enemy reinforcements from moving down to the invasion beaches. With only a dozen men, he engaged and stopped a German panzer column. When his bazooka team killed the German commander, confusion spread in the enemy ranks. Dyas made this pointed observation:

> *Without their leader they didn't know what to do. In the American Army every private is a general—meaning they could adapt. This wasn't the case with the German army. When their chain of command was broken they were helpless and didn't know what to do. It took them a good two or three hours to get a junior officer to organize them.*[217]

Timothy Dyas was somewhat overstating his case. Any unit is adversely affected by the loss of a commander, and German units were able to regroup under such circumstances. However, I believe his main point is valid. The hallmark of American soldiers has always been individual initiative. They think for themselves and do what has to be done. This trait causes nightmares for their officers in peacetime. Young enlisted men are very imaginative in their pranks and subversion of regulations. However, in combat this individualism comes to the forefront.

This trait comes straight from our Founding Fathers, who knew that human dignity and rights flow from God to individual citizens, not to governments or organizations. The individual has always stood at the top of the hierarchy in America, as it is the individual's relationship to God that is sacrosanct. As the Declaration of Independence states, *"We hold these truths to be self-evident, that all men are created equal, that they are endowed by their Creator with certain unalienable Rights."*

Then God said, "Let us make man in our image." ~Genesis 1:26

Memorial

IN JULY 1943, the 505th Parachute Infantry Regiment jumped at night into the hills north of Gela, Sicily, to disrupt enemy communications and to slow reinforcements to the invasion beaches. Even though high winds and navigation errors caused mass confusion among the airborne units, the officers and NCOs (noncommissioned officers) gathered stragglers together to get the job done. In one hard-fought action (described on another day of this month) a series of enemy pillboxes were eliminated along a strategic resupply route leading into Gela.

Sixty-one years later a group of U.S. Navy and Italian officials joined together in a ceremony to honor the American paratroopers who fell in this action. A memorial was built on the site where three German pillboxes are still visible. The names of thirty-nine Americans who lost their lives in the battle are inscribed on the memorial.

The acting mayor of the nearby Sicilian village of Niscemi said, "*These young American Soldiers defended the ideals of freedom and democracy upon which western civilization was founded.*"

"*We give thanks to the American soldiers who fought and died for our liberation, an event that changed the history of our country,*" said the mayor of Gela. "*Yet we see them not as foreigners, but as our heroes for what they did.*"

During the ceremony a minister talked about the courage of the fallen paratroopers and the courage of those American and Italian soldiers serving in the present. "*We ask you to continue instilling that same courage in (these soldiers) who at this moment are putting their lives on the line on foreign soil so that people may be free.*"[218]

> I eagerly expect and hope that I will in no way be ashamed, but will have sufficient courage so that now as always Christ will be exalted in my body, whether by life or by death. ~Philippians 1:20

Infantry advancing with tanks.
(National Archives)

Soldiers making friends during campaign on Sicily.
(National Archives)

To Stay and Fight

CPL. RAY SADOSKI was a rifleman with the 1st Ranger Battalion during the fight for Sicily. At one point he was guarding a group of Italian prisoners near Messina. One of the prisoners who spoke English said to him, "*Hey, how about this—we're going to the States, and you're going to stay here and fight.*"[219]

None of us would want to be a prisoner of war, but the irony of this little quip makes us stop and think. Who gets the better deal—the "captive" sent to safety, or the "free man" who has to go on facing hardship and danger? *If* we could choose, it might be a difficult choice.

There is a parallel here to our view of dying. None of us wants to die. We are programmed instinctively to survive, no matter the circumstance. The thought of our own death is bad enough, but the loss of a loved one is the greatest tragedy that we can imagine. But, here again, we can ask the question, "*Who gets the better deal?*" As Christians, we know where we are going after we die, and we know that a new and better life awaits us there. Is it better to "stay here and fight" or to go to that glorious place where we will be with our Savior?

The apostle Paul wrestled with this question regarding his own life and ministry and described it for us in one of the most eloquent passages in Scripture:

> I eagerly expect and hope that I will in no way be ashamed, but will have sufficient courage so that now as always Christ will be exalted in my body, whether by life or by death. For to me, to live is Christ and to die is gain. If I am to go on living in the body, this will mean fruitful labor for me. Yet what shall I choose? I do not know! I am torn between the two: I desire to depart and be with Christ, which is better by far; but it is more necessary for you that I remain in the body. ~Philippians 1:20–24

Frontline Service

DURING WORLD WAR II the number of Armed Forces chaplains grew thirtyfold from pre-war years. The Army Chaplain Corps expanded to eight thousand, and the Navy to three thousand. Ministers and rabbis from more than forty denominations answered the call to serve their country. These patriotic young men were more than religious leaders. They were counselors, confidants, and friends to their fellow soldiers.

In 1942, each chaplain conducted an average of 53 personal conferences with troubled soldiers each day. Often serving as morale officers, chaplains umpired ball games, organized orchestras, showed films, taught classes and lectured on sex and morality. And of course, they prayed and conducted regular services, typically using available areas like an aircraft flight deck, an apple orchard, a hand-cut hole in a Pacific-island jungle or a makeshift tent for a church; a jeep, packing case or ammunition box for an altar, or a helmet for a yarmulke, the top of a mess kit for a paten or a canteen cup for a chalice.[220]

Typical of these religious leaders who answered their nation's call was the Reverend Paschal Fowlkes, a twenty-six-year-old Episcopal minister from Washington, D.C. He enlisted in the Army and served as a chaplain to a paratrooper regiment. He felt it his duty to join *"the battle for the preservation of democracy and freedom and justice."*[221] Francis Sayre became a Navy chaplain, serving for four years on the USS *San Francisco*. He said that he enlisted *"because the war was on. I wanted to do my part."*[222]

These young men earned a special place in the history of our nation and in the hearts of the men and women they served. During this time of national peril, they combined service to God with service to their nation. Today men and women of faith continue to respond to God's call to help those in trouble, carrying this tradition forward. They include not only those who minister to our Armed Forces, but also those who go out from our churches to inner cities, schools, and third world countries. All these people doing God's work on the "front lines" deserve our admiration, prayers, and financial support.

Each one should use whatever gift he has received to serve others, faithfully administering God's grace in its various forms. ~1 Peter 4:10

A Greater Fellowship

AS THE HOUR for the invasion of Italy drew near, life on a troop-ship made vivid impressions on Cpl. William "Bicky" Kiessel. The compartments were dark, hot, and smelly, with crowded, unwashed bodies. The heavy air was mixed with other foul odors. The folding cots were stacked four high with almost no room to walk. Fortunately, religious services were also memorable in a more positive way:

The energetic chaplains are busy holding services all hours of the day on the various deck levels. Fellows are trying to catch up on years of neglected religion in a few days. And it can be done—and is! The Catholics have Mass, Communion and Confessions while the Protestants preach little, pray much, and sing the favorite hymns of the Church . . . At all these sacred gatherings there is a sincerity and informality that makes for a better and greater fellowship and gives a deeper sense of the intangible value of friends, home, and the eternal verities of life . . . In those services we all wish we'd lived better, been more complimentary and less critical, written home more lovingly and more often, etc. We are finally face to face with life . . .[223]

Kissel ended his letter with the statement, "*Christians never say good-bye. Sooner or later we all meet again.*" This eloquent young soldier obviously was sustained by his faith through difficult times. In his letter, however, he alludes to another aspect of religious worship. Participation in services not only strengthened him personally, but also strengthened the bonds of fellowship with the other soldiers in his unit. This is a great testimony to the power of the body of Christ, which manifests itself whenever Christians come together. We are each able to lead a more victorious life when we are supported and surrounded by our brothers and sisters in Christ.

So in Christ we who are many form one body, and each member belongs to all the others. ~Romans 12:5

Abide with Me

THE TROOPS LEARNED that the regiment would lead the attack next morning on a strongly held enemy position. Worried men stood close together in the makeshift church, a dusty and battered old commercial building about a mile behind the front lines. Stan Scislowski remembered the scene vividly and marveled at how much closer to God he felt in this rustic setting than in the "regular" churches of his past.

When it came time in the service to sing, the words of the old familiar hymn had never been so meaningful. *"The expressions of faith that made up this beautiful hymn crossed my mind, and as we sang, I found myself inserting my own feelings between the lines, feelings that harboured the fear that perhaps I might not be coming back at battle's end."*[224]

The lyrics of "Abide with Me" are meaningful no matter what our own situation may be.

> Abide with me; fast falls the eventide; The darkness deepens; Lord, with me abide.
> When other helpers fail and comforts flee, Help of the helpless, O abide with me.
>
> Swift to its close ebbs out life's little day; Earth's joys grow dim; its glories pass away.
> Change and decay in all around I see; O Thou who changest not, abide with me.
>
> Come not in terrors, as the King of kings, But kind and good, with healing in Thy wings,
> Tears for all woes, a heart for every plea—Come, Friend of sinners, and thus bide with me.
>
> I fear no foe, with Thee at hand to bless; Ills have no weight, and tears no bitterness.
> Where is death's sting? Where, grave, thy victory? I triumph still, if Thou abide with me.
>
> Hold Thou Thy cross before my closing eyes; Shine through the gloom and point me to the skies.
> Heaven's morning breaks, and the earth's vain shadows flee; In life, in death, O Lord,
> Abide with me.[225]

And I will pray the Father, and he shall give you another Comforter, that he may abide with you forever. ~John 14:16 (KJV)

Family Roots

DURING THE CAMPAIGN through Italy, Frank Palilla had an enviable advantage. He spoke fluent Italian. Getting along easily with the natives, he was well supplied with fresh eggs, bread, and other food items. He also had a full canteen of wine most of the time. He shared all this bounty with his comrades, who repaid the favor by keeping him as safe as possible.

The highlight of his military service came when his unit was in a holding area near Bologna, and he was able to hitch a plane ride to Sicily. There he was able to visit Naro, the small Sicilian town where his parents grew up:

> When I announced myself at the barbershop in the piazza the entire town turned out in minutes for a fantastic welcome. It was nothing but overwhelming festivity from there on. We stayed with my mother's identical twin sister for the five days that we were there. The most emotional moments came when I visited the homes in which my parents had lived. In particular, in my father's case not only was I in the room in which he was born, but I was in the presence of the very bed in which he was born. I experienced an unbelievable and everlastingly memorable emotion.[226]

This story is a great testament to the strength of family bonds that transcend time, distance, and even war. God ordained the importance of marriage and made family the foundational unit of society. He exhorted us to *"Marry and have sons and daughters; find wives for your sons and give your daughters in marriage, so that they too may have sons and daughters"* (Jeremiah 29:6). There are few activities more important to God than strengthening and sustaining the family unit.

[Jesus replied], "At the beginning of creation God 'made them male and female.' 'For this reason a man will leave his father and mother and be united to his wife, and the two will become one flesh.' So they are no longer two, but one. Therefore what God has joined together, let man not separate." ~Mark 10:6–9

For Soldiers and Sailors

IN 1941 THE Episcopal Church of the United States published a small booklet for soldiers and sailors that could be carried in their pockets wherever they went. It included an Order of Worship, Holy Communion, prayers, psalms, readings, and hymns. All these were selected to meet the needs of military men and women of that time, and continue to be relevant and uplifting today:[227]

For the Army

O Lord of Hosts, stretch forth, we pray thee, thine almighty arm to strengthen and protect the soldiers of our country. Support them in the day of battle, and in the time of peace keep them safe from all evil; endue them with courage and loyalty; and grant that in all things they may serve without reproach; through Jesus Christ our Lord. Amen.

For the Navy

O eternal Lord God, who alone spreadest out the heavens, and rulest the raging of the sea; Vouchsafe to take into thy almighty and most gracious protection our country's Navy, and all who serve therein. Preserve them from the dangers of the sea, and from the violence of the enemy; that they may be a safeguard unto the United States of America, and a security for such as pass on the seas upon their lawful occasions; that the inhabitants of our land may in peace and quietness serve thee our God, to the glory of thy Name; through Jesus Christ our Lord. Amen.

For World Peace

O Almighty God, who makest even the wrath of man to turn to thy praise; We beseech thee so to order and dispose the issue of this war that we may be brought through strife to a lasting peace, and that the nations of the world may be united in a firmer fellowship, for the promotion of thy glory and the good of all mankind; through Jesus Christ our Lord. Amen.

For God was pleased to have all his fullness dwell in him, and through him to reconcile to himself all things, whether things on earth or things in heaven, by making peace through his blood, shed on the cross. ~Colossians 1:19–20

Hanging Upside Down

Dear Mom, Dad, and Boogie,

Well I've been on my first combat mission and I'm telling you it was plenty jumpy all of the time. It got really interesting too. One of the bombs hung on the side of the bomb bay and wedged itself on the rack. The other bombs as they fell out hit it and wedged it tighter. The arming vane of the bomb was spinning around and the bomb was arming itself in the bomb bay . . . the Bombardier and I got on top of the bomb bay to see what we could do. I was the lighter in weight so I took off my parachute and jacket. I hung down into the bomb bay while he held me around the knees. I worked with both hands getting the bomb loose. I finally got it loose and let it drop out of the open bomb bay.[228]

THIS WAS THE matter-of-fact way Robert Saxton informed his parents of his part in a drama high in the skies over Italy. For his actions the twenty-four-year-old airman was officially cited for heroism and awarded the Soldier's Medal and the Air Medal.

Courage comes in many forms, and, fortunately, is not in short supply on the part of young people today. An amazing example is the story of my church's twenty-six-year-old assistant rector, fresh out of seminary, in his first assignment. Recently, the leaders of the church unexpectedly called him to be *the* rector, responsible for every aspect of administering and shepherding this large, diverse congregation. His decision to accept such a promotion was not easy. He knew that his youthful inexperience and enthusiasm would have to contend with an older congregation and a long history of conservative tradition. In 2008 the Reverend Robert Sturdy prayerfully and courageously accepted this call and all the risks that go with it. Watching him handle his many challenges, I can almost picture him hanging upside down out of a bomb bay. The courage of one of the youngest Episcopal priests in church history has been an inspiration to his congregation and to a whole community.

> For it has been granted to you on behalf of Christ not only to believe on him, but also to suffer for him, since you are going through the same struggle you saw I had, and now hear that I still have. ~Philippians 1:29–30

How Would They Handle This?

GEORGE GRAVES was a corporal with the 504th Parachute Infantry Regiment fighting in the hills of Italy. He wrote a lengthy letter to his father expressing a few rather negative feelings about the Italians' fear and hatred of the Germans. He saw some civilians spitting on German prisoners and others actually threatening them with bodily harm. Even though he was fighting the same enemy, he did not understand this vindictiveness. In the same letter, however, he empathized with what many of these same civilians had to endure:

> We have air raids here about every night, and I have been in those stuffy
> air raid shelters with crying women and children kneeling down and
> praying and wondering how our folks back at home would take this if
> they had to endure it. I am thankful that so far they haven't had to.[229]

If you have ever wondered why Europeans might be so different from Americans, you might consider the fact that generations from practically every country in Europe have spent time in bomb shelters. I don't know how this experience translates into social and political viewpoints later, but it is clearly an historical experience that Americans do not share.

On the personal level, differences in past experience also make it difficult for people to understand each other. Like most married couples, my wife and I have gone through a long process of learning about our respective family histories. We both now have an appreciation of each other's painful experiences in the past that at times still dictate our attitudes and reactions as adults. This knowledge has helped us handle conflict without hurting each other. On any level, the more you understand someone else's past experience, the better chance you'll have of building a meaningful relationship.

The purposes of a man's heart are deep waters, but a man of understanding draws them out. ~Proverbs 20:5

I've Been Blessed

KATHY WALSH loved to sit at her father's feet and listen to his stories. Tom Walsh had lived a hard life, growing up in an orphanage and scrounging for food. In spite of his hardships he always felt that "*God was watching over*," and his thankfulness came through in his stories. His daughter's favorite story was about World War II.[230]

Before going overseas, Tom spent time with one of his few living relatives, a cousin living in California. The cousin had a young daughter who was sick while he was there, and he spent days with her, nursing her back to health. He eventually reached Italy where he was assigned to an airbase near Naples. One evening the Germans bombed his base, and Tom was wounded severely in the head and neck. A rescue crew thought he was dead and actually placed him on a "death pile."

In California, a young girl woke up screaming in the night. "*Uncle Tom!*" she shouted. "*He's all bloody, his head is covered with blood!*" The mother of the little girl, Tom's cousin, called the Red Cross, but was unable to get any information. She was convinced that something had happened to Tom, but she also believed that he had survived. She sent him a telegram, giving him assurance that he would be all right. Meanwhile, an alert medic had discovered that Tom was still alive and had gotten him to a hospital.

After hearing the story, Kathy asked her father, "*Was it ESP? Do you believe in Extra-Sensory Perception, Dad?*" He answered, "*I believe God found a way to let my family know I was all right. The message to my cousin's little girl was God's way of watching over me. I've been blessed, you know!*"[231]

Tom Walsh was a man of faith. He chose to see the events in his life in a positive light and as evidence of God's protection. His faith saw him through his trials and was an incalculable blessing to him and to his daughter.

> Let us then approach the throne of grace with confidence, so that we may receive mercy and find grace to help us in our time of need. ~Hebrews 4:16

They Did It without Complaining

THE ADVANCE UP the Italian peninsula was slow and grueling. Moving forward in the valleys was impossible as long as the enemy held the hills and mountains. Therefore, many battles raged at elevations above 4,000 feet, where winter conditions made the soldier's lives almost unbearable. Keeping these men supplied with the basic necessities for staying alive and fighting was a nightmare in itself. Reminiscent of wars gone by, pack mules and horses were used to move supplies where vehicles couldn't go. Even then, there was a point where the animals could climb no farther, and soldiers had to do the rest. On a typical night, a battalion fighting in the mountains needed eighty-five cans of water, one hundred cases of K rations, ten miles of telephone wire, twenty-five cases of ammunition, one hundred heavy mortar rounds, four cases of first-aid supplies, bags of mail, and countless other items.[232]

All this logistic activity took place at night, since most of it was under enemy observation and artillery fire. Guides were necessary along the route to keep the supply trains from getting lost in the dark. This duty fell, of necessity, on the combat soldiers. The men who shouldered this thankless task were an inspiration to one reporter:

Sickness and exhaustion overtook many . . . so they were sent back down the mountain under their own power to report to the medics there and then go to a rest camp. It took most of them the better part of a day to get two-thirds of the way down, so sore were their feet and so weary their muscles. And then—when actually in sight of their haven of rest and peace—they were stopped and pressed into guide service, because there just wasn't anybody else to do it. So they stayed on the mountainside for at least three additional days and nights . . . just lying miserably alongside the trail, shouting in the darkness to guide the mules. They had no blankets to keep them warm, no beds but the rocks. And they did it without complaining. The human spirit is an astounding thing.[233]

When they hurled insults at him, he did not retaliate; when he suffered, he made no threats. Instead, he entrusted himself to him who judges justly.
~1 Peter 2:23

My Mule

WHEN HE CAME out of the front lines for a brief rest, Richard Ternyey was recruited as a muleskinner. Mules had been found an effective way to move supplies in the rugged Italian mountains, usually at night. Ternyey soon met his mule, Jake. He and Jake had to deliver mortar ammunition to the front lines on a night so dark, "*You couldn't see the hand in front of your face.*"[234] After several hours of hard climbing they reached the forward dump and began unloading.

Suddenly German artillery shells started landing all around them, and everyone scattered in panic looking for holes or ruts to get away from the shrapnel. Ternyey described what happened then:

> *I started frantically searching in the darkness like a blind man for my mule. Everything was in turmoil, a lot of men screaming and yelling. I had no idea where I was. Finally, I found Jake. I didn't have any idea which way to go to my base for fear that I may go the wrong way and be captured by the enemy. For some reason, I can't explain, I thought maybe Jake will have the instinct of finding his way home. So I mounted him, gently patted him on the rump, and he took off. I was scared stiff and prayed that God Almighty will direct this mule back to home base. I finally reached my base safe and sound.*[235]

There are times when we have to give up control. This soldier had little choice but to rely on his mule's instinct. As we face our daily problems, however, we usually do have a choice, and most of us go to great lengths to keep control in our own hands. We are programmed early to "be responsible" and to take care of our own problems. These are admirable traits, but when taken too far interfere with a relationship to God. Our heavenly Father waits for us to come to him. We miss an opportunity when we fail to share our burdens. When we let him take control in the midst of our confusion or uncertainty, we are in the sure hands that will always get us back to "home base."

There you saw how the LORD your God carried you, as a father carries his son, all the way you went until you reached this place. ~Deuteronomy 1:31

Mother's Son

RICKY KIESSEL wrote to his uncle, a World War I veteran, about his experiences in the Italian campaign. He said, "*I've been bombed, strafed, shelled, chased by tanks, sniped at, machine gunned and everything imaginable—and some not. I got knocked about, bruised and scraped but never directly hit.*"[236] He saw a lot of action, but found some of his most difficult times waiting and thinking:

> *The idle period of waiting is nerve wracking. Everything is ready, there is just the period of absolutely nothing to do...You think a lot about the past. People you know or knew and last associations, of home, though not about big things but a lot of silly little trifles or remembrances pop into mind and if you were to stop and figure out "why?" you probably would never know. Thoughts that are precious, moments unreturnable flash past. We are different men since we have been fighting. To a great extent, unfortunately, we have lost our sensitiveness, there is a cold calculating air. We have gone through and experienced what men should not. But at times like these we are mother's sons once more.*[237]

This is a great picture to keep in mind when dealing with other people. That other person, no matter how unattractive or unappreciative, is in fact some mother's son or daughter. That person may have different problems or even values than our own, but in most cases started out just as we did. A mother and/or a father loved them and had high hopes for them. This is even truer of our heavenly Father, who created every human being and loves us all as his own children. He may not like what we are doing at any moment, but he nevertheless has provided for the salvation of every soul. When we deal with others, we need this perspective. Instead of focusing on the differences, we should see first our common bonds as children of God.

Did not he who made me in the womb make them? Did not the same one form us both within our mothers? ~Job 31:15

Ignorance Is Bliss

JAMES COYLE spent his first night at the Italian front wrapped up in half a pup tent, trying to shield himself from a driving rain. The next morning he lined up with others at a chow truck for breakfast. When two German aircraft appeared and began strafing a nearby unit, everyone around Coyle scattered for shelter. He described what he did next:

> I scooted and slid down to the chow truck, climbed up on it, and asked the cook, "Is it OK to get some coffee?" The cook said, "Take the whole d____ truck. I'm getting out of here!" I can't tell you how delicious the pancakes smothered with blueberry and strawberry jam tasted as I sipped my coffee and watched the enemy planes.[238]

There is a well-known paraphrase of a famous Kipling poem,[239] "If you can keep your head when all about you are losing theirs . . . maybe you don't understand the situation!" Here we see a novice displaying a nonchalance foreign to the battle-hardened veterans around him.

As a new Christian I have frequently made the same mistake in my attitude toward evil. When something goes wrong in my life, I usually suspect my own weaknesses and failures, ignoring the fact that there is an enemy in the world who knows me and is seeking to undo my efforts. Victory over this powerful force is more than a matter of self-improvement and takes more than self-will. It takes complete reliance on the power of our Lord and Savior. Ignorance of the presence of evil is not bliss.

Be self-controlled and alert. Your enemy the devil prowls around like a roaring lion looking for someone to devour. Resist him, standing firm in the faith, because you know that your brothers throughout the world are undergoing the same kind of sufferings. ~1 Peter 5:8–9

Hidden Danger

R AY SADOSKI was not happy on the Anzio beachhead. The weather was cold and overcast, and the beach was a wide expanse of open ground, exposed to enemy observation. His officers ordered everyone to dig in for protection from incoming artillery, not sensing a more immediate danger:

> We were set up just to the northeast of Anzio port. The Germans had pulled out so fast that they had left a 20mm Italian anti-aircraft gun sitting there. All our guys were horsing around, getting on the gun and the like. One of our communicators from the command post told me, "Go over to that Italian gun and get that phone wire that the Germans left behind, we can use it." Well, instead of walking all the way out to the gun to unhook the wire, I just grabbed the wire and gave it a yank, and the whole d____ gun went up in a huge explosion. The Germans had rigged that thing to blow up if anybody broke the wire. [240]

Life is full of hidden dangers we don't expect. We take precautions to ensure the safety and well-being of ourselves and families, but over time realize we can't plan for every contingency. The stock market crashes, the other driver swerves, or the spouse misinterprets. Many events are simply beyond our control. When we accept this fact, we open ourselves to a great spiritual blessing. God waits for us to give him control of our lives. The sooner we rely on him, the sooner we will find true peace. When we seek his direction we have a chance to align ourselves with his purpose and the ultimate safety that only God can provide: a secure place in his family and his eternal kingdom.

Do not be anxious about anything, . . . present your requests to God. And the peace of God, which transcends all understanding, will guard your hearts and your minds in Christ Jesus. ~Philippians 4:6, 7

Infantry moving into the Italian hills.
(National Archives)

Tenth Mountain Division at church services in Italy
(National Archives)

One of Three Results

ONE OF THE BLOODIEST battles of the Italian campaign was fought at the little town of Cisterna. The memory of it was a blur to Robert Appel. He knew that he was in the middle of *"hell breaking out all around."*[241] The air was a cacophony of eerie sounds from the metallic missiles that seemed to fill the air around him. He had some amazing observations about the experience:

> *I could actually hear the whirring and swishing sounds of shells whizzing by my ears. It was an unbelievable feeling to know you were literally walking through a labyrinth of metal that seemingly never presented you with an exit. It was a bewildering complexity, so real and so unreal for one to be caught up in—and—yet you knew the outcome would be one of three results. You would either be wounded, killed—or—with God's protective armor plus sheer good luck, you could come through unscathed.*[242]

This soldier was wounded during the battle, but, fortunately, survived to tell us this story. His analysis of possible outcomes accurately summarized what could happen to him physically at that time. It is interesting to note that the same outcomes are also possible in our daily spiritual struggles. Our weaknesses, the thoughtlessness of others, and the dedicated effort of the Enemy all seem zeroed in on slowing and stopping our progress toward God. Unless we are prepared, any of these pitfalls can hurt and even mortally wound us in our faith.

Fortunately, it is also possible that we can survive unscathed, and we are blessed to know that this outcome is not just a matter of sheer luck. The apostle Paul encouraged us to put on the "full armor of God" and place our spiritual safety in the hands of the one who guaranteed it through his own mortal wounds: our Savior, Jesus Christ.

For our struggle is not against flesh and blood, but against the rulers, against the authorities, against the powers of this dark world and against the spiritual forces of evil in the heavenly realms. Therefore put on the full armor of God, so that when the day of evil comes, you may be able to stand your ground.
~Ephesians 6:12–13

Without Faith

PAUL CURTIS was a soldier on the deadly beaches of Anzio. In May 1944 he wrote to his brother, Mitchell, back home in Oak Ridge, Tennessee. Mitchell had asked him to describe his feelings about being in combat, and Paul did his best:

> *I have seen some action—a few hard, hard days in which I saw more than I imagined I ever would. I don't think any man can exactly explain combat. It's beyond words. Take a combination of fear, anger, hunger, thirst, exhaustion, disgust, loneliness, homesickness, and wrap that all up in one reaction and you might approach the feelings a fellow has. It makes you feel mighty small, helpless, and alone . . . Without faith, I don't see how anyone could stand this.*[243]

I am struck by two words in Paul Curtis' letter: *fear* and *loneliness*. Everyone in combat experiences fear. This is a natural reaction whenever death or injury is a possibility. I don't know if everyone experiences loneliness in combat, but I know that I found myself in this state frequently. As an officer, I never felt free to share my deeper thoughts with the men in my unit or with superior officers, and there were rarely fellow company commanders nearby. This left me alone on most occasions with my own fears and uncertainties.

Like Curtis, I now find it hard to see how anyone could stand combat or any other crisis of life without faith. With faith, fear of dying may still exist, but death itself is no threat when you have confidence in the reality of God's eternal kingdom. Loneliness also becomes a non-issue when you have a relationship with God and are able to lift up your concerns to him in prayer. I regret that I did not have such faith while in combat. I would have been a more confident human being and a more effective leader.

Now faith is being sure of what we hope for and certain of what we do not see. ~Hebrews 11:1

Why Do Men Do That?

FELIX SPARKS couldn't stay in the rear. Wounded on Sicily and classified noncombat, he nevertheless hitched a ride on a B-17 bomber to Italy and rejoined his unit. After a period on the stalemated Gustav Line, he led his rifle company in the amphibious assault on Anzio. His unit bore the brunt of a savage German counterattack on February 16, 1944, and suffered severe casualties. He saw more than his share of action and was very emotional about the performance of his soldiers:

I was always amazed at how the American soldier responded in combat because it was a terrible, dirty business. The weather was awful. When you're outside in December, and only have a foxhole to sleep in, and it fills up with water all the time—it's miserable and depressing. But our soldiers learned very fast how to adapt. I loved the rifle company because that's where the action was. We were the ones who went first in any attack. But it always amazed me—why do men do that? Every attack we made, my men knew some of their buddies would be wounded or killed. Yet, when I gave the word, they moved forward without hesitation. They were very good, brave men and I was very proud of them.[244]

There has been a lot of speculation about the motivation of soldiers in combat. Do they perform heroically from a sense of a higher calling or patriotic duty? Or is there a fear of being seen as cowardly? Most of those with combat experience agree that the predominant urge among soldiers is to support their own comrades. No one wants to let a buddy down or endanger him by not being at his side when it counts.

Our fellow Christians need the same kind of support. As we do God's work we all face hard times when we need an understanding shoulder or a helping hand. At those times our brothers and sisters in Christ should not feel alone. We need to be there for them when it counts.

Be devoted to one another in brotherly love. Honor one another above yourselves. ~Romans 12:10

He Was Not Alone

THE 2ND BATTALION fought desperately to hold Mount Battaglia from fierce German counterattacks. Sgt. Harold Flechter had to order his squad to fall back against the enemy onslaught as small arms and artillery fire blanketed his position. To cover the withdrawal of his men, Flechter jumped into a foxhole and began firing a machine gun. As his squad moved down the hill, some of them saw an artillery shell land almost on top of their leader's foxhole.

Later, a search was conducted for Flechter's body, but nothing was ever found. He was listed as missing in action, bringing uncertainty and grief to a family in Kansas. Over time his parents and siblings simply had to accept the fact that he wasn't coming home, and a funeral service was held with an empty casket.

Closure for the Flechter family came in 2005, when a group of Italian civilians found human remains on Mount Battaglia. They also found shoe fragments, pieces of a watch, C-ration cans, and a Catholic prayer card. The card was made of fabric with an image of Jesus Christ left on a protective plastic sheet. DNA and the prayer card identified Harold Flechter. Of all the men missing in his unit, he was the only Catholic. "*We thought it was a miracle,*" his brother said of the discovery and identification.[245]

Peace came to this heroic soldier's family on several levels. They finally knew exactly what happened to Flechter and were able to bury his remains at the foot of his headstone. More importantly, they were comforted by the fact that he did not die alone. His Savior was close at hand with the comfort that only he can give: assurance of a place at his side with God throughout eternity.

> Then he said, "Jesus, remember me when you come into your kingdom." Jesus answered him, "I tell you the truth, today you will be with me in paradise." ~Luke 23:42–43

Still Small Voice

IN 1943 DEAN WILLARD SPERRY of Harvard University published a small booklet titled, *Prayers for Private Devotions in War-Time*. One of his prayers, dated to the seventh century, addressed the "Spirit of Prayer":

> *Dispel for this hour, O Lord, the manifold distractions of the world; that we may be able with quiet minds to receive the promptings of thy still small voice.*[246]

The inspiration for this prayer clearly comes from a story in the Old Testament about the prophet Elijah's encounter with God on Mount Horeb:

> *The LORD said, "Go out and stand on the mountain in the presence of the LORD, for the LORD is about to pass by." Then a great and power-ful wind tore the mountains apart and shattered the rocks before the LORD, but the LORD was not in the wind. After the wind there was an earthquake, but the LORD was not in the earthquake. After the earth-quake came a fire, but the LORD was not in the fire. And after the fire came a gently whisper. When Elijah heard it, he pulled his cloak over his face and went out and stood at the mouth of the cave. Then a voice said to him, "What are you doing here, Elijah?"* ~1 Kings 19:11–13

This story in no way limits how God communicates to man. He can and does speak in any way he pleases. He has revealed himself in Scripture and often speaks to us as we read and study it. He used thunder when address-ing Moses. If he ever speaks to us that way, we don't have to worry about hearing him. However, we know that God speaks most often to us quietly as we pray. He wants us to come to him in prayer and wants us to listen to him in return. Unfortunately, we often allow God's voice to be drowned out by the noise in our lives. Today, it is even worse than when Dean Sperry offered his prayer in wartime. Today we are bombarded by news, entertain-ment, and advertising media that have made a science of commanding our attention. Our "manifold distractions" have multiplied many times over. To have a meaningful relationship with our heavenly Father we must make quiet time and a "quiet mind" our absolutely first priorities.

Be still, and know that I am God. ~Psalm 46:10

Shaken but Grateful

THE BOMBING RUN over Ploesti was a disaster. Vaughn Gordy's B-24 was riddled with flak and two engines were knocked out. One crew member was killed and several others were wounded. As the aircraft started losing speed and altitude, a decision had to be made about the five-hundred-mile flight home over water. Could they make it on two engines? The pilot and engineer finally decided they could. Gordy said, "*With fingers crossed and an appeal to God's help we headed across the Adriatic.*"[247] The crew started throwing every loose item overboard to lighten the ship.

Forty miles later, one of the remaining engines caught fire, and the pilot immediately announced, "*We're going to ditch.*"[248] As the B-24 struck the water with a violent crash, Gordy was knocked unconscious for a moment and woke up to find himself in shoulder-deep water. Someone helped him out the top hatch and into a rubber raft where he soon saw his airplane sink beneath the surface. Fortunately, rescue came soon as an Air Force seaplane appeared over the horizon. Gordy summed up the incident:

> *Four hours after the crash we were back in Italy. Final tally: our tail-gunner was killed in the crash and went down with the plane; our waist-gunner was seriously injured, but survived; but the rest of the crew went back to work the next day, shaken but grateful.*[249]

After ditching at sea, some time off would seem to be in order. Bomber Command, however, seemed to believe that crash survivors should just get over the trauma and get back to work. It is undoubtedly true that the longer you brood about a pain or fear, the harder it will be to get over it later. This applies especially in our relationships. It is always better to clear the air sooner rather than later. Instead of letting a sore spot fester, forgive someone or ask them for forgiveness, and get on with your next assignment.

Still another said, "I will follow you, Lord; but first let me go back and say good-by to my family." Jesus replied, "No one who puts his hand to the plow and looks back is fit for service in the kingdom of God." ~Luke 9:61–62

Three Hymn Books

HORACE MAYCOCK was taken prisoner on Christmas morning 1942. He soon arrived in Camp 70, south of Rome, with thousands of other captured soldiers. Describing this traumatic experience, he said:

It is difficult to convey the true meaning of loss of liberty. Those who have experienced it can fully understand the complete turnaround involved, in which a name becomes a number, the man a machine. It is not easy to adapt to an inflicted mechanical atmosphere, to be thrust suddenly into a world that, at first sight, appears devoid of any under-standing of human rights and feelings.[250]

Under the brutal conditions of captivity, this soldier did find a way to fill the void of human understanding. He and many others made their way to the "churches" organized in their camp. There were Wesleyan, Anglican, and Catholic groups, each of which was a source of strength and encouragement to those who participated.

In November 1943 Maycock was moved to Germany with sixty other prisoners to work on a railroad construction site. As Christmas approached, he took it upon himself to organize a church for this small group. They were all billeted in one room, and this became the sanctuary. He made a rough wooden cross. His only other resources were three old hymnbooks, from which he copied songs onto sheets of black-out paper. With one violin for accompaniment, he held the first service on Christmas morning.

The image of this worship service comes to mind when I am sitting comfortably in my own Episcopal church, surrounded by stained glass, organ music, silver, and linen. I wonder if we come close to the spiritual depth of these men worshipping under much more austere conditions. Probably not. In their circumstance, the need for God was obvious and urgent. Truly, in this sense, blessed are the poor in spirit. We can only approximate this urgency by reminding ourselves of our fallen nature and our constant need for the forgiveness and grace of our Lord and Savior, Jesus Christ.

For where two or three come together in my name, there am I with them.
~Matthew 18:20

We Need to Care

ALBERT THOMAS saw a lot during his service with the 366th Infantry Division. He was a frontline infantryman, sniper, winch operator, and truck driver. With assignments in Italy, France, and the South Pacific, he was never in one place for long. The worst time for him was in the Po Valley during the Allied drive north of Rome. He saw a lot of men wounded and killed, including a good friend whom he was not able to help during the heat of battle. His feelings of sadness and regret stayed with him:

> When it comes down to it we are all just humans here to help each other. Seeing this devastation every day for years takes its toll on you. You come home to things and people don't understand you. You're messed up from all the sadness and cruelty you see. I wish today we could care about each other the way we use [sic] to. No matter the money or things you have we are the same. You only live for so long—we need to care about each other. That's what I discovered to be the most important from being in the war.[251]

We can each benefit from the insights of this veteran who found his own way to cope with suffering. He saw all of war's destruction: cities and countryside devastated, soldiers wounded and killed, civilians rendered destitute. He struggled with all this and eventually concluded that the most important thing for him was to help other people. It is a blessing to see a good man's thoughtful reaction to the horrors of war. It gives us hope that we can each struggle through our trials and disappointments to a better day, focusing less on our own misery, and more on caring for those around us.

"Do you understand what I have done for you?" he asked them. "You call me 'Teacher' and 'Lord,' and rightly so, for that is what I am. Now that I, your Lord and Teacher, have washed your feet, you also should wash one another's feet. I have set you an example that you should do as I have done for you." ~John 13:12–15

He Knew No Enemy

CHAPLAINS HAD to keep records, and the most important were those of deaths and burials. Chaplain Wallace Hale's files grew quite large during his service with the 88th Infantry Division in North Africa and Italy. His combat workbook eventually listed more than a thousand soldiers, with name, rank, serial number, denomination, and location of burial. Many years later, a colleague referred to this workbook while eulogizing Chaplain Hale:

> If you took that manual, you would find page after page after page of German soldiers: their names, their ranks, their units, their location of burial, because Wallace buried them in the Name of the Father, and of the Son, and of the Holy Spirit. Wallace knew no enemy. Wallace saw people as either the sons and daughters of the Living God through Jesus Christ, or he saw them as potential sons and daughters of the Living God. No enemy. They were treated as lovingly, as tenderly, as each and every American soldier.[252]

Hale himself described his role as a chaplain: "*I was a regular army Chaplain who tried to use his religious experiences and knowledge to build men up . . . I stood for fairness, for justice, and for forgiveness in an organization that, at times, tried to ignore these concepts.*"[253]

In a military organization highly focused on its combat mission and the material aspects of war, this man brought a deep concern for individual human beings, regardless of their religious condition or nationality. This is an example that Christians must follow. Jesus died for *all* mankind and focused his own ministry on those most in need. He was criticized for associating with prostitutes and tax collectors, but said, "*The Son of Man came to seek and to save what was lost*" (Luke 19:10). Without Jesus we are all lost, and we share this status with every other human being. We should look at all others as "*potential sons and daughters of the Living God.*"

Here is a trustworthy saying that deserves full acceptance: Christ Jesus came into the world to save sinners. ~1 Timothy 1:15

God Bless America

IRVING BERLIN was a Jewish immigrant who came to the United States when he was five years old. He wrote the great patriotic song "God Bless America" during World War I while serving in the U.S. Army at Camp Upton, New York.[254] Composed for a musical revue, but not used at the time, the song languished in his files for years. In 1938, as war was spreading through Europe, he reintroduced it in an Armistice Day broadcast on the Kate Smith radio show. He included an introduction that is now rarely heard, urging listeners to "swear allegiance to a land that's free" and "be grateful for a land so fair as we raise our voices in a solemn prayer."[255]

Kate Smith sang the song in march tempo with full orchestra and trumpets. It was an immediate sensation and became her signature song. There was even an effort to make it the national anthem, since the words and tune were far more memorable than the complex and more abstract "Star-Spangled Banner."

The distinguishing feature of "God Bless America" is the fact that it is a prayer. It is *not* a statement. It is a plea to God for the protection and guidance this nation has always needed and that only he can provide. When we say it or sing it with this in mind, "God Bless America" is a powerful reminder of our need for him in our personal and national lives.

> Now, our God, hear the prayers and petitions of your servant. For your sake, O LORD, look with favor on your desolate sanctuary. . . . We do not make requests of you because we are righteous, but because of your great mercy. O LORD, listen! O LORD, forgive! ~Daniel 9:17–19

The Slapping Incident

THE CONQUEST OF Sicily almost cost the United States one of its most effective combat generals. During a visit to a field hospital in August 1943, Gen. George Patton physically abused a soldier suffering from a condition euphemistically called "combat fatigue." After talking to a number of wounded soldiers, Patton approached Pvt. Paul Bennet and asked what was wrong with him. The soldier replied, *"It's my nerves,"* and then began to cry.[256]

On hearing this, Patton exploded: *"You are just a . . . coward . . . I won't have these brave men here who have been shot at seeing a yellow* [expletive] *sitting here crying."*[257] He then slapped the man and went on berating him.

When he heard of the incident General Eisenhower quietly reprimanded Patton and required that he apologize to those affected. A few months later, however, Drew Pearson broke the story publicly in a radio broadcast, creating a nationwide scandal.

Patton was harshly condemned by many, but there were others who thought him perfectly justified in forcefully stopping soldiers from shirking their duty. It was easy to give Patton the benefit of the doubt, as he was one of the great combat leaders of the time. There were two sides to this incident that would give a modern ethics class plenty to debate.

On balance, I believe Patton's behavior in this affair has to be condemned. What he did was the result of a temper tantrum on his part and was clearly not a well-thought-out disciplinary action. We're always on dangerous ground when we react to a situation out of anger. Instead of solving the first problem, we create a new one based on our own behavior, and the new problem then takes on a life of its own. There are many biblical warnings about this kind of behavior. In Proverbs we are told, *"A fool gives full vent to his anger, but a wise man keeps himself under control"* (Proverbs 29:11).

If anyone considers himself religious and yet does not keep a tight rein on his tongue, he deceives himself and his religion is worthless. ~James 1:26

Beat VMI

GEN. MARK CLARK was one of the most impressive men I have ever known. I was in his presence many times as a cadet and alumnus during his tenure as president of The Citadel. His reputation always preceded him. He had commanded all Allied forces in Italy during World War II and had been the "Liberator of Rome." His distinguished combat record and imposing physical presence created an aura of greatness.

I once paid a courtesy call after his retirement and found him laughing over a telephone conversation that he had had that day. The Reverend Billy Graham had called to discuss the general's funeral arrangements. General Clark was somewhat aghast at the subject since he was not contemplating that event anytime in the near future, and, when asked about his epitaph, had blurted out: *"Beat VMI!"* He was referring to the Virginia Military Institute, The Citadel's archrival in sports, and was a little concerned that the great religious leader might have been offended by his inappropriate response.

General Clark himself was serious about the religious well-being of his troops and cadets. He ensured that chapel attendance was mandatory at The Citadel, and he always dutifully set the example by being in the front row with his wife, Renie, at every service. During World War II he was quoted as saying, *"I am convinced that a soldier can find strength through prayer. All my life I have found prayer stimulating and comforting, particularly during critical periods."*[258] At that time he wrote an inspirational prayer for his troops:

On The Eve of Battle

On the eve of battle we ask Thee, our Heavenly Father, for strength and courage. We fight, not only for our country, but for our God as well, because we battle for continuance of Christian principles among all men. Give us the strength and the courage to fight well. Help us, in our hour of need, to follow the words of the Bible: "Be of good courage, and let us behave ourselves valiantly for our people, and for the cities of our God."[259] *Give us Thy guidance, Dear Lord, in the hours of crisis that lie ahead. Grant us the power to face our enemies and Thine enemies without fear. And bless, we pray Thee, our families and loved ones at home. Give them comfort and courage and grant them Thy divine protection. These things we ask in Thy name. Amen.*[260]

Remember now thy Creator in the days of thy youth. ~Ecclesiastes 12:1 (KJV)[261]

A soldier stands in a bomb-damaged Italian church.
(National Archives)

B-17 bombing Marienburg, Germany.
(National Archives)

JULY
The Air War

THE MASSIVE USE of air power distinguished World War II from all previous conflicts. Aircraft had limited uses during World War I, and, even though many could foresee great potential for aviation, postwar developments were slow. In the United States, the economic depression of the 1930s caused limited defense budgets and small allocations to military aircraft production. Germany and Japan were among the few countries dedicated to building modern air forces. By 1939, the German Luftwaffe was able to deploy more than four thousand combat aircraft in the invasion of Poland. By contrast, at that time the United States had about two thousand mostly obsolete aircraft scattered around the world. In history's greatest industrial mobilization this number would swell to eighty thousand by 1944. Almost two million men and women were inducted into the air forces to maintain and man this vast aerial armada.

In Europe, American military commanders made an early commitment to daylight, precision bombing of German industrial targets. This task fell to the 8th Air Force under command of Maj. Gen. Carl Spaatz. Under Spaatz, Brig. Gen. Ira Eaker established 8th Bomber Command headquarters in England early in 1942. The workhorses of this campaign were two heavy bombers then starting to roll off production lines in the United States. The B-17 Flying Fortress and B-24 Liberator were both four-engine aircraft capable of flying more than two thousand miles with bomb loads ranging from four thousand to eight thousand pounds. These aircraft required crews of ten or more each, necessitating the training of hundreds of thousands of airmen.

Fighter escorts were an integral part of the air campaign, shepherding the bombers through enemy skies to their targets. Due to the limited range of these fighters, bomber losses were horrendous early in the war. Introduction of the P-51 Mustang improved this situation, and by early 1944, fully escorted missions were flying into Germany with fewer losses.

By the end of the war, the 8th Air Force suffered the loss of about forty thousand airmen killed in action. This was a rate greater than that of any other service. Many thousands more were wounded or went down in enemy territory to become prisoners of war. Some have questioned the effectiveness of the strategic bombing campaign due to the fact that German industrial production increased throughout most of the war. However, it is undeniable that almost the entire Luftwaffe had to be committed to the protection of German cities and millions of men and women devoted to the defense and reconstruction of Germany's infrastructure. Later in the war, German units in the field lost practically all freedom of movement as the skies overhead were dominated by Allied aircraft.

We Pay You

JAMES GOODSON was a nineteen-year-old American who went to England early in the war. He was sure that his country would eventually join the fight, and he wanted to get a head start. He was inauspiciously introduced to the war when his ocean liner, the *Athenia*, was torpedoed and sunk off the Hebrides Islands. He arrived in England with none of his possessions.

> I found a RAF recruiting station and immediately asked if any American could join. No one seemed to know at first if I could but later was told I could but would probably lose my American citizenship when I swore allegiance to the King of England. I told the recruiters that if the king needed my allegiance, he had it. The question of pay arose and I think the fellow said it was seven shillings and six pence a day (less than $2.00). I was heartbroken. I said, 'I've lost everything I have. I don't think I can afford it.' The fellow said, 'No, no, no. We pay you *seven and six*.' I remember thinking, 'These lovable fools. They could have had me for nothing.' To be able to fly a Spitfire and be paid for it was just beyond my wildest dreams.[262]

Goodson flew with the 43rd Squadron of the RAF and eventually with the American Eagle Squadron. He didn't lose his enthusiasm for flying even as the war went on.

During my early years as a Marine officer I often had the identical thought articulated by this young pilot. I couldn't believe that someone was paying me to do what I was doing. Jumping from airplanes and swimming from submarines, I seemed to be living an adventure that most people would pay to experience. I never seemed to lose this enthusiasm for working with other Marines on any kind of mission. After leaving the Marine Corps and working many years for a paycheck, I was blessed to find this feeling again at age fifty-three. When Jesus Christ came into my heart, all the activities in my life became focused on a new mission: living in a way to be worthy of and to advance his kingdom. Every part of my life since then has had a new excitement that transcends any other imaginable adventure.

Whatever you do, work at it with all your heart, as working for the Lord, not men, since you know that you will receive an inheritance from the Lord as a reward. It is the Lord Christ you are serving. ~Colossians 3:23–24

We Won't Do Much Talking

THE STRATEGIC BOMBING campaign of the 8th Air Force played a major part in the eventual Allied victory in Europe. The campaign grew in effectiveness after France was invaded and air superiority gained over the Luftwaffe. Thousands of American bombers swept over northern Europe, penetrating deeper and deeper into German territory.

The beginning of this great buildup was slow and painful. In January 1942 Brig. Gen. Ira Eaker arrived in England to evaluate British bomber operations and to organize the American 8th Bomber Command. In May a small contingent of personnel arrived to set up command headquarters as the actual aircraft were slowly being ferried across the Atlantic. During this time the British continued to fight and bleed almost alone, as no American bombers had yet gone into action against the enemy. In June General Eaker spoke to a group of British dignitaries at High Wycombe, the site of his new headquarters. His words were brief: *"We won't do much talking until we've done more fighting. We hope that when we leave you'll be glad we came."*[263]

This American officer's remarks were simple and appropriate. They were appreciated by his audience and received wide publicity at that time. His humility brought great credit to himself and to his nation. We find numerous biblical reminders of the importance of being careful in our speech:

> *"He who holds his tongue is wise"* (Proverbs 10:19).
> *"The heart of the righteous weighs its answers"* (Proverbs 15:28).
> *"A man of knowledge uses words with restraint"* (Proverbs 17:27).
> *"Even a fool is thought wise if he keeps silent"* (Proverbs 17:28).
> *"Do you see a man who speaks in haste? There is more hope for a fool than for him"* (Proverbs 29:20).

Everyone should be quick to listen, slow to speak and slow to become angry.
~James 1:19

A View from a New Angle

WILLARD RICHARDS was a B-17 waist-gunner on many missions over Europe. He had been in love with airplanes since he was a boy and had a clear recollection from age eleven of his first flight:

> *Taxiing for takeoff was really bumpy, but as we lifted off the ground it became unbelievably smooth. There I was, getting a view of my whole world from a new angle. The big shale pile by the abandoned coal mine, the outline of an old racetrack, the ponds where we skated and fished all came into view. There was the local cemetery and the steel mill where Father worked. The sandstone quarry and the new hospital on the edge of town all looked like blocks on a Monopoly board. My grandfather's farm looked like a postage stamp and our house on the edge of the farm was so small. We descended over the high-tension wires and came in for a really rough landing. The whole flight took about ten minutes, but it changed my outlook on life.*[264]

It is amazing to consider an experience that gives you an entirely new perspective. The birth of our first child was this kind of event, suddenly creating whole new priorities for my wife and myself. There is no change more dramatic, however, than our spiritual awakening. Jesus Christ came into my heart at the end of a long process. But in that one moment of acceptance, my life changed suddenly and completely. I saw other people with new eyes that held no judgment. The Bible came to life as a meaningful source of truth. My church changed from a building into the living body of Christ. It was truly life-changing to experience the perfection of God's love as revealed by his Son. There is no greater change in perspective than the one that comes with a new heart.

This we proclaim concerning the Word of life. The life appeared; we have seen it and testify to it, and we proclaim to you the eternal life, which was with the Father and has appeared to us. ~1 John 1:1–2

A Fifty-Cent Item

ENEMY FIGHTERS came in waves as copilot Vince Mazza wrestled with the controls of his B-24 bomber. The pilot had been killed moments before and the aircraft damaged by an attacking Messerschmitt-109. Crewmen were still trying to remove the dead pilot from the controls as Mazza fought to avoid colliding with other ships nearby. Somehow he kept the battered B-24 in formation, lumbering toward the target: Misburg, Germany.

Suddenly, a 20mm cannon shell exploded in the forward section of the aircraft, destroying the nose turret and blowing out the plexiglass around it. Through this gaping hole a 200 mile-per-hour wind whipped through the interior of the B-24 at minus sixty-seven degrees. Wounded and frostbitten crewmen moved back in the ship to get out of the blast. The pilot stayed at the controls but had increasing difficulty seeing. He felt like his eyes were freezing. He couldn't go down to a warmer altitude because that would further expose his aircraft to fighter attack. Groping around the cockpit, his hand touched a pair of plastic goggles, which he put on over his eyes. He could finally see again to fly the airplane. Vince Mazza forever felt that this fifty-cent item saved his life and the lives of his crew.[265]

That pair of goggles was probably on someone's checklist, and, even though such gear had little intrinsic value, someone had to make sure it was all there. This faithful attention to detail is what saved these men. A Marine 1st sergeant once told me, *"If you take care of the details, the big picture will take care of itself."* Some who pride themselves on being "big picture" people might disagree with this assertion. However, I believe it is valid in the sense that any big task can be broken down into detailed action steps. Success comes in faithfully attending to those small steps. Long ago a little boy took five barley loaves and two small fish with him on an outing to the far shore of the Sea of Galilee. This boy's faithful attention to detail was glorified by Jesus in one of his greatest miracles.

Well done, good and faithful servant! You have been faithful with a few things; I will put you in charge of many things. ~Matthew 25:21

B-24 Liberator bomber.
(U.S. Dept. of Defense)

B-17 Flying Fortress bomber.
(U.S. Dept. of Defense)

A Triumphant Conscience

IN SEPTEMBER 1943 more than four hundred B-17 bombers flew more than five hundred miles against heavy opposition to reach targets near Stuttgart, Germany. On the way, the flight crew of *The Old Squaw* knew that they were in trouble. An attacking enemy fighter had put holes in their right wing tank, which was trailing a mist of leaking fuel. With a slim chance of making it home, the crew faced a fateful decision.

Less than one hundred miles to the south lay neutral Switzerland. Under international law combat crews landing there were interned for the duration of the war. It was well known that living conditions were excellent, not to mention a guaranteed safe return after the war. The navigator of *The Old Squaw* called over the intercom for a vote. He was startled by the response: *"By the time it was my turn to vote, the other nine had all voted to go to England."*[266]

After a harrowing flight and crash landing in the English Channel, one of the crewmen later explained his vote:

> The only thought in my mind was of returning to England and our base. The idea of going to Switzerland and being interned for the war's duration did not take root at all. I had a simplicity of thought and purpose in those days which stood me well. For 45 years I have lived with a triumphant conscience because we made it back to fight again, which was the duty and purpose for which we were pledged.[267]

This is an inspiring testimony to the long-range benefit of making a good, but difficult, choice. We especially need a perspective like this when we wrestle with the problems of family and marriage. Our decisions today can have everlasting consequences to our spouses, children, and ourselves. Doing the right thing may be difficult now, but think of the countless blessings of a "triumphant conscience" in the years ahead.

> The goal of this command is love, which comes from a pure heart and a good conscience and a sincere faith. ~1 Timothy 1:5

A Different View of the War

JIM GOODSON was taken prisoner when his P-51 was shot down over Germany. On the way to a Luftwaffe interrogation center in Frankfurt he was taken off the train in Berlin to change to another line. He learned from a guard that he was at the Friederichstrasse Bahnhof. He was shocked to realize that he was at the site of a major raid scheduled for that day he had helped plan. He also remembered that the Bahnhof was the main aiming point for one thousand bombers. When the air raid warnings sounded at noon he knew what was coming.

> We took refuge in bomb shelters. Because I had taken part in planning the raid, I knew who would be leading the different boxes of bombers and my own fighters would be escorting. It's a very different view of the war, when you're up there at 30,000 feet and you see only little flashes and puffs of smoke. You don't think of people. Sitting in an air raid shelter with Germans all around you, and the crashing, deafening noise above you is something else...It brought home a war pilots very seldom see. Digging women and children out of the rubble we had caused was profoundly affecting.[268]

Few of us ever have an epiphany of this magnitude. We continue through life without realizing how our actions are affecting others. This can be an especially acute problem for men. We often spend years dedicated to careers and causes before looking closely at the effect on our families. Too often it takes a crisis to wake us up to important things we're neglecting. It would be far better to hone our listening skills every day with wives, children, and friends, making sure we know as we go along what our bombs are doing at ground level.

Reckless words pierce like a sword, but the tongue of the wise brings healing. ~Proverbs 12:18

A Greater Hand Than Mine

AFTER SURVIVING a crash landing at sea, several crewmembers of *The Old Squaw* reminisced about their harrowing experience and expressed a belief that something more profound than "luck" was involved:

> *I cannot help but feel that there was something bigger than luck riding with us that day. The fact that we were able to stay with the formation until there were no enemy fighters around, and the fact that our escort arrived shortly afterward might be explained by luck, but when that rescue boat appeared on our course, at just the right moment, I was sure that the Omnipotent was guiding us that day especially. I cannot help but feel, too, that a greater hand than mine or Bob's was on the controls when* The Old Squaw *sat down in the Channel. The captain of the rescue boat told us one last thing which made us thank God for our safety. If we had landed a few miles to the south, we would have been caught in dangerous rip tides. If we had landed a few miles to the north, we would have been in the minefields . . . that particular area was the only place where we could have done so safely.*[269]

Many things had to go right for this crew to survive such a disastrous mission. Even though each detail had a logical explanation in itself, these men saw a miraculous pattern in these details and experienced a deepening of their faith as a result. We always have the same choice. We can accept the logical explanations and even the role of luck in our lives, or we can look more deeply for evidence of God's guiding hand. We know that God created an intricately designed and beautiful universe that we can rightly consider miraculous. Sometimes it takes a child's eyes and sense of wonder to see the miraculous in our own lives.

No eye has seen, no ear has heard, no mind has conceived what God has prepared for those who love him. ~1 Corinthians 2:9

Better Off Angry

IT WAS COMFORTING to see the fighter escort nearby, but, unfortunately, they would not be there long. As the *Luscious Lady* flew further into France, Merlin Miller became more and more nervous at his tail-gun position. This was his second raid on Schweinfurt, deep in German territory, and he knew it would probably be as bad as the first. Alone with his thoughts, there wasn't much to do other than anticipate what lay ahead. As the escorting P-47s peeled off, he went through a familiar mental exercise:

> I said to myself, 'Merlin, get mad, get angry.' I started thinking about the Germans, what they were trying to do to us, what I was going to do to them, anything to stir up my blood and get anger coursing through my system, anything to take away from that feeling of fear I otherwise would have had. By this time I figured out that it was difficult for a person to feel two emotions at the same time. In combat I thought I was better off being angry than afraid.[270]

This airman's strategy for dealing with fear was effective, and it is not uncommon to see athletes use the same approach as they try to get "psyched up" for a big game. However, we should consider war and football the exceptions rather the rule. Anger is usually a destructive emotion and counterproductive to solving our problems. It is always a bad idea to take action against others when upset. We need to be especially careful when we find ourselves with feelings of anger toward God. He is not the cause of our problems, but rather the solution. We are usually the problem. In our relationship with him, we are better off being afraid than angry.

> The fear of the LORD is the beginning of wisdom; all who follow his precepts have good understanding. To him belongs eternal praise. ~Psalm 111:10

Hogie and Wac

MY TWIN UNCLES were pilot and copilot of a B-26 medium bomber. They took off from Rougham, England, on May 17, 1943, to bomb a power plant in Holland, and, with the rest of their entire squadron, never returned. Edward and Arthur Norton, nicknamed "Hogie" and "Wac" were the proud sons of my mother's parents, pioneers of aviation in the small town of Conway, South Carolina, and hometown heroes. They left Clemson College in 1941 to join the Army Air Corps, seeking to answer the call of a nation at war and to pursue their love of flying. At their own insistence, they were together in the same airplane. The deaths of these promising young men was a tragedy for an entire community and my family.

My grandmother was the daughter of a minister and a lifelong pillar of the Presbyterian Church. She made sure her family was well grounded in the Christian faith and faithful in their Christian duties. Even so, this event was a blow that she and my grandfather felt forever after. When the war was over, they sent a poem to be read at a memorial service for another pilot who died with their sons. It captures the devastation that they felt, but also a determination to find a higher meaning in the tragedy:

> *As we trail the weary pathway down the sunset slope of life*
> *As we pass through grievous shadows in this war torn world of strife.*
> *Then our thoughts turn slowly backward to a better, brighter day*
> *When we were building castles and watching you at play.*
> *We had dreams and hopes and visions for your busy little feet*
> *Now we know those dreams and visions never-more your lives shall meet.*
>
> *And now lonely, sad and stricken our one debt to you is plain*
> *To prove that your great sacrifice shall not have been in vain.*
> *So tis us you left behind you who must carry on*
> *Take up the fight you died for till the last great battle's won.*
> *And to you we pledge our promise in the peace that is to be*
> *That we shall never falter that the whole world may be free.*[271]

The righteous perish, and no one ponders it in his heart; devout men are taken away, and no one understands that the righteous are taken away to be spared from evil. Those who walk uprightly enter into peace; they find rest as they lie in death. ~Isaiah 57:1–2

The Weaver

BERT RAMSEY was killed in 1943 when his B-26 medium bomber collided with another aircraft during a low-level attack on a power plant in Holland. A Dutch family buried him there, and his parents later held a memorial service at home in his honor. The service was conducted on November 25, 1945, at the Statesboro, Georgia, Methodist Church. After the congregation sang "Onward, Christian Soldiers," The Reverend Charles Jackson prayed and gave a sermon. A series of tributes to Ramsey and poems to comfort the family were then read. Mrs. Sanford Schulert, whose husband had been killed in the same raid, recited a poem with a special message for the grieving family:[272]

The Weaver

My life is but a weaving Between my Lord and me.
I cannot choose the colors He worketh steadily.

Oft times He weaveth sorrow And I, in foolish pride,
Forget He sees the upper and I the underside.

Not til the loom is silent And the shuttles cease to fly,
Shall God unroll the canvas And explain the reason why.

The dark threads are as needful In the Weaver's skillful hand
As the threads of gold and silver In the pattern He has planned.

This well-known poem provides a unique insight into our relationship with God. God interacts with us as we pray, study, and work together with him to weave the pattern of our lives. This weaving process presents an issue of perspective. Ours is limited by our human nature as we experience events only as they affect us. God's perspective is all encompassing and eternal. A tragedy to us may simply be part of God's plan and even a cause for heavenly celebration. We need to rest in the assurance that God sees the completed tapestry as it unfolds according to his design.

> This third I will bring into the fire; I will refine them like silver and test them like gold. They will call my name and I will answer them; I will say, "They are my people," and they will say, "The LORD is our God." ~Zechariah 13:9

Holes in the Fuselage

THEIR FIRST MISSION was supposed to be a "milk run." They were flying in support of ground troops near Caen, and someone had even decided that flak jackets and helmets wouldn't be needed. Since the flight path was close to the English Channel, Bill Frankhouser looked forward to an easy first day as navigator on his B-17. However, as they approached the target area at an altitude of 14,000 feet, the picture began to change. Bill started to notice tracers coming up from below, although well under his formation. Then a few black puffs appeared closer to their altitude. Suddenly, he found out that he was at war:

> I noticed a one to two-inch-diameter hole as it opened in the aluminum hull close to my right-side gun, and small metallic shavings were propelled inward. This was my first realization that we really were in combat. The Germans were shooting big guns and the plane's hull offered no protection![273]

This story brought back memories of my first time under fire in a helicopter. We were hovering over a hillside in Vietnam, hoisting a wounded Marine through jungle canopy. Suddenly, holes began appearing in the skin of the helicopter. The gunfire was unheard because of the engine noise, making the sensation especially eerie and frightening. Those few moments of being utterly defenseless are burned in my memory. I can't imagine the courage required of these World War II airmen who had to face this extreme vulnerability day after day, week after week. It is gratifying to know that so many of them had a strong faith on which to lean. True comfort during such fearful times can only be found in an eternal perspective and in the assurance of an ultimate safe haven in God's eternal kingdom.

Lord, you have been our dwelling place throughout all generations. Before the mountains were born or you brought forth the earth and the world, from everlasting to everlasting you are God. ~Psalm 90:1–2

Brownie's Faith

THE COAST OF ENGLAND finally came into view, but they knew they weren't going to make it. The B-17 was unable to hold its altitude on its one remaining engine, and settled ever closer to the waves below. Expecting to ditch at any moment, the crew assembled in the radio room and braced themselves for a crash landing. Each became lost in his own thoughts as they looked at each other and waited for the inevitable. One of the crewmen, Elmer Brown, started praying. George Hoyt, the radio operator, remained at his console, sending SOS signals in Morse code. Hoyt looked over at his praying friend for reassurance, and he was not disappointed:

> *Brownie's faith shone as bright as the very sun itself. I remembered him giving me a smile as big as all outdoors. Out my window I saw the choppy and rough sea coming towards us, closer and closer, and I prayed fervently as I continued to beat out those SOS signals.*[274]

Hoyt and others in the crew went on to describe an amazing peace that settled over the group in this tense moment:

> *As we were waiting to hit the water, a complete calm came over us as if 'all is well.'*
>
> *A feeling of absolute calm, just like I was laying under a tree back on the farm . . .*
>
> *(I felt) a great calm take possession of me which language can't describe. I experienced a peace that surpasses all imagination as I watched the whitecaps now flicking by under the wing . . . I called to Brownie and the boys, 'This is it!'*[275]

This smile for a friend in a moment of extreme stress is a strong witness to the power of faith. The faith of this one airman not only reassured him, but, when he let it show outwardly, brought peace to his friends as well. We should always look to our heavenly Father during times of stress with faith that he will hear our pleas. Then, we should also be ready to share a smile with a friend to bear witness to the reassuring power of our faith.

In the same way, let your light shine before men, that they may see your good deeds and praise your Father in heaven. ~Matthew 5:16

Commitment

BUD MAHURIN'S perspective on war began to change in his first dog-fight. A burst from his machine guns hit the ME-110 and, as the enemy aircraft trailed smoke and spiraled down, he could see the tail-gunner slumped over and wounded. He realized suddenly that, *"We're chasing after other human beings, and not just a machine that's flying in the air."*[276] In March 1944 Mahurin himself was shot down and had to bail out of his P-47 behind enemy lines. He came down near Orleans, France, more than 130 miles from the coast. He hid in a field for a day and then made his way to a French farmhouse. The farmer took him to a local member of the Resistance.

During the days that followed he was hidden in haystacks, barns, and basements. Every night he was moved and handed off to another Resistance group. Finally, the difficult arrangements were made for a light plane to pick him up in a field at night. After several failed attempts, he was successfully rescued and flown back to England. His experience gave him another new perspective on war and the dedication of the people who helped him:

> *The Gestapo and German Army were always looking for downed American and British pilots. Whenever the Germans saw a parachute coming down—or they found one of our planes wrecked but no body in it—they would flood the area with search parties. If I got caught, I'd be sent to a POW camp. But if the Resistance guys got caught, they would be executed on the spot.*[277]

This is the measure of true commitment, to be prepared to give your life for a cause. Dying for our faith may be a remote possibility, but, if we are committed to our faith, we need to resolve how we will act when things get difficult. My Bible provides an essay with some pointed advice on this subject: *"In essence, we must consistently choose to love and obey God, even when doing so is hard or mundane. Like a marriage partner, we choose to stick with God 'for better or for worse.' God blesses those who consistently come to him."*[278]

"Because he loves me," says the LORD, "I will rescue him; I will protect him, for he acknowledges my name. He will call upon me, and I will answer him; I will be with him in trouble, I will deliver him and honor him." ~Psalm 91:14–15

Every Day Is Monday

WHIT HILL received his draft notice in September 1941 and promptly enlisted in the Army Air Corps. He was sent to sheet metal repair school to learn the skills needed to fix damaged aircraft fuselages. He went to England with the 91st Bomb Group and soon became a crew chief over seven other men charged with keeping a squadron of B-17 bombers in the air. As the tempo of bombing missions increased, so did the pressure on Hill and his crew.

At the end of each mission the battle and mechanical damage of each returning aircraft was assessed and time to make necessary repairs was estimated. The planes requiring the least amount of work were the first to be repaired. Then there were many shot-up aircraft. The sheet-metal crews would help each other out. There were times when the sheet-metal crews did not get to bed for 72 hours. None of the men from the ground crew—mechanics, electricians, prop specialists, bomb loaders, sheet-metal repairmen had any set daily working hours. Every day was Monday; it was 'work until you drop' and the password for requested tasks was 'how soon?'[279]

I was once amazed by a study showing the morale of postal workers highest during the Christmas season. This seemed counterintuitive at first glance. However, I have learned that most people do respond to a challenge. In fact, many thrive on difficult tasks and take considerable pride in seeing them through. This is a fact of human nature that we should remember in any leadership role. There are always those who thrive on the difficult assignments. They can accomplish great things only if challenged and given opportunities.

Remember this: Whoever sows sparingly will also reap sparingly, and whoever sows generously will also reap generously. Each man should give what he has decided in his heart to give. ~2 Corinthians 9:6–7

God, Get Us Out of Here

JON SCHUELER did not want to be on the mission. He was sick, but had been ordered to fly anyway. To make matters worse, he had to fill in as navigator for a crew he didn't know. After a difficult bombing run over St. Nazaire, his B-17 Flying Fortress finally turned for home and then flew into a real calamity: 120 miles per hour headwinds. The formation seemed to inch toward home as enemy fighters constantly preyed on the struggling bombers.

> It seemed as though we would never get home. We waited for the Focke Wulfs and the Messerschmitts and we watched the Fortresses fall. Falling Forts. I wanted to hold them. I wanted to go down with them. I wanted to go home. I prayed. I prayed, please God . . . don't make this go on and on and on . . . I can't stand this boring repetition, please God, get us out of here and get this over with.[280]

God did answer these prayers, and Jon Schueler returned safely from this mission. However, he was almost shattered by the experience. He was consumed with guilt and the thought that he was responsible for the deaths he had seen. He couldn't sleep, started losing weight, and was eventually taken off flight status. This was a sensitive man who was affected deeply by what he experienced. It is not uncommon for anyone to feel guilt over his or her survival, or even success, when others are not so fortunate. I believe, however, that there is a better response available when things turn out well for us. We can be thankful, as we prayerfully work through these feelings of guilt. Thankfulness is a more positive attitude that will bring us closer to our Father in heaven, the ultimate source of forgiveness for our real and imagined flaws.

Let us draw near to God with a sincere heart in full assurance of faith, having our hearts sprinkled to cleanse us from a guilty conscience and having our bodies washed with pure water. ~Hebrews 10:22

I Will Pay It Gladly

LAVERNE SAUNDERS was an airman and hero of World War II, earning the Navy Cross, Distinguished Service Medal, Distinguished Flying Cross, Silver Star, and Purple Heart. He commanded a bomber group during the Solomon Islands campaign in the Pacific. In one of his famous exploits he was a passenger in a B-17 when the pilot and copilot were seriously wounded by a Japanese fighter attack. Saunders coolly took the controls, ditched the aircraft near an island, and got the crew to safety.

On Christmas Day 1942 he became one of the Army's youngest brigadier generals and took over 7th Bomber Command. Later, he was a key figure bringing the new B-29 bomber into operational service. With 20th Bomber Command he took a B-29 wing to India and China in 1944 and led the first long-range strikes against mainland Japan. In that year he also wrote a moving prayer as an inspiration for military men and women serving around the world:

Help Me to Do My Duty

O God, most merciful and just, look upon this suppliant soldier and help me to do my duty in all things for love of Thee. Make me strong in conflict, brave in adversity, and patient in suffering. Make me vigilant to defend my country against her enemies and proud to carry her cause fearlessly into battle. I do not ask to be preserved free from all bodily harm, and if death is the price I must pay for my country's freedom, I will pay it gladly, trusting in Thy infinite mercy that Thou wilt make a place for me in heaven, there to know peace and happiness for all eternity. Bless and protect my loved ones at home, and grant that my sacrifices on the field of battle may make me worthy of their trust and confidence, through Christ our Lord. Amen.[281]

It is uplifting to see another great military leader of World War II humbly share his faith and help others turn to God for strength to endure whatever hardships lay before them.

O Lord, open my lips, and my mouth will declare your praise.
You do not delight in sacrifice, or I would bring it;
You do not take pleasure in burnt offerings.
The sacrifices of God are a broken spirit;
A broken and contrite heart. ~Psalm 51:15–17

Join Ups in the Dark

THE AIRMEN OF World War II had to face the terrible risks of fighter attack and anti-aircraft fire. Less obvious were the risks associated with accidents. Some of the most dangerous conditions were brought on by the simple phenomenon of darkness. A twenty-year-old B-17 pilot from Tennessee described the difficulty of organizing aircraft in the dark:

> *Daylight joinups were easy. A predawn joinup, a low overcast that you had to climb until you were on top, sometime 18,000 to 20,000 feet and then try to join up was terrible. Scary! Imagine a thousand airplanes trying to line up in groups of thirty-six, spaced two minutes apart in pitch-black darkness and over an exact spot in the English Channel at a precise time, make the orderly, perfect formation envisioned by the men behind armor-plated desks, you get a feeling for the high risk of collision . . . When it did happen, two 65,000–pound, four-engine aircraft loaded with bombs and 2,780 gallons of high octane made a very untidy mess.*[282]

During my military service I was always amazed at how difficult it was to do anything in the dark. A simple task like navigating a small unit from point A to point B was challenging. Coordinating units maneuvering in the field could be fraught with confusion.

There is a parallel here to our spiritual lives. When we try to live without God at the center of our lives, we experience a special kind of darkness. Simple things become complicated. Forgiving others for their mistakes should be easy and effortless. However, without God, we get wrapped up in our own hurt feelings. Without God's light guiding our way, we stay confused within ourselves. Our own desires and motives lead us along truly dark and confusing paths. Only with God's light can we see the straight path that we need to be walking with him.

Then your light will break forth like the dawn, and your healing will quickly appear; then your righteousness will go before you, and the glory of the LORD will be your rear guard. ~Isaiah 58:8

Ploesti

T HE B-24'S FLEW *"straight into a scene that resembled the background of a medieval painting of hell."*[283] Raging fires, black smoke, flak bursts, and tracers filled the air over the oil refineries of Ploesti, Romania. One hundred seventy-seven American bombers flew thirteen hundred miles from North Africa to attack the strategic target providing thirty percent of Germany's oil. Flying at tree top level in daylight, under radio silence, the daring raid was difficult to coordinate and highly dangerous. Instead of arriving simultaneously over the six refineries, the B-24s came in a few at a time to face alerted anti-aircraft batteries and fighter opposition. On that day in August 1943 forty-four aircraft went down with the loss of almost five hundred men. Five earned the Medal of Honor.

Twenty-one-year-old Capt. Richard Butler of San Diego, California, was a volunteer for the Ploesti mission. He and many others faced the unknown and their own fear with the most effective source of comfort known:

> *I was the co-pilot of our B-24 and Walt Bunker was the pilot. Walt was anything but a religious man, so I was surprised, as we were going out across the Mediterranean, to see Walt pull out one of the small Bibles we were issued and start reading it. I always carried mine with me and I got it out and read some Psalms. I had read from the Good book on other missions, but I had never seen Walt reading from a Bible. That kind of gives you an idea about how serious we were taking this mission.*[284]

There are many psalms that reassure us during difficult times. Psalm 23 is the best known and most memorized. I have found the transcendent imagery of Psalm 91 a special source of encouragement when I am fearful: *"He who dwells in the shelter of the Most High will rest in the shadow of the Almighty"* (Psalm 91:1). Scripture such as this enables us to turn our attention away from our earthly concerns and toward our Father in heaven. Even though the dangers that we face may not go away, we know from his Word that God, through his Son, has assured us of his *eternal* protection.

You will not fear the terror of night, nor the arrow that flies by day, nor the pestilence that stalks in the darkness, nor the plague that destroys at midday. ~Psalm 91:5–6

Redemption

GEORGE MCGOVERN was a famous member of the "Greatest Generation." During World War II he was a bomber pilot with thirty-five combat missions to his credit. He later became a congressman and senator from South Dakota and the Democratic candidate in the 1972 presidential election.

He expressed one regret about the war. As he pulled away from the target on one of his last missions over Austria he received word that a five-hundred-pound bomb was hung up in the bomb bay. The bomb was armed, making it impossible to land safely. Working feverishly, several crewmen tried to free the deadly projectile. Unfortunately, it came loose as the bomber flew over a small farm. McGovern looked down in horror as the bomb destroyed a cluster of houses on the farm.

For forty years he lived with a sense of guilt over this incident. In 1985 he was lecturing at the University of Innsbruck and, in response to a question from a television reporter, described his regret about the accidental bombing of those farmhouses. That night an elderly Austrian farmer called the television station with a message for the senator:

> *"Tell the American senator that it was my farm. We saw this low bomber coming, where all the others that had come over earlier were way up above. I got my wife and three daughters out of the house and we hid in the ditch, and no one was hurt. You can tell him that I despised Adolf Hitler, even though my government threw in with him."*[285]

When he heard these words, George McGovern was finally able to sigh in relief. He said, *"After all those years, I got redemption."*[286] Every thinking person involved in war comes away with some sense of guilt. I believe that God honors such pangs of conscience and offers each of us a path to our own redemption.

Therefore, there is now no condemnation for those who are in Christ Jesus, because through Christ Jesus the law of the Spirit of life set me free from the law of sin and death. ~Romans 8:1–2

The Wrong Seat

GEORGE MCGOVERN was the son of a Methodist minister and grew up in a household that took faith and morals seriously. After the war he attended theological seminary to pursue an interest in applying Christian ethics to practical life. He was a student minister for about a year, until he decided on a different career path that took him into teaching and eventually politics. In a 2003 article he talked about his service in the war and his ambivalence about God's role in it:

> As a World War II bomber pilot, I was always troubled by the title of a then-popular book, God is My Co-pilot. My co-pilot was Bill Rounds of Wichita, Kansas, who was anything but godly, but he was a skillful pilot, and he helped me bring our B-24 Liberator through thirty-five combat missions over the most heavily defended targets in Europe. I give thanks to God for our survival, but somehow I could never quite picture God sitting at the controls of a bomber or squinting through a bombsight deciding which of his creatures should survive and which should die.[287]

I agree with the observation that God doesn't squint through bombsights or pick targets for destruction in war. The title of the book mentioned doesn't necessarily imply that either, but is instead intended to convey the idea that God was there with the author, protecting him during his missions. Others, including myself, have also been troubled by the title of this book, but for a different reason. If God is our copilot, then the implication is that he is along for the ride, watching out for us and protecting us during dangerous moments. However, if he is the pilot, then *he* has the controls. The bumper sticker says it best:

If God Is Your Co-pilot,
YOU ARE IN THE WRONG SEAT

"For I know the plans I have for you," declares the LORD, "plans to prosper you and not to harm you, plans to give you hope and a future." ~Jeremiah 29:11

A Prayer of Thanks

ED BRANDT stared up at the German Me-262 diving directly toward him. From the nose compartment of his B-26 bomber, he had a clear view. The yellow-nose jet bore in straight at his aircraft and then passed close in front, without firing his cannon. There was little time to enjoy this "good fortune." Ahead, another six-plane formation seemed to erupt as a B-26 exploded and crashed into two others. The intercom came alive with shouting gunners calling out enemy aircraft.

On April 26, 1945, the 17th Bombing Group made an all-out effort to destroy the German airbase at Lechfield, home of the new German jet fighter, the Me-262. With an incredible airspeed outclassing Allied fighters, these aircraft were proving a serious threat. This raid was opposed by large numbers of the deadly Me-262s and proved to be the most costly of the war for the 17th. When his ship landed at home base Brandt learned that most of his squadron had not returned. He and his crew said a prayer of thanks for having survived this battle, which turned out to be their last combat mission of the war.

Years later Ed Brandt learned that one of the German pilots involved in the Lechfield battle had written an account of his part in the action. He described how he had dived on a formation of B-26s only to have his 20mm cannon malfunction when he pressed the trigger. This was probably the occurrence that saved Brandt and his fellow crewmen on that day. He could only reiterate his prayer of thanks to God for another miraculous occurrence that had enabled him to survive one of the most dangerous missions of the war.[288]

When I was in great need, he saved me. Be at rest once more, O my soul, for the LORD has been good to you. For you, O LORD, have delivered my soul from death. ~Psalm 116:6–8

P-51 Mustang fighter.
(U. S. Dept. of Defense)

P-47 Thunderbolt fighter.
(U. S. Dept. of Defense)

Repetitive Training

CHIP BORK was on his second strafing run trying to knock out a German tank when *"all hell broke loose."* Ground fire ripped through his P-47 fighter, wounding him severely and starting a fire in the cockpit. In a state of shock and semiconsciousness, he was only vaguely aware of the next few moments. His first clear recollection was a loud pop as he looked up to see his parachute open above him and himself floating free of his spiraling aircraft.

Later, witnesses helped him piece together what happened. When the fire started he turned his plane upside down, unlatched and opened the canopy. He unfastened his seat belt and pushed the stick forward to safely bail out. Then he pulled the rip cord to deploy his chute. He remembered none of this. He was thankful that he had his Catechism and Prayer Book in his pocket at the time, and felt that it was *"a miracle that I survived."* He was also thankful for the training that had prepared him for this moment:

> *I would quarrel about doing certain things over and over, things that I felt I already knew how to do, but my instructor insisted that I do them again just to make sure that I understood and got it right. I have often thought back to the day when I was shot down over St. Lo, and the subconscious actions I took to save my life in that emergency situation. I must give credit to heroes of mine, those very farsighted Pilot Training Instructors, for the grueling and repetitive training they put me through. I shall never forget them.*[289]

This story is a tribute to demanding teachers everywhere. I have the same affectionate respect for my high school algebra teacher, Mr. S. L. Lemmon. He was the toughest teacher I ever had. Under his wary eye generations of students did the hard, repetitive work necessary for a solid grounding in algebra. We are blessed to have educators who set high standards and who have the moral courage to hold themselves and their students to them. Such teachers are surely doing God's work in this world and richly deserve our appreciation.

> Not many of you should presume to be teachers, my brothers, because you know that we who teach will be judged more strictly. ~James 3:1

Sixty-two Missions and an Outcast

A WORLD WAR II pilot told a sad story about a member of his squadron. He called him Captain "Johnson" for sake of anonymity. This man suffered extensive injury from a bad parachute landing when his aircraft was shot down on a bombing mission over Germany. With sixty-two missions to his credit, he only needed three more to go home. However, he refused to fly again. This became a source of great controversy within the squadron where most felt that, *"If I have to fly, then he has to fly."* This festered for a while until one day he was gone.

Fifteen years later the squadron had a reunion, and our storyteller relates what happened when a certain member appeared:

> *Who should walk in but our old friend Captain Johnson. No one spoke to him. Many just turned their backs on him. I felt sorry for him. But while we were risking our necks over Germany and losing good men, he was curled up and whining under a blanket. He flew with us, but not a single man considered him to be one of us.*[290]

I understand the attitude of these airmen who served their country so honorably, and I intend no criticism of them. They earned the right to feel how they felt. I relate this story simply to illustrate the contrast between the value systems of our world and that of God's kingdom. In this world Captain Johnson flew sixty-two missions, fell apart, and became an outcast. In the world of our Savior, Jesus Christ, he could have done the wrong thing sixty-two times and still have had a way to reclaim his status as "one of us." Repentance would be required, but forgiveness would be certain.

Then Peter came to Jesus and asked, "Lord, how many times shall I forgive my brother when he sins against me? Up to seven times?" Jesus answered, "I tell you, not seven times, but seventy-seven times." ~Matthew 18:21–22

The Greatest Compliment

THE MISSION WAS a navigator's nightmare. The bombing run to Karlsruhe should have been an eight-hour trip, but bad weather forced the formation to make frequent course changes. Frank Federici was lead navigator for a flight of six B-24s and felt that they were "touring Germany." By the time they were over the target he was hearing complaints from the other aircraft that fuel and oxygen were in short supply.

At this point Federici recommended a complete departure from the planned route that had been ordered for the mission. He took his lead aircraft down to an altitude of 500 feet and headed straight for home base, ignoring orders. At such low altitude he had to do the navigating job of his life. Cloud formations required constant maneuvering and new sets of calculations for each course change. He said later, *"I could have used one hundred twenty seconds in a minute instead of sixty!"*[291]

Federici reached his base in England with ten minutes fuel to spare. However, instead of congratulations, he and his pilot received reprimands for violating their orders. He was almost too tired to care:

> I decided that sleep was more important (than eating) and started walking in the snow toward our Quonset hut. As I walked toward the hut, I was tempted numerous times to lie in the snow and go to sleep. However, I continued to walk to the hut, when suddenly I was confronted by another navigator who caught up to me and said, "Thanks a lot, Frank." He was one of the navigators in an aircraft flying in our six-ship formation back to base. I have considered his "thank you" as the greatest compliment received during my seventy-nine years! He was thanking me for saving his life.[292]

To have your work judged positively by someone you respect is one of life's great rewards. We should also remember, however, that our work can have eternal consequences as well. Although our salvation in Jesus Christ is guaranteed, when our work for him is judged worthy, we will be rewarded. Someday, every one of us will want to hear our Savior say, *"Well done, good and faithful servant"* (Matthew 25:21, 23).

The fire will test the quality of each man's work. If what he has built survives, he will receive his reward. If it is burned up, he will suffer loss; he himself will be saved, but only as one escaping through the flames. ~1 Corinthians 3:13–15

The Hunters

AFTER THE BATTLE OF BRITAIN, Royal Air Force Spitfires and Hurricanes were usually employed as escorts for Allied bombers over Europe. Lt. Johnnie Johnson flew many of these missions in his Spitfire, and by the end of the war was the highest-scoring RAF pilot. He made some interesting observations about his fellow aviators:

> It is fascinating to watch the reactions of the various pilots. They fall into two broad categories . . . the hunters and the hunted. The majority of the pilots, once they have seen their names on the board, walk out to their Spitfires for a pre-flight check and a word or two with their ground crews. They tie on their mae-wests, check their maps, study the weather forecast and have a last-minute chat with their leaders or wingmen. These are the hunters.
>
> The hunted . . . turned to their escape kits and made quite sure that they were wearing the tunic with the silk maps sewn into a secret hiding-place; that they had at least one oilskin-covered packet of French francs, and two if possible; that they had a compass and a revolver and sometimes specially made clothes to assist their activities once they were shot down.[293]

Johnnie Johnson obviously put himself in the "hunter" category. He may be implying that he was braver than some of his fellow pilots, or at the very least more optimistic. Maybe he and the other hunters just didn't have very good imaginations. Whatever the case, I think that we can assume that these pilots were more positive in their actions and more effective in the air.

Focusing on the negative has never been good for pilots or for anyone else. Jesus Christ came into this world to direct our attention in a new and positive direction. He brought the message that we can't work our way to God by eliminating the negatives in our lives. We will never be good enough on our own. By simply accepting God's forgiveness through his Son, we take the one positive step necessary to gain a place in his kingdom. We continue this positive focus as we live in the body of Christ and joyfully share the truth of this gospel message.

Therefore no one will be declared righteous in his sight by observing the law; rather, through the law we become conscious of sin. But now a righteousness from God, apart from law, has been made known, to which the Law and the Prophets testify. This righteousness from God comes through faith in Jesus Christ to all who believe. ~Romans 3:20–22

249

The Men Were Noble

THE ROUTINE STARTED at 2:30 a.m. The B-17 crewmen stumbled out of bed, dressed in the cold, and plodded through the rain and mud to breakfast. Then they began assembling in the briefing room. Someone yelled, *"Attention!"* as the commanding officer walked down the center aisle and mounted the stage. Everyone finally came awake as the mission for the day was announced.

Jon Schueler paid close attention to every detail. As navigator for the *Bad Check* (named in hope that she would always come back) he carried a lot of responsibility on his shoulders. After the pre-mission briefing he and the rest of his crew climbed aboard their aircraft.

> *As long as the momentum of activity was going, everything would be OK. I felt the excitement, the blood coursing through my veins. I felt the intensity of it. We would start the engines reving and I'd lay out my charts and have everything ready, oxygen mask, parachute. Check all the dials. Computer, pencils, Weems plotter. Milt Conver would be making wisecracks. We could feel the plane being readied, we could feel the vibration of readiness of men moving back and forth at their dials, controls and guns. Everything was OK. We were a team and we knew each other and loved each other. The men were truly noble.[294]*

These feelings are not uncommon in combat. You grow very close to others when you share an important mission and some degree of hardship or danger. Twenty-five years after having such an experience, I rediscovered the same kind of intense feeling for others in the body of Christ. There is no mission that brings men and women closer together than working to bring others into the family of God. Everyone contributes unique gifts to the task, and every gift is prized by all. The key ingredient that holds this great and noble family together is the love of Jesus Christ for every member, which all the members share freely with each other.

But in fact God has arranged the parts in the body, every one of them, just as he wanted them to be. If they were all one part, where would the body be? As it is, there are many parts, but one body. ~1 Corinthians 12:18–20

The Missions Had to Be Flown

ARLY IN THE WAR scattered British and Australian forces, often with obsolete equipment, tried to oppose the Japanese advance through East Asia. Many Royal Air Force pilots were still flying biplanes that proved easy prey to the modern Japanese Zero fighters. As comrades failed to return from missions, it became ever harder for the survivors to keep going up. One airman commented on his own feelings and on a fellow pilot's determination to oppose the enemy invasion of Sumatra:

> *We were terribly fearful, some of us literally shaking . . . But the missions had to be flown and it was then that I saw real valour . . . not just flashes of it but as a part of every member's daily life. A special bravery seemed to be generated, where fear was greatest . . . The courage that we saw was in the calm before the storm, of very young men . . . doing something that petrified them . . . But they did it because it was their duty.[295]*
>
> *I think of Bob's sheer guts on that day only with deep admiration. He was going on a mission . . . to find a Japanese sea force, to try to break through its fighter and anti-aircraft screens and bomb it. Scared stiff like everyone who had to make such attacks, he was so overwrought that he actually vomited on the tarmac as he went to climb into his Hudson. But he just vomited, shook his head, climbed aboard and took off.[296]*

Could anything be more difficult than finding courage in a losing cause? These airmen knew that defeat was inevitable, but continued to find the will to do their duty. Many times we, as Christians, are discouraged by far less formidable risks. We think that certain people are hopeless and that any effort on our part to share the gospel would be futile. When we hear moral issues being discussed and sense we're in the minority, we sometimes feel that our solitary voice will have no effect. At these times, we need the courage of these RAF pilots, who were able to leave the bigger picture in the hands of a higher authority while focusing on their individual responsibilities. Courage is action in the face of possible embarrassment or failure.

I tell you the truth, anyone who has faith in me will do what I have been doing. He will do even greater things than these, because I am going to the Father.
~John 14:12

The Real Hero

THE CHAPLAIN was up before dawn with the aircrews, sharing their last moments before another mission. He listened to the briefings and assignments, and followed their route laid out with tape across the map. As he looked at the young airmen he was almost overcome with feelings of love and fear. He knew them well, and he admired and loved them deeply. He also knew that, *"For some of them it was the dawning of their last morning in this world."*[297] For all of these men he was a link to home, and, as always, he gravely received their messages. This morning he was deeply moved when one man asked him to, *"Tell my mother I know she is the real hero."*[298]

The chaplain pondered the bond between mothers and sons and concluded that both were soldiers with difficult roles to play in a difficult war, but . . .

> *The greatest soldiers are the mothers of men. While men go to battle-fronts mothers endure a bloodless martyrdom. Theirs is fortitude's braver part, for their hearts, life-laced and "love-laced" to their sons, must endure the hungering interval when human hate makes them childless in motherhood, long before they face the sorrows of death.*[299]

The chaplain's thoughts turned to history's greatest example of a heroic woman, the mother of our Savior. *"Enduring her sufferings, by her compassion, Mary then became the strength and consolation for sorrowing mothers through the ages. She who had seen the shadow of death over His whole life from the crib to the Cross, could do nothing to help her dying Son."*[300] May God bless all mothers who have to stand aside as their sons go into harm's way. They send them into the world with the gift that is the most Christ-like of all gifts: a mother's love.

When Jesus saw his mother there, and the disciple whom he loved standing nearby, he said to his mother, "Dear woman, here is your son," and to the disciple, "Here is your mother." ~John 19:26–27

We Trusted in Prayer

AFTER A PARTICULARLY harrowing mission through heavy flak Tommy Hayes landed his P-51 at home base in England. He described what happened as his aircraft finally rolled to a stop: *"I climbed out of the cockpit, got on my hands and knees in the mud to kiss the good earth and thank the Lord."*[301] When his crew chief realized what he was doing, he got down beside him and joined in.

Hayes was a veteran pilot from Portland, Oregon. He had seen action early in the Pacific flying P-40s and had been with the 357th Fighter Group in England since its first combat mission. He was a little older and wiser than many of his fellow pilots, eventually rising to command a squadron of P-51s flying escort missions deep into Germany. He saw more than his share of aerial combat and downed eight German aircraft. His family at home was never far from his mind.

> *When I left the States for Europe, I left my wife and daughter of sixteen months. We each had a job to do and we talked about that. I know the stress was greater for her than for me. She wrote me a letter every day. We lived our lives together by our letters. It helped when I shot down a plane and the local paper or radio had a story or a few words on the local boy, Major Hayes. If she hadn't had a letter for a week or more, at least on this date she knew I was okay. I was not a drinking man. We both trusted in prayer.*[302]

A priest once used a simple blackboard diagram to illustrate how a couple can strengthen their relationship. He drew two separate lines from the bottom of the board converging into one point at the top. The lines represent our separate lives and can, in fact, go in any direction. However, if both parties in a marriage continually strive to grow nearer to Christ at the top of the board, they will also grow closer to each other, as their lines converge. This has been an enduring image in our marriage as my wife and I have tried to keep our focus on this common goal, to be one in love and service to our Lord.

> So they are no longer two, but one. Therefore what God has joined together, let man not separate. ~Matthew 19:6

What Would I Do?

MAX WOOLLEY bailed out of his P-38 fighter at 18,000 feet. Wounded by ground fire on the way down, his descent seemed to take forever. His parachute was riddled by bullets and almost useless by the time he hit the ground hard near Charleroi, Belgium. In a dazed state, fully expecting to be captured, he was instead picked up by a Belgian family and taken to their home. Woolley stated later that during this time, *"Prayer was the greatest source of inspiration for me . . . It gave me strength, consolation, and a way to talk, to plead for help and life itself."*[303] The Belgian family hid him from the Germans and gave him all the care that they could:

> *They sacrificed their safety and gave me the best they had to offer, a place to rest, food from their sparse pantry, wet towels to subdue the stifling heat from being crammed into an eighteen-inch high enclosure and to wipe the blood and infected pus that oozed from my wounds for almost two months.*
>
> *I've often asked myself, 'Could I befriend a bloody, dirty, wounded man whom I had never before seen, share my scant supply of food, jeopardize the safety and welfare of myself and my family?'*[304]

Each of us would have to agonize over this question. What would I do? Looking at our "WWJD" (What would Jesus do?) bracelets, we know what we *should* do. Jesus answered the question emphatically while explaining the phrase "love your neighbor" to a legal expert. He told the story of the man who was robbed and beaten beside the road. He was passed by a priest and a Levite, both "religious" men, who did not stop. A Samaritan, even though considered a foreigner, did stop to render assistance. Even though we know that we should follow the example of the Samaritan, few of us would find the courage within ourselves to do what the Belgian family did in this story. There is only one source of such strength, and that is Jesus Christ himself. When we prayerfully ask, "What would Jesus do?" we can also expect him to give us the resources to do it.

"Which of these three do you think was a neighbor to the man who fell into the hands of robbers?" The expert in the law replied, "The one who had mercy on him." Jesus told him, "Go and do likewise." ~Luke 10:36–37

To Stay at Home

THE GREAT RADIO commentator Edward R. Murrow announced soberly, *"Berlin last night wasn't a pretty sight. In about thirty-five minutes it was hit with about three times the amount of stuff that ever came down on London in a night-long blitz. This is a calculated, remorseless campaign of destruction."*[305] He was reporting what he actually saw while accompanying a Lancaster four-engine bomber on a nighttime raid over the German capital.

The citizens of Berlin lived in the middle of this remorseless campaign for two years. Anti-aircraft guns, searchlights, and fighter aircraft provided a strong defense for the city, and, early on, inflicted heavy losses on the enemy formations daring to venture this deeply into Germany. Still, the bombers came, and the people of the city had to cope with the mounting destruction. After every raid, they did whatever they could to repair their homes and neighborhoods. One Berliner poignantly tried to explain what kept them going:

> We repair because we must repair. Because we couldn't live another day longer if one forbade us the repairing. If they destroy our living room, we move into the kitchen. If they knock the kitchen apart, we move over into the hallway. If only we can stay 'at home.' The smallest corner of 'at home' is better than any palace in some strange place.[306]

We can't understand an "air war" or bombing campaign without considering the effects on all the human beings involved. Most of this month has been seen from the perspective of the airmen flying their hazardous missions. We must also remember that the destruction on the ground was even more horrendous. By understanding and remembering the suffering on both sides we are bound to more soberly consider how to resolve our present and future conflicts. War has always and will always exact a terrible price in human suffering.

> David said to Solomon: "My son, I had it in my heart to build a house for the Name of the LORD my God. But this word of the LORD came to me: 'You have shed much blood and have fought many wars. You are not to build a house for my Name, because you have shed much blood on the earth in my sight.'"
> ~1 Chronicles 22:7–8

Shipbuilders at work.
(Franklin D. Roosevelt Presidential Library)

AUGUST
War on the Home Front

A S AMERICA witnessed the disappointing aftermath of World War I and struggled through the Great Depression of the 1930s, a strong isolationism gripped the nation. Even into 1941 public sentiment remained strong against involvement in the wars spreading over Europe and the Far East. This attitude changed completely and irrevocably when Japan bombed Pearl Harbor. After President Franklin Roosevelt gave his famous speech to a joint session of Congress declaring December 7, 1941, *"a date which will live in infamy,"* Congress voted unanimously, except for one vote, to approve a declaration of war. America entered the war with a complete unity of purpose.

The war effort soon touched every strata of the nation's economic and social life. The military draft had the most obvious and profound effect. By the end of the war more than ten million men were inducted into the armed forces. The absence of these men affected families and businesses in many ways. Women not only had to take care of their households, but they also had to take over many essential jobs. To attract women into the industrial workforce, a campaign was launched featuring "Rosie the Riveter," an attractive, patriotic, and efficient assembly line worker. Eventually, more than three million women worked in war production plants.[307]

The war consumed vast amounts of the country's agricultural and industrial output. Production of automobiles, houses, and appliances almost came to a halt, as assembly lines were turned over to tanks, trucks, ships, and ammunition. The Ford Motor Company created the world's largest assembly line in Willow Run, Michigan, where the production of B-24 Liberator bombers reached 428 per month.

Ship construction was revolutionized under the leadership of Henry J. Kaiser. Abandoning the traditional keel-up procedure, Kaiser introduced a modular construction method where sections of a new ship were constructed away from the final assembly site. These large sections were then brought together and welded into finished ships. By the end of the war, sixteen U.S. shipyards had delivered 2,580 Liberty ships, the largest production run of a single ship in history.[308] Overall, the United States increased its shipbuilding capacity by more than 1,200 percent, producing 5,200 naval and cargo vessels during the war.

By 1944 the War Department was consuming 40 percent of the gross national product, and many commodities such as meat, sugar, butter, coffee, gasoline, tires, and clothing were being rationed to the civilian populace. Ration books were issued with colored stamps worth different point values. Items were displayed on store shelves with labels indicating their cost in cash and ration points. A customer could make a purchase if he had enough stamps and cash, *if* there was something on the shelf. Gasoline was probably the most critical item with most people receiving coupons for three gallons per week. To supplement food supplies, Victory Gardens sprang up everywhere, as individual families joined the effort to feed the nation.

In spite of the hardships of the war, and perhaps to some extent because of them, there was a remarkable unity across the country. The entertainment industry vigorously supported the troops and the government's War Bond campaigns. Churches rallied behind the war effort, as nearly every American was convinced of the moral rightness of the Allied cause. More than ten thousand chaplains were provided to the armed forces and countless ministries were initiated to support the troops at home and overseas. The nation's leaders and citizens prayed for the safety of their loved ones and for victory in the greatest struggle in history. Never before or after has America been so united.

Face to the Coal

DURING THE DARKEST days of the war there was trouble in England's coal mines. Workers were leaving the mines to enlist in the army. Many young men wanted to be fighting in the front lines, not digging coal out of the ground, and coal production was in jeopardy when the nation needed it most. Winston Churchill went to the mines to deliver a speech and to give the miners a vision of the future:

He pictured for them what would take place when the Nazis were beaten and the war was over. He said there would be a great parade honoring all who sacrificed for victory. First, there would be the Royal Navy sailors who had battled Hitler at sea. Then would come the Royal Air Force pilots who had fought the Luftwaffe in the skies. Then would come the Royal Army soldiers who had fought at Dunkirk. Last of all would come a long line of sweat-stained, soot-streaked men in miner's caps. Someone would cry from the crowd, *"Where were you during the dark days of our struggle?"* And from ten thousand throats would come the answer, *"We were deep in the earth, with our faces to the coal."*[309]

Churchill's vision was powerful. With tear-streaked faces the miners went back to work with the firm belief that every piece of coal they brought out of the earth was vital to the survival of their nation. They knew that their work might be mundane and seem unglamorous, but that it was necessary to the larger cause. This story has been used many times to inspire others in addition to these miners. We know that, as Christians, our service to God can often take mundane forms. It was Jesus himself who washed the feet of his disciples. He did this to focus their attention, and ours, on service to other people. He might be telling us to keep "our faces to the needs of others," and to rest in the knowledge that there is no such thing as mundane service in his name.

Now that I, your Lord and Teacher, have washed your feet, you also should wash one another's feet. I have set you an example that you should do as I have done for you. ~John 13:14–15

Prayer and Sacrifice

MARY ALICE PINNEY was twelve years old when the Second World War began. She vividly recalled President Roosevelt's radio address declaring that December 7th would forever be *"a date that will live in infamy."* Her most vivid recollection of the war was the united effort that she saw on the home front:

> *One of the most important things I have ever seen in the world it was something I saw then that I haven't seen in any war since. Any church, any synagogue, any place that held any religious practice, what-so-ever, sent prayers, and I mean, everywhere for the people fighting in the war. And it never stopped until long after the war. I have never seen any kind of support the way our town supported the troops in World War II. The home front sent food, supplies, and clothes, anything we had on hand to help them. We were rationed painfully, it didn't matter how rich or poor you were, everyone was sharing in the loss.[310]*

In *The Screwtape Letters,* C. S. Lewis masterfully presents letters from a senior devil to his younger nephew instructing him on the fine points of winning humans away from the "Enemy" (God). He had some startling insights about why war might not be as good for the devil's cause as might be expected:

> *I must warn you not to hope too much from a war. Of course war is entertaining. The immediate fear and suffering of the humans is a legitimate and pleasing refreshment for our myriads of toiling workers. We may hope for a good deal of cruelty and unchastity. But, if we are not careful, we shall see thousands turning in this tribulation to the Enemy, while tens of thousands who do not go so far as that will nevertheless have their attention diverted from themselves to values and causes which they believe to be higher than the self.[311]*

Mary Alice Pinney has illuminated C. S. Lewis' point. During the trials of wartime, many Americans did come closer to God and to each other through mutual prayer and sacrifice. Fortunately, war isn't necessary to bring us to this condition. Whenever we put our individual concerns aside in support of a worthy goal, we have the potential of drawing closer to others and to God.

> What is more, I consider everything a loss compared to the surpassing greatness of knowing Christ Jesus my Lord, for whose sake I have lost all things.
> ~Philippians 3:8

Stockings

WITH A "War Ration Book" families were allowed to buy limited amounts of food, clothing, shoes, coffee, tires, gasoline, and other essentials, based on the size of the family. People learned to use everything sparingly and to waste nothing. Even razor blades were re-sharpened. Butter was so scarce that a vegetable-oil substitute was invented, called *margarine*. Posters appeared in the stores saying, *"Do with less so they'll have enough."* The shortage of consumer goods was severe in all areas, but in one case affected women particularly. Lourelei Prior was a female defense worker in Fort Wayne, Indiana. She explained:

> We couldn't get stockings either—all the silk was used for parachutes and nylon hadn't been invented yet. Now, stockings didn't matter at the plant. There, all the gals wore tight clothing and pants and a hat and safety glasses—and no jewelry—because of the heavy machinery. But no gal or new bride wants to be seen in a skirt without stockings! So when I would go out with Herb, sometimes to make it look like I had on stockings, I would draw a black line up the back of my legs with an eyebrow pencil to make it look like I was wearing silk stockings.[312]

Like most Americans this woman took the shortages caused by the war with good humor and ingenuity, and made the best of what she had. She expressed the attitude of most civilians toward these hardships and gave us good advice for the present day:

> In our house we didn't grumble about the shortages . . . I had four brothers-in-law who were in the service. If giving up a little bit helped the boys "over there" and would bring them back sooner, it was fine with us . . . We just thanked God for what we did have.[313]

When times are good, be happy; but when times are bad, consider: God has made the one as well as the other. ~Ecclesiastes 7:14

North Platte Canteen

BY DECEMBER 1941 the east-west rail lines across the United States were filled with troop trains. A small group of citizens in the little village of North Platte, Nebraska, took note of this fact and decided to try to do something for all these servicemen passing through their town. On Christmas Day the first team of five volunteers waited at the depot with baskets of sandwiches and little bottles of cold milk. During the ten-minute stop, they moved along the train passing out these treats to the hungry and appreciative men crowded into the cars. Soon the whole town and surrounding region were involved in supporting the North Platte Canteen, which became famous for this unusual and unexpected hospitality. For the duration of the war, the little town of twelve thousand fed hundreds of thousands of troops passing through—without the benefit of government aid and in spite of food shortages and rationing.

One of the women who worked in the Canteen from the beginning was Elaine Wright. Her husband was a railroad employee, and her son was in the Navy. One day word spread throughout North Platte that Elaine had received the dreaded telegram informing her and her husband that their son had been killed in action. No one saw her for several days, until one morning she walked into the Canteen. There was a long and uncomfortable silence, as no one knew what to say to her. She finally said to them: *"I can't help my son, but I can help someone else's son."*[314]

Some wise person once said, *"You can be bitter, or you can be better."* Elaine Wright epitomized the "better" approach to dealing with grief. There is no more effective way to soothe your own pain than doing something for someone else. Seeking a higher purpose in service to others is the surest way to move beyond yourself and your grief.

> Your attitude should be the same as that of Christ Jesus: Who, being in very nature God, did not consider equality with God something to be grasped, but made himself nothing, taking the very nature of a servant. ~Philippians 2:5–7

Patience with Humanity

EARLY IN THE WAR Ernie Pyle went to North Africa as a correspondent. Already famous for his human-interest stories, he spent most of his time with troops in the front line, writing about the war from their perspective. He was able to report on the transition of these young Americans from civilians to warriors, and he conveyed his belief that they were adapting to the demands of combat and were measuring up well as soldiers. Speaking for them and himself, he wrote, *"The new war finally became the normal life to us."*[315] In one poignant article he focused on a profound change within himself, which he considered a "personal redemption":

> [There is] *a new patience with humanity that I've never known before. When you've lived with the unnatural mass cruelty that mankind is capable of inflicting upon itself, you find yourself dispossessed of the faculty for blaming one poor man for the triviality of his faults. I don't see how any survivor of war can ever be cruel to anything, ever again.*[316]

The reporter's inclination toward forgiveness of human faults and patience with others are healthy sentiments, and his message is a positive one. Those who have witnessed cruelty on a large scale should be especially averse to inflicting it on a personal level. However, I believe it would be a mistake to consider our own faults trivial when compared with the larger evils of war. War is a product of human weakness and reflects these "trivial" faults on a larger scale. In other words, we are all sinners, and our sin is what causes human conflict at the personal and the international level. Only when we fully accept this fact about ourselves can we understand our desperate need for a savior and redeemer.

Here is a trustworthy saying that deserves full acceptance: Christ Jesus came into the world to save sinners. ~1 Timothy 1:15

Comforting a Mother

USUALLY THE FOLKS at home did their best to cheer up their sons and daughters overseas. Occasionally, however, a soldier had to encourage a loved one back home. Chaplain Walter Hanley was serving in New Guinea when he learned that his mother in Ohio was extremely ill with little hope of recovery. He also had little hope of getting home on leave. He did his best to comfort her with a letter:

> *You have been a good mother to us all, and all that we children have we owe to you. With Clarence's and Papa's deaths, your ill-health for years and the depression, your life has been a hard one—and yet your faith & your prayers have given you the strength to go on. When the train pulled out of the station I think you knew you would never see me again, and your strength has encouraged me all of these months. If God asks of you this sacrifice—for my work was needed here for these boys, I know you will have the strength to make it. The other priests here said their masses, as I did, this morning for you, and I know Almighty God will care for you . . . Whatever good I may be able to do in the priesthood will be a testimony of your prayers and your struggles to bring me there . . . I know that Papa and Clarence are waiting for you and that our prayers will be for you every day until you join them in heaven.[317]*

This letter is an inspiring insight into a strong family. This strength obviously derives from a mother's faith that has brought her family close to God and to each other. With this faith they were able to deal with the hardships of war and pain of death with confidence and hope. Faith and family remain the surest sources of strength to meet the constant challenges of this world.

> Children, obey your parents in the Lord, for this is right. "Honor your father and mother"—which is the first commandment with a promise—"that it may go well with you and that you may enjoy long life on the earth." Fathers, do not exasperate your children; instead, bring them up in the training and instruction of the Lord. ~Ephesians 6:1–4

Family Relationships

DURING THE WAR women on the home front took on new roles. Edith Sokol married Victor Speert in 1942 and moved from base to base with him fourteen times over the next two years. When Victor was deployed to Europe in 1944 Edith got a job in a day care center. Before long she was named director of the True Sisters Day Care Center in Cleveland. Her new responsibilities were important and challenging. In October 1945 she wrote to her husband about how she thought she was changing:

> Last night Mel and I were talking about some of the adjustments we'll have to make to our husbands' return. I must admit I'm not exactly the same girl you left—I'm twice as independent as I used to be and to top it off, I sometimes think I've become "hard as nails"— hardly anyone can evoke any sympathy from me. No one wants to hear my troubles and I don't want to hear theirs. Also—more and more I've been living as I want to and I don't see people I don't care about—I do as I d____ please. As a whole, I don't think my changes will affect our relationship, but I do think you'll have to remember that there are some slight alterations in me.[318]

Of necessity, many women became more independent during the war years. Large numbers left their homes to enter the workforce, representing a new phenomenon in our culture. Those women staying at home also became used to shouldering more responsibility and to making decisions on their own. In the decades since the war these trends have continued and have presented challenges within the family. Fortunately, even though the culture has changed, our guidelines for successful family relationships have not. The Bible continues to be our authority. God ordained that marriage should be a relationship of such depth that it reflects Christ's own all-consuming and sacrificial love for his church. In this sense it is a partnership between a husband and wife who love each other and submit to each other unselfishly and generously.

Submit to one another out of reverence for Christ. Wives, submit to your husbands as to the Lord . . . Husbands, love your wives, just as Christ loved the church and gave himself up for her to make her holy . . . each one of you also must love his wife as he loves himself, and the wife must respect her husband. ~Ephesians 5:21, 22, 25, 33

BUY WAR BONDS

War bond poster.
(National Archives)

World War II recruiting poster.
(National Archives)

Women working on a B-17 bomber.
(National Archives)

For Those Who Suffer

ROY CAMPANELLA was a baseball player during World War II and was one of the first African Americans to play in the major leagues. As catcher for the Brooklyn Dodgers, he played in five World Series and was a league All-Star eight times. In 1958 his career ended when he was paralyzed in an auto accident. While going to therapy every day at the Institute of Physical Medicine and Rehabilitation in New York City, he noticed a bronze plaque on the wall inscribed with a poem written by an unknown Confederate soldier. After reading it twice, he was filled with *"an inner glow that had me straining to grip the arms of my wheelchair."*[319]

A Creed For Those Who Have Suffered

I asked God for strength, that I might achieve.
I was made weak, that I might learn humbly to obey...
I asked for health, that I might do greater things.
I was given infirmity, that I might do better things...
I asked for riches, that I might be happy.
I was given poverty, that I might be wise...
I asked for power, that I might have the praise of men.
I was given weakness, that I might feel the need of God...
I asked for all things, that I might enjoy life.
I was given life, that I might enjoy all things...
I got nothing I asked for—but everything I had hoped for.
Almost despite myself, my unspoken prayers were answered.
I am, among men, most richly blessed![320]

If we can look at our trials in life as opportunities to grow closer to God and to be a more effective witness for him, then truly every trial can be a blessing, to ourselves and to others. The courage to adopt this attitude doesn't come from within. Only in Jesus Christ can we find the inner resources to lead such a life.

> That is why, for Christ's sake, I delight in weaknesses, in insults, in hardships, in persecutions, in difficulties. For when I am weak, then I am strong.
> ~2 Corinthians 12:10

I'll Wait for You Forever

COUPLES SEPARATED by the war were affected in different ways. Some could not stand the strain. Fortunately, some not only endured but even grew stronger. Relying on God and their faith, Ruth Kwall and Joseph Portnoy remained true to each other through a long engagement. When Joseph could get a three-day pass they were finally married in 1943. Ruth wrote a letter affirming where the strength in their relationship came from:

> I want to tell you again, more surely than ever, that no matter how long or hard the siege may be I'll wait for you forever. I know, and darling you must too, that God in heaven will guard this precious thing and help preserve it and us for a time when the world will need tangible examples to show it that war does not end things; that good, beautiful emotions live on forever. I'm nineteen, Joe, but I know deep down inside me that the emotion I feel, that we feel is older, is mature—that it has made me grow to more of the sort of person you'd have me be. War isn't funny and I know we'll be tested even further than we ever dreamed could be possible.[321]

Echoing these feelings, Joseph responded, *"You are wise to rely on your complete faith that everything will turn out right for us, and knowing that you think like that, I also feel free to exercise my faith."*[322] This couple is a living testament to a great spiritual truth: if two people strive to grow closer to God, they will inevitably grow closer together. As they put God at the center of their relationship, Ruth and Joseph Portnoy experienced a deepening of their love in spite of the hardships and separation of wartime.

And this is love: that we walk in obedience to his commands. As you have heard from the beginning, his command is that you walk in love. ~2 John 6

Miracle of Radio

WORLD WAR II was the first war in which radio played an important role in civilian and military communications. The science of sending code and voice transmissions through the airways was pioneered in the early 1900s, and the first commercial broadcast stations were licensed in the 1920s. One of the earliest practical uses for this new technology was communication with ships at sea, making the U.S. Navy an early and vigorous proponent of its military use. By the early 1940s commanders were able to stay in regular although sometimes tenuous contact with their ships and units around the globe. Within the civilian community, families gathered around their radio sets to be entertained and to hear the latest news of the war.

The following prayer was written by a well-known Navy chaplain in 1944 giving thanks for this marvelous invention:

Thanksgiving for Radio Communication

Infinite God, who hast founded the known upon the unknown, and hast hidden the secrets of Thy universe beneath the twin cloaks of silence and invisibility: Who has dared Man to divine the meaning that there lies hidden, and has made Man of such a disposition that he can find no satisfaction as long as there remains one unanswered question: We thank Thee for the mind and spirit, the indefatigable energy and the questing intelligence of those scientists and technicians in physics and electricity, who took Thy cosmic dare, and by the force of their insatiable curiosity and their persistent imagination made possible radio communication and brought forth from the silence of electricity the beauty of sound and from the invisibility of light the beauty of color. Thou who hearest our unspoken prayers across the unimaginable abyss of eternity; we thank Thee for all those who have helped Man to enter into communication with Man across the echoless miles with a wonder and fidelity that is akin to prayer. Amen.[323]

The final thought in this prayer is startling and thought provoking, comparing the communications of man through the ether with prayer to God. It is something to ponder.

> What other nation is so great as to have their gods near them the way the LORD our God is near us whenever we pray to him? ~Deuteronomy 4:7

Missing in Action

Marjorie and Rowland Gaunt were married in Cranston, Rhode Island, in August 1943. Within a few weeks, Rowland received his navigator's wings and assignment to a B-17 bomber squadron in England. In March 1944 Marjorie received the dreaded telegram informing her that her husband was missing in action. For months, she lived in the limbo of not knowing. She continued her letters and her prayers in spite of the agonizing uncertainty. In November, with dwindling hope, she wrote:

> *Wherever you are, I know you must feel my love for you. My love has grown stronger each day and it is just bursting for expression. I've told you many times how much I love you, and I am so thankful for that now . . . Please, darling . . . keep your eyes uplifted and trust in God. I've prayed continually for His protection over you and His guidance during these long trying months. I pray for Him to give you patience and to bless you and make you strong. Oh, that I might bear it for you. I would gladly die that you might come back to those that love you and live gloriously to serve humanity and God . . . Be strong, my darling. May God give you courage, patience and strength that will carry you triumphantly through your ordeals to lasting peace, gentleness and love.*[324]

Unfortunately, these prayers were not answered as Marjorie hoped they would be. Rowland was lost at sea in February 1944 when his B-17 was shot down off the coast of Denmark. It was not until 1945 that she was officially informed of his death by the War Department. Marjorie's courage and faithfulness sustained her during this long ordeal and are a strong witness to the power of faith in such a bleak time. Her prayers may not have been rewarded in this life as she had hoped, but we can rest in the assurance that God's will was accomplished and that this brave couple will triumphantly find lasting peace and love together in eternity.

And the two will become one flesh. So they are no longer two, but one. Therefore what God has joined together, let man not separate. ~Mark 10:8–9

Physical Separation

ERMAN SOUTHWICK was inducted into the Army in 1943 and served in Europe for most of the war. He was sustained during this separation by a lively correspondence with his wife, Flora, at home in Marietta, Ohio. Her words made a moving case that she and Erman were not really separated by the miles between them:

> *When I get a letter from you I try to make a mental picture of all the things you tell me and then knowing you as I do I work out just how you reacted to what you said and the expression on your face. It makes me feel so close to you and through every line of your letters is the assurance over and over again of your love and that gives me a safe warm feeling inside. You see, darling, I just love you so much, I don't really recognize any separation from you. They can separate us physically and that is pretty hard to take sometimes but when there is complete emotional and intellectual unity between two people to really separate them is impossible.*[325]

This couple demonstrates the biblical model of marriage: *"So they are no longer two, but one. Therefore what God has joined together, let man not separate"* (Matthew 19:6). Even though separated by time and distance, they remained united in spirit. The marriage relationship is intended to be an everlasting bond between a man and a woman reflecting the depth of our relationship with our Savior, Jesus Christ. With the words *"complete emotional and intellectual unity"* this young woman perfectly captures the essence of that higher unity promised by the apostle Paul. In one of the most moving passages of Scripture, we receive a vision of the spiritual unity in Jesus Christ that will prevail through every hardship:

For I am convinced that neither death nor life, neither angels nor demons, neither the present nor the future, nor any powers, neither height nor depth, nor anything else in all creation, will be able to separate us from the love of God that is in Christ Jesus our Lord. ~Romans 8:38–39

Pocket Prayers

IN 1941 THE Episcopal Church of the United States published a small booklet for soldiers and sailors that could be carried in their pockets wherever they went. It included an Order of Worship, Holy Communion, prayers, psalms, readings, and hymns. All these were selected to meet the needs of military men and women. Some of the prayers are especially poignant and universally relevant:[326]

For God's Help

Grant us, O Lord, in all our duties thy help, in all our perplexities thy counsel, in all our dangers thy protection, and in all our sorrows thy peace; for the sake of Jesus Christ our Saviour, Amen.

Grant us, Lord, we beseech thee, the spirit to think and do always such things as are right; that we, who cannot do any thing that is good without thee, may by thee be enabled to live according to thy will; through Jesus Christ our Lord. Amen.

For Fidelity

Teach us, good Lord, to serve thee as thou deservest; to give and not to count the cost; to fight and not to heed the wounds; to toil and not to seek for rest; to labour and not to ask for any reward, save that of knowing that we do thy will; through Jesus Christ our Lord. Amen.

For Loyalty

Almighty God, grant us thy gift of loyalty. For our homes, give us love and obedience; for our country, sacrifice and service; for our Church, reverence and devotion; and in everything make us true to thee; through thy Son, our Saviour Jesus Christ. Amen.

For Loyalty to Our Homes

Grant, O Lord, to those in the service of their country who have left wives and children at home, a steadfast loyalty through all the days of separation, that returning at length to their beloved they may know the joy of unbroken fidelity; through Jesus Christ our Lord. Amen.

The Lord has heard my cry for mercy; the Lord accepts my prayer. ~Psalm 6:9

Pride and Anguish

GABRIEL NAVARRO was a first-generation immigrant from Mexico living in Houston, Texas. His son, Porifirio, was a Marine corporal fighting somewhere in the Pacific. Mr. Navarro's letter to his son reflects the mixture of intense pride and anxiety felt by World War II parents:

It has been one year to the day that, courageous and optimistic, full of faith and love of country, you left our side to join the armed forces of America. The forces of Democracy and Liberty. Twelve months of absence, during which time our thoughts and my paternal affection have followed you step by step across an ocean full of dangers . . . My heart stops beating when I think of death extending its wings over your head.

The courage and enthusiasm which you demonstrated upon leaving us to answer your country's call, which needs the help of its children, filled me with satisfaction and pride. And you may be sure that your mother, who gave you life, also covers you with benedictions and prayers, just as your mother country covers you with its flag.[327]

I believe that the most difficult test of faith for any person is to have a son or daughter in a life-threatening situation. This anxiety is prolonged and even more acute during wartime, when duty calls the child to face danger over a long period of time. We might see the higher purpose and feel pride in their devotion to an important cause. Nevertheless, as the parents of today's military men and women can attest, the worry is still crushing. There is only one source of effective relief from this degree of anxiety, and that is our Savior, Jesus Christ. During his ministry he explained and modeled the perfect love that our heavenly Father has for his children. He is always there to ease our burdens and to take our anxieties upon himself. His constant care and concern is the ultimate source of comfort in this life and in the eternal future.

Look at the birds of the air; they do not sow or reap or store away in barns, and yet your heavenly Father feeds them. Are you not much more valuable than they? Who of you by worrying can add a single hour to his life? ~Matthew 6:26–27

Rationing

B^{Y EARLY} 1943 shortages of food, gasoline, and other war materiel were beginning to be felt throughout the nation. Renee Pike gave a sense of what it was like on the home front in letters to her husband, George:

Rosie the Riveter poster. (National Archives)

> *Boy, what I wouldn't give for a nice banana. But that is just wishful thinking. I don't think anyone in America has seen a banana for over six months . . . the civilian population is certainly feeling the shortage of food-stuffs now. Last week we didn't have a scratch of butter in the house from Monday until Friday . . . It's a lot worse on we people in the country than it is on the city folks. They can go out and get some kind of meat every day while we have plenty of meatless days up here. They can also stand in line for 2 or 3 hours for a pound of butter, but up here there are no lines as there is no butter . . . Yesterday I didn't take any meat . . . because I'm sick of the same thing. You see, the thing that they have the most of is sausages but people can't keep eating the same thing every day.*[328]

Since our more recent wars in Vietnam and the Middle East have produced so much controversy, many are amazed at the national unity evidenced during World War II. This letter gives us an insight into how that unity came in large part from the sense of shared sacrifice by both the military and civilian populace. Every American had his or her part to play. Our subsequent armed conflicts have not touched most of the nation other than our military servicemen and their families. Somehow, we have been involved in wars where large numbers of our citizens have had no underlying perception that the nation's survival was at stake. If we are going to send our sons and daughters to war, it should be a matter of our survival as a nation, and the effort should involve sacrifice on the part of every American.

Has any other people heard the voice of God speaking out of fire, as you have, and lived? Has any god ever tried to take for himself one nation out of another nation, by testings, by miraculous signs and wonders, by war, by a mighty hand and an outstretched arm, or by great and awesome deeds. . . ?
~Deuteronomy 4:33–34

Sex Rank

MEN ARE GENERALLY clueless about what women are thinking. One anonymous member of the British Women's Auxiliary Air Force revealed some startling insights into her own thoughts about what she termed, *"The Great Man-Chase."*

> *To get a man is not sufficient. It's easy to get a man. In fact it's difficult not to. The desirable qualities are rank, wings, looks, money, youth in that order. Rank is unbelievably important . . . the height of sex-rank is commission and wings. Higher commission, the better. Sergeant pilots and ground commissions tie for second place. This includes Army officers. Ground stripes come a poor third. In terms of "looks" I include charm, personality, etc. This counts only as a narrow comparison viz Pilot Officer A is better than Pilot Officer B because he is more charming, but we'd rather go out with Pilot Officer B who is not charming, than with Sergeant C who is (and he's good looking too).[329]*

It's hard to know how serious these comments were meant to be. I tend to think that this young girl from a bygone era was having some fun with her readers. However, there is clearly some truth revealed in this little essay. In *The Screwtape Letters*, C. S. Lewis also gives us some truth about sexual attraction in his own unique tongue-in-cheek fashion. We hear the older devil instructing his nephew on the physical type of woman best suited for his "patient":

> *This question is decided for us by spirits far deeper down in the Lowerarchy than you and I. It is the business of these great masters to produce in every age a general misdirection of what may be called sexual "taste." They do this by working through the small circle of popular artists, dressmakers, actresses, and advertisers who determine the fashionable type. The aim is to guide each sex away from those members of the other with whom spiritually helpful, happy, and fertile marriages are most likely.[330]*

The ironic humor in this passage makes us laugh, until we realize the seriousness of the truth being presented. We have an adversary seeking to direct our attention away from those qualities in others most beneficial to our spiritual health and long-term happiness. When we are drawn to the superficial and trivial aspects of appearance and personality, we pass up the opportunity to find deeper relationships based on character. This insight is important in our friendships, but is absolutely critical to our selection of potential lifelong partners.

> Her children arise and call her blessed; her husband also, and he praises her: "Many women do noble things, but you surpass them all." Charm is deceptive, and beauty is fleeting; but a woman who fears the LORD is to be praised.
> ~Proverbs 31:28–30

The Conductor

DENTON DABBS enlisted in the Naval Air Corps in 1942. His hometown was Chattanooga, Tennessee, and his first assignments were to bases in Alabama during the different stages of his training. After a few weeks at Cortland, he spent three months at Montgomery for pre-flight instruction, and then ended up at Decatur for flight school. All these towns lay along the Southern Railway's main line from Memphis to Chattanooga. On weekend leaves he had the way to get home, if not the funds to pay for all the trips he would have liked. This problem was unexpectedly solved on his first trip.

Soon after boarding the train at Cortland the conductor observed his uniform and asked him if he was going home on leave. Denton told him that he was. The conductor then told him to keep his ticket, that he might want to use it again. The same conductor extended that privilege as long as the train rides continued. Denton Dabbs would never forget this small kindness.

> I still remember the old gentleman who was the conductor on that train and how nice he was to me. He made his job pleasant by being friendly with all of the passengers. I can still picture his face and his conductor's uniform with shiny brass buttons and the little bill-cap he wore on his head. Somehow he knew I was just a kid in a topsy-turvy world torn apart by the war, going home to see someone I loved. He might have had kids of his own out there somewhere, but somehow he knew that little piece of paper I held in my hand was important to me and maybe I would get another chance to visit home. He was a kind old gentleman and I shall always remember him.[331]

Jesus told his disciples that he would remember those in heaven who were kind to him when he was in need. His listeners wondered: What could they possibly do to help the Son of God? We wonder the same thing and are not even sure how we would recognize him if we saw him. Jesus gave us the simple answer. We serve him when we serve those we meet every day.

I tell you the truth, whatever you did for one of the least of these brothers of mine, you did for me. ~Matthew 25:40

The Dream

IN DECEMBER 1943 Jennie Cesternino dreamed of her son, Leonard, who at that time was fighting in Italy. She described the dream in a letter to him:

> You know son I'm feeling happy today. The reason is I dreamed about you last night and I saw you very plain in my dreams and that made me very happy. It was just like really seeing you.
>
> I dreamed you came in from work from Tony's and you came in all smiles and you said to me Ma you better send my pants to the cleaners because I have a date for tonight.
>
> It really made me happy to see you even though it was only a dream . . . [332]

Unfortunately, Leonard was mortally wounded in action at about this time. The family believes that his death occurred on the night of his mother's dream. Perhaps this is one of those tragic coincidences that make an interesting story. Or, could this be an example of God's amazing grace, giving a mother and son a last reunion? I prefer to believe the latter. After being separated by time and distance for many months, Mrs. Cisternino and Leonard were given a moment together in anticipation of a greater reunion to come. The poet, Robert Browning, described his faith that he would be together again with his beloved wife in heaven:

> For sudden the worst turns the best to the brave.
> The black minute's at end,
> And the elements' rage, the fiend voices that rave,
> Shall dwindle, shall blend,
> Shall change, shall become first a peace out of pain.
> Then a light, then thy breast,
> O thou soul of my soul! I shall clasp thee again,
> And with God be the rest![333]

Brothers, we do not want you to be ignorant about those who fall asleep, or to grieve like the rest of men, who have no hope. We believe that Jesus died and rose again and so we believe that God will bring with Jesus those who have fallen asleep in him. ~1 Thessalonians 4:13–14

The Risen Soldier

FRANCIS SPELLMAN, the Archbishop of New York and later Cardinal, hated the war and its powers of destruction. At times it seemed to him that God's kingdom of love on Earth was almost at the point of being overwhelmed. He felt that this blanket of darkness was in danger of covering the planet, unless mankind could learn the lesson of peace from the soldiers doing the fighting. He saw these brave young men and women as Christ-like figures, willingly exposing themselves to death in the hope that something good would grow from their sacrifice. He grew to love and respect these soldiers and wrote a moving poem in tribute to them and the cause for which they had to fight:

I am the risen soldier; though I die
I shall live on and, living, still achieve
My country's mission—Liberty in truth
And truth in Charity. I am aware
God made me for this nobler flight and fight,
A higher course than any I had deemed
Could ever be; and having found my course,
Whether I ground my plane on the home field
Or plunge a flaming banner from the skies,
I shall not turn again to petty things,
Nor change my plan of life till God has sealed
My papers with His seal. And if it be
My blood should mingle reverently with Christ's,
His Son's, in this my final missioning,
Shall I not whisper with my dying breath—
"Lord, it is sweet to die—as it were good
To live, to strive—for these United States,
Which, in Your wisdom, you have willed should be
A beacon to the world, a living shrine
Of Liberty and Charity and Peace."[334]

We can only pray that our nation continues to fulfill God's purpose as a beacon of freedom to the world, and that America will always be worthy of such a prayer.

> But he was pierced for our transgressions, he was crushed for our iniquities; the punishment that brought us peace was upon him, and by his wounds we are healed. ~Isaiah 53:5

Our Love Is of God

ISABEL ALDEN and Maurice Kidder were students together at the University of New Hampshire. They were married in 1935, the year Maurice graduated. He attended a theological seminary in Boston and entered the Army as a chaplain when the war broke out. Separated for three years, Isabel wrote countless letters. On hearing the news of the Normandy invasion, her sense of danger was heightened, as well as her faith in the relationship between God, her husband, and herself. At that fearful time she wrote:

> I have thousands of things I could say right now. I am about to take the train for Boston . . . for I simply feel I have to go someplace where I can worship . . . We shall be closer than ever, I feel sure. Do not lose courage, and do everything the best possible that you can. I know you will be a tower of strength to your men. I know too that God will be with you, not in the sense of miraculously taking care of your physical body, but taking care of your spirit so that it can withstand whatever comes upon it.
>
> I am not alarmed. I am excited. I am relieved with a terrible relief. I am afraid, but I know your fear is infinitely worse than mine. I love you to the utmost that I am capable of, and our love is of God. Be with God, and you are with me, as I am with you.[335]

From a dark time in our history Isabel has given us a witness to the power of a sustaining faith. She was confident in her husband's love because she knew that that love was from God and was blessed by God. With God at the center of a relationship, we can be assured that it will remain strong through every trial. When our love for God is intertwined with our love for another person, no physical event will impact our spiritual unity with that person or with our heavenly Father.

I have given them the glory that you gave me, that they may be one as we are one: I in them and you in me. May they be brought to complete unity to let the world know that you sent me and have loved them even as you have loved me. ~John 17:22–23

D-Day Prayer for the Troops

DURING THE EVENING of June 6, 1944, as American, British, and Canadian troops were fighting to establish a beachhead on the coast of Normandy, President Franklin Roosevelt went on the radio to lead the nation in a D-Day prayer:

> *My fellow Americans: Last night, when I spoke with you about the fall of Rome, I knew at that moment that troops of the United States and our allies were crossing the Channel in another and greater operation. It has come to pass with success so far.*
>
> *And so, in this poignant hour, I ask you to join me in prayer:*
>
> *Almighty God: Our sons, pride of our nation, this day have set upon a mighty endeavor, a struggle to preserve our Republic, our religion, and our civilization, and to set free a suffering humanity.*
>
> *Lead them straight and true; give strength to their arms, stoutness to their hearts, steadfastness in their faith.*
>
> *They will need Thy blessings. Their road will be long and hard. For the enemy is strong. He may hurl back our forces. Success may not come with rushing speed, but we shall return again and again; and we know that by Thy grace, and by the righteousness of our cause, our sons will triumph.*
>
> *They will be sore tried, by night and by day, without rest—until the victory is won. The darkness will be rent by noise and flame. Men's souls will be shaken with the violences of war.*
>
> *For these men are lately drawn from the ways of peace. They fight not for the lust of conquest. They fight to end conquest. They fight to liberate. They fight to let justice arise, and tolerance and goodwill among all Thy people. They yearn but for the end of battle, for their return to the haven of home.*
>
> *Some will never return. Embrace these, Father, and receive them, Thy heroic servants, into Thy kingdom.*[336]

Tomorrow, the president's prayer is continued for the nation.

You are not a God who takes pleasure in evil; with you the wicked cannot dwell. The arrogant cannot stand in your presence; you hate all who do wrong. ~Psalms 5:4–5

D-Day Prayer for the Nation

AFTER ASKING for God's protection over the servicemen in danger on the beaches of Normandy, President Roosevelt continued with his prayer, asking God for unity and courage throughout the nation. With this heartfelt plea he completed his radio broadcast on June 6, 1944, the night of D-Day:

And for us at home—fathers, mothers, children, wives, sisters, and brothers of brave men overseas, whose thoughts and prayers are ever with them—help us, Almighty God, to rededicate ourselves in renewed faith in Thee in this hour of great sacrifice.

Many people have urged that I call the nation into a single day of special prayer. But because the road is long and the desire is great, I ask that our people devote themselves in a continuance of prayer. As we rise to each new day, and again when each day is spent, let words of prayer be on our lips, invoking Thy help to our efforts.

Give us strength, too—strength in our daily tasks, to redouble the contributions we make in the physical and the material support of our armed forces.

And let our hearts be stout, to wait out the long travail, to bear sorrows that may come, to impart our courage unto our sons wheresoever they may be.

And, O Lord, give us faith. Give us faith in Thee; faith in our sons; faith in each other; faith in our united crusade. Let not the keenness of our spirit ever be dulled. Let not the impacts of temporary events, of temporal matters of but fleeting moment—let not these deter us in our unconquerable purpose.

With Thy blessing, we shall prevail over the unholy forces of our enemy. Help us to conquer the apostles of greed and racial arrogances. Lead us to the saving of our country, and with our sister nations into a world unity that will spell a sure peace—a peace invulnerable to the schemings of unworthy men. And a peace that will let all of men live in freedom, reaping the just rewards of their honest toil.

Thy will be done, Almighty God. Amen[337]

But I, by your great mercy, will come into your house; in reverence will I bow down toward your holy temple. Lead me, O Lᴏʀᴅ, in your righteousness because of my enemies—make straight your way before me. ~Psalms 5:7–8

This Is Your Daddy

JERRY'S FATHER joined the Army in 1944, a few months after she was born. After basic training he was sent to the war zone in Italy where he served for two years. Jerry had memories of getting together with other service families and playing with the other children. She also remembered her mother's letters that she always sealed with a freshly applied lipstick kiss. On one occasion Jerry was allowed to wet her own mouth with orange juice and apply an "orange juice kiss." She had generally pleasant memories of her wartime experience because her mother was so good at sheltering her from the tension and anxiety that she experienced. She did clearly remember the day her father came home.

> At last the day arrived when my father was due to come home. Yes, he had survived combat and the attendant challenges of being away from home and family for so long. I was staying with my grandparents while Mom went to the train station to pick him up. When they arrived, I was upstairs in my grandparents' bath tub. I remember hearing large footsteps bounding up the stairs two at a time, followed by this tall, young man entering the bathroom. To this day I can vividly hear my grandmother saying "This is your daddy." He grabbed me out of the tub, and we began our bonding process that had been delayed for more than two years.[338]

We know that there were many unhappy endings to family separations during this and every other war. That fact is what makes this heartwarming story of reunion so uplifting. We have a little reminder from history, if we need it, of how precious our families are. We should look at them every day with the eyes of a returning soldier and a long-separated daughter.

The jailor brought them into his house and set a meal before them; he was filled with joy because he had come to believe in God—he and his whole family. ~Acts 16:34

It's Too Hard

MYRA STRACHNER continued to write her boyfriend, Pvt. Bernie Staller, even after he was reported missing in action. Her last letter was written on April 18, 1945, the day before news of his death arrived.

> Today I cried again. I haven't since the day the president died. I was lying on my bed in the afternoon today and I found my lips forming words, "It's too hard! It's too hard!" over and over again, and when I realized what I was saying I started to cry quietly. Then I went into the den and played some of the songs that mean something to us and I cried hard for a little while . . .[339]

While it is often said that the Lord doesn't give us more than we can bear, I'm sure this woman and countless others mourning the loss of loved ones felt inadequate to deal with the pain of their loss. Even those of us who know Jesus as our Lord and Savior are not promised a pain-free life. When Jesus walked this earth, he allowed his good friend Lazarus to die and be buried by his grief-stricken sisters. The pain was real, even though three days later Jesus brought Lazarus back to life for the glory of God and so that many people's faith would be increased.

Today, God does not choose to reveal himself through resurrecting the dead. Instead, he is glorified when his children experience trials and suffering and yet remain faithful to him. In the midst of Job's epic suffering, Job's wife told him to *"curse God and die"* rather than continue to live with the physical and emotional pain (Job 2:9). But Job refused, and God was glorified. (JG)

[Job] replied, ". . . Shall we accept good from God, and not trouble?" In all this, Job did not sin in what he said. ~Job 2:10

Dear John

C PL. SAMUEL KRAMER wrote to *Yank* magazine in September 1943 to claim the shortest "Dear John" letter ever received in the European Theater. His letter was duly published, to the amusement of countless readers: *"Mr. Kramer: Go to hell! With love, Anne Gudis."*[340]

This "loving" couple met in 1942, before Sam was posted to England. There followed a stormy three-year correspondence, reaching a climax of sorts with this letter. They continued writing, however, often with similar acrimony. Over time, amazingly, the situation improved. In June 1944 Anne would write, *"All I can do is tell you how very much you mean to me and how I long for the day when we can be together again."*[341] After the war, they did come together and were married in 1945. A long, successful marriage with three children followed.

This is a story of perseverance that should inspire any married couple. Relationships do become stormy at times, and one or both partners say things that wound the other. The lesson here is clear: keep talking. In this case, the couple kept on writing, which eventually accomplished the same purpose. They worked through their self-inflicted wounds to recapture those things about each other that attracted them in the first place. My mother's advice was to never go to sleep on an argument. This can sometimes be difficult to do literally, but the basic advice is the same: keep on talking until you resolve the problem. And every time you take the first step to reconcile, remember that Jesus himself is on your side, for in every situation, *"Blessed are the peacemakers"* (Matthew 5:9).

For God is not a God of disorder but of peace. ~1 Corinthians 14:33

Candlelight Service

IN 1943 A GROUP of women in Brooktondale, New York, began printing a newsletter called the *Brooktondale Bugler*, with information about local events and their hometown servicemen stationed around the world. The paper carried an article about a special service held on December 30, 1944:

> *At the morning service of the Nazarene Church in Brooktondale, Dec. 30th, a candle lighting service was held in honor of those in Service of our Country from our community. Dr. Howard Miller delivered the message in conjunction with the service. His subject was, "The relationship of Home, Church, and Country."*

> *A row of nineteen candles was placed in front of the Altar and as the Pastor, Rev. Stanford Ernest read the name of the man or woman in service, the mother, wife, or sister, lighted a candle in his or her honor. Rev. Ernest offered a prayer for their safe return and Miss Betty Miller very impressively sang "Keep the Home Fires Burning."*

> *Two beautiful flags, the American and the Christian, were presented to the Church by Dr. Howard Miller and Mrs. Miller.*[342]

The 2007 population of Brooktondale was 2028. It may have been smaller or larger in 1944, but probably not by much. Nineteen young people serving in the armed forces represented a large portion of this small town. This prayerful and thoughtful community support had to be encouraging and uplifting for those doing their duty away from home. We pray that so many will never again be involved in a war, but that, whatever the number, those who go into harm's way for us will always be so honored. As the popular World War I song says, *"Keep the home fires burning, while your hearts are yearning . . ."*[343]

> Greater love has no one than this, that he lay down his life for his friends.
> ~John 15:13

Letter to MacArthur

MAIL SERVICE and information from the Southwest Pacific theater was slow and sporadic. A Chicago woman, Mrs. Nels Neslund, could not get news about her wounded son, Robert, and finally went to the top for help. On January 1, 1945, she wrote a letter that was part entreaty and part prayer directly to General MacArthur:

> *This is the first prayer of nineteen forty five, that our boys come home safe and sound. It is written on the first minute of the new year and if God ever listened to a prayer I hope it is this one . . .*
>
> *Please take care of my boys, let Robert get well, let him stay in the hospital till he is . . . and please God hold your healing hand over the mind and spirit and physical well being of all the soldiers in the Philippines and all over the world, for if each one of them has a mother or a wife whose prayer joins with mine this first hour of 1945 I am sure the strength of it, the strength of all the combined prayers of this day will be able to move mountains . . .* [344]

Unfortunately, General MacArthur's response to this appeal is not known. He must have been moved by the eloquence of this distraught woman appealing to him and to God at the same time. She may have had little faith in the Army, but the depth of her faith in God shows through in her inspiring appeal to God and other mothers. This is the kind of faith that brings individuals and families through difficult times and enables them to deal with whatever worldly crisis besets them. God freely offers the same spiritual protection and support to his people whenever we turn to him for it.

My soul finds rest in God alone; my salvation comes from him. He alone is my rock and my salvation; he is my fortress, I will never be shaken. ~Psalm 62:1–2

If You'll Sort the Socks

HOURS AFTER STEPPING off his landing craft into knee-deep water, Smith Shumway looked down at Omaha Beach from the high ground. Below him lay an amazing scene. Ships and landing craft stretched as far as he could see. Many were still circling offshore and others were coming into the beach. Airplanes were roaring overhead, and shells were bursting everywhere. The beach was littered with men and machines. It was a sight he would never forget and, unfortunately, one of the last sights he would ever see.

Soon after, Shumway's life was changed forever by an exploding anti-tank mine. Advancing through the hedgerows of Normandy, he was only a yard behind a tank when it blew up. The horrendous explosion riddled him with shrapnel and thrust him into darkness. Over the following days he had to accept the fact that he was permanently blind.

The young officer spent the next two years in hospitals and rehabilitation centers, recovering from his wounds and adapting to his blindness. His progress was amazing. In 1946 he was hired by the state of Maryland as a rehabilitation counselor for the blind. He soon began visiting factories to show managers and blind workers that they could do many tasks previously thought impossible for a blind person. He became one of the most successful counselors in the nation at placing the sightless in industrial jobs. He also gradually worked up the confidence and courage to propose to his college sweetheart, Sarah Bagley. He told her, *"If you'll sort the socks and read the mail, I can do the rest."*[345] Sarah consented, and they were happily married. Shumway summed up the peaks and valleys of his life and explained the powerful source of his motivation: *"I felt that my heavenly Father had blessed me and spared my life for a reason."*[346]

> For I tell you the truth, many prophets and righteous men longed to see what you see but did not see it, and to hear what you hear but did not hear it.
> ~Matthew 13:17

An Unexpected Benefit

COMBAT CONDITIONS had a way of dissolving denominational differences. Chaplains found themselves ministering to the men and women around them regardless of their religious affiliation or even non-affiliation. One Catholic chaplain with the 93rd Division found 98 percent of his troops Protestant and still worked tirelessly to provide religious support to every man. A Baptist chaplain and a Catholic chaplain worked together with the Marines going into Tarawa, and both became popular with the troops of each other's faith. A war correspondent observed them in action and commented, *"Denominational distinctions did not mean much to men about to offer up their lives."*[347]

The military chaplains of World War II practiced an ecumenism born of necessity. From their combat experiences many of these chaplains also found a deeper personal faith that tended to further blur denominational differences. This cooperative spirit was a blessing to millions of men and women in uniform and would eventually bless the nation as well. Inevitably, these chaplains returned home to bring better understanding between the faiths. One historian described the phenomenon:

> *The American and Allied sense and hope for a better future included a perhaps unexpected benefit as chaplains returned after the war to their churches, schools, and communities. The nature of their service in combat stripped away many of the traditional icons and trappings; the faith of many chaplains was deepened by this return to the basics. There was also a significant growth in ecumenical spirit and understanding. At the battalion aid stations and the burial sites, the chaplains, regardless of their own faith, knew and used appropriately the counsel, prayers and last rites befitting the soldier who was sick, wounded, dying, or just plain afraid and exhausted.*[348]

There is one body and one Spirit—just as you were called to one hope when you were called—one Lord, one faith, one baptism; one God and Father of all, who is over all and through all and in all. ~Ephesians 4:4–6

No Self-Righteousness

SAMUEL MOOR SHOEMAKER was rector of Calvary Episcopal Church in New York from 1925 to 1952. He is best remembered for his work helping formulate the Twelve Step Program for Alcoholics Anonymous. During World War II many of his sermons addressed the war effort, and his words were not always soothing to his listeners. He lashed out at the immorality that he saw in the nation, comparing America to a "spoiled child." He did support the war effort, determining it a "grim necessity" and an opportunity for nations to again choose democracy. However, he abhorred any self-righteousness on the part of his countrymen:

> No war can ever be a clear-cut way for a Christian to express his hatred of evil. For war involves a basic confusion. All the good in the world is not ranged against all the evil. In the present war, some nations that have a great deal of evil in them are yet seeking to stand for freedom . . . against other nations which have a great deal of good in them but yet are presently dedicated to turning the world backwards into the darkness of enslavement.[349]

These words can be applied to individuals as well as to nations. Every human being has the potential for good as well as evil. And every "good" person falls short of God's expectations. Christians especially must understand this truth. By definition, a Christian is a fallen human being whose only value comes from the grace of God and trust in Jesus Christ. There is no room for a "holier than thou" attitude toward any other human being. Samuel Shoemaker was right to remind Americans then and now that self-righteousness is even more destructive when evidenced by a nation.

Do not say to yourself, "The LORD has brought me here to take possession of this land because of my righteousness." No, it is on account of the wickedness of these nations that the LORD is going to drive them out before you.
~Deuteronomy 9:4

Pass the Ammunition

O N DECEMBER 7, 1941, the USS *New Orleans* was moored along Berth 16 at the Navy Yard, Pearl Harbor, undergoing engine repairs while on shore power. As soon as the Japanese air attack began, the general quarters alarm sounded, and the crew scrambled to their battle stations. The sky was filled with attacking aircraft, and, in a few moments, all of the *New Orleans'* air defense weapons were firing at a fever pitch. The ship's chaplain, Cdr. Howell Forgy, moved about the ship, giving encouragement to the men. He himself was inspired by a group of sailors passing shells to one of the five-inch gun mounts:

> *The big five-inch shells, weighing close to a hundred pounds, were being pulled up the powerless hoist by ropes attached to their long, tube-like metal cases. A tiny Filipino messboy, who weighed little more than the shell, hoisted it to his shoulder, staggered a few steps, and grunted as he started the long, tortuous trip up two flights of ladders to the quarterdeck, where the guns thirsted for steel and powder. A dozen eager men lined up at the hoist. The parade of ammunition was endless, but the cry kept coming from topside for more, more, more . . . The boys were putting everything they had into the job, and it was beginning to tell on them . . . Minutes turned to hours. Physical exhaustion was coming to every man in the human endless-chain of that ammunition line. They struggled on. They could keep going only by keeping faith in their hearts.*
>
> *I slapped their wet, sticky backs and shouted, "Praise the Lord and pass the ammunition."****

This phrase soon became well known and was incorporated into a song by Frank Loesser. Reflecting a more innocent age and the religious character of America at that time, it became a popular hit. The song told the story of a chaplain who laid aside his Bible to man the guns, while shouting what was to become one of the most famous phrases of World War II.

> There is a time for everything, and a season for every activity under heaven: . . .
> A time to tear and a time to mend,
> A time to be silent and a time to speak,
> A time to love and a time to hate,
> A time for war and a time for peace. ~Ecclesiastes 3:1, 7–8

*** Langer, *World War II*, p. 30. Quoting from the book, "*. . . And Pass the Ammunition,*" by Howell M. Forgy.

World War II Navy recruiting poster.
(National Archives)

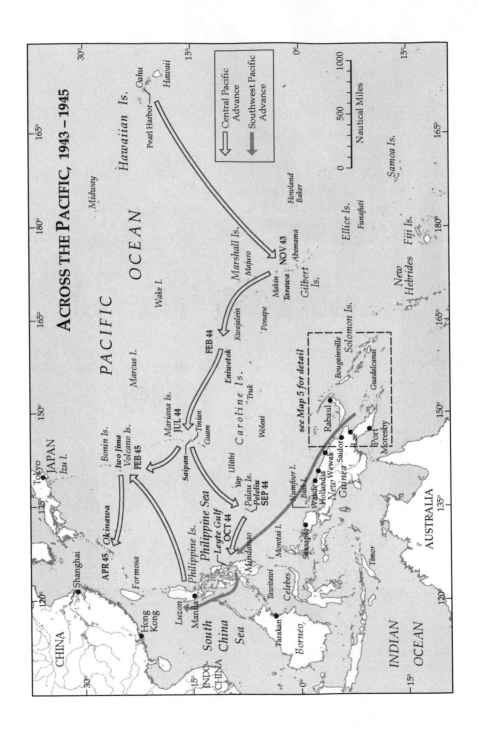

ACROSS THE PACIFIC, 1943–1945

Central Pacific Advance

Southwest Pacific Advance

Nautical Miles

1000

500

0

PACIFIC OCEAN

Hawaiian Is.

Pearl Harbor

Oahu

Hawaii

Midway

Marshall Is.

Majuro

NOV 43

Makin

Tarawa

Abemama

Gilbert Is.

Howland

Baker

Ellice Is.

Funafuti

Samoa Is.

New Hebrides

Fiji Is.

Wake I.

Marcus I.

FEB 44

Kwajalein

Eniwetok

Ponape

Truk

Caroline Is.

Woleai

JAPAN

Tokyo

Izu I.

Bonin Is.

Iwo Jima

Volcano Is.

FEB 45

Mariana Is.

JUL 44

Tinian

Guam

Saipan

Yap

Ulithi

Palau Is.

Peleliu

SEP 44

Okinawa

APR 45

Shanghai

Formosa

Hong Kong

Philippine Is.

Philippine Sea

Luzon

Manila

Leyte Gulf

OCT 44

Mindanao

CHINA

INDO-CHINA

South China Sea

Tarakan

Borneo

Celebes

Tawitawi

Morotai I.

Sansapor

Timor

Numfoor I.

Biak I.

Wakde

Hollandia

New Guinea

Wewak

Saidor

Lae

Port Moresby

Rabaul

see Map 5 for detail

Bougainville

Solomon Is.

Guadalcanal

AUSTRALIA

INDIAN OCEAN

30°

15°

0°

15°

30°

120°

135°

150°

165°

180°

165°

150°

135°

120°

SEPTEMBER
The Central Pacific Campaign

ADM. ISORUKU YAMAMOTO, the architect of the Japanese triumph at Pearl Harbor, warned his superiors early in the war that if the conflict lasted more than a year he would not be able to guarantee success against the United States. In 1943, his worst nightmare was realized as America's industrial might began to show itself in the Pacific. By that time, the U.S. 5th Fleet was operating with six heavy *Essex* class aircraft carriers, thirteen smaller carriers, twelve battleships, and large numbers of cruisers, destroyers, and support ships. Commanding this armada was the hero of Midway, Vadm. Raymond Spruance. The spearhead of the fleet was its four Fast Carrier Task Groups, each with four aircraft carriers and an escort of supporting surface ships. The ground combat element was the V Amphibious Corps, commanded by Maj. Gen. Holland M. Smith, affectionately known as "Howlin' Mad" by the Marines under him. Having anticipated the coming battles in the Pacific for more than a decade, the Marines were ready with the equipment and tactics for an island-hopping campaign against defended beaches.

After considerable debate between Army and Navy planners, the Joint Chiefs decided that priority in the Pacific would go to a Navy and Marine Corps drive directly at Japan, while MacArthur's Army forces would continue their advance through New Guinea toward the Philippines. Step one of the Central Pacific campaign would be the coral atoll of Tarawa in the Gilbert Islands.

The main objective at Tarawa was the tiny two-mile-long island of Betio, the only fortified position on the atoll and site of an airfield. On November 21, 1943, five thousand Marines of the 2nd Marine Division made a difficult landing on the lagoon side of the island across a wide expanse of shallow reef. In three days of savage fighting more than one thousand Marines were killed attacking strongly fortified positions that had proven impervious to inaccurate naval and air bombardment. Bunkers with six-foot-thick roofs made of logs, sand, and corrugated iron had to be assaulted by individual squads with rifles, hand grenades, and satchel charges. Valuable lessons were learned at Tarawa that would benefit upcoming operations, including the necessity of longer and more accurate pre-assault fire support.

As U.S. forces captured the Marshall Islands in February 1944, the Japanese were forced to a new inner perimeter stretching from the Mariana Islands to the Palaus and western New Guinea. The garrisons east of this line were given the suicidal mission of sacrificing themselves to make the U.S. advance as slow and costly as possible. The assaults on Saipan and Peleliu were accordingly contested to almost the last man. D-Day on Saipan was June 15, 1944, nine days after the invasion of France. Marine and Army units sustained more than sixteen thousand casualties overcoming the thirty-two thousand defenders. The attack on Peleliu in September proved to be the costliest amphibious operation in history, with forty percent casualties.[350]

In conjunction with these land operations the Pacific Fleet fought a series of important naval engagements that further reduced Japanese military strength in the Pacific. In one two-day period U.S. carrier aircraft and submarines inflicted a crippling blow to Japanese naval air power, destroying three hundred aircraft and three carriers in the Philippine Sea. These operations in the Central Pacific in 1944 brought the war ever closer to mainland Japan. Air bases in the Marianas enabled long-range bombers to reach Tokyo, while new naval bases prepared the way for the long-awaited U.S. return to the Philippines.

War of Attrition

IN A 2004 SPEECH to 1st Marine Division veterans, Secretary of the Navy Gordon England drew some interesting comparisons between the Marines' foes in World War II and today's conflict in the Middle East:

> There is a parallel between 9/11 and the island and battle of Peleliu. By 1944, the Japanese recognized that they could not match American firepower and tactics in the air, on the sea, or in land warfare. Therefore, at Peleliu, they shifted their strategy from a war for victory to a war of attrition. Japanese commanders had orders to seek a 'stalemate' in which they would inflict the highest possible cost to Americans in blood and time . . .
>
> What makes Peleliu so significant is that in the face of this new strategy and warfare, the 1st Marine Division did not hesitate—or lose its will. The Marines pressed on until the Japanese were defeated. Despite heavy losses, the Marines would not be deterred.[351]

The secretary pointed out that he was four years old when America fought the first 'ism' of his lifetime: fascism. His granddaughter was four years old on September 11, 2001, when America went to war against terrorism. Once again Marines face foes seeking to spill as much blood as possible. This time the targets are civilians as well as soldiers.

In both these wars, Secretary England asserted that the decisive factor has been and continues to be the courage and sacrifice of American men and women in uniform:

> The raw courage and determination that prevailed in the caves and jungles of Peleliu continues today in Kandahar, Baghdad, Al Kut, Tikrit, Najaf . . . and other places where the 1st Marine Division carries on. It's still about our people . . . God bless each of you, God bless this magnificent Corps, and God Bless America.[352]

Our Armed Forces continue to serve us heroically today, and we continue to pray the same prayer expressed by Secretary England: "May God bless our men and women in uniform, and may God always bless America."

Therefore, I urge you, brothers, in view of God's mercy, to offer your bodies as living sacrifices, holy and pleasing to God—this is your spiritual act of worship. ~Romans 12:1

The Spiritual Campaign

THE WAR WAS closing in on the Christian missionaries of the Dutch East Indies. Dr. Robert Jaffrey, the Head of Mission, knew that in the short run his work would be interrupted. However, like a great general, his vision for a greater campaign in the future inspired optimism. To one of his fellow missionaries he outlined his strategy for "conquests" ahead:

> With a steady hand and the voice of one assured of victory, he traced upon the map our coming campaign: the Natuna and Anambas Islands; Sumatra—ferreting out and mopping up those pockets of satanic resistance in the central and southern districts; the final liberation of the Punans of Borneo's hinterland; Bali, firmly held in the grip of the enemy, would be freed, its iron gates yielding under the onslaught of faith and prayer. He paused to give praise to our Commander in Chief for spiritual battles fought and won in some of the smaller islands, then moved on to Misool, the Isle of Demons, the Bird's Head of New Guinea, the Wissel Lakes area, the Zwart and Memberamo River Valleys, down either side of the Carstenz backbone—and at last his finger came to rest over the Grand Valley of the Baliem.[353]

The person hearing these words was awed at this magnificent display of *"a faith that never staggers at the promise of God . . . of a burning love that counts not life dear unto itself, but is expendable for God; and of a vision that is never dimmed."*[354] We also are inspired by this insight into the heart of a great missionary. We know that no significant works can be accomplished without a vision. When God gave Moses one of the greatest missions in history, he also gave him a magnificent vision of what he was going to accomplish:

> The LORD said, "I have indeed seen the misery of my people in Egypt. I have heard them crying out because of their slave drivers, and I am concerned about their suffering. So I have come down to rescue them from the hand of the Egyptians and to bring them up out of that land into a good and spacious land, a land flowing with milk and honey." ~Exodus 3:7–8

Our Faith Is Complete

GEORGE SYER was a staff sergeant with the 96th Division. He had only ten days with his newborn son, John Paul, before shipping out to the Pacific in July 1944. Trying to be optimistic, but fearing the worst, he wrote a letter to John Paul to tell his son that he loved him and to give him a future understanding of his father's beliefs:

> *Two months have gone now since you were born. Mother has since sent pictures that I treasure . . . Yes two months, and tonight I am on the threshold of another adventure of life. Tomorrow we board ship to go overseas. I do not fear to go knowing that I too must share the responsibility of fighting for my country. I have no desire to kill, son, only to save life, but there are times like these that one can't understand, but seek to serve God and also my country seems the only true course to take.*
>
> *I go with faith that the Lord shall bring me back safe from the conflict. However should the Lord decide that my service has ended, and I fall on foreign soil, my faith will be satisfied to its fullest by Him who is wise and better than I could ask or expect.*
>
> *The answer to our faith is always complete, even though the answer is not according to your own will. A paradox, yes but that is God's privilege and power.*[355]

Fortunately, John Paul was reunited with his father after the war and, so, had more than this letter to guide him through his formative years. The letter is nevertheless a powerful insight into one man's beliefs. The phrase, *"answer to our faith"* is thought-provoking and worth pondering in itself. I take it to mean the final realization of the truth of what we believe, that is, the realization we receive when we actually meet our Savior in heaven. How and when this occurs is not up to us, although we know that the answer we receive when that time comes will certainly be full and complete, even beyond what we expect. The paradox lies in the fact that we who are worth so little ultimately receive so much.

Now faith is being sure of what we hope for and certain of what we do not see. ~Hebrews 11:1

How to Pray

THE THIRTY-SHIP convoy left Guadalcanal on September 4, 1944, headed north slowly at seven knots. The speed was dictated by the tank landing ships (LSTs), with their clamshell bow doors and cargoes of amphibious tractors. Four assault waves were embarked for the ten-day journey to Peleliu, a small island six hundred miles east of the Philippines. Bruce Watkins was one of the Marines aboard who had never heard of this remote little island. He had a lot of time to think about what he had left behind and to pray about what lay ahead:

> *I remember leaning on the ship's rail, alone for once, my thoughts on my much-loved wife of 14 months. I knew she would be praying for me, although she could not know the hour of our peril. Brought up in a Christian home, it was natural for me to turn to God and ask for His help. I asked for sharpness of mind to make the right decisions quickly for those who depended on me. Somehow I felt it was wrong to ask for my personal safety, but I asked for strength to fight no matter how badly I might be wounded. And so the last hours passed. Soon there would be no time for reflection.[356]*

This was a thoughtful man who was able to turn to God as he faced an unknown and dangerous future. I found it very intriguing that he would not pray for his own safety. Perhaps he was conscious of the fact that many would die in the upcoming invasion, and he did not want to selfishly put himself ahead of others. Or perhaps he thought that God's plan might include his death and to pray otherwise would be futile. I've had similar thoughts to these and questions about what to ask of God. I have come to believe that I can ask God for anything, after prefacing my request with a heartfelt *"Thy will be done, Lord."*

Then the word of the LORD Almighty came to me: "Ask all the people of the land and the priests, 'When you fasted and mourned in the fifth and seventh months for the past seventy years, was it really for me that you fasted? And when you were eating and drinking, were you not just feasting for yourselves?'" ~Zechariah 7:4–6

Marines assaulting a bunker on Tarawa.
(National Archives)

Religious service behind the lines.
(National Archives)

Thirty-Second Prayers

THEY CALLED IT the *"night of the mortars."* The Japanese defenders on Peleliu found the range to the Marines' position and kept firing round after round all through the night. Incoming mortar fire is especially unnerving because it comes in from an almost vertical angle with only a quiet, whistling sound. Open foxholes offer little protection, and there weren't even many of those due to the hard coral surface. Many of the rounds detonated in the trees, showering shrapnel on the men huddled below.

Bruce Watkins was a platoon leader with 1st Marine Regiment, landing with the first wave at Peleliu. Contrary to expectations, the resistance was well organized and fanatical. He and his men fought for every foot of terrain and, over two days, suffered many casualties. On the second night the mortar fire started, and Watkins moved among his men as best he could, giving first aid and encouragement. At one point he heard a comforting sound:

> *A Catholic Marine in the next hole was praying with his rosary and it inspired me to employ what I had come to call my 30–second prayers. I'm sure that God received a great deal of communication that night. Mine went something like, "Father, let me do my job and do it well. I don't ask You to save me, but help me to be a good leader. If I must be hit, give me the strength to carry on and Your will always be done."*[357]

I've always felt that God would rather hear frequent thirty-second prayers than have us wait for "suitable" occasions to pray longer. In fact, so long as it is heartfelt, this kind of prayer is the perfect way to bring God into our daily lives. We can always manage a short prayer before a meeting, an important phone call, or a trip. I believe that this is what the apostle Paul meant by his advice to *"pray continually"* (1 Thessalonians 5:17).

Then Jesus told his disciples a parable to show them that they should always pray and not give up. ~Luke 18:1

Time to Think

THE SECOND DAY on Peleliu was another day of intense combat. It started abruptly for the Marines of Bruce Watkins' battalion with an incoming barrage of heavy-caliber fire on their hilltop position. Large chunks of rock and shrapnel were flying everywhere and casualties were mounting. Watkins realized he couldn't keep his men in such an exposed position and ordered them back down the hill. He was the last to leave and experienced his most frightening moment of the war when an arm-sized shell fragment whizzed by his head, cutting his helmet strap.

On flat ground below the ridge, Watkins spent the rest of the day dodging sniper fire as he went about the task of reorganizing his men and preparing a new defensive line tied in with the rest of the battalion. Just before nightfall several amphibious tractors brought the first delivery of food. Spam sandwiches and grapefruit juice were the special for the day. As darkness and rain settled in, the Marines experienced their first lull in the action. Watkins recalled:

> This night was relatively quiet and I had more time to think about myself. We were wet, filthy, and our lips were burnt. I had a fungus infection in my crotch and a smashed finger from the night before. I guess it was the first time I had really noticed. I have often thought officers and NCOs with their constant responsibility had an advantage in that there was little time to think about themselves. The private(s), on the other hand, often had time to reflect and wonder what crazy order they would be given next, fearing the worst.[358]

Responsibility is sometimes a burden, but seen from this perspective, is *always* a blessing. Self-absorption is probably the closest we come to hell on Earth, and when we are responsible for someone or something else, our focus is outside ourselves. Fortunately, we don't have to be commissioned officers to have this change of outlook. Every foot soldier in God's kingdom has opportunities to tend to the needs of others, serving them at home, in church, and in the workplace.

Do nothing out of selfish ambition or vain conceit, but in humility consider others better than yourselves. Each of you should look not only to your own interests, but also to the interests of others. ~Philippians 2:3–4

No Atheists

FATHER WILLIAM CUMMINGS became a military chaplain by accident. He was teaching school in Manila when the Japanese invaded the Philippines in 1942. When his school was destroyed, he hitched a boat ride across Manila Bay to join the American and Filipino soldiers fighting on the Bataan Peninsula. All through the siege of Bataan and the final days of Corregidor he ministered to the beleaguered troops around him and became a source of comfort and inspiration to many. He felt that spiritual support was more critical than ever in a combat situation, articulating to a war correspondent his belief that, *"There are no atheists in foxholes."*[359] This now-famous comment took on a life of its own when the correspondent flashed the quote across the seas to America and the rest of the world.

The ordeal for Cummings and many other U.S. servicemen would follow with the eventual surrender of Corregidor and imprisonment by the Japanese. Under the most inhumane conditions imaginable, he said, *"There are so many men here. I cannot help them all, but if I can help a few, then maybe God will feel my life justified. When I worry about their suffering, I don't have time to think of myself."*[360] Father Cummings' last days were spent on a Japanese prison ship. He died in the arms of one of his beloved soldiers reciting the Lord's Prayer. He is memorialized on Chaplains Hill in Arlington National Cemetery.[361]

> For I am not seeking my own good but the good of many, so that they may be saved. Follow my example, as I follow the example of Christ. ~1 Corinthians 10:33–11:1

The Voice of a Man Who Believed

OF ALL THE PRISONERS held by the Japanese during the war, the worst fate befell those placed on a series of prison ships, called "hell ships" by those who were on them. In 1944, as the Allies advanced on the Philippines, the Japanese began loading thousands of prisoners into the cargo holds of old steamships for relocation to Formosa and Japan. The conditions were unspeakable. The crowding was so severe there wasn't room for everyone to even sit down at one time. Food and water were almost nonexistent, as temperatures below deck soared above 120 degrees. Buckets were lowered to serve as latrines. Disease and death ravaged the victims of this tribulation.

On a particularly suffocating night, the cries of anguish on one of these ships grew louder and louder as the tormented prisoners seemed on the verge of a hysterical outbreak. The voice of Chaplain William Cummings suddenly rang out over the clamor. One of the men recalled an amazing transformation:

> Father Cummings began to speak. The sound was clear and resonant and made me feel he was talking to me alone. The men became quiet.
>
> "Our Father who art in heaven, hallowed be Thy name. Thy kingdom come. Thy will be done on earth as it is in heaven." . . . The voice went on. Strength came to me as I listened to the prayer, and a certain calmness of spirit.
>
> "Have faith," he continued. "Believe in yourselves and in the goodness of one another. Know that in yourselves and in those that stand near you, you see the image of God. For mankind is in the image of God."[362]

When he spoke these words it completely changed those who heard them, as the witness reported, *"For a while sanity returned to the faces around me . . . some of us continued to be held by the strength of that voice, the voice of a man who believed and who wanted us to believe."*[363] It is truly miraculous that a man could see God in a miserable and hysterical mass of humanity such as this. His faith was a powerful witness to God's love for the men on that prison ship then and for us blessed to read about it today.

Brothers, as an example of patience in the face of suffering, take the prophets who spoke in the name of the Lord. As you know, we consider blessed those who have persevered. ~James 5:10–11

God's Timing

ROBERT TAYLOR was pastor of the Fort Worth Baptist Church when he joined the Army in 1940. He was sent to the Philippines where he was assigned as chaplain to the 31st Infantry Regiment. Immediately after war was declared, Taylor's unit went into action against the Japanese on the Bataan Peninsula. During this campaign he earned the Silver Star for rescuing wounded soldiers under enemy fire. When the Philippines surrendered, he became a prisoner of war and ministered to thousands of fellow captives in the Cabanatuan camp hospital. In 1944 he spent fourteen weeks in solitary confinement for smuggling food and medicine to patients.[364] One prisoner, known to be an atheist, called Taylor a *"tower of strength."*[365] Another prisoner observed a dying soldier ask Taylor how to have a relationship with God:

> *The young man, cognizant of his spiritual indifference in the past, asked if it was all right to straighten things out with God just because one was about to die. Taylor responded to the young soldier by telling him that God's response to our need is not based on our timing but on his great love for us. On that day, by the power of God, that young man gave his life to Christ. Afterwards, the young man reached up, took his dog tags, and with a jerk broke the chain and handed them to Taylor. As he placed them in the chaplain's hand, he squeezed it gently and a wide smile crept over his face.*[366]

This is a story of one man's faithfulness and God's timing. By his faithful service, Robert Taylor earned the respect of the soldiers around him and became an effective witness to the power of the gospel. He was the right person at the right time for this soldier, who was able with Taylor's gentle guidance to put his faith in Christ at the time and place that God intended. We are called to be equally faithful in his service. We must gently share the gospel when appropriate and patiently wait for God's timing to bring about the hoped-for result.

And the God of all grace, who called you to his eternal glory in Christ, after you have suffered a little while, will himself restore you and make you strong, firm and steadfast. ~1 Peter 5:10

Droplets on a Parched Heart

WHEN THE MARINES invaded Saipan, Saburo Arakaki was an eighteen-year-old student at the local vocational school. Forced into the hills by the fighting, he evaded the Americans for months. He finally surrendered to one of the detention camps where he found great tension between those who favored continued resistance and those who were convinced the war was over. The young and idealistic Arakaki was persuaded to murder two Japanese civilians who were leaders of the "defeatist" group. The teenaged assassin was soon caught, tried, and sentenced to death. Months later, while awaiting his execution, he learned that his sentence had been commuted to life in prison.

With no hope for the future, Arakaki was sullen and hateful toward his captors. About a year into his sentence, someone gave him a small booklet written in Japanese. He saw it was a short course in Christianity and knew he wanted nothing to do with anything western, much less religion. Yet his longing to read anything in his own language temporarily overcame his intense antagonism. He was soon reading about the Bible and amazingly found the words being absorbed into his heart. He described his feelings:

> [The Bible] is truly an ancient book, but it has continued to be read even today. In it is something precious that captivates the hearts of people. In it is hidden the profound wisdom of God . . . No matter how many times one reads the Bible, there is always fresh meaning in its words—words that will satisfy the longings of the heart.[367]

The effect of Scripture on this young man was profound, as one who knew him observed: "*These words sank into Saburo's heart like precious droplets of water soaking into the arid desert sands. He read on, brushing aside the thought that this was the Christian Bible he was reading about.*"[368] By God's written Word alone, a transformation was begun in the heart of this bitter young man.

The secret things belong to the LORD our God, but the things revealed belong to us and to our children forever. ~Deuteronomy 29:29

I Do

A S SABURO ARAKAKI read through his booklet on Christianity while imprisoned in Hawaii, he began to learn about Jesus Christ. He identified with the fact that this man had been falsely accused and executed for something he did not do, and yet taught about mercy and offered forgiveness of sins to the world. As Arakaki's resistance seemed to melt, he longed to read more about this intriguing figure. He got his wish when he unexpectedly received a Japanese language New Testament that he began reading under a single light bulb in a dark basement of the prison. One passage from John, chapter 12, penetrated deeply into his heart, as he thought to himself,

> *Jesus says that . . . He came not to judge, but to save the world. A sinner can be saved. The agony that I suffered fighting against approaching death as a convict on death row can't possibly compare with the final agony of those two men that I killed. Now the only thing I can do is to ask for forgiveness from God and pray that they rest in peace.*[369]

A deep emotion overcame him as the tears flowed down his face. On his knees, he looked up and cried out, *"God, thank You so much."*[370] The words of another verse also seemed to propel him further in this new direction: *"Therefore, if anyone is in Christ, he is a new creation"* (2 Corinthians 5:17). At that moment he knew that Jesus was in his heart, and he knew that he wanted to be baptized. Not long after, he received permission to go to a local church where the pastor asked him the all-important question, *"Saburo, do you believe that the Lord Jesus Christ is your personal Savior?"* The convicted assassin responded passionately: *"I do."*[371]

> I have come as a light into the world, that whoever believes in Me should not abide in darkness. And if anyone hears My words and does not believe, I do not judge him; for I did not come to judge the world but to save the world.
> ~John 12:46–47

Corpsman

THE MEDAL OF HONOR citation for Fred Faulkner Lester reads in part:

Quick to spot a wounded Marine lying in an open field beyond the front lines...Lester unhesitatingly crawled toward the casualty under a concentrated barrage from hostile machine guns, rifles, and grenades. Torn by enemy rifle bullets as he inched forward, he stoically disregarded the mounting fury of Japanese fire and his own pain to pull the wounded man toward a covered position.[372]

Hospital Corpsman
Fred Lester
(U.S. Navy)

Fred Lester was one of a special breed of heroes, dear to all Marines: the Navy corpsman. These men served with Marine units in every campaign of World War II, providing life-saving first aid in and beyond the front lines. They became integral parts of the units they served, sharing every hardship and danger. One officer spoke for all Marines with this comment:

I never saw a Corpsman refuse to go to a Marine's aid, no matter how exposed the position, even if the wound was assumed to be fatal. No Marine could write about the war without praising the Navy Corpsmen. These men, who had joined the Navy expecting at least warm chow and a good bed, got stuck with dirt, mud, blood, and Marines. They became, however, one of us, much admired for their unceasing courage in coming to our aid. Their casualty rate was just as great as ours.[373]

The Navy Hospital Corps has a long tradition of medical service going back to the beginning of the Navy. Many doctors and corpsmen have served valiantly on ships and in combat area field hospitals. To Marine "grunts" of the past and present, however, medical attention when it counts comes from the "doc," who always responds to the call, *"Corpsman up!"* May God continue to bless those who so bravely and selflessly serve their fellow men.

> But a Samaritan, as he traveled, came where the man was; and when he saw him, he took pity on him. He went to him and bandaged his wounds, pouring on oil and wine. Then he put the man on his own donkey, took him to an inn and took care of him. ~Luke 10:33–34

Children of God

CARLOS QUINTANA'S wounds left him speechless for six years. During the battle for Saipan a mortar fragment pierced his mouth, severed a major artery, and damaged the nerves controlling his tongue. He was hospitalized for the remainder of the war, eventually ending up in San Diego. Unable to eat or talk, his weight dropped to eighty-nine pounds, and he had to be fed intravenously. In spite of his suffering he maintained a positive attitude thanks to his strong belief in God. Using linguistic exercises he made slow progress in regaining movement of his tongue, and, after six years, recovered to a somewhat normal condition.

Carlos also recovered in his personal life. He married, had three children, and began working with young people. He helped found a youth center called Barrio Station, designed to keep kids off the streets of San Diego. He was driven to do something significant in service to others because he felt God had given him a new life after he had come so close to death. He knew that his calling was to help children: *"The most important thing for all of us is our duty to educate, guide, and support our children because they represent the future of our country and the security of our freedom."* Besides, he said, *"We're all children of God."*[374]

I was once standing at a playground with a friend, looking on as our children played together. He turned to me and said, *"I'll bet God enjoys watching us have a good time, as much as we enjoy seeing our children play."* This was one of my most lasting insights into the loving nature of our heavenly Father. We are truly *his* children.

> If you then, though you are evil, know how to give good gifts to your children, how much more will your Father in heaven give the Holy Spirit to those who ask him! ~Luke 11:13

A Drumstick or a Wing?

NAVY CHAPLAINS were at the scene of every Pacific island campaign. They didn't carry weapons, but in every other way were part of the Marine units they served. Their job was, of course, the most difficult of all: looking after the souls of young Marines. One chaplain described his routine: *"In combat our main action was to go from place to place, unit to unit, and start out early in the morning and go till dark, just visiting one unit after the other and many times just have a very brief service. We had some very small hymn books . . . and some Testaments I could carry in my map case, and we would just gather a few men together in a bomb crater or defilade. . . ."*[375]

Another chaplain used a special type of ministration:

> *He had a canvas gas-mask carrier slung over each shoulder. In one carrier he had Scotch whiskey, in the other fried chicken. As he knelt by each young, frightened, wounded Marine, he was invariably asked, "Am I going to be OK?" "Sure you are!" was the cheerful answer. "While you are waiting to be evacuated, would you rather have a drumstick or a wing?" The young Marine would be so surprised he would forget about himself. Then, when the chaplain asked if he wanted to wash it down with a swig of Scotch, he couldn't believe he was hearing correctly amidst all of the confusion, noise, and death all around him.*[376]

Watching this chaplain in action, one doctor said, *"That man probably saved more young lives from dying of shock than will ever be known."*[377] These Navy chaplains worked on many levels, both spiritual and physical, as they tried to do God's work under the most difficult conditions imaginable. These examples show how simple kindness and a familiar routine can be invaluable in the midst of chaos. We can try to bring the same calming comfort to others overcome by wounds or fear in the midst of a personal crisis. A casserole comes to mind. Drumsticks or wings? Or maybe a swig of Scotch.

> He makes me lie down in green pastures, he leads me beside quiet waters, he restores my soul. ~Psalm 23:2–3

Knee Work

JIMMY ADCOCK was a medic serving with the 40th Infantry Division on Guadalcanal, New Britain, and the Philippines. He was awarded the Silver and Bronze Stars for heroism during these campaigns. During his time in the service he spent long hours shooting craps with his payday money on the floor of various sordid places, an activity that he jokingly referred to as *"knee work."* Then one day a Lutheran chaplain who had gotten to know him said, *"Jim, you could be on your knees praying for your needs. God will provide you information you'll delight in the rest of your life."*[378] Adcock was moved by the chaplain's interest and began attending catechism classes. He eventually decided to make the *"big move in (his) life,"* accepting Jesus Christ as his Savior. In 1943 he was baptized and became a Christian.

Before landing in the Philippines, he wrote to his wife, Ramona, that, *"We are one together by Him, even though physically we are apart. There will come the day when we will look back on these years that war has separated us, but we will do so lovingly and with thanks to Him that we are again together."*[379]

Jim Adcock was sustained by his new faith during the rest of the war, having confidence that he would eventually return to his wife so they could raise a family together. He did return home safely, and the couple eventually had three daughters. Jim would later comment: *"I am proud to say all my children and grandchildren are baptized believers who are serving God with their time and talents."*[380]

It is amazing to contemplate the good done by one chaplain befriending an aimless soldier in wartime. He introduced him to Jesus Christ and a new kind of "knee work" that changed his life, gave him confidence in the future, and impacted future generations of his family.

> Come, let us bow down in worship, let us kneel before the LORD our Maker; for he is our God and we are the people of his pasture, the flock under his care.
> ~Psalms 95:6–7

I'll Prove He's a Bum

COL. GREGORY BOYINGTON was one of the great heroes of Marine Corps aviation. He shot down twenty-eight Japanese aircraft, earned the Medal of Honor, and was a prisoner of war for twenty months. As the commander and oldest member of Marine Fighter Squadron 214, he earned the nickname "Pappy," and his unit of replacement pilots became known as the "Black Sheep Squadron." One of his many exploits is recounted in his Medal of Honor citation:

"Pappy" Boyington
(U. S. Marine Corps)

> *Major Boyington led a formation of twenty-four fighters over Kahill on 17 October and, persistently circling the airdrome where sixty hostile aircraft were grounded, boldly challenged the Japanese to send up planes. Under his brilliant command, our fighters shot down twenty enemy craft in the ensuing action without the loss of a single ship.*[381]

Boyington was shot down over Rabaul in January 1944. Bailing out at low altitude, he was injured and captured by the Japanese. When he was finally repatriated after his prison ordeal, he was in extremely poor health and was medically discharged from the Marine Corps. His life after the war took a further tragic turn as he battled a new enemy: alcoholism. During a disastrous period he went through three wives and a series of uninspiring jobs. Due to the heavy smoking that went with his drinking, he almost died of emphysema. He once proclaimed that his drinking addiction was, *"no doubt the most damning thing in my character."*[382]

Boyington was rehabilitated somewhat in the 1970s by Alcoholics Anonymous and the television series, *Baa Baa Black Sheep*, based on his best-selling book. In the final line of the book, he wrote: *"If this story were to have a moral, then I would say: 'Just name a hero and I'll prove he's a bum.'"*[383] Pappy Boyington had been humbled by his life experiences, but will nevertheless be remembered always as one of the great combat leaders of World War II.

> I know, O LORD, that a man's life is not his own; it is not for man to direct his steps. Correct me, LORD, but only with justice—not in your anger, lest you reduce me to nothing. ~Jeremiah 10:23–24

The Definition of Courage

I N THE ASSAULT on Guam the Marines lost one of their best chaplains. The youthful, redheaded Tony Conway was enormously popular with both officers and enlisted because of his quiet nature and the intense interest he showed in every man. Unfortunately, he was killed when a Japanese shell struck his landing craft just as it reached the shore.

As if he had some premonition of what lay ahead, Conway wrote his parents on the afternoon before the invasion of Guam, suspecting that this could be his last letter to anyone:

> *Dear Pop and Mom and Everyone:*
>
> *It isn't too often I have to write a letter like this one. This is a pre-invasion letter. We go into Guam tomorrow. I am not so much afraid now, but tomorrow morning, no doubt, I will be plenty scared . . .*
>
> *If the worst should happen to me, know that it is God's will, and I gave my life for the Church and the God who rules it. I took the vow at ordination to obey. My work here is obedience at its best.*
>
> *Yes, no doubt, I will be doubly scared on this major operation. Christ was scared when He was going to His death, for He cried out "Father, if it be possible, let this chalice pass from me." He did it for me, I must do it for Him. I'd go in if it were even to save one soul.*
>
> *All the good I am going to do in there makes me courageous for "Courage is fear that has said its prayers." And there is no greater prayer than squaring souls away for God.*[384]

I have never seen a better definition of *courage*. By taking our fears to God in prayer, we are able to face any challenge in his strength. Courage is knowing we have access to this strength and that it will sustain us, no matter what threatens our physical or spiritual safety.

His divine power has given us everything we need for life and godliness through our knowledge of him who called us by his own glory and goodness.
~2 Peter 1:3

When the Roll Is Called

JAKE DESHAZER was laid to rest in March 2008. The World War II Doolittle Raider and Christian evangelist received full military honors. Hundreds of people honored the man who had suffered three years as a prisoner of war in Japan and then returned after the war to start twenty-three churches and bring many thousands of Japanese citizens to Jesus Christ. One of his children said, *"He wouldn't want this service to be about his accomplishments. He'd want Jesus to get all of the credit."*[385]

During the funeral there was a rifle salute, and a lone bugler blew taps. A B-1 bomber flew over from the modern equivalent of Jake's old squadron, the 34th. The casket flag was folded and presented to his wife. The sergeant in charge of the honor guard said, *"Jake's a hero. This is why we do military honors, to honor people like Jake. He's history."*[386] The service itself was simple. The pastor said a few words and prayed. Then everyone sang a hymn that was Jake's favorite, and one dear to the heart of many airmen, "When the Roll Is Called Up Yonder":

When the trumpet of the Lord shall sound, and time shall be no more,
And the morning breaks, eternal, bright and fair;
When the saved of earth shall gather over on the other shore,
And the roll is called up yonder, I'll be there.

On that bright and cloudless morning when the dead in Christ shall rise,
And the glory of His resurrection share;
When His chosen ones shall gather to their home beyond the skies,
And the roll is called up yonder, I'll be there.

Let us labor for the Master from the dawn till setting sun,
Let us talk of all His wondrous love and care;
Then when all of life is over, and our work on earth is done,
And the roll is called up yonder, I'll be there.[387]

And I saw the dead, great and small, standing before the throne, and books were opened. Another book was opened, which is the book of life. ~Revelation 20:12

Mascot

THE USS *SAMUEL B. ROBERTS* was ready for combat. Newly constructed, outfitted, and manned by an eager crew, she was ready to leave Norfolk for the Pacific theater. She needed just one more crew member. After an evening ashore involving more than a small amount of drinking, several enlisted men smuggled a little black dog back aboard. It wasn't long before Capt. Bob Copeland found out about this unauthorized stowaway on his ship.

As the sailors waited nervously to find out what was going to happen, Copeland called for the ship's doctor and chief yeoman. He informed them that they had a new crew member that needed a complete physical exam and official service record. After these formalities, the little mutt was named "Sammy," adopted as the ship's mascot, and given the rank of seaman 2nd class. He quickly became a valuable part of the ship's company. Someone made him a little kapok life vest. An article appeared in the ship's newsletter that Sammy had a girlfriend in Tokyo and had selected the *Roberts* as the fastest way to cross the Pacific.

For a young man of thirty-three years, Bob Copeland was a uniquely mature and talented leader. He never hesitated to exert his authority as captain of his ship, but he did so in a way that gained the respect of the men. He frequently stopped to talk with them and to ask about their families and girlfriends. Gestures of this kind, including the adoption of Sammy as mascot, showed his human side to the crew. This human touch also introduced a few warm feelings into an otherwise cold sea-going life. Bob Copeland knew the importance of his mission. He also knew that he would not be able to accomplish that mission without an effective, close-knit team. By his actions, he demonstrated a great Christian truth, that bonds of affection between men are even more powerful than the bonds of authority.[388]

For the law was given through Moses; grace and truth came through Jesus Christ. ~John 1:17

Overwhelming Odds

"A large Japanese fleet has been contacted. They are fifteen miles away and headed in our direction. They are believed to have four battleships, eight cruisers, and a number of destroyers. This will be a fight against overwhelming odds from which survival cannot be expected. We will do what damage we can."[389]

BOB COPELAND, captain of the destroyer escort USS *Samuel B. Roberts*, spoke these words to his crew and turned his little ship to face a menacing enemy fleet. The *Roberts* was part of a destroyer screen protecting six escort aircraft carriers off the coast of Leyte in October 1944. The Japanese fleet had come undetected through the San Bernardino Strait the night before and now announced its presence with salvos of 3,200-pound projectiles fired from its18-inch guns.

Outmatched in size, firepower, and speed, the *Roberts* and three other destroyers nearest the enemy fleet launched a desperate attack. They laid a smokescreen to give some cover to the carriers and opened up with their 5-inch guns, which could do little more than annoy the massive Japanese warships. Their only effective weapons were torpedoes, which had to be fired at close range. The *Roberts* steamed ahead through a mounting hail of naval gunfire to within four thousand yards of the enemy battle line to launch her torpedoes and score a hit on an enemy cruiser. The little warship in return suffered devastating and fatal damage from multiple shell strikes. Within a few hours the *Roberts* went down stern first with the loss of ninety crewmen.

Two other destroyers were lost that morning in one of the most gallant actions in U.S. naval history. By sheer determination the sailors of this tiny force slowed and disorganized the Japanese advance, buying time for air attacks to turn the tide of the battle. Admiral Nimitz stated: *"The history of the United States Navy records no more glorious two hours of resolution, sacrifice, and success."*[390] This would be the last surface engagement of the war and one of the finest hours of the U.S. Navy.

> Saul replied, "You are not able to go out against this Philistine and fight him; you are only a boy, and he has been a fighting man from his youth."
> ~1 Samuel 17:33

40mm guns in action against attacking aircraft.
(National Archives)

Burial at sea for sailors killed in action.
(National Archives)

Powder in the Scuttle

THE DESTROYER USS *Heermann* churned ahead at maximum speed toward the Japanese cruiser formation. Incoming shells spouted huge geysers in a rainbow of colors all around the little ship. Red, yellow, and green dye marked the rounds from different enemy guns. The *Heermann* was trying desperately to screen the wounded and badly listing escort carrier, *Gambier Bay*, by laying smoke and disrupting the enemy advance. She had only her 5–inch guns to bear on the larger Japanese ships closing in.

The *Heermann*'s five mounts kept up a steady cadence as each gun crew worked feverishly through the loading cycle over and over again. Fifty-four-pound projectiles came up the shell hoists to be fused and hand-loaded into the breeches. Twenty-eight-pound powder bags were pushed up through scuttles for loading behind the projectiles. The smell of cordite and human sweat became overpowering, especially for the men below decks in the confined spaces of the handling rooms. One sailor described the experience:

> *Round after round I take from Sacco, placing it in the scuttle. As the previous round is removed, I push up a new one and secure it in its seat. Forty, fifty rounds, then the violent action of the ship, a brief pause. Just enough time to bring up more shells from the lower handling room. Many times more, rapid fire, no time for thought. Keep a powder charge in the scuttle. No talk, only Sacco's orders to keep the lower hoist moving. The human machine works flawlessly. We still know nothing of the happenings around us. No feelings, no interruptions, just keep a powder in the scuttle.*[391]

As happens so often in combat, we see men working together to do a job with no idea of the bigger picture around them. They had to get their part done while having faith that others would do theirs and that the overall battle would be fought wisely. This remains a powerful metaphor for our lives in Christ. We try to use our gifts conscientiously in his service while resting in the confidence that he is in control of the outcome.

But those who hope in the LORD will renew their strength. They will soar on wings like eagles; they will run and not grow weary, they will walk and not be faint. ~Isaiah 40:31

Reaching Back

THE MODERN GUIDED missile frigate USS *Samuel B Roberts* was commissioned in 1986, a direct descendant of the World War II ship of the same name lost at Leyte Gulf. In memory of his ship's ancestor, the captain, Cdr. Paul X. Rinn, had a bronze plaque made with an image of the first *Roberts* and a roster of her crew engraved on it. The plaque was prominently displayed on the quarterdeck of the ship and was a key point in the indoctrination of each new crew member.

In 1988 the new *Roberts* struck a mine while escorting Kuwaiti oil tankers in the Persian Gulf. With a fractured keel and twenty-five-foot hole in the hull she was taking on massive amounts of seawater and in imminent danger of sinking. Captain Rinn thought, *"I'm not sure we can save this ship, but we've got to try. . . ."*[392] Working feverishly through a long night he and a determined crew saved the ship. During the night the bronze plaque on the quarterdeck took on a new significance.

In 2001 Paul Rinn was the featured speaker at a reunion of the World War II-era sailors of the *Samuel B. Roberts* and her sister destroyers. Rinn described in detail the heroism of his crew in saving the modern-day *Roberts*. He then told them the story of the bronze plaque with *their* names engraved on it:

> It sent a chill through me on the night of the mining, as we were fighting to save the ship, to see crew members passing the plaque and reaching out and touching it, not just one or two guys but seemingly everyone who passed it. Clearly they were bonding with the heroism of the past.[393]

And so, these sailors of a new era reached back into the past to connect with the courage and struggle of those who had gone before. They were reaching back to the men who had experienced the same fears and hopes, and who had fought the same battle: to save a ship and each other.

A friend loves at all times, and a brother is born for adversity. ~Proverbs 17:17

The Proud and the Humble

MICHAEL CONWAY was a Navy chaplain and one of the great heroes of World War II. When the USS *Indianapolis* was torpedoed and sunk in the Philippine Sea, he and nine hundred other sailors were left adrift. Few lifeboats survived the catastrophe, and most of the men had only their kapok life jackets. Father Conway made it his duty to swim from group to group offering spiritual support and encouragement. After three days and nights of tireless effort, the young priest quietly slipped beneath the surface and was gone.

In a *Saturday Evening Post* article, one of the survivors later recalled the chaplain holding services the day before the *Indianapolis* went down, and needing two mess decks to accommodate the large, overflow crowd. He was always popular with Catholic and Protestant sailors alike. It was reported that in this service, *"He spoke on the parable of the Pharisee and the Publican (or tax collector in modern translations), likening them to two sailors appearing before the captain of the ship."*[394]

Unfortunately, the details of this sermon are lost, but it is not difficult to grasp the intended image: Two sailors accused of breaking regulations stand before the captain for judgment. One is unrepentant and defensive. He argues about the regulation itself and cites how often others break it. He will not admit a mistake. The other sailor has little to say, except to confess his guilt and express his remorse. Looking at each man's similar service record, the captain makes the same decision you or I would make, and confirms the point made by Jesus in his great parable: the humble and remorseful are treated mercifully and justified by their earthly superiors and God. Jesus has little to offer those who justify themselves.

For everyone who exalts himself will be humbled, and he who humbles himself will be exalted. ~Luke 18:14

The Seagull

THEY ATE THE fourth and last orange on the sixth day. It was their last source of nourishment. An even deeper sense of doom settled over the men packed together in the three small life rafts, adrift on the Pacific Ocean. Hunger, thirst, sunburn, open sores, and untreated wounds magnified their sense of despair.

All the odds seemed stacked against this little group, except for one thing in their favor. Among them was the famous airman and World War I ace Eddie Rickenbacker. The ex-military man considered himself the senior of the group, based on his experience, and felt that it was his role to hold the rest together. He became a lonely voice of encouragement. When the food ran out and discouragement seemed to peak, he started prayer meetings twice a day, with Scripture readings from a New Testament belonging to one of the men. The procedure was for each man to read a passage fitting to the occasion, even if some had never read from the Bible before. Rickenbacker found new meaning and a special beauty in the words of Psalm 23 and Matthew 6:31–34.[395]

There were a few cynics in the group at first, until the afternoon of the eighth day. After a Scripture reading and prayer for deliverance, what Rickenbacker termed "a small miracle" occurred. As he was dozing, a seagull landed on his head. With great care he slowly reached up and somehow grasped the bird's legs. They finally had a little food, but, more importantly, had bait for the fishhooks, which had been useless up until then. Their survival was insured. Rickenbacker said later: *"There was not a one of us who was not aware of the fact that our gull had appeared just after we had finished our prayer service. Some may call it coincidence. I call it a gift from heaven."*[396]

> So do not worry, saying, "What shall we eat?" or "What shall we drink?" or "What shall we wear?" For the pagans run after all these things, and your heavenly Father knows that you need them. But seek first his kingdom.
> ~Matthew 6:31–33

Mama Planted the Seeds

EDDIE RICKENBACKER was a great man. He was a hero of two wars, a pioneer of aviation, and a highly successful businessman. He seemed blessed with boundless energy and an ingrained optimism. He endured suffering and faced death more than once. After a disastrous airline crash he literally willed himself back from death, which he described as, *"the sweetest, tenderest, most sensuous sensation. Death comes disguised as a sympathetic friend. It is easy to die. You have to fight to live."*[397] He fought this fight more than most men.

The source of this man's amazing strength of character was a deep religious belief that he acquired as a boy and strengthened during his eventful life:

> *Never, even during my most mischievous escapades, had I lost faith in God. Mama had planted the seeds of religion too deeply in all of us for that. All through my childhood there was a warm, continuing family ritual. After supper . . . Mother would ask one of us to bring in the Bible . . . [She] would open it and begin to read. Her favorite passages were the Sermon on the Mount and the 23rd Psalm, and they are the ones I remember best. She would often stop reading to discuss the meanings behind the Scriptures and how we could apply the principles of Christianity to everyday life.*
>
> *It was my mother who taught us to pray . . . But formal prayer was only the beginning. Mama taught us that the Lord above was a friendly God, a Presence who was interested in our problems and sympathetic to them. Thanks to her influence, I have always talked to God in my prayers . . . full of confidence that He listens and responds.*[398]

This passage presents a perfect prescription for the spiritual development of children. A warm and secure family atmosphere provides the foundation. Reading Scripture together teaches biblical knowledge, and also serves to bring the family closer together. Finally, the parent who explains the power of prayer and leads his or her children by example into a deeper appreciation of it gives them a lifelong resource and path to their own relationship with God. Scripture, prayer, and family form a powerful basis for spiritual growth.

> But as for you, continue in what you have learned and have become convinced of, because you know those from whom you learned it, and how from infancy you have known the holy Scriptures, which are able to make you wise for salvation through faith in Christ Jesus. ~2 Timothy 3:14–15

Payback

FRED HARGESHEIMER bailed out of his P-38 fighter over New Britain, an enemy-held island seven hundred miles north of Australia. For seemingly unending days and nights he struggled through the mountainous terrain and dense jungle. Fighting exhaustion and discouragement, he recalled his youthful days as an Episcopalian lay reader and recited the 23rd Psalm over and over every day: *"Surely goodness and mercy will follow me..."*399 On the thirty-first day a group of natives found him in wretched condition and took him to their little village of Ea Ea, on the north coast of the island. There they nursed him back to health and hid him from frequent Japanese patrols. Eight months later, he was rescued by submarine.

After the war, Fred returned to Ohio where he started work, married, and had children. As time went by, he kept thinking of Ea Ea and the people who had saved him. In 1960, with his family's blessing, he used their vacation money to make the eleven thousand-mile trip back to New Britain. There he got the sense that maybe a simple "thank you" wasn't enough for these wonderful, but extremely poor people.

During the next ten years Fred raised money at home and made several trips back to New Britain to build a school, a library, and a clinic. He started a small oil palm farm, which proved a valuable source of revenue to the village. In 1970 he and his wife moved there to teach in the school. He explained, *"These people were responsible for saving my life. How could I ever repay it?"*400

Fred Hargesheimer didn't just repay a debt. He demonstrated a Christ-like love for these people whom he came to know so intimately. He gave more to them of his time and his money than they had any reason to expect. Christ demonstrated a love even greater than this by giving up his very life for a world that did not deserve it. This is a love that flows from the nature of God and is fortunately not based on the merits of mankind.

All have sinned and fall short of the glory of God, and are justified freely by his grace through the redemption that came by Christ Jesus. ~Romans 3:23–24

Seventy-eight Degrees

A WAR CORRESPONDENT wrote a graphic description of one of the Navy's smallest ships:

> A DE, my friend, is a Destroyer Escort. It's a ship long and narrow, something like a destroyer but much smaller. They are rough and tumble little ships. Their decks are laden with depth charges. They can turn in half the space of a destroyer.
>
> They roll and they plunge. They buck and they twist. They shudder and they fall through space. They are in the air half the time, under water half the time, their sailors say they should have flight pay and submarine pay both.[401]

The men of USS *Conklin* (DE-439) experienced their share of rolling and plunging during antisubmarine duty in the Pacific. In June 1945, however, they were struck by a typhoon with seas of a magnitude seldom seen by any sailor. After a night of violent wind and waves, the storm reached its peak at about 5:00 a.m.

Suddenly the men on the bridge saw an incredibly huge wave building off the port bow. Seconds later they were thrown around like matchsticks as the little ship was knocked over on her side. Three sailors were killed as the ship lost all power and fuel oil flooded the decks. The *Conklin*'s inclinometer measured a roll of seventy-eight degrees, past the point of no return for a ship of her type. After seventy-two degrees the laws of physics decreed that she should keep rolling. In the next instant, however, another wave struck the ship at just the right angle to knock her upright.

The *Conklin* survived her ordeal thanks in part to the desperate efforts and superb seamanship of her crew. Most of them, however, ever after felt that they had experienced a miracle and the hand of God acting to save their little ship and their lives.[402] Human hands could not have brought the *Conklin* back from a seventy-eight–degree roll.

He got up and rebuked the wind and the raging waters; the storm subsided, and all was calm. "Where is your faith?" he asked his disciples. ~Luke 8:24–25

Turn On the Lights

ON JUNE 19, 1944, Japan committed all its remaining carrier forces in an attack on the U.S. invasion fleet at Saipan. During an eight-hour air battle over the Philippine Sea the Japanese carriers were practically stripped of their aircraft as 375 were shot down by American flyers. The next day a U.S. carrier force under Adm. Marc Mitscher was released from its defensive role at the beachhead to seek out the enemy aircraft carriers.

After a long day of empty searching, a scout plane finally sighted the Japanese fleet late in the afternoon. Mitscher knew that a strike at that distance would mean a night recovery of his own aircraft, for which his pilots were not trained. He nevertheless felt the need to seize this fleeting opportunity to strike a decisive blow, and so launched his aircraft as darkness was approaching. At about sunset this strike found and successfully sank one Japanese aircraft carrier and damaged two others.

Now, in total darkness, more than two hundred American pilots found themselves low on fuel and looking for a place to land. The U.S. carriers were steaming toward them, but, as always, were under blackout conditions to protect against air and submarine attack. As some aircraft were starting to run out of fuel, Mitscher faced another crucial decision: to risk his ships or his aircrews. He finally turned to his chief of staff and said, *"Turn on the lights."*[403] Suddenly the fleet was illuminated with running lights, flight deck lights, and star shells exploding overhead. Landing signal officers with fluorescent batons waved in the aircraft. One naval officer on the scene called this, *"One of the war's supreme moments."*[404]

By dispelling the darkness, Mitscher recovered most of his pilots and won one of the greatest naval victories of the war. The darkness surrounding the U.S. fleet on that night is symbolic of the world that Christians find all around them. We have many opportunities to make decisions and to take risks of our own to shine the light of Jesus Christ into those dark places.

When Jesus spoke again to the people, he said, "I am the light of the world. Whoever follows me will never walk in darkness, but will have the light of life." ~John 8:12

Yamamato

IN 1939 ISOROKU YAMAMOTO became commander in chief of the Japanese Combined Fleet. This promotion culminated a brilliant career of naval command at all levels, including two tours of duty in the United States. From his experience he knew more about America than most Japanese, and, consequently, did not favor going to war against America. In a speech before the war he said:

> Most people think Americans love luxury and that their culture is shallow and meaningless. It is a mistake to regard the Americans as luxury-loving and weak. I can tell you Americans are full of the spirit of justice, fight, and adventure. Also their thinking is very advanced and scientific. Lindberg's solo crossing of the Atlantic is the sort of valiant act which is normal for them. That is a typically American adventure based on science. Do not forget American industry is much more developed than ours—and unlike us they have all the oil they want. Japan cannot beat America. Therefore we should not fight America.[405]

These views were not popular with the many pro-war factions in Japan, who were already angry over Yamamoto's opposition to his country's other military adventures. His rise to overall command against such heated opposition was an indication of his brilliance and his reputation among his peers.

This great admiral is seen as a tragic figure of history because he was ultimately drawn into fighting the war that he didn't believe he could win. The choice he had to make was hard: whether to continue his opposition and step down, or to devote his keen intellect to making the best fight possible. It is difficult in retrospect to know what would have happened if he had done more to oppose the war.

As we live our own lives in an uncertain world, we also face difficult decisions. Fortunately, they are seldom of this magnitude, even though they can be extremely stressful from our perspective. We are blessed to know that we are never on our own when we face hard choices. In our times of uncertainty we can turn to God through the spiritual resources that are always available to us: Scripture, prayer, and the loving advice of fellow Christians.

This day I call heaven and earth as witnesses against you that I have set before you life and death, blessings and curses. Now choose life, so that you and your children may live. ~Deuteronomy 30:19

Do We Believe in Prayer?

DAN SNADDON grew up in a small town in Scotland, joined the Royal Army Medical Corps, and became a prisoner of war when the Japanese captured Singapore. For almost four years he lived in utter deprivation and was witness to horrible abuses against himself and his fellow prisoners. His story is an amazing witness to the power of his relationship with God and how his prayers sustained him through conditions that seem impossible for anyone to have endured.

After he was released he had time to reflect on what prayer meant to him. He first thought of his mother's promise to *"go (every morning) into your bedroom at 8 am and kneel at your bed and pray for you."*[406] He thought of his hometown church and all his brothers and sisters in Christ who kept praying for him, even when they didn't know if he was dead or alive. He concluded firmly that, *"I believe that God answers prayer."*[407] He then went on to challenge other Christians about the strength of their beliefs:

> *Worldly men laugh when Christians mention the power of prayer. We are not altogether surprised at this, but let us take ourselves to task. Do we really believe in prayer? I am inclined to believe that deep down in our hearts we really doubt the power of prayer, although we acknowledge the power with our lips. This was my own experience, but prayer is real. It is something tangible. I have found out from my own personal experience that prayer moves the hand of Him who moves the universe. God answers prayer. It is one of the most powerful and potent means that God has put into the hands of the believer. In fact, one has written that 'Satan trembles when he sees the weakest saint upon his knees.'*[408]

We know that God does not always cure the sick or save those in danger. If we believe the apostle Paul's words that "to die is gain" (Philippians 1:21), we can safely assume that God's plan is at work no matter the outcome. But we can take even stronger encouragement from Dan Snaddon's witness that he has seen God respond to specific prayers, and, especially, that he has been sustained through the direst possible circumstances by his relationship with God through prayer.

Be joyful always; pray continually; give thanks in all circumstances, for this is God's will for you in Christ Jesus. ~1 Thessalonians 5:16–18

Old Glory flies over a U.S. aircraft carrier.
(National Archives)

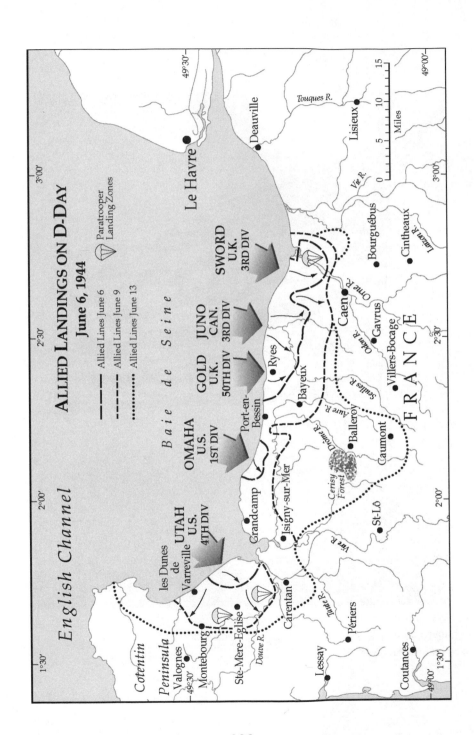

ALLIED LANDINGS ON D-DAY
June 6, 1944

Paratrooper Landing Zones

Allied Lines June 6
Allied Lines June 9
Allied Lines June 13

English Channel

Baie de Seine

Cotentin Peninsula

les Dunes de Varreville

UTAH
U.S.
4TH DIV

OMAHA
U.S.
1ST DIV

GOLD
U.K.
50TH DIV

JUNO
CAN.
3RD DIV

SWORD
U.K.
3RD DIV

Le Havre

Deauville

Touques R.

Lisieux

Bourguébus

Cintheaux

Caen

Orne R.

Odon R.

Gavrus

Villers-Bocage

FRANCE

Ryes

Bayeux

Seulles R.

Port-en-Bessin

Grandcamp

Isigny-sur-Mer

Aure R.

Balleroy

Drôme R.

Cerisy Forest

Caumont

St-Lô

Carentan

Taute R.

Vire R.

Douve R.

Ste-Mère-Église

Montebourg

Valognes

Lessay

Périers

Coutances

Miles

OCTOBER
The Invasion of France

D-DAY FOR THE invasion of France was June 6, 1944. General Dwight Eisenhower's mission was simply stated:

> You will enter the Continent of Europe, and, in conjunction with the other United Nations, undertake operations aimed at the heart of Germany and the destruction of her armed forces.[409]

After months of preparation and years of fighting on the periphery, the time had finally come to strike directly at Germany with the aim of ending the war. The scale of Operation Overlord was unlike anything seen before. Three airborne divisions jumped into inland landing zones ahead of the beach landings. Five divisions made an amphibious assault over a fifty-mile-wide swath of the Normandy coast, ahead of fifty more divisions that would eventually pour in to take the battle into Germany. More than five thousand vessels and eleven thousand aircraft were assembled for this massive undertaking, and artificial harbors were created along the beaches to handle the massive logistical flow.

The German units manning the coastal defenses of Normandy were well prepared by this time and offered bitter resistance at almost every point. The first waves of the American 1st Division were hit hardest crossing Omaha Beach. The moment the landing craft ramps went down, they were decimated by accurate machine gun and artillery fire from positions dominating the beach. The high ground was taken by the end of D-Day thanks to the initiative and courage of small-unit leaders and individual soldiers.

Fortunately for the Allies, on a strategic level, the German high command was surprised at the timing and location of Overlord. Even as the Normandy landings were unfolding, they continued to expect the main invasion further north where the beaches were better. Also, the weather seemed to play a miraculous role in events by giving a brief window of opportunity for the invasion during a prolonged period of otherwise impossible conditions. Massive Allied air attacks added to the German confusion and further hampered movement of reserves that could have assisted forces defending the beaches.

By the end of D-Day, one hundred seventy-five thousand Allied troops and fifty thousand vehicles were ashore along the Normandy coast. The cost in lives and materiel was high, but by any measure, the invasion was a complete success. The British had returned and the Americans had finally arrived on the continent of Europe.

The Change Was Electric

FOR THE INDIVIDUAL soldiers the buildup to D-Day was long and tedious. Isolated at bases throughout England, they were kept as busy as conditions permitted but were told little. Everything was a secret, and no loose talk was permitted. Everything had a number: the tents, the vehicles, the men themselves. Many felt they were without identity among countless thousands of others waiting to do an uncertain job at an indefinite time in the future. One correspondent observed that, *"It simply drove the mind into a fixed apathy."*[410] On June 3 the same correspondent was finally able to report a profound change in this sullen atmosphere:

> *That evening the soldiers were told the plan and what they had to do. The change was electric. The suspense was snapped. A wave of relief succeeded it. Now that the future was known and prescribed everything would be easier. We were to embark the following afternoon. We would sail during the night. H-Hour was the following morning. . . . As the men stood in their ranks listening to the colonel you could feel the confidence growing. Here at last was something practical and definite, something to which one could adjust oneself.*[411]

We each deal with a lot of uncertainty in life as we face the indefinite future. We don't know what crisis waits next with our families, our jobs, or other things we haven't thought of yet. For me these daily concerns often seem to merge into a vague and semiconscious anxiety. I am always better off when I take the time to deliberately and prayerfully focus on each concern and, with God's help, formulate some kind of action plan. God wants to either take our worry away or help find us find a way to do something specific about it. Like the men of D-Day we find relief when we know what we face and what we have to do.

Do not be anxious about anything, but in everything, by prayer and petition, with thanksgiving, present your requests to God. ~Philippians 4:6

The Great Crusade

ON THE EVE OF D-Day, General Eisenhower published a leaflet for every member of the invasion force, to inform, to inspire, and to seek God's blessing:

British soldier reads D-Day message.
(Eisenhower Presidential Library)

> *Soldiers, Sailors and Airmen of the Allied Expeditionary Force! You are about to embark upon a great crusade, toward which we have striven these many months. The eyes of the world are upon you. The hopes and prayers of liberty-loving people everywhere march with you. In company with our brave Allies and brothers in arms on other fronts, you will bring about the destruction of the German war machine, the elimination of Nazi tyranny over the oppressed peoples of Europe, and security for ourselves in a free world. Your task will not be an easy one. Your enemy is well trained, well equipped and battle-hardened. He will fight savagely. But this is the year 1944! Much has happened since the Nazi triumphs of 1940–41. The United Nations have inflicted upon the Germans great defeats, in open battle, man-to-man. Our air offensive has seriously reduced their strength in the air and their capacity to wage war on the ground. Our Home Fronts have given us an overwhelming superiority in weapons and munitions of war, and placed at our disposal great reserves of trained fighting men. The tide has turned! The free men of the world are marching together to Victory! I have full confidence in your courage, devotion to duty and skill in battle. We will accept nothing less than full Victory! Good Luck! And let us beseech the blessings of Almighty God upon this great and noble undertaking.*[412]

As we have seen before, national leaders were not reluctant to call their troops and nation to God during the crucial moments of World War II. D- Day was one of those times. The spiritual humility of America's leaders and the prayerfulness of her citizens kept the nation focused on God, the true source of American unity and strength that had sustained the nation throughout its history.

I lift up my eyes to the hills—where does my help come from? My help comes from the LORD, the Maker of heaven and earth. ~Psalms 121:1–2

Creating a Bond

BOB BENVENUTO enlisted in the Navy in 1943 as a seventeen-year-old. When he finished boot camp, he found his name on a roster of men heading to an unknown destination—beginning an almost indescribable odyssey. It started, with more than a thousand others, on a waterfront pier in New York, where he waited for two weeks. Finally, his group was marched onto the *Queen Mary*, which arrived in Scotland five days later. After another week he went by train to Southhampton, England, where he was herded into an open field early in the morning to wait all day in the rain for a ship to arrive. At 1:00 a.m., after his personal "longest day," a large ship came into the loading ramp and opened huge clamshell doors. Bob went aboard LST (Landing Ship Tank) 279 to receive the biggest surprise of his life:

> *I was amazed! At two a.m. we went on board exhausted . . . And surprise of all surprises, awaiting us, in spite of the hour, were hot showers and a turkey dinner. The Captain welcomed us aboard and explained that he was aware of our ordeal and sorry for the delay in bringing the ship in. He had ordered the cooks to prepare the special dinner and directed the chief engineer to open the fresh water showers just for us. To make our welcome complete he advised and allowed us to sleep in til mid day. And so it was, that we became shipmates of, and part of the crew of the LST 279. The concern and compassion of the captain (Lt. James T. Beard) had created a bond that night between his new crewmen, ship's company and 'his' ship, that lasted throughout the entire European tour of duty.*[413]

This story gives food for thought on the subject of hospitality. Are we doing all we can to welcome guests into our churches? If we are truly mission-oriented, these are the most important people at every service, not our friends and fellow church members. The first experience of a visitor can shape his or her attitude toward the message and body of Christ for a long time to come. An unexpected kindness may have a lasting and even an eternal impact.

> For I was hungry and you gave me something to eat, I was thirsty and you gave me something to drink, I was a stranger and you invited me in. ~Matthew 25:35

Gen. Eisenhower gives encouragement to paratroopers.
(Eisenhower Presidential Library)

Church service before invasion.
(National Archives)

Shipboard Service

THE TROOPSHIP weighed anchor at 6:30 p.m., moving south into the gathering darkness. The night was not totally black and the outline of untold numbers of other ships could be seen on all sides. The lanes through the minefields had been cleared and marked, and the ships moved through uneventfully. At about 9:00 p.m. someone came on the ship's public address system to read D-Day messages from the Navy admirals and General Eisenhower. Not long after, the ship moved past a line of battleships, waiting in the darkness.

Later still, one of the unit chaplains held a service on the quarterdeck. He stood on top of a packing crate as the troops gathered around. The ship was rolling by then in heavy seas and several men had to support the chaplain to keep him from falling off his perch. The troops crowded round in their life belts and steel helmets, seeking comfort in the chaplain's words and familiar passages of Scripture. In the words of the old hymn, "Abide with Me," they found special reassurance of God's presence on a dark night:[414]

> Abide with me; fast falls the eventide; The darkness deepens: Lord with me abide.
> When other helpers fail and comforts flee, Help of the helpless, O abide with me.
>
> Not a brief glance I beg, a passing word; But as Thou dwell'st with Thy disciples, Lord,
> Familiar, condescending, patient, free. Come not to sojourn, but abide with me.
>
> Thou on my head in early youth didst smile; And, though rebellious and perverse meanwhile,
> Thou hast not left me, oft as I left Thee, On to the close, O Lord, abide with me.
>
> I need Thy presence every passing hour. What but Thy grace can foil the tempter's power?
> Who, like Thyself, my guide and stay can be? Through cloud and sunshine, Lord, abide with me.[415]

He that dwelleth in the secret place of the most High shall abide under the shadow of the Almighty. I will say of the LORD, He is my refuge and my fortress: my God; in him will I trust. ~Psalms 91:1–2 (KJV)

The Soldier's Load

THE BRITISH STEAMER *Princess Maude* arrived at her designated spot off Omaha Beach at midnight. The American troops aboard were supposed to be sleeping, but few were able. Many went topside to gaze at the thousands of other vessels in the invasion armada, while others congregated in small groups to talk and pass the time. At 2:00 a.m. the mess decks were opened for breakfast. Finally it was time to get ready. Chuck Hurlbut, a combat engineer, described what happened next:

> Then you put your stuff on. We all had new olive-drabs. I think we had long johns. We had a field jacket. And then they gave us these impregnated coveralls. They were so stiff and unwieldy they could almost stand up by themselves. They had been specially treated with some solution that would withstand gas. You put those on. And on top of that, you had your belt, your gas mask, a bandolier of bullets. And your cartridge belt had a bayonet, a canteen, a first aid packet, and more bullets. Your helmet. I made sure the chinstrap was down. And your rifle. And your backpack, which had your mess kit, your shovel, and your incidentals. There's 50 or 60 pounds of stuff.[416]

Fifty to sixty pounds is probably a conservative estimate of the weight on these soldiers. Rations, grenades, and engineer equipment are not even mentioned. They had a lot to prepare for to carry out their mission in the invasion. In reading this passage, you might recall that the apostle Paul also urged us to, *"Put on the full armor of God,"* so that we can perform our mission in his service. Most of this armor is defensive in nature, except for one item: the sword of the spirit. God's Word is our offensive weapon guaranteeing victory over every evil power threatening us.

Stand firm then, with the belt of truth buckled around your waist, with the breastplate of righteousness in place, and with your feet fitted with the readiness that comes from the gospel of peace. In addition to all this, take up the shield of faith, with which you can extinguish all the flaming arrows of the evil one. Take the helmet of salvation and sword of the Spirit, which is the word of God. ~Ephesians 6:14–17

Soldiers of Our Savior

THE PARATROOPERS knew the time had come when they were given live ammunition. The days had been long in the crowded airfield hangars with endless briefings, calisthenics, chow lines, and waiting. There had already been one twenty-four-hour postponement and everyone's nerves were on edge. Pvt. 1st Class Leslie Cruise realized the long wait was almost over. To his load of k-rations, canteens, first-aid pack, extra clothing, M-1 rifle, and bayonet, he added a belt full of 30-caliber ammunition and two extra bandoliers, plus fragmentation and smoke grenades, and a 9-inch anti-tank mine.

(Eisenhower Presidential Library)

As he checked his gear he patted his left breast pocket where he kept his most important item: a small New Testament that his mother had given him. Thinking of his Bible, he said a quiet prayer to himself: *"God help me to commit myself to the task ahead and help me to be a good soldier, and save me from harm."*[417] He knew that he and his fellow soldiers would need the power of God in the night and days ahead.

Early in the evening of June 5 Cruise attended to one final preparation before donning his equipment. He gathered with others for a chapel service led by his chaplain, Capt. George "Chappie" Wood. During the service the chaplain said a prayer for the paratroopers that Leslie never forgot:

> *Almighty God, our Heavenly Father: Who art above us and beneath us, within and around us, drive from the minds of our paratroopers any fear of the space in which thou art ever present. Give them the confidence in the strength of thine everlasting arms, endue with clear minds and pure hearts that they may participate in the victory which this nation must achieve in thy name and through thy will. Make them hardy soldiers of our country as well as thy son, our Savior, Jesus Christ. Amen.*[418]

Pray also for me, that whenever I open my mouth, words may be given me so that I will fearlessly make known the mystery of the gospel. ~Ephesians 6:19

Moment of Reckoning

SHORTLY BEFORE 11:30 p.m. the converted Royal Air Force bomber began rolling down the runway at Keevil airfield. Members of the 12th Yorkshire Parachute Battalion, laden with their equipment and weapons, were huddled in the bay, deep in their own thoughts. As the wheels of the aircraft ceased to roll, Capt. Philip Burkinshaw realized they were airborne. He vividly recalled his thoughts at that moment:

> My mind was awhirl with mixed emotions and, I must confess, some fears, particularly the fear of being afraid. Would we be dropped on or near to the dropping zone, or perhaps due to change in the weather or wind speed, or a fault in navigation, well behind enemy lines; would I find the rendezvous; how would I shape up in front of my platoon in the stark reality and unaccustomed horrors of battle, and would I command and guide them as they deserved. The moment of reckoning was inexorably approaching for me, as it was for thousands of others in the air, on land and on sea.[419]

Anyone who has experienced combat can identify with Captain Burkinshaw's fears. Most would agree that the fear of not measuring up in the eyes of others is acute, especially before going into action for the first time. No one knows how he or she will react in a crisis until that "moment of reckoning." We should all realize, of course, that such a moment is ahead for every human being. We are all approaching the end of life and the great unknown at a speed we cannot measure. Our last moment may arrive in due course or unexpectedly. God has provided the one and only way to alleviate our instinctive fear of this event. Through his Son, we are assured that our "moment of reckoning" will be a joyous reunion, as we take our place with him in eternity.

But now that you have been set free from sin and have become slaves to God, the benefit you reap leads to holiness, and the result is eternal life. For the wages of sin is death, but the gift of God is eternal life in Christ Jesus our Lord. ~Romans 6:22–23

Lips Moving Wordlessly

THE BRITISH WAR correspondent sat nervously in the eerie glow of the aircraft's interior red lights. The paratroopers' faces appeared slightly blue and the tips of their cigarettes white as they joked among themselves and waited. After a sharp turn over the coast the exterior lights and rotating beacons of all the aircraft in the formation were extinguished, giving them a ghostlike quality as they headed out over the Channel toward their Normandy drop zones. The correspondent described the final minutes before this group of men would start the invasion of Europe:

> *Someone called out: "Ten minutes to go." The paratroop commander talked quietly to his men. A final briefing. I shall never forget the scene up there in those last fateful minutes, those long lines of motionless, grimfaced young men burdened like pack-horses so that they could hardly stand unaided. Just waiting... So young they looked, on the edge of the unknown. And somehow, so sad. Most sat with eyes closed as the seconds ticked by. They seemed to be asleep, but I could see lips moving wordlessly. I wasn't consciously thinking of anything in particular, but suddenly I found the phrase "Thy rod and Thy staff" moving through my mind again and again. Just that and no more.*[420]

The apparent tranquility of this scene is betrayed by the many lips "moving wordlessly" in the semidarkness. Who can imagine the inner turmoil of a group of men facing a night parachute drop into enemy territory? The dangers multiply as each man visualizes all that can happen. I have great empathy for the unfortunate souls who had only the cold comfort of their own thoughts in these moments. Fortunately, we know there were many who had a place to go outside themselves. Moving lips is sure evidence that some were seeking God in this fearful moment. Prayer is the only activity I know of that guarantees us a way outside ourselves. We need to build this bridge with God during the quiet times in our lives so that it will be there during those fearful moments when our minds want to multiply the dangers ahead.

> Because Jesus lives forever, he has a permanent priesthood. Therefore he is able to save completely those who come to God through him, because he always lives to intercede for them. ~Hebrews 7:24–25

Trees

AS THE C-47 neared the drop zone it was bouncing furiously. Turbulent air and flak were giving the paratroopers a rough ride. Malcolm Brannon was number 15 in a stick of eighteen jumpers, and, with all his gear, weighed about three hundred pounds. To stand up and hook up to the static line were not easy tasks, and to remain standing was almost impossible as the aircraft rose and fell violently. As the light flashed green and the jumpmaster shouted, *"Go!"* he pushed those in front as he was pushed from behind, out the door into the darkness.

Within seconds Brannon felt the sharp and reassuring jolt of his opening canopy. Enemy tracers were lacing the air around him, and he began praying for his friends and for himself. As he neared the ground he became aware that he was drifting backwards. Fearing a bad landing with his heavy equipment, he tried unsuccessfully to maneuver his parachute so that he could hit the ground facing forward. As time ran out, he tensed for the worst. Suddenly there was a *swish* as he passed through the limbs of a tree and a slow deceleration as he came to a stop one foot from the ground. He said later, *"I was under HIS guidance—I knew and I said, 'Thanks.'"*[421] Amazingly, he was also reminded in that moment of an old poem expressing reverence for the same thing that had saved him:

> *I think that I shall never see A poem lovely as a tree.*
> *A tree that looks at God all day, And lifts her leafy arms to pray;*
> *Poems are made by fools like me, But only God can make a tree.*[422]

Only God can make a tree, and only God can give a frightened soldier the faith that a greater power is with him in the midst of danger.

> And the LORD God made all kinds of trees grow out of the ground—trees that were pleasing to the eye and good for food. In the middle of the garden were the tree of life and the tree of the knowledge of good and evil. ~Genesis 2:9

Broken

THE YOUNG FRENCH girl was fast asleep when the walls of her house seemed to shake. She then heard loud voices and got out of bed to see what was happening. The nine-year-old Marie-T Lavieille opened the door to the kitchen and saw a strange sight. A large man was seated in the middle of the room. His face was painted black, and he was wearing a helmet with leaves and a khaki uniform full of pockets. He was holding his right arm and speaking words that she could not understand. Her mother and brothers stood around him as he kept saying over and over, *"Broken, broken."* After a while, the injured man bandaged his own shoulder and gave Marie a chocolate bar from one of his pockets. One of her brothers drove him somewhere to get medical attention. It was a night she would never forget. Her family had helped an American paratrooper of the 82nd Airborne Division. Marie later said of the incident:

> *'Broken'—this first English word remains burned in my memory. For me, I was just 9 years old—and because of this extraordinary experience—I became an English professor, often serving as an interpreter during ceremonies of the anniversary of D-Day.*[423]

Sometimes we forget how impressionable a child can be. My wife and I once met an extremely talented illustrator of children's books. I will never forget his concern for how a young mind might perceive his artwork. He was convinced that a violent image could be fixed in the memory of a child, with lasting consequences. In our present age of television and video games this seems like an almost quaint notion: to guard the images and protect the minds of our children. The story of Marie and the paratrooper is a reminder of how important it is to keep trying, no matter how difficult is seems. A child's images are lasting. We need to make sure that as many as possible are wholesome and uplifting.

> But if anyone causes one of these little ones who believe in me to sin, it would be better for him to have a large millstone hung around his neck and to be drowned in the depths of the sea. ~Matthew 18:6

Forward Observer

HOURS BEFORE DAYLIGHT on D-Day four men in a rubber boat approached Omaha Beach. Three Navy frogmen dropped off into the water. The fourth man, Lt. William Smith, continued to the beach where he crawled ashore in darkness and dug a shallow foxhole for protection. His dangerous mission was to get to the beach undetected and to adjust naval gunfire by radio.

Lieutenant Smith, or "Smitty" as he was called, understood his overwhelming responsibility. He had landed in North Africa and Sicily, and knew what the weapons hidden above him could do to troops and landing craft. He was a twenty-seven-year-old veteran, handpicked for this new and untried assignment, and had trained for weeks in the difficult art of coordinating the fire of moving ships against stationary targets.

Smitty was also a very religious man. When he packed his duffel bag, the last thing in and the first thing out was his Bible. When he wasn't on the job, his first priority was reading it, and he did this every night without fail. He also turned to God frequently in prayer. His son later described how he prepared for his D-Day mission:

> *He had long ago resolved himself to the near certainty of his own death. He was going to call fire as long as he had a single breath in his body. He would leave his own fate, and thus the fate of many of those coming ashore in his sector, to God . . . he asked only that God look out for them. As usual, there was no thought of his personal safety. On this day God certainly had more important things to think about than him.*[424]

At the end of a long and harrowing day on Omaha Beach, Smitty turned off his radio and thanked God, not for his own survival, but that he had been able to do his job successfully. He also said a prayer for *"those brave, brave men that had fallen in service to their nation, and their God."*[425] He was awarded the Bronze Star for his heroic actions on D-Day.

Sing to the LORD a new song, for he has done marvelous things; his right hand and his holy arm have worked salvation for him. ~Psalms 98:1

Field Marshal Rommel inspecting beach defenses.
(Eisenhower Presidential Library)

Landing craft ramp goes down on a Normandy beach.
(National Archives)

I Didn't Feel Too Good

THE BOAT RIDE TO Omaha Beach was somewhat peaceful—until the ramp of the landing craft went down. Sgt. Hy Haas looked out on a scene of pure terror. Smoke and machine-gun bullets filled the air. The sound of mortar and artillery shells exploding was ear-splitting. Haas went into the water first to scout for mines, and then drove his self-propelled anti-aircraft gun off the landing craft into the water. It was pandemonium. He had been on the beach only a few minutes when an officer ran up to him gesturing to a point ahead. There was a German bunker blocking the advance to the bluff overlooking the beach. Through a clearing in the smoke, Haas got a clear shot at the bunker and destroyed it.

This proved to be an important action in the drama on Omaha Beach. Haas had opened up one of the vital egress routes off the beach, allowing his comrades to advance onto the high ground beyond. Not long after, he was moving past the destroyed bunker:

There were the Germans we had shot. They were in an awful state. And you could say, "Look, thousands of our guys were hit, and I don't know how many dead." Yet when I saw what we had done, I didn't feel too good. Because I had never really hurt anybody before. Those Germans were our enemies, and yet to see those guys bleeding from the mouth . . . They just lay out there on the bunker. I don't know if they lived or not.[426]

We read the description of battles and see the casualty figures, and think that we understand what happened. However, we either have to see it for ourselves, or we have to read a first person account such as this, to truly grasp the tragedy. Combat is not a video game. Men inflict real pain and suffering on each other, and many do not survive. Fortunately, humanity does not disappear entirely, as the conscience of this young soldier proves. He did his job, but he didn't feel good about it. Hopefully we will always find young men of such character to defend our nation.

How much more, then, will the blood of Christ, who through the eternal Spirit offered himself unblemished to God, cleanse our consciences from acts that lead to death, so that we may serve the living God! ~Hebrews 9:14

Follow Me

THE FIRST WAVE to hit Omaha Beach was devastated. As the ramp dropped on his landing craft, Chuck Hurlbut stepped into the water and quickly saw the ranks of his unit shredded by enemy gunfire. He struggled through the surf to the sound of explosions, small arms fire, and the cries of wounded soldiers. Somehow he made it across the beach to the dune line, where he found more devastation and chaos. He didn't know where he was or where the others in his unit were. There were no leaders, only other scared and disoriented soldiers like himself. Looking seaward he saw landing craft burning and bodies all over the beach. The rumor swept through the dispirited men that the invasion on Omaha Beach had failed and that those there were stranded. He wondered where they would go. Into the water? At this dark moment he witnessed an amazing phenomenon:

> All of a sudden, a guy here, a guy there, a sergeant here, "Come on guys, let's go get them." They started up. They got these snipers along the way. They blew out a pillbox. About 1 o'clock, 1:30, up on a hill, way up on the horizon, I saw some Yankees, waving, "Come on up! Come on up!" And whoever those guys were, they were the heroes. They lacked the leadership but they had that initiative, the soldier quality, that said, "We're not gonna die here. Let's go get these guys!"[427]

The hallmark of American fighting men in World War II and in the present day is summed up in one word: initiative. When officers are not physically present, small-unit leaders and individual soldiers step up to do what needs to be done. This is partly due to training, and partly due to something in the American character. The individualism and personal responsibility that we see in our soldiers are by-products of the freedom that they enjoy as Americans. This freedom was God's gift at the founding of this nation and the reason he has blessed America throughout much of her history.

It is for freedom that Christ has set us free. Stand firm, then, and do not let yourselves be burdened again by a yoke of slavery. ~Galatians 5:1

Fieldstripping an M-1

JAMES JORDAN was in the first wave on Omaha Beach. His landing craft took a direct hit from an artillery shell that killed many of his fellow soldiers instantly. He went into the water and found himself sinking under the weight of a seventy-five-pound pack and weapon. Fortunately, he was able to ditch all his gear, make his way back to the surface, and swim to shore. He recalled, *"As badly as things had begun for me, once I made the beach, it got worse."*[428] Picking up an abandoned M-1 rifle, Jordan moved forward under heavy machine-gun fire to a seawall where he found what was left of his platoon. He described what he did next:

> *I then discovered the rifle I had picked up from the beach wouldn't fire, probably due to being clogged with sand. I picked up a second rifle that was on the beach close to the sea wall. This one wouldn't fire either. After the third rifle I found wouldn't fire, I realized I would have to clean it in order to have a functioning weapon. So, while still behind the sea wall, I stripped down the M-1 and cleaned the trigger housing with a toothbrush that I still had from one of my pockets. That one worked.*[429]

This story reminded me of my first training as a Marine officer candidate at Quantico, Virginia. Fieldstripping and cleaning our rifles was a daily ritual. To emphasize the importance of a clean weapon, our young sergeant-instructor told us how he had lost his rifle cleaning kit while fighting in Korea and had used his toothbrush for weeks to clean his M-1. At the time, the concept of putting a clean rifle ahead of oral hygiene was not easy for a group of college boys to swallow. Just like Private 1st Class Jordan in this story, we all learned differently later. Without a functioning weapon, a Marine or soldier in combat is pretty useless and helpless.

In his letter to the church at Ephesus, the apostle Paul described the spiritual armor available to Christians, including our primary and only offensive weapon: *"the sword of the Spirit, which is the word of God"* (Ephesians 6:17). Burnishing this sword through frequent study and application should be our own daily ritual.

Put on the full armor of God so that you can take your stand against the devil's schemes. ~Ephesians 6:11

First through the Wire

HARLEY REYNOLDS was supposed to land after the first assault wave on Omaha Beach. However, the first wave was late and his was early. He quickly lost men in his machine-gun section as he tried to get a foothold on the fire-swept beach. Trying to explain it, he said, *"Confusion doesn't describe it."* For a while his constant thought was, *"What's keeping me up? I must be hit. Too many bullets were flying not to be hit."*[430]

The first cover he spotted was a raised roadbed running along the beach where he found respite from the heavy fire. He gathered his men there as best he could, trying to figure out what to do next. Barbed wire on the road and a wire fence beyond blocked the advance. The incoming tide would soon make his safe spot untenable.

Help soon arrived in the form of a small soldier with a long bangalore torpedo. Exposing himself to enemy fire, the soldier moved up to slide the torpedo under the wire and then inserted a fuse lighter. When the charge detonated Reynolds didn't hesitate:

> *My head was three or four feet from the torpedo and I was closest to the path it blew in the wire. My men were behind me better than we had even done in practice. I went through the trip wire high stepping just as we did on obstacle courses. I was running so fast I hadn't made up my mind what to do about the wire fence until I faced it. I literally dove through in a sideways dive . . . Troops on the beach seemed to be holding back but not for long.*[431]

Staff Sergeant Reynolds was later credited with being the first man through the barbed wire on this beach. He played a critical role in opening the way for others to fight their way forward to the high ground needed to secure the beachhead. For his heroic actions he was awarded the Bronze Star, French Croix de Guerre, and Purple Heart. His courage inspired many others on Omaha Beach and continues to inspire us today.

Be strong and courageous. Do not be terrified; do not be discouraged, for the LORD your God will be with you wherever you go. ~Joshua 1:9

To Train for the Kingdom

Be strong!
We are not here to play, to dream, to drift.
We have hard work to do and loads to lift.
Shun not the struggle,
Face it: 'tis God's gift.[432]

THIS POEM WAS prominently posted on Lt. John Burkhalter's trunk and gave a glimpse of his character. Burkhalter was a highly decorated chaplain with the 1st Division, landing early on Omaha Beach on D-Day. He had been ordained in 1935 and served as pastor of a Florida church until he enlisted in the Army in 1942 at age thirty-three. He was a former National Championship high school football player and professional boxer for eight years. With the 1st Division, he was awarded the Silver Star for gallantry in action after heroically exposing himself to enemy fire to recover casualties. He looked and lived like a true combat chaplain, as evident in a colleague's description:

> *He stands before his congregation in a faded fatigue uniform, feet braced, chest thrown out, jaw thrust forward. His strong-looking hands hold firmly to the hymn book. He stands there, a powerful figure, his eyes meeting every man's glance like a boxer looking for an opening. When he talks he speaks like a coach addressing a group of athletes in training. He doesn't harangue or plead or scold. His words carry his own conviction and confidence in what he is saying. This is the way to train for the Kingdom of God, he implies in his manner, hands on hips, head thrust forward slightly. These are the things to do. This is how to do them.*[433]

If you believe the axiom that, *"young men don't need counselors, they need role models,"* you can visualize this man as a perfect military chaplain. His appearance, his attitude, and his faithfulness inspired men who were not easily impressed, as he successfully took the Word of God into a difficult and dangerous venue. His life was an inspiration then and now to live and act boldly for God's kingdom, epitomizing the words of the old hymn: *"Stand up, stand up for Jesus, ye soldiers of the cross!"*[434]

> David said to the Philistine, "You come against me with sword and spear and javelin, but I come against you in the name of the LORD Almighty, the God of the armies of Israel, whom you have defied." ~1 Samuel 17:45

I Was Talking to Him

CHAPLAIN JOHN BURKHALTER suffered with his men on Omaha Beach. He saw landing craft obliterated by direct hits and countless men cut down as they tried to reach the shore. He saw wave after wave pile up on the beach, unable to advance. Every advantage seemed to be with the Germans and every disadvantage with his troops. Through it all he prayed earnestly, with faith that only God could see anyone safely through such a nightmare. In retrospect he was certain that he would never forget those moments. He knew that during the ordeal he had drawn very close to God. In a letter to his wife, he explained:

> *Nobody can love God better than when he is looking death square in the face and talks to God and then sees God come to the rescue. As I look back through hectic days just gone by to that hellish beach I agree with Ernie Pyle that, "it was a pure miracle we ever took the beach at all."[435] Yes, there were a lot of miracles on the beach that day. God was on the beach D-Day; I know He was because I was talking to Him.[436]*

This story must surely prove beyond doubt that it is possible to find God in any situation. If this man could survive Omaha Beach with that conviction, we can have faith that God will be with us in our day-to-day crises. We can also see here an even more amazing attribute of God. Our relationship with him actually grows stronger as our plight worsens and our reliance on him deepens. We may have to look back to see it, but our personal lows can be and often are our spiritual highs. Have faith that, no matter what pain you are in, he is there when you keep *"talking to Him."*

I will proclaim the name of the LORD. Oh, praise the greatness of our God! He is the Rock, his works are perfect, and all his ways are just. A faithful God who does no wrong, upright and just is he. ~Deuteronomy 32:3–4

Soldiers help each other off the beach.
(National Archives)

Medics give aid to the wounded.
(National Archives)

Hero of Omaha

JOSEPH DAWSON never considered himself a professional soldier. Even so, he was an infantry company commander and one of the great heroes of D-Day. After his landing craft was hit and almost wiped out, he reached Omaha Beach where he found groups of disorganized soldiers trying to stay alive in the maelstrom. He gathered those nearest him and began moving forward under the withering fire. Attacking through a minefield, he was wounded but continued to lead the assault until the high ground overlooking the beach was taken. His group was one of the first to penetrate the enemy beach defenses on D-Day, and Dawson himself was later awarded the Distinguished Service Cross. His citation reads in part:

> With absolute disregard for his own personal safety, Captain Dawson moved from his position of cover on to the mine field deliberately drawing the fire of the enemy machine guns in order that his men might be free to move. This heroic diversion succeeded and his combat group crossed the beach to move into the assault on the enemy strongpoint. During this action, Captain Dawson was wounded in the leg. In a superb display of courage in the face of heavy enemy fire, Captain Dawson although wounded, led a successful attack into the enemy stronghold.[437]

Dawson was offered a full commission in the regular army after the war, but chose instead to return to civilian life. He said, *"I was a civilian that was granted the opportunity to defend my country."*[438] In writing about his actions on D-Day he displayed great reverence and humility over his success and survival:

> It is awesome, even now, to me to see how we could possibly have survived, because the terrain there is remarkable in that it has the high ridge overlooking the beach itself, in such a dramatic way . . . It was only just the luck of God that allowed me to find a little opening which permitted us to get off of the beach. I've always felt a degree of humility as well as thanking God for having had the opportunity for making a break which allowed us to proceed off of Omaha.[439]

The fear of the Lord teaches a man wisdom, and humility comes before honor.
~Proverbs 15:33

Take the Skillet off the Stove

GEORGE DAVISON was one of many black American soldiers to land on the Normandy beaches on D-Day. He was a member of a barrage balloon battalion responsible for protecting the invasion beaches from air attack. These soldiers had to go in under fire and operate from foxholes on the beach. Their balloons were tethered to cables designed to keep enemy aircraft above strafing altitude along the shoreline.

Davison was a very religious man, and his spiritual strength came through in letters to his wife, Mary, and son, Richard. He told them, *"I have been to church and Sunday school and asked for forgiveness of everything I (have) ever done to anyone and prayed . . . After laying in my hole in the ground and listening to bullets go over my head bursting beside me, not more than reaching distance away, I have come to the conclusion that there is one with more power than the walking, would stand by me and see me home again."*[440]

He especially felt God's hand supporting him at the crucial moments when he approached the beach in a landing craft filled with ammunition:

As a truck went down the ramp, I grabbed on to the racks and this truck went out of sight so I let go . . . So there I am in that water, with too much weight, so I shrugged my shoulders and off went my musette bag . . . all the time this was happening the enemy was putting down a steady stream of cross fire, we were let off in to deep waters. I believe the Lord was on my side because if he would have let just one of those tracers hit those 105 howitzer shells it would have been all over. You could have taken the skillet off the stove cause the gas would have been gone![441]

It is inspiring to hear the story of a soldier's simple faith during a dangerous time. His belief in a caring God sustained him on the beaches of Normandy and is the kind of faith that will sustain each of us through any crisis.

> Praise be to the Lord, to God our Savior, who daily bears our burdens. . . . Our God is a God who saves; from the sovereign LORD comes escape from death.
> ~Psalms 68:19, 20

He Speaks French

AFTER THE EXCITEMENT of serving on a landing craft during the assault on Omaha Beach, Albert Berard's life settled into a dull routine offloading supplies in the port of Cherbourg. When convoys started running to Paris, he and some friends saw a chance to relieve the boredom. Without asking anyone, they left their unit and hitched a ride on a truck headed east. Late that night they were dropped off on the outskirts of Paris, where they did in fact begin quite an adventure. Fortunately for the group, Berard spoke fluent French and quickly made friends everywhere he went. He and his friends were welcomed as conquering heroes. One family in particular adopted the sailors and held a banquet in their honor. The mother of the family wrote a letter to Berard's mother with a heartfelt message:

> We are pleased to have with us this evening your son, Albert, along with three of his comrades. We would like to compliment you on the pleasant manner in which he speaks French, in a manner which is correct, well-bred, and educated. Not knowing you, we hope that you will receive good news from all your children that might be in harm's way and that all return in good health. This evening this French family is experiencing a very good time and sincerely holds you in our thoughts . . . May God protect you always.[442]

The hospitality shown these young Americans was warm and genuine. After years of Nazi occupation, the French people were grateful to their allies for their liberation. These bonds of affection have continued to the present day, despite occasional political disputes on the national level. On a personal level, most French men and women have a soft spot for any American who shows a willingness to try to speak their language. Such an effort is always pleasing to God, as he blesses any attempt to reach out to others while trying to understand their point of view.

Carry each other's burdens, and in this way you will fulfill the law of Christ.
~Galatians 6:2

The Nun

L T. JIM PENTON'S tank destroyer unit moved into Vire at dusk. His men dug in among the ruins of the French village as German artillery fire continued to fall all through the night. As the sun came up they surveyed the damage done to their vehicles and equipment. They also noticed a convent to the rear of their position when the amazing sound of morning bells chimed, joining the wail of the German 88s. They then saw an even more amazing sight. A solitary nun began moving through the village feeding and watering the livestock, milking the cows, and collecting eggs. She worked serenely through the morning even while the German artillery kept the soldiers huddled in their foxholes. Lieutenant Penton described his reaction:

> *I know that our most argumentative and skeptical atheist was duly fascinated and impressed by that display of the power and force of that Sister's faith—and complete fearlessness . . . It was not the sudden, stimulated and short-lived courage which drives a man to risk hot lead on a daring dash to aid a buddy, to me, it was far more than that . . . It was the picture of a mellowed and complete faith—it was serenity of mind and soul amidst man's savagery of arm and spirit.*[443]

Not all of us will ever feel that adrenaline surge that bolsters courage in the heat of the moment. Far more often, we would do well to follow the example of this nun and go about our daily tasks resolved to meet our own responsibilities, whatever they may be. It may be tiresome, ordinary, and unglamorous. It may be a quietly precarious position. But we must continue to perform our tasks with the conviction that God will take care of us as he sees fit. (JG)

Whatever you do, work at it with all your heart, as working for the Lord, not for men. ~Colossians 3:23

The Little Pocket Bible

BEFORE GOING ashore on Utah Beach, someone handed Louie Havard a pocket Bible that he carefully placed in the left breast pocket of his uniform jacket. He didn't think too much about it after that due to the heavy fighting on D-Day and afterward. His unit, Company L of the 4th Division, remained in almost constant contact with the enemy as it fought inland.

A few days later Havard was seriously wounded near Cherbourg. He was struck in the chest by shrapnel, which would have entered his heart, except for the presence of the little pocket Bible in his chest pocket. The book deflected the metal fragment just enough to miss his heart and go into his left arm. He was evacuated to a field hospital where he underwent the first of many operations. After his first surgery, the doctor presented him the Bible that was in his pocket and told him that it had saved his life. Years later, Havard's daughter observed that she and two succeeding generations also owed their lives to that Bible.[444]

We are amazed at the story of one small Bible deflecting a piece of shrapnel and extending a man's life. His family joyfully accepted this event as a miracle and a blessing to themselves and untold descendents to come. Even more amazing is the knowledge that every Bible contains all that is necessary to save human souls, and that millions have been blessed by the power of this great book. Every human being is able to claim this greater miracle through the life-changing message revealed in its pages. Through Jesus Christ we are offered the unearned gift of a relationship with our Father in heaven during this life and throughout eternity.

All Scripture is God-breathed and is useful for teaching, rebuking, correcting and training in righteousness, so that the man of God may be thoroughly equipped for every good work. ~2 Timothy 3:16–17

No Distant Unknown

PVT. 1ST CLASS Albert Kishler fought with the 9th Army in Europe. In December 1944 he wrote to a friend to describe his thoughts during combat. Like many others who faced constant fear he felt God's presence.

> *Sunday—God's Day. The man who said that there are no atheists in fox-holes had hit the nail on the head. When the sun goes down and darkness steals in, life to the infantrymen becomes nothing more than a gust of wind. The nights are long, fifteen hours and cold and you are invariably dug in the middle of a sugar beet field—Germany is all beet fields, orchards, and towns. To get back to the foxhole, there you are—a grenade in one hand, more handy, and your other hand fingering your BAR [Browning Automatic Rifle]—it's you and good old Mother Earth and God. And when the time comes that you leave that hole and charge across several hundred yards of enemy territory with machine guns burning, 88's and mortars thinning your numbers, God is never forgotten. To us, death is no distant unknown . . .[445]*

When we live in relative prosperity and good health, death can be a remote possibility—in fact, it can be a distant unknown. Unfortunately, as we go about the routine of our lives, God himself can become a distant unknown. Albert Kishler's story reminds us how this can change in a life-and-death situation. With such a reminder, we know we should not wait for a crisis to think seriously about our relationship to God. The goal of our Christian walk should be to grow constantly closer to him through daily prayer, study, and worship. God wants us to share our hopes and to give our fears to him, whether great or small. As our relationship with him grows and deepens, his presence will be an immediate comfort to us on a daily basis and in the crises that we must inevitably face.

And now, O Israel, what does the LORD your God ask of you but to fear the LORD your God, to walk in all his ways, to love him, to serve the LORD your God with all your heart and with all your soul. ~Deuteronomy 10:12

It Might as Well Be in a Church

IT WAS A STRANGE church service. The little Belgian village was in ruins after being fought over only a few days before. Battle-weary veterans came back from the front lines to join in. Replacements coming up also took part. It was an unusual mixture of dirty and clean uniforms, expressionless stares and boisterous enthusiasm. The men from the front lines had seen too much, the replacements too little. Tanks and jeeps were pulled up all around the little church where an American chaplain and a Belgian priest were conducting an ongoing service for anyone who could stop. One soldier described the scene as the chaplain recited the Lord's Prayer:

As he neared the end, German 88s started to drop nearby. No one moved. Just as he finished, a shell landed quite near the church. Normally, men would have been making a mad dash for cover, but for some strange reason, nobody moved—we just stood there. Then behind me on the opposite side of the church, a man with a deep voice started reciting the 23rd Psalm, and soon everyone joined in. The shelling continued, but it seemed that the voices of the men became stronger. I guess the thought was, if we are going to die, it might as well be in a church.[446]

Psalm 23 (KJV)

The LORD is my shepherd; I shall not want.
He maketh me to lie down in green pastures: he leadeth me beside the
still waters.
He restoreth my soul: he leadeth me in the paths of righteousness for his
name's sake.
Yea, though I walk through the valley of the shadow of death, I will fear
no evil: for thou art with me; thy rod and thy staff they comfort me.
Thou preparest a table before me in the presence of my mine enemies:
thou anointest my head with oil; my cup runneth over.
Surely goodness and mercy shall follow me all the days of my life: and I
will dwell in the house of the LORD forever.

Fate

IN JUNE 1944 Arnold Brown took command of Company G of the 358th Infantry Regiment fighting in France. His company had seen a lot of action and had suffered fifty percent casualties in recent engagements. He had three days to reorganize for the next attack on the Island of Seves. On the day of the battle he learned a lesson:

> There was one sergeant, I couldn't get him out of his foxhole to join us for the attack. He was squatted down below ground level, and he was frozen with fear. After this attack, which was also a failure, I went back to check on him. There he was, crouched down in that foxhole in the same position I'd last seen him. The only difference was, he had a hole in his steel helmet. For him to get killed like that it took a treeburst artillery shell, and a piece of shrapnel had to go straight down into that foxhole. The lesson I learned was, if it's your time you cannot hide. I decided that I may get it, but I'm going to be doing my job when I do. If he had joined us in the attack, he might be alive today.[447]

I had a similar experience in Vietnam that haunted me for a long time. Due to a premonition, one of my men refused to go with his unit on an operation. I sent him back to a rear area intending to deal with him on our return. Unfortunately, the man was killed by a rare rocket attack on the base. My feelings then were similar to those of the officer in this story. As a Christian, however, I have come to see a different lesson in these incidents. I believe that these men did not meet some preordained "fate." They were killed by random and senseless acts of war. In any dangerous situation we can take measures to minimize our risks, and we can pray for God's protection. Our actions and prayers can make a difference. One thing is for certain: our prayers will always bring us closer to God, our ultimate source of comfort and peace.

Moreover, no man knows when his hour will come: As fish are caught in a cruel net, or birds are taken in a snare, so men are trapped by evil times that fall unexpectedly upon them. ~Ecclesiastes 9:12

All Right, God

MACHINE-GUN FIRE from a German pillbox had stopped their advance. Myron Eberle moved forward to try to get the attack moving, when enemy mortar shells started falling all around him. He described his experience in the next few moments as, *"the most vivid of my entire life"*:

> *While issuing orders, the thought popped into my mind with no prelim-*
> *inary warning, that "I was going to die, right now!" My response was*
> *not spoken, but it was none the less a response, and it was, "Well, all*
> *right God, if it is time." And with my response came over me the most*
> *peaceful, serene, joyous feeling that everything was going to be wonder-*
> *ful and death was going to be a marvelous experience.*[448]

Almost in the same instant, a mortar shell struck right beside the awestruck soldier. Eberle himself was unhurt by the blast and survived the battle with the belief that God had given him a special message. He felt that he had received assurance for the rest of his life that *"death will not be very frightening when we actually get there . . . God does indeed want us for his own."*[449]

As Christians we know the truth of this soldier's revelation. Our Savior conquered death for us and waits to receive us in a wonderful place. Even though we understand this, we are still inspired by this story and find our faith strengthened by this soldier's experience. One man's reassurance from God is reassuring to us all. Death is truly nothing to fear. God does want us for his own.

> When the perishable has been clothed with the imperishable, and the mortal with immortality, then the saying that is written will come true: "Death has been swallowed up in victory."
> "Where, O death, is your victory?
> Where, O death, is your sting?" ~1 Corinthians 15:54–55

D-Day Message

IN THE SPRING OF 1944 Barbara Sanz started writing to Lester McClannen, a good friend of her brother. At that time she was a divorced mother of two, and he was an Army cryptographer stationed in England. On June 6th Barbara learned of the D-Day invasion and heard the president's radio address that night. She was profoundly moved by this news and wrote an emotional letter to Lester:

> Now I understand why I have not heard from you. The "Day" has come. I can't explain the feeling I had when I first heard of the Invasion. I heard it when I walked in the (beauty) shop this morning, I was stunned. We all knew it was coming and were happy that it is started, so it can all end soon. When it actually happens it's a shock. It was such a gloomy day, rained all day. That didn't help much. We had the radio going all day.
>
> The President gave a prayer tonite that the nation was to join. Believe me, when I say I put my whole heart and soul in that prayer and will continue to pray knowing that you and the other boys have help and come out on top.[450]

I believe that Barbara Sanz's response to the president's prayer was representative of the vast majority of Americans on that fateful day in 1944. It was natural to hear a call to God in a time of such crisis, and it was natural to respond. I believe that God heard and answered those prayers. If America were called to prayer in that manner today, I believe that millions would respond in the same way. We can only pray that God will continue to hear our prayers and that our nation will continue to be worthy of his blessing.

> But let all who take refuge in you be glad; let them ever sing for joy. Spread your protection over them, that those who love your name may rejoice in you. For surely, O LORD, you bless the righteous; you surround them with your favor as with a shield. ~Psalms 5:11–12

Christian Soldiers

ON JUNE 6, 1944, Flora Southwick of Marietta, Ohio, wrote her husband, Erman, after learning of the invasion of France:

> Today we have lived history. I can't even describe my sensations when I turned on the radio this morning. Somehow there is a feeling of relief that things have actually started . . . I am not very optimistic about things coming easily but I can face the future with my chin up and I know that whatever the future holds for us we shall face with courage and dignity . . . Just took time out to hear the President and then heard Fred Waring's musical group do "Onward Christian Soldiers." The most beautiful arrangement I have ever heard . . .[451]

"Onward, Christian Soldiers" was a favorite hymn of my childhood and sung often in the Kingston Presbyterian Church in Conway, South Carolina. It was also sung at the funeral of President Dwight Eisenhower at the National Cathedral in March 1969. I am sure the hymn was popular during the World War II era due to its martial flavor and stirring theme. The military overtone may be less in vogue in modern times, but I believe the words of this great hymn are still an invigorating call to action for Christians to unite in the cause of carrying Christ's gospel to the world:

> Like a mighty army moves the church of God;
> Brothers, we are treading where the saints have trod.
> We are not divided, all one body we,
> One in hope and doctrine, one in charity.
>
> Crowns and thrones may perish, kingdoms rise and wane,
> But the church of Jesus constant will remain.
> Gates of hell can never gainst that church prevail;
> We have Christ's own promise, and that cannot fail.
>
> Onward, Christian soldiers, marching as to war,
> With the cross of Jesus going on before.[452]

Endure hardship with us like a good soldier of Christ Jesus. ~2 Timothy 2:3

Weather for Overlord

THE SEQUENCE OF weather events surrounding Operation Over-lord is one of the most miraculous stories of World War II. The D-Day invasion was vastly complex and had many meteorological requirements. A low tide at first light was needed to expose beach obstacles to the assault waves. A full moon after midnight the night before was necessary for airborne operations. June 5 and 6 came closest to meeting these conditions.

Additionally, however, the winds could not be too strong for landing craft and paratroopers. The clouds could not be too low for aircraft. Surf conditions had to be acceptable. The chief meteorologist estimated the odds of all these requirements being met in early summer on the coast of France as fifty or sixty to one.[453] On June 4 a stormy English Channel seemed to bear out these odds. D-Day on the 5th had to be canceled.

From the German perspective, May seemed a more likely month for the invasion. During periods of good weather in May, coastal defense forces were put on maximum alert. When the weather turned bad in early June, readiness was relaxed and some units were withdrawn from the coast for exercises inland. Conditions were so bad that reconnaissance aircraft could not fly. General Rommel felt that action was so unlikely that he left his headquarters for a visit to Germany.

With ships at sea and all of his forces poised to go, General Eisenhower and his staff agonized over each weather report. A slim chance for a break on June 6 was forecast. The moon and tides would not be right again until June 19–20. On this slim hope, Ike finally announced, "OK. We'll go."[454] The weather was not perfect. It was just bad enough to lull the German defenders and just good enough to allow the essential Allied landing operations to proceed successfully.

When gale force winds struck the Normandy coast on June 19–20, General Eisenhower sent his chief meteorologist a note saying how thankful he was that they went when they did. He would not have had a second chance. Thanks to this miraculous weather pattern, the greatest invasion in history succeeded.

> Then the Lord sent a great wind on the sea, and such a violent storm arose that the ship threatened to break up. ~Jonah 1:4

In Case of Failure

Our landings in the Cherbourg-Havre area have failed to gain a satis-factory foothold and I have withdrawn the troops. My decision to attack at this time and place was based on the best information available. The troops, the air and the Navy did all that bravery and devotion to duty could do. If any blame or fault attaches to the attempt it is mine alone.

— Gen. Dwight D. Eisenhower, July 5, 1944[455]

THIS MESSAGE, if broadcast, would have announced one of the greatest disasters in history: the failure of the Allied invasion of Normandy. It is difficult to imagine the ramifications of such a scenario. Would Germany have had time to fully develop its jet aircraft, missile, and nuclear technologies and to ultimately prevail in "Fortress Europe?" Would the Soviets have conquered more or even all of Europe? Would the United States have eventually used nuclear weapons against Germany?

None of these questions can be answered and, fortunately, don't have to be. General Eisenhower's message was a handwritten note found in his belongings by an aide weeks after the invasion. He never had to deliver it to the public.

Although never used, Eisenhower's "in case of failure" message provides two great insights into the events of D-Day. First, we see into the character of the Supreme Commander himself, with more evidence that he was a decent man. He would never have considered pointing a finger at subordinate commanders or the weather. Second, we have another reminder of just how uncertain success was on D-Day. In retrospect, many events of history may seem inevitable. Only when we go back and look at the details do we see how precarious those events were. The "in case of failure" message fully documents that success on this momentous day was not inevitable.

We should obviously be thankful for the skill of the commanders and the bravery of the troops who achieved this great victory. We should also be thankful for a God whose merciful providence made it possible.

No eye has seen, no ear has heard, no mind has conceived what God has prepared for those who love him. ~1 Corinthians 2:9

D-Day Remembered

ON JUNE 6, 1984, President Ronald Reagan gave a speech com- memorating the fortieth anniversary of the D-Day invasion. He spoke to a group of veterans assembled at Pointe du Hoc, overlooking the beaches of Normandy. In his moving talk, he asked rhetorically why men like these would put aside their instinct for self-preservation and risk their lives to overcome such overwhelming obstacles. What inspired them?

We look at you, and somehow we know the answer. It was faith and belief; it was loyalty and love.

The men of Normandy had faith that what they were doing was right, faith that they fought for all humanity, faith that a just God would grant them mercy on this beachhead or on the next. It was the deep knowledge—and pray God we have not lost it—that there is a profound, moral difference between the use of force for liberation and the use of force for conquest. You were here to liberate, not to conquer, and so you and those others did not doubt your cause. And you were right not to doubt.

You all knew that some things are worth dying for. One's country is worth dying for, and democracy is worth dying for, because it's the most deeply honorable form of government ever devised by man . . .

Something else helped the men of D-Day: their rock-hard belief that Providence would have a great hand in the events that would unfold here; that God was an ally in this great cause. And so, the night before the invasion . . . General Matthew Ridgway on his cot, listen(ed) in the darkness for the promise God made to Joshua: "I will not fail thee nor forsake thee."

These are the things that impelled them; these are the things that shaped the unity of the Allies.[456]

We pray that what inspired our heroes of D-Day will continue to inspire and unify our nation during the troubled times that will inevitably come in the future. We hope and pray that America will continue to put God's will and his guidance ahead of all other worldly concerns.

> The LORD himself goes before you and will be with you; he will never leave you nor forsake you. Do not be afraid; do not be discouraged. ~Deuteronomy 31:8

President Reagan speaks at the 40th Anniversary of D-Day.
(National Archives)

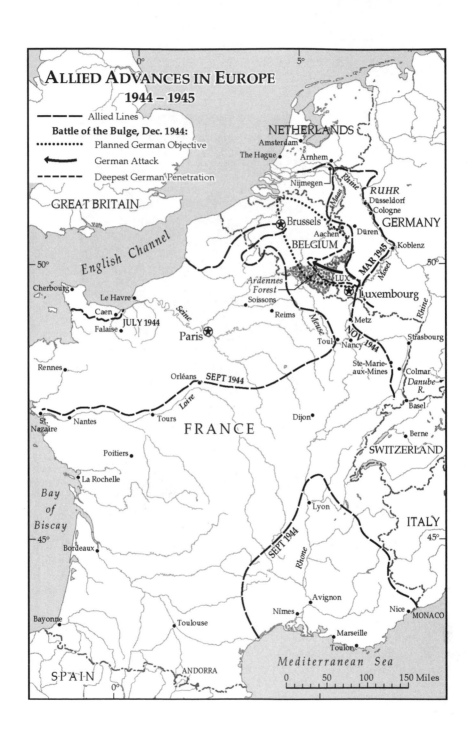

ALLIED ADVANCES IN EUROPE
1944 – 1945

— — — Allied Lines

Battle of the Bulge, Dec. 1944:

• • • • • • • • • • Planned German Objective

◄——— German Attack

— – — – — Deepest German Penetration

GREAT BRITAIN

NETHERLANDS

Amsterdam
The Hague
Arnhem
Nijmegen

Rhine

Maas

RUHR
Düsseldorf
Cologne

GERMANY

Brussels

Aachen
BELGIUM
Düren
Koblenz

English Channel

MAR 1945

Mosel

Ardennes
Forest

LUX

Cherbourg

Le Havre
Caen
JULY 1944
Falaise

Soissons

Reims

Luxembourg

Seine

Paris

Meuse

Metz

NOV 1944

Nancy

Strasbourg

Toul

Ste-Marie-
aux-Mines

Colmar

*Danube
R.*

Rennes

Orléans
SEPT 1944

Rhine

Basel

St.
Nazaire
Nantes
Tours

Loire

Dijon

Berne

FRANCE

SWITZERLAND

Poitiers

La Rochelle

*Bay
of
Biscay*

Lyon

ITALY

Bordeaux

SEPT 1944

Rhone

Bayonne

Toulouse

Avignon

Nîmes

Nice
MONACO

Marseille
Toulon

SPAIN

ANDORRA

Mediterranean Sea

0   50   100   150 Miles

NOVEMBER
Victory in Europe

BY THE END of June 1944, one million Allied troops had crossed the Normandy beaches onto French soil. After weeks of hard fighting, the port of Cherbourg was taken, followed by a massive air and land assault centered on the town of St. Lo, enabling the first decisive Allied breakout from the beachhead in late July. Progress eastward was rapid from this point, as other American and French units landed on the Mediterranean coast and began advancing from the south. By early September Paris was liberated, and a continuous Allied line was soon established from the Swiss border to the English Channel.

With Soviet armies closing from the east and almost continuous bombing of industrial sites from the air, the Nazi high command concluded that the defense of France was futile. German forces were pulled back and consolidated behind the natural barrier of the Rhine River network. Although the first German city, Aachen, was captured in October, the Allied advance slowed almost to a standstill due to bad weather and mounting supply problems.

As freezing temperatures and cloudy weather started to settle over central Europe in late 1944, Hitler conceived a bold offensive campaign to relieve the pressure on his reeling army. On December 16 his generals launched an eleven-division assault through the Ardennes Forest aimed at Brussels and Antwerp. In a stroke, Hitler sought to split the Allied armies and to deny the Allies the vital port facilities at Antwerp. This desperate move had little chance of ultimate success, but still caught the Allies by surprise and seriously disrupted their planned offensive operations. The ensuing Battle of the Bulge was fought bitterly over a two-week period. The focal point was at Bastogne, where the 101st Airborne Division held out even though cut off and surrounded. When the weather cleared just before Christmas Day and Patton's 3rd Army advance units arrived, the issue was decided. By early January all German forces were eliminated from the "bulge," with the loss of two panzer armies and eight hundred tanks. There would be no further offensive efforts by the German army.

After the Battle of the Bulge it was only a matter of weeks before the Allied armies continued to push to the east. In March 1945 the Rhine

River barrier was forced at several points, as the German defenses began to collapse all along the front. The British and Canadian armies on the left flank raced for the German North Sea ports. The American 1st and 9th armies advanced on the Ruhr Valley, cutting off Germany's main industrial region from the rest of the country. Patton's Third Army, meanwhile, attacked east along the Danube toward Czechoslovakia.

As the war was nearing an end, General Eisenhower made a controversial strategic decision with long-range consequences for the postwar era. He did not attempt to capture Berlin. Stopping short and directing his forces southward at other objectives, he allowed the Soviets uncontested control of the German capital. As Red Army forces encircled Berlin, Hitler finally committed suicide on April 29. By strange coincidence, Franklin Roosevelt and Benito Mussolini also died within days of the German leader's death. Shortly thereafter, a German provisional government accepted surrender terms and a cease-fire. At Eisenhower's headquarters, Marshal Alfred Yodl signed the formal document:

We, the undersigned . . . hereby surrender unconditionally to the Supreme Commander, Allied Expeditionary Force, and simultaneously to the Supreme High Command of the Red Army, all forces on land, sea, and in the air who are at this date under German control.[457]

At 11:01 p.m. on May 8, 1945, World War II in Europe came to an end.

Bonhoeffer

DIETRICH BONHOEFFER was a German Christian during World War II. He was a Lutheran theologian, pastor, and leader of the Confessing Church, which opposed the anti-Semitic policies of the Nazis. Arrested by the Gestapo in April 1943 and imprisoned in a series of camps, he was finally hanged at Flossenburg on April 9, 1945, a few weeks before that city was liberated. While in prison, he wrote parts of his great work, *Ethics*, including a treatise on the role of the church in the modern world:

> *The way of Jesus Christ, and therefore the way of all Christian thinking, leads not from the world to God but from God to the world. This means that the essence of the gospel does not lie in the solution of human problems, and that the solution of human problems cannot be the essential task of the Church.*
>
> *The Church's word to the world is the word of the incarnation of God, of the love of God for the world in the sending of His Son, and of God's judgment upon unbelief. The word of the Church is the call to conversion, the call to belief in the love of God in Christ, and the call to preparation for Christ's second coming and for the future kingdom of God.*[458]

Bonhoeffer articulated a unique and timeless perspective on the relationship between the Church and God. The church is God's vehicle for redeeming the world, not the world's vehicle for bringing its problems to God. This perspective is as vital today as ever.

This is what is written: The Christ will suffer and rise from the dead on the third day, and repentance and forgiveness of sins will be preached in his name to all nations. ~Luke 24:46–47

Bonhoeffer on Freedom

IN 1944 DIETRICH BONHOEFFER wrote an essay titled, "Stations on the Way to Freedom." Its message is especially poignant considering his state of imprisonment at the time he wrote it. In this masterful work he addressed the subjects of self-discipline, action, suffering, and death. Each of these will be highlighted over the next several days.

Self-discipline

If you set out to seek freedom, you must learn before all things
Mastery over sense and soul, lest your wayward desirings,
Lest your undisciplined members lead you now this way, now that way.
Chaste be your mind and your body, and subject to you and obedient,
Serving solely to seek their appointed goal and objective.
None learns the secret of freedom save only by way of control.[459]

Bonhoeffer presents here an apparent paradox. To be free, we must be in control. This seems contradictory, until we realize the extent to which we can be governed by our passions. When our whims and desires rule our behavior, we are truly imprisoned. When we have no firm foundation we are out of control and at the mercy of the world's expectations and our own uncertain judgment. Only when Jesus Christ controls our lives are we truly free to live as we are intended: with joyful hope in him and a sure purpose in service to his kingdom.

Jesus replied, "I tell you the truth, everyone who sins is a slave to sin. Now a slave has no permanent place in the family, but a son belongs to it forever. So if the Son sets you free, you will be free indeed." ~John 8:34–36

Action and Freedom

IN HIS SECOND STATION on the way to freedom, Dietrich Bonhoeffer calls us away from the realm of abstract thought and good intentions to the real world of action.

Action

Do and dare what is right, not swayed by the whim of the moment.
Bravely take hold of the real, not dallying now with what might be.
Not in the flight of ideas but only in action is freedom.
Make up your mind and come out into the tempest of living.
God's command is enough and your faith in him to sustain you.
Then at last freedom will welcome your spirit amid great rejoicing.[460]

We have read many stories about men and women who took action during time of war, in spite of their fears and the uncertainty of the times. Wartime seems to present situations requiring practical action rather than abstract ideas. There are times when the same applies in our spiritual lives. We all need times of quiet study and contemplation. However, this kind of activity is not an end in itself. These times are meant to prepare us to take action in service to God's kingdom. We know that faith without works is dead. We don't work our way to God, but if he is within us, we will want to do great things for him.

When we are tempted to feel too ill-equipped to accomplish anything for God, remember that it is not our ability that God is interested in, but our availability. Moses was convinced he was the wrong man for the job of leading the Israelites out of Egypt. But God told him, *"I will be with you"* (Exodus 3:12). In the same way, the apostle Paul tells us why we should never feel inadequate: *"I can do everything through him who gives me strength"* (Philippians 4:13). (JG)

> You foolish man, do you want evidence that faith without deeds is useless? . . . As the body without the spirit is dead, so faith without deeds is dead. ~James 2:20, 26

Suffering and Freedom

DIETRICH BONHOEFFER suffered persecution and imprisonment for his Christian beliefs. For him to consider his suffering an integral step on his way to freedom is one of the most amazing witnesses ever recorded.

Suffering

> *See what a transformation! These hands so active and powerful*
> *Now are tied, and alone and fainting, you see where your work ends.*
> *Yet you are confident still, and gladly commit what is rightful*
> *Into a stronger hand, and say that you are contented.*
> *You were free from a moment of bliss, then you yielded your freedom*
> *Into the hand of God, that he might perfect it in glory.*[461]

Elsewhere in this book are stories of American and Japanese soldiers who suffered in prison and, through this suffering, found freedom in Christ. Out of the depths they discovered a new and better life. While few of us today will experience the tribulation of a prisoner of war camp, there will come a time in each of our lives when we will discover our own suffering. It could be chronic pain or a terminal illness, losing a loved one, battling depression, or simply a gnawing sense of being unfulfilled.

We need to understand that God uses these experiences to draw us closer to him. Have you noticed that we experience the most growth when times are difficult? When circumstances are easy, we have no reason to rely fully on the Lord. In the Psalms we see how David handled suffering. Psalm 10 begins with a cry of desperation: *"Why, O LORD, do you stand far off?"* (v. 1). But by the end of the same chapter, David comes to rely on his knowledge of God's character. May our own trials be times of honestly seeking the Lord. (JG)

> You hear, O LORD, the desire of the afflicted;
> You encourage them, and you listen to their cry,
> Defending the fatherless and the oppressed,
> In order that man, who is of the earth, may terrify no more. ~Psalms 10:17–18

Death and Freedom

A FTER EXPLORING the subjects of discipline, action, and suffering, Dietrich Bonhoeffer came to the final and ultimate step toward freedom—death itself.

Death

Come now, highest of feasts on the way to freedom eternal,
Death, strike off the fetters, break down the walls that oppress us,
Our bedazzled soul and our ephemeral body,
That we may see at last the sight which here was not vouchsafed us.
Freedom, we sought you long in discipline, action, suffering.
Now as we die we see you and know you at last, face to face.[462]

Throughout this devotional are stories of miraculous survival and answered prayers. However, we know that many prayers, from our human perspective, were not answered. During World War II thousands of soldiers and sailors paid the ultimate price and did not return home. Bonhoeffer here speaks for these brave men and women, revealing the ultimate survival that was theirs as Christians: eternal life with their Lord and Savior. Only a Christian can face death with this joyful hope. We know what waits for us. And only when we part with this temporary dwelling place of earth can we enjoy our homecoming reunion with the Lord and all his saints who have gone before us.

The apostle Paul eagerly anticipated meeting Jesus again face to face: *"We are confident, I say, and would prefer to be away from the body and at home with the Lord"* (2 Corinthians 5:8). And yet, he did not allow himself to dwell on that heavenly future so much that he neglected his earthly tasks: *"So we make it our goal to please him, whether we are at home in the body or away from it"* (2 Corinthians 5:9). We should also anticipate death with confidence, knowing it is the passage to heaven; and yet continue in the good works God has given us to do here on Earth until he calls us home. (JG)

For to me, to live is Christ and to die is gain. ~Philippians 1:21

The Church Must Confess

BEFORE HE WAS executed, Dietrich Bonhoeffer voiced criticism of the German Lutheran Church for its compromises with the Nazi government:

> The church must confess that she has witnessed the lawless application of brutal force, the physical and spiritual suffering of countless innocent people, oppression, hatred, and murder, and that she has not raised her voice on behalf of the victims and has not found ways to hasten to their aid . . . By her own silence she has rendered herself guilty because of her unwillingness to suffer for what she knows is right.[463]

James Dobson has used this quote to point to the present day church's passivity on the issue of abortion.[464] I am not qualified to comment on the validity of this criticism. Many individual Christians and churches have worked diligently in this area, especially to give viable choices other than abortion to troubled expectant mothers. I am very much in favor of this approach on the personal level. I am not so certain of what is appropriate on the political level. I believe churches and Christian groups are on dangerous ground when they seek power through the political process, no matter how worthy the cause. We certainly make our primary duty of bringing Christ's message to the world more difficult for ourselves if we are perceived as trying to coerce others in matters of conscience. Our Founding Fathers wisely preempted this issue as they wrote the Constitution. Christians should be thankful for this freedom of conscience and for the freedom to use persuasion in changing the conscience of others.

This is the covenant I will make with them after that time, says the Lord. I will put my laws in their hearts, and I will write them on their minds. ~Hebrews 10:16

Don't Disgrace Your Name

JOE GRASER WAS serving with Patton's 3rd Army in Europe when he learned that his younger brother, Don, back in Ohio, had been inducted into the Army. He wrote a heartfelt letter to his brother giving him advice on being a soldier and a man:

> As Mom always said you are judged by the company you keep, so don't be to [sic] hasty at first with whom you run around with, wait a while then pick out a buddy or so . . . you will see it's very easy to give your religion up, while in the service, since no one is there to remind you about it, but always live the way you were brought up, over two years ago when I came in Mom told me, to be careful & never to disgrace my name, that is something that has always been on my mind, in whatever I do & surely has been a guidance to me.[465]

My first thought on reading this letter was that telling a loved one not to "disgrace his name" sounds like advice from a bygone era. Today it almost seems a quaint notion. What would a young person now consider disgraceful? For many in today's culture, probably little short of being caught committing a felony. Yet, the biblical imperative stands, to "*Honor your father and mother.*" We do this by giving them respect and by doing nothing to bring them embarrassment or shame. I think it reasonable to expand the scope of this injunction to the family as well, so that our actions honor them and bring credit to them in the larger community.

It is also important to remember that our Lord Jesus taught us an even more expansive view of how we should live in relation to these commands. We are called to fulfill these obligations out of love rather than obedience. When his love fills our hearts, we are able to lovingly bring honor to him, to our parents, and to our families. In love, we will never disgrace his name or our own.

> I will put my laws in their minds and write it on their hearts. I will be their God, and they will be my people. ~Jeremiah 31:33

I Precede You

K IM MALTHE-BRUUN was a Danish partisan sentenced to die for smuggling weapons to a resistance group. He wrote a last letter to his mother trying to comfort her with his thoughts about life after death:

> *I am an insignificant thing, and my person will soon be forgotten, but the thought, the life, the inspiration that filled me will live on. You will meet them everywhere—in the trees at springtime, in people who cross your path, in a loving little smile. You will encounter that something which perhaps had value in me, you will cherish it, to become large and mature.*
>
> *I shall be living with all of you whose hearts I once filled. And you will all live on, knowing that I have preceded you, and not, as perhaps you thought at first, dropped out behind you . . . Follow me, my dear mother, on my path, and do not stop before the end.*[466]

This young man's expectations are not unlike many today. There is pale hope that something of himself will live on in the memory of others. He knows intuitively that he has thoughts and inspirations that are not going to die. But what happens to them?

We need to appreciate the power of the gospel message to bring hope to those with this mindset. In Christ Jesus we are blessed to know exactly where we're going. The young man in this story also has an intuition that in dying, he will go ahead of the living to a place where they will eventually come. Vague speculation is not necessary here either. Jesus has assured us: *"I am going there to prepare a place for you"* (John 14:2). Likewise, I believe it is true that, when our time comes, we in turn go to prepare the way for others. This is our joyful hope in Jesus Christ: he conquered death for us, so that we and our loved ones can be with him forever.

And if I go and prepare a place for you, I will come back and take you to be with me that you also may be where I am. You know the way to the place where I am going. ~John 14:3–4

Pray for Ourselves

GENERAL PATTON asked his chaplain a startling question: *"How much praying is being done in the Third Army?"* The chaplain admitted that there were probably few prayers being said, other than by the unit chaplains themselves. The general leaned back in his swivel chair, looked at the other man intently, and declared:

> *Chaplain, I am a strong believer in prayer. There are three ways that men get what they want; by planning, by working, and by praying . . . But between the plan and the operation there is always an unknown. That unknown spells defeat or victory, success or failure. It is the reaction of the actors to the ordeal when it actually comes. Some people call that getting the breaks; I call it God. God has His part, or margin in every-thing. That's where prayer comes in. Up to now, in the Third Army, God has been very good to us. We have never retreated; we have suffered no defeats, no famine, no epidemics. This is because a lot of people back home are praying for us. We were lucky in Africa, in Sicily, and in Italy, simply because people prayed. But we have to pray for ourselves, too.*[467]

There is plenty of room to question General Patton's theology. To con-sider praying one of three ways for men to *"get what they want"* is a very limited view of God and prayer. However, there is not much room to ques-tion his sincerity. He was genuinely thankful for the success of his army and mindful that it was not all due to his own military brilliance. General Patton provides a great example of a leader who is able to look beyond himself and to give credit to prayer and to God for his success. While times were good, he looked forward to the trials ahead and urged his men to stay close to God, reminding them and himself that, *"We have to pray for ourselves."*

Seek the LORD while he may be found; call on him while he is near. ~Isaiah 55:6

Prayer for Clear Weather

ON DECEMBER 8, 1944, General George Patton directed that every man in the 3rd Army pray for cessation of the rains that had bogged down the Allied advance. A chaplain drafted the prayer that was then printed on two hundred fifty thousand three-by-five-inch cards and distributed to the troops:

> *Almighty and most merciful Father, we humbly beseech Thee, of Thy great goodness, to restrain these immoderate rains with which we have had to contend. Grant us fair weather for Battle. Graciously harken to us as soldiers who call Thee that, armed with Thy power, we may advance from victory to victory, and crush the oppression and wickedness of our enemies, and establish Thy justice among men and nations. Amen.*[468]

I had always considered this prayer a little bit of semi-sacrilegious theater on Patton's part, until I read the story of the man who wrote it. Col. James H. O'Neill was chaplain of the 3rd Army and knew General Patton well. He vouched for the sincerity of Patton's religious belief and of this appeal for God's help. He considered the general to be a man who, *"had all the traits of military leadership, fortified by genuine trust in God, intense love of country, and high faith in the American soldier."*[469]

Two days after the prayer cards were distributed, the German 6th Panzer Army took advantage of the bad weather and poor visibility, launching their great last-ditch offensive through the Ardennes Forest. After stunning successes in the first few days, the fate of the German advance was sealed on December 20 when the weather cleared, allowing Allied air attacks to turn the tide of the battle. George Patton prayed for clear weather, and he got it—at one of the most crucial moments of the war.

He got up and rebuked the wind and the raging waters; the storm subsided, and all was calm. "Where is your faith?" he asked his disciples. ~Luke 8:24–25

American troops advancing into Germany.
(National Archives)

Crossing the Rhine in assault boats.
(National Archives)

A Hymn Book in One Hand

ON DECEMBER 27, 1944, the 551st Parachute Infantry Battalion launched a night raid on Noirefontaine signaling the first Allied offensive of the Battle of the Bulge. The moon was full and the night so cold that enemy land mines failed to detonate in the frozen ground. Charles Fairlamb was a radio operator with the battalion and found himself in the middle of a hard-fought battle lasting through the night.

The next morning the 551st assembled for a long-overdue Christmas service. Still close to the front lines and exhausted, they gathered in a wooded area with faces still painted black and weapons ready. Fairlamb described the scene:

> *It was cold and snowing, and nearly half the men had lost their voices because of bad weather. The trees, mostly pine, were beautifully covered with snow and decorated with tinsel which the Germans had been dropping to make our radar ineffective. It was the most impressive Christmas service I've ever attended. I don't believe that anyone could be any closer to the real Christmas than we were that day. But it made you feel kind of funny standing there worshipping God while you had a helmet on your head, a hymn book in one hand, and a rifle in the other.*[470]

The contrast is stark. The peace of Christmas in the middle of combat. A hymn book and a rifle. This story could serve a useful purpose in reminding us to be thankful for the relative tranquility of our daily lives and worship. Or, in some cases, this story might mirror our daily lives. Sometimes our time in church is only a brief interlude to prolonged conflict, anger, or anxiety. When we find ourselves in such a state, it is time to take stock of our relationship with the Savior. It takes a certain amount of spiritual discipline, including regular prayer, study, and service, to keep Jesus at the center of our lives when we're not in church. Only then will the rest of our lives take on that same sense of order and tranquility that we find in the sanctuary.

Be joyous always; pray continually; give thanks in all circumstances, for this is God's will for you in Christ Jesus. ~1 Thessalonians 5:16–18

Guardian Angel

A S HIS COMPANY was fighting to take the German town of Dillin-gen, Arnold Brown saw a building that offered good observation of the enemy occupied area of the city. He climbed two flights of stairs and found a two-man forward observation team using the same vantage point to call in artillery fire. As soon as he arrived, the strangest phenomenon of his life occurred. He called it his "vision."

His mind suddenly became like a movie screen and he could see German soldiers with their distinctive helmets. The soldiers had a radio and were beaming in on his position. They were transmitting this information to an artillery battery where the guns were being aimed and prepared to fire. As this picture filled his mind he became confused:

> I hesitated. I thought, "What should I do? Should I tell these men to move? If I tell them to move and nothing would happen, they'd think I was cracking up. . . ."
>
> When I hesitated, I felt something pushing me toward the stairway, just like wings, pushing me. When that occurred, I didn't hesitate. When I got down off the last step, an artillery shell exploded in that room and killed both of those men.
>
> This was my evidence that I was going to survive this war, and that I did have a guardian angel.[471]

We know that there are many biblical references to angels. This soldier's amazing witness seems to confirm that these heavenly beings continue to do God's work in the modern age as well. The Bible tells us that angels were created by God to act as his servants, to relay messages from God, give encouragement and guidance, and provide protection. Arnold Brown's confidence that a guardian angel was looking over him is a powerful witness to the continued existence of this special way that God can directly touch our lives.

> He thought he was seeing a vision. They passed the first and second guards and came to the iron gate leading to the city. It opened for them by itself, and. . . . When they walked the length of one street, suddenly the angel left him. Then Peter came to himself and said, "Now I know without a doubt that the Lord sent his angel and rescued me from Herod's clutches." ~Acts 12:9–11

Malice toward None

AFTER DAYS OF vicious fighting the American paratroopers brought in a wounded German soldier to their company commander. He had lain out all night in subzero weather with a severe wound in his leg from a .50 caliber bullet. Both of his arms and legs were frozen, and he was begging to be shot. The company commander later recalled:

> *I couldn't do it. I asked for a volunteer. Even if he survived, he'd have to have both arms and legs amputated, and this could have been a mercy killing. But these battle hardened soldiers that had been fighting Germans a few minutes before would not volunteer. One soldier, out of sympathy for the suffering and bravery of this soldier, lit a cigarette and held it to his lips. Another soldier brought him a hot cup of coffee and held it so he could get coffee until we got the litter jeep up there and sent him to the rear.*[472]

On another battlefield a British lieutenant described the attitude of his men toward enemy prisoners immediately after an intense battle: *"We treated them very kindly, bringing in their wounded and giving them cigarettes. It is strange, but we are very poor haters."*[473]

These Allied soldiers exemplified the Christian moral code for the merciful treatment of a defeated enemy articulated eighty years earlier by a great American president: *"With malice toward none, with charity for all, with firmness in the right as God gives us to see the right . . ."*[474] Fortunately for us, mercy is an attribute of God himself, and he fully expects us to show this quality toward others, even in the heat of conflict.

My judgments flashed like lightning upon you. For I desire mercy, not sacrifice, and acknowledgment of God rather than burnt offerings. ~Hosea 6:5–6

The Only Clean Thing

THE GERMAN ATTACKS were almost continuous. The remnants of a British airborne unit was holding on to its tenuous position in a battered school building as casualties mounted and ammunition dwindled. Their mission was to defend the eastern side of the Rhine River bridge at Arnhem until relieved. Hours of waiting had turned into days, as the relief column was hopelessly delayed in heavy fighting. Meanwhile, an officer in the school building described the scene:

> *By morning I had to issue more Bensedrine to face the dawn attack. No one had now had any sleep for seventy-two hours. The water had given out twelve hours ago and food twenty-four hours ago . . . The men themselves were the grimmest sight of all: eyes red-rimmed for want of sleep, their faces, blackened by fire-fighting, wore three days' growth of beard. Many of them had minor wounds, and their clothes were cut away to expose a roughly fixed, blood-soaked field dressing. They were huddled in twos and threes, each little group manning positions that required twice that number. The only clean things in the school were the weapons. These shone brightly in the morning sun, with their gleaming clips of ammunition beside them.*[475]

Clean weapons shining in the midst of a dirty and chaotic battle scene presents a powerful image. It reminds us of God's armor, designed to protect us from the evils of the world. Although mostly defensive in nature, it also includes one powerful offensive weapon: *"the sword of the Spirit, which is the word of God"* (Ephesians 6:17). When this weapon is kept burnished through constant study and application, we are prepared for the spiritual battles and chaos of this world.

The night is nearly over; the day is almost here. So let us put aside the deeds of darkness and put on the armor of light. ~Romans 13:12

Your Cross

JIM KOERNER saw too much. In fighting with the 10th Armored Division he saw buddies wounded and killed by small arms fire, artillery, mines, and booby traps. In December 1944 he was separated from his unit and captured by the Germans, suffering constantly from exposure, hunger, and Allied bombing attacks. After the war he continued to suffer nervous depression and had to take tranquilizers to function. His father had committed suicide before him, and twice, in his confused state, he held a gun to his own head. He declared that his salvation came in a prayer that he found in the wallet of a deceased friend:

Your Cross

The everlasting God has in His wisdom foreseen from eternity the cross that He now presents you as a gift from His inmost heart. The cross He now sends you He has considered with His all-knowing eyes, understood with His divine mind, tested with His wise justice, warmed with His loving arms, and weighed with His loving hands to see that it be not one inch too large and not one ounce too heavy for you. He has blessed it with His holy name, anointed it with His grace, perfumed it with His consolation, taken one last glance at you and your courage, and then sent it to you from heaven, a special greeting from God to you and alms of the all merciful love of God.[476]

I now carry this prayer in my own wallet as a constant reminder that God will not give me more to do or to bear in this life than I can handle. With Him beside me I can endure any trial and see any task through to completion. Jesus said, *"Anyone who has faith in me will do what I have been doing. He will do even greater things than these, because I am going to the Father"* (John 14:12). We can have faith that, whatever cross we bear, it is the cross that he has given us. He will also give us the strength to carry it.

If anyone would come after me, he must deny himself and take up his cross daily and follow me. ~Luke 9:23

Chaplain's Letter

IN DECEMBER 1944, Chaplain (Col.) James O'Neill published a Training Letter to the 486 chaplains of the 3rd Army under his supervision. At the request of his commanding general, more than three thousand copies of the letter were printed so that distribution could be made to unit commanders as well. The subject was prayer:

> *Our glorious march from the Normandy Beach across France to where we stand, before and beyond the Siegfried Line, with the wreckage of the German Army behind us, should convince the most skeptical soldier that God has ridden with our banner.*
>
> *As chaplains it is our business to pray. We preach its importance. We urge its practice. But the time is now to intensify our faith in prayer, not alone with ourselves, but with every believing man, Protestant, Catholic, Jew, or Christian, in the ranks of the Third United States Army.*
>
> *Urge all of your men to pray, not alone in church, but everywhere. Pray when driving. Pray when fighting. Pray alone. Pray with others. Pray by night and pray by day. Pray for the cessation of immoderate rains, for good weather for Battle. Pray for the defeat of our wicked enemy whose banner is injustice and whose good is oppression. Pray for Victory, Pray for our Army, and pray for Peace.*
>
> *Now is not the time to follow God from 'afar off.' This Army needs the assurance and faith that God is with us. With prayer, we cannot fail.*[477]

The apostle Paul urged the Thessalonians to *"pray without ceasing"* (1 Thessalonians 5:17 KJV). Chaplain O'Neill gives us a simple explanation of this difficult concept. We can certainly pray in church or any other quiet place. However, we can also converse with God while walking, driving, or in the midst of a crowd. When Jesus said to *"go into your room, close the door and pray to your Father"* (Matthew 6:6), he was telling believers to go within themselves. We can do this anywhere. What goes on within, between God and us, is more important than the place where it happens.

And the Lord said, "Listen to what the unjust judge says. And will not God bring about justice for his chosen ones, who cry out to him day and night?"
~Luke 18:6–7

Nativity Scene

IN THE OPENING days of the Battle of the Bulge the advancing German forces overran the 106th Infantry Division and took more than seven thousand prisoners. Chaplain Paul Cavanaugh was among this group of unfortunate men who found themselves herded onto trains without heat or food in bitter winter conditions. For days they suffered from extreme cold and hunger as they traveled farther and farther east. They were finally discharged from the train to a prison camp at a place called Bad Orb, Germany. Forced into makeshift barracks, they found little improvement in their living conditions. Food was scarce, heat nonexistent, and the guards brutal.

In this desolate situation Chaplain Cavanaugh and the men of the 106th observed Christmas Eve 1944. Under these conditions they came closer to the actual poverty of the Nativity scene than could possibly be experienced in an actual church. As the men huddled together to fight the cold, the chaplain spoke a few words that he later thought might have been the *"best Christmas sermon he would ever give."* He talked to them about the blessed night in another faraway place long before, when God demonstrated for all time his love for mankind. He assured his fellow soldiers that this love continued for each one of them individually, in spite of their misery and isolation. He told them that God's love was present even there in the frozen barracks of a prisoner-of-war camp.[478]

The chaplain prayed, *"Lord, grant peace to the world. . . . Grant that the peace which Christ, who is called the Prince of Peace, came to bring us may be established all over the world."* In the deep silence lasting through the night after this impromptu service, Paul Cavanaugh felt at long last that all was *"still and calm and peaceful"* over this modern nativity scene.[479]

Peace I leave with you; my peace I give you. I do not give to you as the world gives. Do not let your hearts be troubled and do not be afraid. ~John 14:27

Prayer in a Burning Tank

CHARLES ZIERS was the new man in a veteran crew. He looked to the old-timers for support in his first action. His sergeant told him, *"Ziers, just keep your eyes and ears open and do as I have shown you and you'll come out on top."*[480] These were the last words spoken to him by the sergeant. Ziers' Sherman tank was part of the leading element in an attack on enemy hilltop positions holding up the division advance toward Cologne. Incoming fire was heavy. Suddenly there was a brilliant flash and explosion, and everything went dark.

Not knowing at first if he was dead or alive, Ziers slowly began to smell gasoline and gun powder. He realized that his tank was on fire and that his fellow crewmen were either dead or gone. He knew that he had to get out of the tank before it exploded, but the barrel of the main gun was blocking his hatch. Bleeding and in pain, the trapped soldier *"prayed like never before."*[481] Ziers passed out again briefly, and, when his head cleared, suddenly knew he was going to get out of that tank. He said, *"Thank you Lord,"* and started looking for the way. He finally saw it:

> There was a narrow passage of about 2 ft. leading across to the driver's compartment. If I could fit through that tiny space I would be home free. After many attempts I finally took off all of my clothes . . . with still no success. The smoke got thicker and I became more desperate. Finally I found a bucket of grease under my seat and smeared it all around the hole. Still no luck. I smeared the rest of the grease all over my body and then somehow with the Grace of God, I was free.[482]

This story has such an obvious spiritual meaning that it is practically a sermon by itself: if you find yourself in a tight spot, *"Pray like never before."* God will show you a way. Unfortunately, we often have to come to our wit's end to reaffirm this truth for ourselves. We should always remember that God is waiting for us to bring our problems and our crises to him.

You will not have to fight this battle. Take up your positions; stand firm and see the deliverance the LORD will give you. ~2 Chronicles 20:17

Christic, The Risen Soldier

Christ, The Risen Soldier

ARCHBISHOP FRANCIS SPELLMAN'S classic *The Risen Soldier* was published in 1944. This little book was a poignant tribute to the men and women serving their country in wartime. It was adamant in its denunciation of war but profuse in its praise for those bearing the burden of it. Throughout the book he drew parallels between these soldiers and a greater Soldier, the greatest sacrificial figure of all time: Jesus Christ.

> *Yes, it was another Soldier, One Who had vision and a mission beyond the grave, a Soldier Who died for something good—to save His fellow men . . .*
>
> *He is a warrior "Heaven-flung and heart fleshed." He too is wearing a helmet, "the helmet of salvation." He is armed with "the sword of the spirit against the rulers of the world of this darkness, against the spirits of wickedness in high places." He too is a Pilot to all who go down to the sea in ships, to all who take wings and fly through the air, to all who walk human pathways.*
>
> *This Soldier said: "He that shall lose his life for my sake shall find it." . . . All men were His brothers and to them He gave a new commandment, that they love one another. He was a Captain who bivouacked with his men, sharing privations and hardships.*
>
> *The other Soldier returns to tell me that Love never sacrifices in vain. He bids me look with shining eyes towards the day when men, "shall turn their swords into ploughshares and their spears into sickles."*[483]

The greatest Soldier has also been called the Prince of Peace. His message of love and forgiveness opened the sure path to God and ultimate peace for every human being. We may not see peace on Earth until the end days, but on the personal level, it is available in our lives every day. Our Lord and Savior waits for our response.

He came and preached peace to you who were far away and peace to those who were near. For through him we both have access to the Father by one Spirit. ~Ephesians 2:17–18

They Gave All They Had

A S AMERICAN SOLDIERS advanced through Europe they encountered vast numbers of refugees whose plight was stark and heartbreaking. The war had shattered their homes, families, and communities. Chaplain Rabbi David Eichhorn had a special concern for the beleaguered Jewish remnants scattered through each country. In the little village of Rosieres-aux-Salines he found twenty-two Jewish women, aged sixty-eight to ninety-seven, whose husbands had been deported early in the war. The wives were left deliberately as a burden on the rest of the village. The chaplain found them in two rooms of a hospital, dirty and half-starved. After supplying food, clothing, and fuel to keep them alive, he went about raising money for their continued care. His account is uplifting:

> The soldiers in the past two weeks have given me over $800 to help these and other Jewish refugees who needed help. God bless the American Army and American Jewish soldiers. There is no other Army like it in the whole world. I had to plead with these men not to give me as much as they wanted to give. Many of them wanted to empty their pockets and give me all they had.[484]

We know there are many biblical imperatives enjoining us to be charitable. *"Blessed is he who has regard for the weak"* (Psalms 41:1). *"He has scattered abroad his gifts to the poor, his righteousness endures forever"* (Psalms 112:9). *"A generous man will himself be blessed, for he shares his food with the poor"* (Proverbs 22:9). We are also very specifically called to direct our charitable efforts to the widows and orphans. Without husbands and fathers they are in special need of the material and spiritual support of the body of Christ.

Religion that God our Father accepts as pure and faultless is this: to look after orphans and widows in their distress and to keep oneself from being polluted by the world. ~James 1:27

389

Miracle of the Rock

ISAAC AVIGDOR was one of ten thousand Jews transported in 1944 from Poland to the Mauthausen concentration camp in Austria. There he was put on the infamous "Quarry Detail," removing by hand large rocks blasted from a mountainside. After each dynamite blast, the prisoners were ordered to carry away a large rock to the disposal area. Being the new man on the detail, Avigdor hesitated after the first explosion while the others rushed in to pick up the rocks of manageable size. He could find only a boulder that he could barely lift. At first he tried to carry it in his hands, then on each shoulder. Soon, his shoulders were bleeding, and he was lagging behind. He knew that laggards were usually shot and that thousands had already died in the same situation. As he stumbled and fell, he knew that this was the end for him.

> *I didn't care anymore: let them shoot me, or throw me off the mountain, and I let the rock drop to the ground. And the miracle happened: the rock hit the ground and split in two. Quickly, unnoticed by any one, I picked up one of the pieces and resumed marching. There may have been a natural crack in the rock that caused it to split the moment it received a blow. None the less, a threefold miracle happened to me: the rock split; I had enough presence of mind to realize at once to take advantage of what had happened; no one noticed.*[485]

In recalling this incident, Avigdor thought of another rock made famous in the Old Testament. Jacob used a stone for a pillow as he dreamed of a ladder to heaven. He made the stone a pillar and declared, *"This stone . . . will be God's house"* (Genesis 28:22). There are other occasions in the Bible where God uses rocks miraculously. Moses drew water from the rock at Horeb to satisfy the thirst of the Israelites and to demonstrate God's presence (Exodus 17:6). An angel caused fire to come from a stone to give Gideon a sign of God's favor (Judges 6:21). I believe that we can accept Isaac Avigdor's witness as evidence of God performing another miracle with a rock, in a time much closer to the present day.

Fire flared from the rock, consuming the meat and the bread. And the angel of the LORD disappeared. When Gideon realized that it was the angel of the LORD, he exclaimed, "Ah, Sovereign LORD! I have seen the angel of the LORD face to face!" ~Judges 6:21–22

He Never Spared Himself

PADDY CREAN was an Irish priest from Dublin. He joined the British Army in 1941 and served with distinction as a military chaplain for more than twenty years. During World War II he landed at Normandy with the 29th Armored Brigade and saw action in Belgium, Holland, and Germany. For his heroic service he was made a Member of the Order of the British Empire (MBE). After the war he served with two United Nations peacekeeping missions to the Congo. Father Crean wrote many letters home during the war, revealing his low-key personality and deep faith. Soon after D-Day, he wrote,

> *After 16 days at this second front thank God I am safe and well. We are in France as you know and everything is going well. I am overwhelmed with chaps all clamouring for the comforts of the Faith and I must say whatever dangers there may be and there are some of course, it is all well worth it. I have been up to the front quite a lot and been shelled once! However, God is Good.*[486]

His qualities as a chaplain were illustrated in the citation for his MBE:

> *Possessing a quiet, sincere and likeable character, he has always been on the best of terms with all ranks. He has never spared himself in his work and has afforded great assistance and comfort to many. He has made constant visits to the wounded, often in advanced medical posts and has throughout shown great keenness and organizing ability in arranging clubs and rest rooms, which have not been confined to those of his own creed.*
> *He has been a strong rock to those of his own flock, and has throughout taken the greatest interest in all matters pertaining to the welfare of the troops. He has set a very fine example and has made a great contribution to the happiness and wellbeing of the men.*[487]

Paddy Crean is another distinguished example of a clergyman who heroically and selflessly served his nation, his fellow soldiers, and his God during wartime. In sacrificing for others, he never spared himself.

You, my brothers, were called to be free. But do not use your freedom to indulge the sinful nature; rather, serve one another in love. ~Galatians 5:13

Call on the Lord

DESMOND STEPHENSON was a British paratrooper wounded and captured by the Germans in Holland. He was taken to a makeshift, overcrowded hospital that came under attack from artillery fire. Shells were exploding everywhere, blowing out the hospital's doors and windows. As he huddled with others in a stairwell, he had an amazing and uplifting experience:

> A voice seemed to say to me, "Why not call on the Lord and ask him to take care of you," and I did. I prayed to him for protection and guidance and immediately my shattered nerves were steadied and I was able to look at others and steady them without feeling the same. I had a new life and in the midst of all this noise and tumult I had a peace of mind unknown to me before. It was wonderful to have a joy unspeakable, and since then my Jesus has stood by me most wonderfully.[488]

Desmond's faith provided him reassurance and spiritual comfort through many ordeals. He was taken to a prison camp near the Polish border where he was held until the Russian advance forced an evacuation to the west. In the coldest part of the winter of 1944 he walked for twenty-eight straight days and slept in the snow every night, huddled together with other prisoners for warmth. Whoever had to sleep on the ends of a row often did not survive the night. Food was practically nonexistent.

Throughout this desperate experience, Desmond continued to pray and to put his faith in God's providence. Whenever he found shelter or food, he gave God the credit and his profound thanks. Looking back he was able to say, *"I feel sure that he brought me through all this to prove to me his goodness and mercy."*[489] Desmond's life after the war was one of service to his church and fellow men, in gratitude for his own salvation on the battlefield.

He guarded him as the apple of his eye, like an eagle that stirs up its nest and hovers over its young, that spreads its wings to catch them and carries them on its pinions. The LORD alone led him. ~Deuteronomy 32:10–12

It Was Done by Men

WINTER IN THE Ardennes Forest meant overcast skies, deep snow, and frigid temperatures. In the Battle of the Bulge the German Army attempted to use these conditions to their advantage. The element of surprise and lack of Allied air cover almost gave them the victory in this last-ditch campaign to stave off defeat. The fighting was brutal, and the struggle to survive the elements was equally intense. One unit of the 101st Airborne Division was reduced from 170 to 58 men within a few days of constant enemy contact fighting around Bastogne.

It was an individual soldier's battle, as one related: *"If you're fighting a war in a ditch, the whole war is in that ditch. . . . When you're in a hole, pinned down by mortars and machine guns have you in a crossfire, it's impossible to get a sense of the overall picture."*[490]

The toll was heavy on these isolated soldiers, fighting the enemy and the elements: *"We went seventy-two days we didn't shower, we shaved with cold water out of a steel helmet, and washed one foot at a time; in case Germans hit us again, or you got called to attack . . . We had lice, scabies, and I had trench mouth so bad I could move my teeth around with my tongue."*[491] On seeing these battle-weary men, a reporter observed, *"Everyone seems about the same age, as if weariness and strain and the unceasing cold leveled all life."*[492] The same reporter summarized the Battle of the Bulge and eloquently gave credit for the outcome where it was due:

> *There were many dead and many wounded, but the survivors contained the fluid situation and slowly turned it into a retreat, and finally, as the communiqué said, the bulge was ironed out. This was not done fast or easily; and it was not done by those anonymous things, armies, divisions, regiments. It was done by men, one by one—your men.*[493]

We live on; beaten, and yet not killed; sorrowful, yet always rejoicing; poor, yet making many rich; having nothing, and yet possessing everything. ~2 Corinthians 6:9–10

German soldier surrenders.
(National Archives)

Once there was a church.
(Franklin D. Roosevelt Presidential Library)

A German Soldier's Prayer

IN AUGUST 1944 the tide of the war had turned against the Axis
forces. A German soldier wrote his parents a heartfelt letter expressing
his concern for them and faith in God's protection:

Dear Parents,

*A time of uncertainty, apprehension and fear is now beginning for you
as well. I pray sincerely that God gives you courage each day, and that
you don't sink into worry but hold onto the certainty that your prayers
will be heard. Rest assured and be happy! That is my wish and my plea
to you. Don't be afraid, even during the days when you hear nothing and
can know nothing about how things are for me. Everything that I experience and am permitted to live through in these times reassures me that
I will be kept safe for you, for God does nothing by halves. I shall come
through these dangers. God granted me life through you. For that I am
always grateful to you.*

Your son, Friedrich[494]

The prayers of this soldier and his parents were not answered in the
way they wished. Friedrich was killed in September 1944, days after writing this letter. We know that thousands of other Christian families, both
German and American, were disappointed in the same way during this
horrendous war. Does this mean that all those prayers were in vain? I fervently believe that this was not the case. God heard every one of those
prayers, and those praying received a blessing of more lasting significance
than life or death on this earth. It is the amazing nature of God, the
almighty creator of the universe, to also be our loving Father who allows
us to approach him in our private thoughts. Through our prayers we have
an opportunity to grow closer to him and to understand his desires for
us. A few minutes in his presence are worth a lifetime outside of it. He
doesn't guarantee our safety, but he does guarantee to hear us and to be
with us no matter how terrible our circumstance.

Let us then approach the throne of grace with confidence, so that we may
receive mercy and find grace to help us in our time of need. ~Hebrews 4:16

Prisoner of the Lord

LAWRENCE DONKIN served with a British infantry unit in the North African campaign. His capture by German troops in Tunisia was the start of an amazing odyssey. He was held in an Italian prisoner-of-war camp until Italy surrendered and his guards walked away. After weeks of evading the Germans he made his way to Switzerland where he was interned until 1944.

After the war Donkin returned to his home and wife in England. On a day in 1950, while starting out to sea, his wartime experiences flooded back into his memory, and he began to recall the many miraculous incidents that had enabled him to survive the war. His weapon had mysteriously jammed just before his capture, preventing him from firing at that moment, saving his life. On a dark night in Italy he had bumped into an iron bar that saved him from falling into a deep pit. Most important of all, while evading the Germans, he had picked up a New Testament lying on a schoolroom floor and had started reading it. In all these events, he became convinced that he was seeing *the preserving Hand of God and His saving grace.*[495]

Reading from the New Testament that he brought home from Italy, he came to Chapter 11 of Matthew and Jesus' compelling invitation: *"Come unto me, all ye that labour and are heavy laden, and I will give you rest. Take my yoke upon you, and learn of me, for I am meek and lowly in heart: and ye shall find rest unto your souls. For my yoke is easy, and my burden is light"* (Matthew 11:28–31 KJV). Donkin's response to that invitation changed his life forever:

> So, I was drawn to the Lord Jesus and responding to his words, "Come unto me," I received him as my Lord and Saviour, so, I, a sinner by nature was saved...I who was a prisoner of war and escaped am now a prisoner of the Lord Jesus Christ, and, after 40 years, I have never wanted to escape from him, nor will I ever want to.[496]

All things have been committed to me by my Father. No one knows the Son except the Father, and no one knows the Father except the Son and those to whom the Son chooses to reveal him. ~Matthew 11:27

God Is All You've Got

JAMES NORTON wrote to his parents on April 15, 1945, describing that day as the *"second-happiest day of my life."* He was finally able to write home and to tell them about the happiest day of all: when he was liberated from a German POW camp. Norton had been wounded and captured four months earlier during the Battle of the Bulge and described his captivity as *"living hell."* He also described an important change within himself as he confronted the possibility of dying:

> *Death has faced me many times in the past months and by the grace of my Lord and Savior I am here today to write this letter. I always considered myself a good Christian until I was captured, and then I learned what a fool I had been and what it really means to have faith and the power of prayer. I prayed day and nite, and these prayers were heard . . .*[497]

This young soldier's experience reflects a very real spiritual truth. Christians often experience a closer relationship to God during times of stress. Rick Warren described this phenomenon: *"Your most profound and intimate experiences of worship will likely be in your darkest days— when your heart is broken, when you feel abandoned, when you're out of options, when the pain is great—and you turn to God alone . . . You'll never know that God is all you need until God is all you've got."*[498] If we come closer to God in a stressful situation, we can be thankful that we have been so blessed. Our continuing challenge, however, is to seek God in our everyday activities, without waiting for the next crisis.

We despaired even of life. Indeed, in our hearts we felt the sentence of death. But this happened that we might not rely on ourselves but on God. ~2 Corinthians 1:8–9

I Go and Prepare a Place

T HE CHAPLAIN scanned the sky anxiously. After waiting for hours, he could see his airmen returning to base from the day's mission. He counted their numbers as he tried to pray each one safely back home. He gazed at the rain-swept runway and waited until the last plane was on the ground before facing the reality that all had not returned. With a sorrowful heart, he took the letter given him hours earlier from his pocket:

Dear Mother and Dad:

Strange thing about this letter; if I am alive a month from now, you will not receive it, for its coming to you will mean that after my twenty-fifth mission, God has decided I've been on earth long enough and He wants me to come up and take the examination for permanent service with Him . . .

Some things a man can never thank his parents enough for, they come to be taken for granted through the years: care when a child and countless favors as he grows up. I am recalling now all your prayers, your watchfulness—all the sacrifices that were made for me, when sacrifice was a real thing and not just a word to be used in speeches . . .

I die with many things to live for. But the loss of the few remaining years unlived together is as nothing compared to the eternity to which we go, and it will be well worthwhile if I give my life to help cure a sickened world, and if you and I can help to spare other mothers and fathers and younger generations from the griefs of war . . .

Pray for me; be proud of me, for I am proud of you. As you have done through the years for me, so now I do for you, and await your coming to me.[499]

This young airman's letter is a sad but powerful witness to a strong faith. This is the faith available to all Christians, who rest in the certain knowledge of where they are ultimately going and in the fact that loved ones will eventually be with them in that blessed place. From God's perspective, those who go sooner are even more fortunate than those temporarily left behind.

In my Father's house are many rooms; if it were not so, I would have told you. I am going there to prepare a place for you. And if I go and prepare a place for you, I will come back and take you to be with me that you also may be where I am. ~John 14:2–3

Nazi Gold

IN EARLY APRIL 1945 the little German village of Merkers fell to the lead elements of General Patton's 3rd Army. Soon after, two military policemen stopped a pregnant French woman on the road to Merkers and gave her a ride into town. As they passed the entrance to a mine, the woman told them that this was the place where the Nazis stored their treasure. The soldiers passed this comment up the line, setting off an amazing chain of events.

It was soon discovered that the mine did indeed hoard the wealth of the Third Reich. There were more than eight thousand bars of gold bullion, more than two thousand bags of gold coins from various nations, and billions of Reichmarks stored in boxes. More than four hundred paintings were found, including works by Rembrandt, Raphael, van Dyck, Monet, Manet, and Renoir. In a separate cache, more than two hundred suitcases, trunks, and boxes were found containing jewelry, watches, dental work, gold and silver items of all kinds, and currency. This was identified as S.S. loot from private dwellings throughout Europe and from concentration camp victims.[500]

The contents of the Merker mine were removed to Frankfurt, Germany, where the long postwar process of restitution began. A Tripartite Gold Commission was established to get this wealth back into the hands of its rightful owners. In 1998 the Commission performed its final act by turning over its last stock of gold to the Nazi Persecution Relief Fund for Holocaust survivors.

There has probably never been a more pointed demonstration of the futility of amassing great material wealth in this life. Jesus warned that we should not store up treasures on Earth. Lasting wealth is found only in our spiritual lives. By making daily deposits of prayer and service to God, we build our accounts in his kingdom and accumulate the wealth that only comes from a relationship with him.

But store up for yourselves treasures in heaven, where moth and rust do not destroy, and where thieves do not break in and steal. For where your treasure is, there your heart will be also. ~Matthew 6:20–21

Liberation of Paris.
(National Archives)

Allied commanders toast victory.
(National Archives)

400

Our Strength and Shield

THE WAR IN EUROPE IS ENDED!
SURRENDER IS UNCONDITIONAL;
V-E WILL BE PROCLAIMED TODAY

*T*HE NEW YORK TIMES headline of May 8, 1945, was emphatic and joyful. The war in Europe was finally over. The victory was won. The celebrations could begin around the world. In England, at this historic moment, King George VI gave a radio broadcast and thoughtfully turned the world's attention to God and to the obligations of the future. Starting with the words, *"Today we give thanks to Almighty God for a great deliverance,"* he called his nation and the world to remember God's blessing in this great victory:

> *There is great comfort in the thought that the years of darkness and danger in which the children of our country have grown up are over and, please God, forever. We shall have failed, and the blood of our dearest will have flowed in vain, if the victory which they died to win does not lead to a lasting peace, founded on justice and established in good will. To that, then, let us turn our thoughts on this day of just triumph and proud sorrow; and then take up our work again, resolved as a people to do nothing unworthy of those who died for us and to make the world such a world as they would have desired, for their children and for ours.*
>
> *This is the task to which now honour binds us. In the hour of danger we humbly committed our cause into the Hand of God, and He has been our Strength and Shield. Let us thank him for His mercies, and in this hour of Victory commit ourselves and our new task to the guidance of that same strong Hand.*[501]

God's hand was evident in many events of World War II and in the lives of many who endured it. If we ever wonder if God is still on our side as a nation, we should note the words of one of our great presidents, Abraham Lincoln: *"It is my constant anxiety and prayer that I and this nation should be on the Lord's side."*[502]

You are the God who performs miracles; you display your power among the peoples. With your mighty arm you redeemed your people. ~Psalms 77:14–15

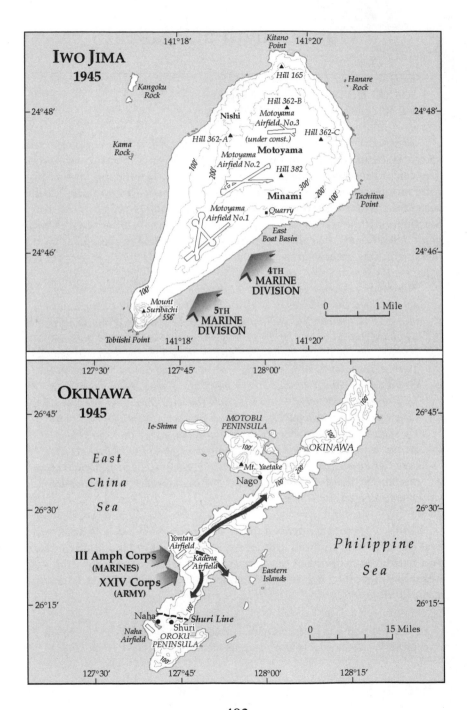

IWO JIMA
1945

141°18'   141°20'

Kitano
Point

24°48'   24°48'

▲ Hill 165

Kangoku
Rock

Hill 362-B
Motoyama
Airfield No.3
(under const.)

Nishi

Hill 362-A ▲   ▲ Hill 362-C

Kama
Rock

Motoyama

Motoyama
Airfield No.2   ▲ Hill 382

Minami

■ Quarry

Tachiiwa
Point

24°46'   24°46'

Motoyama
Airfield No.1

East
Boat Basin

Hanare
Rock

100'
200'
300'
200'
100'

**4TH
MARINE
DIVISION**

Mount
Suribachi
556'

100'

**5TH
MARINE
DIVISION**

Tobiishi Point   141°18'   141°20'

0   1 Mile

OKINAWA
1945

127°30'   127°45'   128°00'

26°45'   26°45'

Ie-Shima

MOTOBU
PENINSULA

100'

E a s t

OKINAWA

C h i n a

▲ Mt. Yaetake

100'
200'

Nago ●

S e a

26°30'   26°30'

P h i l i p p i n e

Yontan
Airfield

S e a

III Amph Corps
(MARINES)

Kadena
Airfield

Eastern
Islands

XXIV Corps
(ARMY)

26°15'   26°15'

Naha ●

100'

Shuri Line

Naha
Airfield ● Shuri
OROKU
PENINSULA

100'

0   15 Miles

127°30'   127°45'   128°00'   128°15'

402

DECEMBER

Victory in the Pacific

ON OCTOBER 20, 1944, a radio broadcast rang out through the Philippine Islands from the beaches of Leyte: *"This is the Voice of Freedom, General MacArthur speaking. People of the Philippines! I have returned. By the grace of Almighty God our forces stand again on Philippine soil."* With these uplifting words the campaign to liberate this vital island chain began. Within two months Leyte was taken, and then, in January 1945, MacArthur's forces invaded the main island of Luzon. Fighting would continue against fierce enemy resistance throughout the islands until the final surrender of Japan.

Also in October 1944 one of the greatest naval battles in history was fought as three Japanese fleets converged on Leyte Gulf in an all-out effort to destroy the landing forces assembled there. Over a three-day period the U.S. fleet sank thirty-six enemy warships, rendering the Imperial Japanese Navy largely ineffective as a fighting force. On the last day of the battle, the Americans had their first taste of a new enemy "tactic," the suicide bomber. The aircraft carrier *St. Lo* was lost that day to a Kamikaze attack. By the end of the war, five thousand Japanese aviators would kill themselves this way, wreaking massive destruction on Allied ships and sailors.

By early 1945 American war planners finally faced the ultimate question of the Pacific war: how to bring about the surrender of Japan. Up until that time, the fanatical and suicidal resistance encountered in every battle seemed to prove that an invasion of the Japanese home islands would be required by the fall of the year. As these plans were formulated, two key intermediate objectives were identified: Iwo Jima and Okinawa. Both were needed for air and naval bases closer to Japan, and both were heavily defended. By this time the Japanese had developed new tactics that put their main defenses well away from the beaches, with deep bunkers and interconnecting tunnels practically impervious to air and naval bombardment.

Instead of taking five days as estimated, the conquest of Iwo Jima took almost a month. Admiral Nimitz, commenting on the fierceness of the battle and the high casualty rate, said, *"Among the Americans who served on Iwo Island uncommon valor was a common virtue."*[503] The most inspiring image of the war came when a group of Marines was photographed raising an American flag on Mt. Suribachi, the most prominent terrain feature of the island.

The seizure of Okinawa was also a protracted and costly operation. Two Marine and two Army divisions made the initial assault on April 1, and it was not until late June that the island was declared secure. Casualties among the ground troops were severe, and Kamikaze attacks rained down on the ships at sea during the entire operation.

As preparations for a November invasion of the Japanese home islands continued, a B-29 bomber, flying from the Marianas Islands, dropped an atomic bomb over Hiroshima on August 6. A day later the Soviet Union declared war on Japan and invaded Korea. Then another atomic bomb was dropped, this time on Nagasaki. The powerful factions within the Japanese government that had continued to insist on a fight to the bitter end were finally silenced by the overwhelming need to stop the rain of destruction. Hostilities were brought to an end on August 15, 1945. The formal surrender ceremony was held on September 2 aboard the USS *Missouri* in Tokyo Bay. The Japanese foreign minister, General MacArthur, and Admiral Nimitz signed the documents, followed by representatives of every Allied nation. World War II was finally and mercifully over.

God Be Merciful

THE LITTLE EPISCOPAL *Prayer Book for Soldiers and Sailors* was a complete resource for worship, prayer, and study. It included Bible passages that were especially useful for military men and women. One of these was Jesus' classic parable of the proud man and the humble man:

The Pharisee and the Publican

And he spake this parable unto certain which trusted in themselves that they were righteous, and despised others: Two men went up into the temple to pray; the one a Pharisee, and the other a publican. The Pharisee stood and prayed thus with himself, God, I thank thee, that I am not as other men are, extortioners, unjust, adulterers, or even as this publican. I fast twice in the week, I give tithes of all that I possess. And the publican, standing afar off, would not lift up so much as his eyes unto heaven, but smote upon his breast, saying, God be merciful to me a sinner. I tell you, this man went down to his house justified rather than the other: for every one that exalteth himself shall be abased; and he that humbleth himself shall be exalted. (Luke 18:9–14 KJV)

The little prayer, *"God be merciful to me a sinner,"* is the key to our faith in Jesus Christ. I say it earnestly every day. Jesus came into the world to save sinners, and, until we acknowledge our own hopeless condition, there is nothing he can do within us; there is no room for his saving grace.

This Scripture passage is especially fitting for the last month of this book, devoted to *victory* in World War II. It is an appropriate reminder of the danger of pride, which can cause us to stumble at the personal and the national level. In this war America achieved complete and total victory over all her enemies. A thankful humility was appropriate then and continues to be our best posture as a nation now, as we acknowledge God's grace and our countless blessings.

Fourth Inaugural Address

ON JANUARY 20, 1945, Franklin Roosevelt was inaugurated for an unprecedented fourth term of office as president of the United States. At that time the Battle of the Bulge was raging in Europe and the invasion of Iwo Jima was about to start. The war was far from over, and uncertainty about the future still gripped the nation. In his inaugural address Roosevelt sought to share a vision of hope and peace for the world based on his faith in God's guidance:

> As I stand here today, having taken the solemn oath of office in the presence of my fellow countrymen—in the presence of our God—I know that it is America's purpose that we shall not fail. In the days and the years that are to come we shall work for a just and honorable peace, a durable peace, as today we work and fight for a total victory in war . . .
>
> We can gain no lasting peace if we approach it with suspicion and mistrust—or with fear. We can gain it only if we proceed with the understanding and the confidence and the courage which flow from conviction.
>
> The Almighty God has blessed our land in many ways. He has given our people stout hearts and strong arms with which to strike mighty blows for our freedom and truth. He has given to our country a faith which has become the hope of all peoples in an anguished world.
>
> So we pray to Him now for the vision to see our way clearly—to see the way that leads to a better life for ourselves and for all our fellow men—to the achievement of His will to peace on earth.[504]

President Roosevelt's comments perfectly reflect America's situation in the present time, and his prayer remains totally relevant today. Human beings are clearly not capable of achieving peace on Earth by means of their own resources. Only in God will this sought-for state ever be found.

The plans of the LORD stand firm forever, the purposes of his heart through all generations. Blessed is the nation whose God is the LORD, the people he chose for his inheritance. ~Psalms 33:11–12

3

Fourth Honeymoon

AN ANONYMOUS Navy Armed Guard sailor left a diary of his experiences on the merchant ship SS *Russell A. Alger*. In November 1944 the *Alger* set sail from New York City as part of a larger convoy headed across the Atlantic to North Africa and Belgium. This was the beginning of another long separation between a young sailor and his wife. After saying goodbye to her he wrote these words:

> *As I watched New York's famous skyline fade from view in the dim, early morning light I recounted the many happy hours Margaret and I spent together in the brief period of just less than two weeks that had slipped away during the stay in port preceding the journey that had just started. We had jokingly referred to it as our "fourth honeymoon," since ours was a wartime marriage and each subsequent meeting was another honeymoon. We were so accustomed to these brief meetings, with the necessity for living each moment to its fullest, that sometime we caught ourselves wondering what it will be like to live in a peaceful world without the tender farewells and joyous meetings. I am certain that the meeting, however brief, is so much better than being away from each other for a year or more. I fear that there will be many adjustments that will have to be made when the war is over, especially amongst those couples who have been separated for long periods.* [505]

We can call this "looking on the bright side." This young man had many reasons to feel sorry for himself. Repeated separations were painful for him and his wife. However, he was wise enough to realize that many wartime separations were measured in years rather than months. Others were having an even harder time.

We need this same perspective as we deal with our own problems from day to day. No matter how difficult our situation, we can be confident that it could be worse. More importantly, no matter how difficult our situation, there is always much for which we can be thankful. A thankful heart is more pleasing to God than one preoccupied with problems, and thankfulness can be the perfect basis for a growing relationship with him.

Sing to the LORD, you saints of his; praise his holy name. For his anger lasts only a moment, but his favor lasts a lifetime; weeping may remain for a night, but rejoicing comes in the morning. ~Psalms 30:4–5

A Soul-Stirring Sight

THE USS *FRANKLIN* was a World War II Essex-class aircraft carrier, affectionately known to her crew as *"Big Ben."* On the morning of March 19, 1945, she was maneuvering close to Japan when a lone enemy bomber attacked suddenly, dropping two bombs that penetrated deep into the ship, causing immense devastation and widespread fires. As the fires grew in intensity, secondary explosions started from the ship's ammunition stocks. Casualties were everywhere.

From this scene of chaos arose one of the war's greatest heroes. Lt. Cdr. Joseph O'Callahan was *Big Ben*'s chaplain and a very impressive figure. His physical appearance was commanding and his past accomplishments as a collegiate track star, writer, and university professor were legendary. His actions on this day are best recounted in the citation for his Medal of Honor:

> *Lieutenant Commander O'Callahan groped his way through smoke-filled corridors to the open deck and into the midst of violently exploding bombs, rockets and other armament. With the ship rocked by incessant explosions, with debris and fragments raining down and fires raging in ever increasing fury, he ministered to the wounded and dying, comforting and encouraging men of all faiths; he organized and led firefighting crews into the blazing inferno on the flight deck...Serving with courage, fortitude and deep spiritual strength, Lieutenant Commander O'Callahan inspired the gallant officers and men of the Franklin to fight heroically and with profound faith in the face of almost certain death.*[506]

This was the only Medal of Honor awarded to a chaplain in World War II. His commanding officer called O'Callahan, *"The bravest man I ever saw."*[507] Another officer described his actions as *"a soul stirring sight."*[508] With a white cross painted on his helmet Joseph O'Callahan bravely went beyond the call of duty and distinguished himself and the Savior whom he served.

For God did not give us a spirit of timidity, but a spirit of power, of love and of self-discipline. ~2 Timothy 1:7

An Unseen Enemy

IWO JIMA MEANS "sulfur island," and the rotten egg smell of sulfur gas pouring out of steaming rock beds permeated the air. By the time the Marines landed there was practically no vegetation remaining over a moonscape of cratered volcanic sand and rocky ridges. They soon realized that they were engaged in a two-dimensional battle. They were fighting *on* Iwo Jima, whereas the Japanese defenders were *under* Iwo Jima. The island had been turned into one of the greatest underground fortresses ever seen.

For months Korean laborers, military engineers and demolition experts had built fortified positions and interconnecting tunnels throughout the island, stocked with ammunition and food. The Japanese soldiers waited in these mutually supporting underground fortifications for the Americans to come to them. Each had a printed "battle vow" before him in his cave: *"Each man will make it his duty to kill ten of the enemy before dying."*[509]

For the Marines, this was largely a battle against an unseen enemy. One historian remarked, *"There were Marines who fought on Iwo Jima for the entire six-week campaign who never saw a living enemy soldier."*[510] One Marine said, *"It was an eerie landscape. While you couldn't see them, you had a feeling that the Japanese had you always in their sights."*[511]

Christians also face an enemy that amazingly remains largely unseen in the world around them. Satan has succeeded in trivializing his own image to the extent that few take even his existence seriously. The little red figure with a pitchfork is more of a joke than a threat to anyone's eternal survival. It is well to ponder the evil that we see at work in the world and how well organized it often seems to be. And we need to renew our understanding of this enemy's nature through Scripture: *"The devil prowls around like a roaring lion looking for someone to devour"* (1 Peter 5:8). Knowledge of such an enemy is essential to our spiritual survival.

For such men are false apostles, deceitful workmen, masquerading as apostles of Christ. And no wonder, for Satan himself masquerades as an angel of light. ~2 Corinthians 11:13–14

Marines advancing on difficult terrain.
(National Archives)

Church service on Okinawa.
(National Archives)

Emergency Landing

DURING THE BATTLE for Iwo Jima, the Marines suffered their highest casualty rate of the war. For the first time, there were more American dead and wounded than Japanese. One rifle company landed with 235 men, received seventy replacements during the battle, and suffered 240 casualties, more than 100 percent of its original strength. Twenty-seven Medals of Honor were awarded, reflecting the heroism of the men and the savagery of the fighting.

On March 4 the battle for the island was still raging when the Marines received an unexpected visitor. A B-29 bomber flew past Mount Suribachi, dipped down, and slammed onto the partially repaired airstrip. As the aircraft skidded to a stop at the northern end of the runway, the name *Dynah Might* could be seen painted on the nose. Enemy fire started falling near the aircraft. Taxiing back to the other side of the airfield out of range of the enemy guns, the sixty-five-ton behemoth came to a stop. The crew jumped out of the aircraft, fell on their hands and knees and kissed the runway. Hundreds of Seabees and Marines cheered their throats dry, as one Marine observed, *"What a contrast! Here were men so glad to be on the island they were kissing it. A mile or two to the north were three Marine divisions who thought the ground . . . (was) not even good enough to spit on."*[512]

The *Dynah Might* brought a tangible demonstration to the Marines of what they were fighting for on Iwo Jima. By war's end more than two thousand U.S. aircraft would land on the little island, and thousands of other airmen would be saved. From time to time we all need some tangible reminders of what we're striving for. Our mission as Christians is to save souls, and there is nothing more motivating than to hear about a success. Share your own witness with your brothers and sisters in Christ. You never know when your words will be the very encouragement that someone else needs to carry on in their work for the Lord's kingdom.

> You will be my witnesses in Jerusalem, and in all Judea and Samaria, and to the ends of the earth. ~Acts 1:8

Nurses

AS SOON AS Iwo Jima Airfield No. 1 was cleared of enemy mines and the runways were repaired, transport aircraft from Guam began arriving to evacuate the seriously wounded. At that time a group of twelve nurses had just arrived on Guam to work in the field hospital there. Norma Crotty was one of the first to learn that she would accompany a flight to Iwo Jima and care for wounded Marines on the return trip. After an anxious five-hour flight, she suddenly found herself in the middle of a combat zone for the first time. She could hardly believe the lack of color in a desolate landscape filled with dirt, smoke, and noise. To her it was like *"living in a newsreel."*[513]

She soon found the aid station, where thirty of the most seriously wounded were selected for evacuation. They were taken to the waiting aircraft and put on bunks stacked four high. Since there were no doctors on the return flight, Norma and one corpsman were on their own taking care of their patients. Her memories of these men were vivid and lasting:

The fellows were so much younger than us, seventeen or eighteen years old, and some of them looked younger than that. Like little boys. And they wanted their mothers, and we sort of became their mothers and comforted them. They were all very courteous and appreciative of anything we did. As much as we did for them medically, I think it was the comforting that was most important to them, and to us. Mostly, they wanted to talk to us, and they enjoyed watching us comb our hair and put on lipstick. They'd ask us to do that. The feeling of closeness to these boys I didn't have again until I had children.[514]

There are few things as pure as a nurse's love for her patients or a mother's love for her children, both of which are illustrated in this story. It is an incredible realization that both are but a pale reflection of God's love for us. In spite of the fact that we turn away from him and continually disappoint him, he continues to treat us as his own children. In the greatest demonstration of love ever known, he sent his Son to live in the world, to teach us, to suffer for us, and to redeem us to himself.

God demonstrates his own love for us in this: While we were still sinners, Christ died for us. ~Romans 5:8

Divine Wind

A N IMPORTANT EVENT in Japanese history occurred in the year 1281 when the Mongol emperor Kublai Khan invaded the island nation with an overwhelming army and naval armada. Vastly outnumbered, the Japanese fought back, but were saved only by an unseasonable typhoon that scattered the invasion fleet. This incident was considered an intervention by divine providence and remembered as the Kamikaze—or Divine Wind.

In 1944, facing the inexorable Allied advance toward the home islands, the Japanese military turned to a desperate measure. A modern "divine wind" of suicide bombers was unleashed on the American fleet. The first wave of Kamikazes hurtled down at Leyte Gulf in the Philippines in October 1944, where the escort carrier *St. Lo* became the first victim of the new tactic. These attacks built to a crescendo at Okinawa where thirty-six ships and landing craft were destroyed. It is estimated that by war-end 4,900 U.S. sailors were killed by as many as 5,000 Kamikaze attacks.[515]

In May 1945 a twenty-three-year-old Japanese pilot wrote his last letter home before his one and only mission:

> *Dear Parents: Please congratulate me. I have been given a splendid opportunity to die. This is my last day. The destiny of our homeland hinges on the decisive battle in the seas to the south where I shall fall like a blossom from a radiant cherry tree. I shall be a shield for His Majesty and die cleanly along with my squadron leader and other friends.*[516]

The individual courage of this Japanese airman cannot be denied. It is the policy of intentional suicide that is so abhorrent to our value system. Our concern for human life stems from our loyalty to a God who created us in his image and places eternal value on every human soul. Even in wartime Americans have and will hopefully always continue to conserve lives, whether they be our own troops, civilians, or even enemy combatants. No human life is expendable.

Then God said, "Let us make man in our image, in our likeness, and let them rule over the fish of the sea and the birds of the air, over the livestock, over all the earth, and over all the creatures that move along the ground." ~Genesis 1:26

USS *Bunker Hill* burns after suicide attack.
(National Archives)

God Is My Co-Pilot

ROBERT SCOTT was one of World War II's most famous aviators. He was credited with thirteen aerial victories while flying his P-40 Warhawk over China. He flew as a volunteer with General Claire Chennault's Flying Tigers and then as commander of the 23rd Fighter Group of the China Air Task Force. He returned to the United States in 1943 to a hero's welcome and nationwide speaking tour. While still on active duty he wrote his wartime memoir, *God Is My Co-Pilot,* and served as technical advisor to Warner Brothers for the movie production of his book. Colonel Scott wrote a heartfelt prayer to share his faith with other military men and women:

Prayer of a Fighter Pilot

O God, My Father, The Great Referee of earth and sea and sky, be with me in combat and adversity. Strengthen my love for the land that has given me birth and make me worthy of the sacrifices of my fathers in hewing America from the wilderness they found. Endow me with the courage to face danger in spite of fear. Make me resolve that the blood of my fathers was not shed in vain and that regardless of cost—our way of life shall endure. Keep me physically strong that I may better defend my home and my native land. Keep me mentally awake that my enemies may never again strike with surprise and deal with me in treachery. Uplift my morals that I may better maintain the honor of my country and reverence of my forefathers. Let duty to God and country be my most sublime aspirations, and kindle my heart and soul with the determination to die rather than yield the ideals of my world. O God, My Father, whatever duty befalls me when my country calls, may I acquit myself as worthy of Thy Guidance.

And when my combat's over and my flying days are done
I will store my ship forever in the airdrome of the sun.
Then I'll meet the Referee, Great God, my Flying Boss,
Whose Wingspread fills the heavens from Polaris to the Cross.
. . . Amen[517]

Where were you when I laid the earth's foundation? Tell me, if you understand. Who marked off its dimensions? Surely you know! Who stretched a measuring line across it? On what were its footings set, or who laid its cornerstone—while the morning stars sang together and all the angels shouted for joy? ~Job 38:4–7

Faith Will Help

CHAPLAIN HERB VAN METER wrote many letters to the families of fallen heroes and with great effort did his best to personalize each one. In April 1945 he wrote to the family of James Emory, a Marine killed on Iwo Jima.

> *As we left Iwo Jima you would know how hard it was to leave behind those who fought beside me. As the transport left the anchorage the troops stood silently, reverently at attention in their honor. Eyes were fixed on the flag flying in the Division cemetery over their graves. It was a holy moment. Words cannot express the thoughts that rise in a man's heart at such a time. There were men thinking of James as there were men whose thoughts were with those who lie beside him under those white crosses. There were prayers and there were tears. We will not forget.*
>
> *Time alone will heal the pain of separation from your son. Pride will help you face it now: pride in one who gave his life to his nation, pride in having given a gift so great. Faith will help: faith in those great causes for which Jim risked and gave his life, faith in the dedication of our people and nation to those causes. And most of all there is faith in Almighty God to help you, faith in Him who gives us life and in whose providence it is taken from us. God grant you that faith.[518]*

It is one thing to believe that God is sovereign in the giving and taking of life when all our loved ones remain with us. To cling to that knowledge when a son has died, however—especially in the brutal circumstances of war—is taking that faith to an entirely new level. My own faith has not been tested in this way, and I pray that yours has not either. But to help safeguard our faith before it is even placed in the refiner's fire, we would benefit from remembering to place our faith in the unchanging person of God and his son, Jesus Christ, rather than measuring our faith by our circumstances. (JG)

> I am the LORD, and there is no other. I form the light and create darkness, I bring prosperity and create disaster; I, the LORD, do all these things. ~Isaiah 45:6–7

We the Living

ON MARCH 21, 1945, a cemetery on Iwo Jima was dedicated to the fallen Marines and sailors of the 5th Marine Division. Chaplain Roland Gittelsohn delivered a moving sermon with echoes from Abraham Lincoln's address at another great battlefield—Gettysburg:

> This is perhaps the grimmest, and surely the holiest task we have faced since D-Day. Here before us lie the bodies of comrades and friends. Men who until yesterday or last week laughed with us, joked with us, trained with us . . . Men who fought with us and feared with us . . . Now they lie here silently in this sacred soil, and we gather to consecrate this earth in their memory.
>
> It is not easy to do so. Some of us have buried our closest friends here. We saw these men killed before our very eyes. Any one of us might have died in their places. Indeed, some of us are alive and breathing only because men who lie here beneath us had the courage and strength to give their lives for us. To speak in memory of such men as these is not easy. Of them, too, can it be said with utter truth: 'The world will little note nor long remember, what we say here. We can never forget what they did here.' . . . These men have done their job well. They have paid the ghastly price of freedom. If that freedom is once again lost . . . the unforgivable blame will be ours, not theirs, so it is we, 'the living' who are here to be dedicated and consecrated.[519]

Every person who has lived through war thinks of lost comrades with feelings of sadness and guilt. We survived, and they did not. Chaplain Gittelson articulately spells out our only recourse. We have to live our lives in honor of those who gave theirs. To do this, we have to be a force for peace in the world, in our communities, and in our families. In this noble endeavor we have an all-powerful ally—the Prince of Peace, Jesus Christ.

Blessed are the peacemakers, for they will be called sons of God. ~Matthew 5:9

To Live Together

In the 1940s the military services reflected the racial prejudice and seg-regation then pervading American society. Black American units were organized in each branch of the Armed Forces, but were not used in direct combat roles at first. Later in the war, this began to change as the long, slow process of improving racial relations gained momentum in the services and nation.

At Iwo Jima's battlefield cemetery Chaplain Roland Gittelsohn, a Jewish rabbi, took a bold step for that time by addressing the issues of race and religion. He reminded the living of their eternal bonds with the fallen and one of their most important obligations to honor their memory:

> We dedicate ourselves, first to live together in peace the way they fought and are buried in this war. Here lie men who loved America because their ancestors generations ago helped in her founding, and other men who loved her with equal passion because they themselves or their own fathers escaped from oppression to her blessed shores. Here lie officers and men, Negroes and Whites, rich men and poor—together. Here are Protestants, Catholics and Jews—together. Here no man prefers another because of his faith or despised him because of his color. Here there are no quotas of how many from each group are admitted or allowed. Among these men there is no discrimination. No prejudices. No hatred. There is the highest and purest democracy.[520]

This sermon was reprinted in the thousands and made its way back to the States in untold numbers of letters home. It was also picked up by newspapers, magazines, and radio broadcasts. It was one of many seeds planted during the war that would grow slowly and painfully toward a color-blind America.

Have we not all one Father? Did not one God create us? Why do we profane the covenant of our fathers by breaking faith with one another? ~Malachi 2:10

A Sorry Swap

THE HUMAN COST of the war was at times overwhelming. A chaplain walked through a new graveyard in the Philippines lined with thirty-five hundred freshly painted white crosses. He looked at the ages of the fallen soldiers buried there and noticed that practically every one was eighteen or nineteen years old:

> *For this, some poor woman labored for nine months, brought the child into the world, took care of every need, watched him grow up, proud, and this is the way it ends? There's got to be a better way.*[521]

Another chaplain received many answers to his letters of condolence. Most were gracious and thankful for his help. A few were bitter, as this one from the parents of an only son killed on Iwo Jima:

> *Did he die quick, with a rifle bullet or was he blown all to h___ with a mortar or torn up by shrapnel? Did he last long enough to see the flag go up on Suribachi? . . . We spent eighteen years raising this boy and it took eighteen months for the Marines to finish the job, and we have an engraved certificate to show that he died for liberty. You will have to admit that it is a . . . sorry swap.*[522]

This letter may not have been typical, but it was honest. Other parents and loved ones may have accepted their losses more graciously, but their pain was just as deep. It is a natural and a good thing to glorify our sons and daughters who have fallen in wartime fighting for our nation. We rightfully consider them heroes. It is a good thing also to understand and remember the cost of this sacrifice. Mothers, fathers, spouses, siblings, communities all suffer losses that are at times almost impossible to bear. These tragedies shatter lives and affect untold future generations. While condemning war and the human failures that cause it, we pray to see that day envisioned by the prophet Isaiah:

He will judge between the nations and will settle disputes for many peoples. They will beat their swords into plowshares and their spears into pruning hooks. Nation will not take up sword against nation, nor will they train for war anymore. ~Isaiah 2:4

Common Denominator

A JEWISH CHAPLAIN gave this thoughtful description of his ministry to soldiers during World War II:

I find most of my work with men of Protestant and Catholic faiths. Moving about clearing stations, mobile hospitals, rest centers and reserve units . . . one cannot merely seek his own fellow worshippers. Every boy is equally important—and a smile looks as good on anyone. We forget that we are this faith or another and emphasize the common denominator of fellowship. When they bring them in on a litter covered with mud, blood-soaked, with fear and shock in their faces, you can't tell what they are until you look at their dog tags. To serve such men is my privilege.[523]

Military chaplains have always functioned on many levels. As representatives of their faith they have a role in sharing their beliefs with those in spiritual need. As representatives of different denominations they provide the familiar forms of worship that are meaningful to those denominations. On a more basic level, however, they try to represent God to others by bringing a simple, godly concern to every man and woman. This caring touch in the midst of often-desolate surroundings has been of incalculable comfort to many thousands, regardless of their religious affiliation or nonaffiliation. The common denominator is the fact that *all* are truly God's children. Many of these chaplains have shared the dangers and discomforts of combat duty around the world and have earned the gratitude of generations of soldiers, sailors, and airmen.

> After this the Lord appointed seventy-two others and sent them two by two ahead of him to every town and place where he was about to go. He told them, "The harvest is plentiful, but the workers are few." ~Luke 10:1–2

Ace of Aces

EDDIE RICKENBACKER was one the greatest heroes of World War I and II. As leader of the famous 94th Aero, "Hat in the Ring," Squadron he posted twenty-six victories over enemy aircraft in the First World War, earning the distinction of "Ace of Aces." For his heroism in aerial combat he was awarded nine Distinguished Service Crosses and the Medal of Honor. After the war he went into the business world as owner and manager of the Indianapolis Motor Speedway and chief executive officer of Eastern Airlines.

In 1941 Rickenbacker was involved in a near-fatal airplane crash near Atlanta and was hospitalized for months. While still recovering from multiple injuries sustained in the crash, be agreed to become the personal envoy of the secretary of war, Henry Stimson. He traveled around the world to give encouragement to armed forces personnel and to gauge the effectiveness of U.S. tactics and equipment.

While flying from Hawaii to the island of Canton in 1942, his B-17 ditched in the middle of the Pacific. With seven other survivors, he spent twenty-four days lost at sea. He credited prayer and the miraculous arrival of a seagull for his survival. He was a devout Christian and wrote the following heartfelt prayer. When he spoke of the "valley of the shadow of death," he had more first-hand knowledge than probably any other living man.

O Lord, I thank thee for the strength and blessings thou hast given me, and even though I have walked through the valley of the shadow of death, I feared no evil, for thy rod and thy staff comforted me even unto the four corners of the world. I have sinned, O Lord, but through thy mercy thou hast shown me the light of thy saving grace.

In thy care we are entrusting our boys and girls in the Services scattered throughout the entire world, and we know that in thee they are finding their haven of hope. Be with our leaders, O Lord; give them wisdom to lead us to a spiritual victory, as well as a physical one. And until that day, be with those at home—strengthen them for whatever may lie ahead . . . In Jesus' name I ask it. Amen.[524]

You prepare a table before me in the presence of my enemies. You anoint my head with oil; my cup overflows. Surely goodness and love will follow me all the days of my life, and I will dwell in the house of the LORD forever. ~Psalms 23:5–6

Safety in God's Will

DARLENE DEIBLER spent four long years in a Japanese prison camp. Separated in 1942 from her missionary husband, she never saw him again. She was still a captive when she learned more than a year later that he had died in another camp. At the end of the war, a friend brought a letter from her husband written to her on his deathbed. Along with expressions of love he wrote poignantly of one regret: *"My darling, I have wished 1001 x's that I had taken you away from here. I am concerned for your safety."*[525] Darlene's reaction to her husband's letter revealed the strength of her faith:

> It took me a long time to finish the letter. I didn't want to stain it with tears. I was so grieved that he felt he should have taken me away. Both of us had agreed that we should remain, and that decision was reached only after much prayer. "Lord, I trust that You reminded him that it was You Who impressed upon both our hearts that we should not leave. I have been safer here, overshadowed by Your love, than I would have been anywhere else on this earth, outside of your will!"[526]

It is difficult to appreciate the power of this statement without knowing the full extent of the hardships and danger faced by this woman during her captivity. Suspected of spying by the Japanese secret police, she was starved and beaten repeatedly. She frequently thought that her execution was imminent. She survived debilitating diseases and frequent bombing attacks. For her to declare that during all this she was safer there, in God's will, than she would have been elsewhere is one of the most amazing testaments of faith I have ever read. It is inspiring to witness the power of such a sure relationship with God. After praying for guidance and listening for an answer, Darlene Deibler was confident that she was doing what God wanted her to do. With this knowledge she was able to face every hardship without regret.

Although the Lord gives you the bread of adversity and the water of affliction, your teachers will be hidden no more; with your own eyes you will see them. Whether you turn to the right or to the left, your ears will hear a voice behind you, saying, "This is the way; walk in it." ~Isaiah 30:20–21

The Planets Had Fallen

DURING HIS FIRST two months as vice president, Harry Truman seldom saw Franklin Roosevelt and received little information on critical wartime developments. He knew nothing about the atomic bomb or problems with Russia, problems that suddenly became his to solve when Roosevelt died on April 12, 1945. Shortly after taking the oath of office, he told reporters, *"Boys, if you ever pray, pray for me now. I don't know if you fellas ever had a load of hay fall on you, but when they told me what happened yesterday, I felt like the moon, the stars, and all the planets had fallen on me."*[527]

President Truman.
(Harry S. Truman Library)

Harry Truman also prayed for himself. He was a life-long Baptist, believing that his church gave *"the common man the shortest and most direct approach to God."*[528] He had a favorite prayer that he had used since high school, as a bank clerk, farmer, public official, and, now, as president of the United States:

> *Oh Almighty and Everlasting God, Creator of Heaven, Earth and the Universe:*
> *Help me to be, to think, to act what is right, because it is right; make me truthful, honest and honorable in all things; make me intellectually honest for the sake of right and honor and without thought of reward to me. Give me the ability to be charitable, forgiving and patient with my fellow men—help me to understand their motives and their shortcomings—even as Thou understandest mine!*[529]

Harry Truman was known as an honest and plainspoken man. His religion was an important part of his life although he didn't put much value in the form of it or in intermediaries. As he put it, *"I've never thought that the Almighty could be impressed by anything but the heart and soul of the individual."*[530]

The God who made the world and everything in it is the Lord of heaven and earth and does not live in temples built by hands. ~Acts 17:24

Potsdam

ON JULY 26, 1945, the United States, Great Britain, and China issued the Potsdam Declaration defining acceptable surrender terms with Japan. It was somewhat brutal in its directness and threatened Japan's *"prompt and utter destruction"* if not accepted. However, it also proposed a road to recovery and reconciliation. The following are excerpts:

> *We do not intend that the Japanese shall be enslaved as a race or destroyed as a nation, but stern justice shall be meted out to all war criminals, including those who have visited cruelties upon our prisoners. The Japanese Government shall remove all obstacles to the revival and strengthening of democratic tendencies among the Japanese people. Freedom of speech and religion and of thought, as well as respect for the fundamental human rights, shall be established.*
>
> *The occupying forces of the Allies shall be withdrawn from Japan as soon as these objectives have been accomplished and there has been established in accordance with the freely expressed will of the Japanese people a peacefully inclined and responsible Government.*[531]

Within days this declaration was rejected forcefully by the Japanese prime minister and was followed by days of continued conflict and devastation. It nevertheless eventually formed the basis of American policy toward postwar Japan and provided the structure for one of the most successful reconstructions in history. It was a reflection of America's oft-reiterated war aims to defeat tyranny and restore freedom. Neither conquest nor revenge was part of this agenda.

I was witness to the final restoration of occupied territory, when, in 1972, sovereignty over Okinawa was returned to the government of Japan. The postwar occupation of Japan was not without problems or flaws, but history shows that ultimately these benign policies, based on an elevated view of human nature, indeed did bring recovery and reconciliation to a devastated nation.

"Though the mountains be shaken and the hills be removed, yet my unfailing love for you will not be shaken nor my covenant of peace be removed," says the LORD, who has compassion on you. ~Isaiah 54:10

Consumed by Your Anger

A FEW DAYS AFTER the atomic bomb destroyed Hiroshima, the Reverend Kiyoshi Tanimoto was summoned to the deathbed of a parishioner suffering from burns and radiation sickness. Mr. Tanimoto, himself suffering from the shock and fatigue of dealing with the widespread misery, offered an Old Testament reading from his Japanese-language pocket Bible: *"For a thousand years in Thy sight are but as yesterday when it is past, and as a watch in the night. Thou carriest them away as with a flood; they are as asleep . . . For we are consumed by Thine anger and by Thy wrath are we troubled . . ."*[532]

Isaac Watts used these words from Psalm 90 to convey a New Testament message in one of the greatest Christian hymns ever written:

Our God, Our Help in Ages Past

Our God, our help in ages past, Our hope for years to come,
Our shelter from the stormy blast, And our eternal home.
A thousand ages in Thy sight Are like an evening gone;
Short as the watch that ends the night Before the rising sun.
Time, like an ever rolling stream, Bears all its sons away;
They fly, forgotten, as a dream Dies at the opening day.
Our God, our help in ages past, Our hope for years to come,
Be thou our guard while troubles last, And our eternal home.[533]

This hymn gives a masterful portrait of our mighty Lord and of his perspective on time and humanity. From his viewpoint our lives truly go by in a flash, and, on Earth, we are quickly forgotten. However, this hymn goes further to highlight another facet of God's character. God loves us and provides an eternal home for us to be with him. Through his Son, he gives us the sure way to forgiveness, peace, and everlasting life. The degree of our pain and hardship in this life no longer matter. We can find comfort in God's perspective and in the hope that he gives us for the future.

> I tell you the truth, whoever hears my word and believes him who sent me has eternal life and will not be condemned; he has crossed over from death to life.
> ~John 5:24

Fearful Loneliness

MISS TOSHIKO SASAKI lost everything on the day Hiroshima was bombed. Her home was destroyed and her parents and younger brother died. She suffered a compound fracture of her leg, months of nightmarish pain, and a permanently crippled condition. As she grew more and more depressed and morbid, she was befriended by a German missionary priest, himself a survivor of the bomb blast. The priest walked great distances to see her in spite of his own pain and weakness. He carefully introduced religion into their talks, which she at first bitterly resisted. She had a hard time with the idea of a loving God that would allow the suffering she had seen. Over time, the priest's patient faithfulness changed her heart, and she became a Christian.

After recovering from her wounds Sasaki worked in a retirement home for old people and eventually became its director. She found that her greatest gift as a Christian was the ability to help others die in peace:

> She had seen so much death in Hiroshima after the bombing, and had seen what strange things so many people did when they were cornered by death, that nothing now surprised or frightened her. The first time she stood watch by a dying inmate, she vividly remembered a night soon after the bombing when she had lain out in the open, uncared for, in dreadful pain, beside a young man who was dying. She had talked with him all night, and had become aware, above all, of his fearful loneliness. She had watched him die in the morning. At deathbeds in the home, she was always mindful of this terrible solitude. She would speak little to the dying person but would hold a hand or touch an arm, as an assertion, simply, that she was there.[534]

We all seem to worry about finding "the right thing to say" to a dying person and their loved ones. If we are able to share God's love and provide spiritual comfort with words, we should certainly do so. However, this story is an inspiring reminder that our presence and touch are usually more important than what we say to a person facing the end of life.

And God raised us up with Christ and seated us with him in the heavenly realms in Christ Jesus, in order that in the coming ages he might show the incomparable riches of his grace, expressed in his kindness to us in Christ Jesus. ~Ephesians 2:6–7

Divine Providence

AFTER THE WAR President Harry Truman took part in a dedication ceremony for the New York Presbyterian Church in Washington, D.C., where many presidents, including Abraham Lincoln, had worshipped. He took the occasion to express some heartfelt views on America's relationship to God and the world.

> We talk a lot these days about freedom—freedom for the individual and freedom among the nations. Freedom for the human soul is, indeed, the most important principle of our civilization. We must always remember, however, that the freedom we are talking about is freedom based upon moral principles. Without a firm moral foundation, freedom degenerates quickly into selfishness and license.
>
> I do not think that anyone can study the history of this Nation of ours—study it deeply and earnestly—without becoming convinced that divine providence has played a great part in it. I have the feeling that God has created us and brought us to our present position of power and strength for some great purpose.
>
> It is not given to us to know fully what that purpose is. But I think we may be sure of one thing. That is, that our country is intended to do all it can, in cooperation with other nations, to help create peace and preserve peace in this world. It is given to us to defend the spiritual values—the moral code—against the vast forces of evil that seek to destroy them.
>
> This is a hard task. It is not one that we have asked for . . . But we need not be afraid, if we have faith.[535]

Every point made by President Truman is applicable to America today. God has continued to bless this great nation. Never before in history have any people had such complete freedom to set their own moral and spiritual course. It is as if God has perfected freedom in America and waits to see what each person will do with it. As Christians we must live and demonstrate this enduring truth to others: that the ultimate purpose of our lives and our freedom is to seek and find God.

> God did this so that men would seek him and perhaps reach out for him and find him, though he is not far from each one of us. "For in him we live and move and have our being." ~Acts 17:27–28

Silent Night

On December 24, 1942, the 7th Marine Regiment was relieved from the front line on Guadalcanal after ninety-six consecutive days of combat. Edward Andrusko and his battle-weary comrades marched to the relative safety of the beach area to wait for embarkation. That night he and many other Marines attended a memorable Christmas Eve service in a coconut grove beside Henderson Field. The makeshift altar was covered by a tent, and coconut logs served as pews. Bomb shelters were close at hand. Andrusko observed, *"It was a beautiful service with candles, caroling, prayer for peace on Earth, and memorials to our dead and wounded."*[536]

Suddenly, however, the air raid warning sounded. The chaplain, a seasoned combat veteran himself, calmly asserted that he was going to continue with the service, but pointed to the air raid shelters for all who wanted to seek a safer place. Most of the Marines stayed in the dark outdoor church, illuminated by a single candle. An amazing scene unfolded:

> *Soon we heard the drone of enemy planes and the whistling of their bombs and explosions approaching closer and closer.*
>
> *Instantly the dark night was brightly illuminated by our large searchlights . . . nearby batteries of our anti-aircraft cannons blasted away . . . The guns fired loudly and rapidly, and their high overhead explosion bursts would light up the sky. . . . Our bright red tracers added to the awesome fireworks display. More bombs fell, but soon passed us by.*
>
> *We sang "Silent Night, Holy Night. All is calm. All is bright," as the enemy planes passed slowly overhead. After a while their bombs fell further and further away from us. Our prayers and carol singing must have been heard through the din of battle, and answered, for soon the all clear was sounded. No one was hurt at our church service. That was our first and last Christmas Eve midnight mass on Guadalcanal Island.*[537]

An angel of the Lord appeared to them, and the glory of the Lord shone around them, and they were terrified. But the angel said to them, "Do not be afraid. I bring you good news of great joy that will be for all the people. Today in the town of David a Savior has been born to you; he is Christ the Lord." ~Luke 2:9–11

Looking for the Star

THERE WAS PLENTY of bad news from the European front on December 24, 1944. The German offensive through Belgium and Luxembourg, known as the Battle of the Bulge, had been launched on December 16 with devastating effect. V-1 rockets, or "buzz bombs," were bringing a new rain of terror on England's cities. On Christmas Eve Flora Southwick wrote her husband, Erman, a letter filled with mixed emotions:

> *The war news has been in the past few days disheartening to say the least and to me it brings the sad thought that our physical separation may be longer. My heart aches for those who are suffering and dying during what should be a season of gladness. And I have great compassion for those who have lost loved ones . . .*
>
> *Tonight I shall look for the Christmas star and you in France will also be looking for it. Real clouds or the clouds of battle may obscure it but we shall know it is high in the sky sparkling as brightly as ever and bringing its promise of peace and love to all men and women of good will. . . . This Christmas Eve I am strangely happy and I can say to you, darling, a Very Merry Christmas.*[538]

Christmas can be the loneliest of lonely times when we are separated from home and loved ones. This young woman bridged the gulf between her and her husband by turning their mutual attention to a common reference point, the Christmas star. Even in the most difficult circumstances, Christmas is the time of supreme hope. When we focus on the magnitude of the event and realize that this was the turning point in history when God came into the world, we can experience the peace that comes with this special season, in spite of our worldly tribulations. Just as this couple did in World War II, we can find peace in the wonder of this glorious event and draw closer to all other Christians around the world as we look together for the brightly sparkling star.

> They went on their way, and the star they had seen in the east went ahead of them until it stopped over the place where the child was. When they saw the star, they were overjoyed. ~Matthew 2:9–10

Christmas on a Corvette

CORVETTES WERE small naval vessels used in convoy escort duty. They were smaller than destroyers and had even fewer amenities for the crew. The quarters were cramped, and the ride was rough, especially in the North Atlantic during the winter months. Frank Curry spent several years on board the Canadian Navy corvette HMCS *Kamback*, operating out of Newfoundland and Nova Scotia. After a rough at-sea period the *Kamback* returned to port on December 24. Curry described his first shipboard Christmas and the brief opportunity to relax for a day:

> *Christmas Day—and what a day. My first one aboard a ship, but, from the looks of things, not my last. Up at 0800 (among our rare gifts, and a most welcome change). We hosed down the decks and cleaned ship. Decorated our mess decks and tied a small Christmas tree to the masthead— apparently another old, old tradition of the sea. I got feeling pretty merry on the punch which the Old Man fixed personally in the seaman's messdeck. We had a tremendous dinner—all the officers in a very congenial mood for a change—they were almost human.*[539]

In our modern world it is easy to lose appreciation for simple pleasures. On this Christmas Day during wartime, this seaman didn't receive a lot of extra benefits. Sleeping late, a special punch, and a good meal were about all there was. The ship still had to be cleaned in spite of the occasion. Still, these little amenities were appreciated and made this a special day.

It would be well if we could also do less during the Christmas season and enjoy the simple pleasures of our family and the Christmas story. It has unfortunately become trite to say that we need to "put Christ back into Christmas." Nevertheless, this is the only way that we will ever simplify this increasingly turbulent time of year. Our entire purpose should be to focus on the Christ child and the beauty of his story: *"For God so loved the world that he gave his one and only Son"* (John 3:16).

> The Word became flesh and made his dwelling among us. We have seen his glory, the glory of the One and Only, who came from the Father, full of grace and truth. ~John 1:14

Merry Christmas

IN DECEMBER 1944, while war continued to rage in Europe and the Pacific, President Roosevelt gave a radio address, trying to bring a moment of peace to the nation. In his 1944 Christmas Address he said:

> *It is not easy to say 'Merry Christmas' to you, my fellow Americans, in this time of destructive war.*
>
> *Nor can I say 'Merry Christmas' lightly tonight to our armed forces at their battle stations all over the world—or to our allies who fight by their side. Here, at home, we will celebrate this Christmas Day in our traditional way—because of its deep spiritual meaning to us; because the teachings of Christ are fundamental in our lives; and because we want our youngest generation to grow up knowing the significance of this tradition and the story of the coming of the immortal Prince of Peace and Goodwill.*
>
> *But, in perhaps every home in the United States, sad and anxious thoughts will be continually with the millions of our loved ones who are suffering hardships and misery, and who are risking their very lives to preserve for us and for all mankind the fruits of His teachings and the foundations of civilization itself.*
>
> *The Christmas spirit lives tonight in the bitter cold of the front lines in Europe and in the heat of the jungles and swamps of Burma and the Pacific islands. Even the roar of our bombers and fighters in the air and the guns of our ships at sea will not drown out the messages of Christmas which come to the hearts of our fighting men.*[540]

In today's politically correct world, it is amazing and uplifting to hear a great former president say to the nation, *"Merry Christmas,"* and acknowledge *"the coming of the immortal Prince of Peace."* The nation was undoubtedly more spiritual at that time and more conscious of its Christian heritage than it is today. This should not discourage us now, however. God is still sovereign; our nation is where God wants it to be. Freedom of conscience prevails, and our mission as Christians is clear. The nation and world need the Christmas message more than ever and await our personal, loving proclamation of it.

Suddenly a great company of the heavenly host appeared with the angel, praising God and saying, "Glory to God in the highest, and on earth peace to men on whom his favor rests." ~Luke 2:13–14

If Only in My Dreams

EVEN IN MODERN times it is hard for many to think of Christmas without thinking of Bing Crosby. In 1942 he sang "White Christmas" in the movie *Holiday Inn*. The next year he recorded the melancholy but hopeful "I'll Be Home for Christmas." Both of these songs have become enduring Christmas classics, and both had their origins in the bleakest period of World War II, when there was no end to the war in sight. "I'll Be Home for Christmas" in particular struck a chord with every GI away from home and with every loved one at home waiting for his or her return—especially the last line:

> *I'll be home for Christmas*
> *If only in my dreams.*[541]

I have spent my share of Christmases away from home. One of the most dreary was a monsoon-soaked holiday season in Vietnam. By far the most poignant was a Christmas separated from my wife and new daughter. Aboard an amphibious ship in the South China Sea, Christmas 1972 was a lonely experience in close quarters with hundreds of other Marines. I spent long moments looking over the guardrail into an empty sea, thinking of home and Christmas. I was there, but "only in my dreams." May God bless those servicemen and women this Christmas season who are a long way from home, doing their duty, but wishing they were with loved ones in a happier place.

> When times are good, be happy; but when times are bad, consider: God has made the one as well as the other. ~Ecclesiastes 7:14

Thank God We Lost the War

DARLENE DEIBLER was preparing to return to the United States after being liberated from a Japanese internment camp and four years of captivity. The young missionary was approached by a Japanese officer with a surprising declaration:

> Some people would not understand if I said this to them, but I think you will. I'm thanking God we lost the war. I really mean that! We are a proud people, and if we had won the war, the doors of Japan would never again have opened to missionaries. Many people would say I was a traitor to my country, but I love my country and my people enough to suffer the humiliation of defeat, that they might have the opportunity I have had of hearing that Christ is the Son of God, and that He died for all. There are many among the soldiers of my country who are now asking questions. There is a receptivity to my ministry, since the worship of our ancestors has failed to give us the victory. They are searching, and I ask that you pray for them.[542]

No one would ever wish for a personal, family, or national disaster. Unfortunately, such events will inevitably happen. At such times, we can only pray for the strength of faith evidenced by this Japanese Christian. In the face of a national tragedy, he saw hope that more in his country would turn to the true God. In the wake of the 9/11 terrorist attacks America saw an apparent resurgence of faith across the land. "God Bless America" was seen everywhere. Unfortunately, as conditions returned to normal, these displays subsided. I pray that it won't take a devastating disaster to bring about a more widespread and lasting return to faith among our own "proud people." On a national or a personal level, when prosperity blinds us to our dependence on God's mercy and the importance of God in our lives, it is surely a curse.

"Indeed, it is easier for a camel to go through the eye of a needle than for a rich man to enter the kingdom of God." Those who heard this asked, "Who then can be saved?" Jesus replied, "What is impossible with men is possible with God." ~Luke 18:25–27

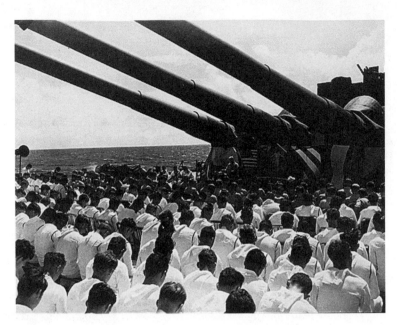

Religious services on the USS *South Dakota*.
(National Archives)

Gen. MacArthur signs the surrender documents.
(National Archives)

It Must Be of the Spirit

ON SEPTEMBER 2, 1945, Gen. Douglas MacArthur made a radio broadcast to the American public from the site of the surrender ceremony in Tokyo Bay. Always eloquent, the great general conveyed his deep concern about the destructiveness of modern war and the need for a spiritual resurgence to prevent even worse conflicts in the future.

> Today the guns are silent. A great tragedy has ended. A great victory has been won . . . The holy mission has been completed and in reporting this to you, the people, I speak for the thousands of silent lips, forever stilled among the jungles and the beaches and in the deep waters of the Pacific which marked the way . . . A new era is upon us . . .
>
> We have had our last chance. If we do not devise some greater and more equitable system, Armageddon will be at our door. The problem is theological and involves a spiritual recrudescence and improvement of human character that will synchronize with our almost matchless advance in science, art, literature, and all material and cultural developments of the past 2,000 years. It must be of the spirit if we are to save the flesh.[543]

The apostle Paul pleaded with the Galatians for the same kind of spiritual revival within their society. He perfectly contrasted for all time the difference between a life of the flesh and a life of the Spirit:

So I say, live by the Spirit, and you will not gratify the desires of the sinful nature. For the sinful nature desires what is contrary to the Spirit, and the Spirit what is contrary to the sinful nature. They are in conflict with each other, so that you do not do what you want. But if you are led by the Spirit, you are not under law.

The acts of the sinful nature are obvious: sexual immorality, impurity and debauchery; idolatry and witchcraft; hatred, discord, jealousy, fits of rage, selfish ambition, dissensions, factions and envy, drunkenness, orgies, and the like. I warn you, as I did before, that those who live like this will not inherit the kingdom of God.

But the fruit of the Spirit is love, joy, peace, patience, kindness, goodness, faithfulness, gentleness and self-control. Against such things there is no law. Those who belong to Christ Jesus have crucified the sinful nature with its passions and desires. Since we live by the Spirit, let us keep in step with the Spirit. ~Galatians 5:16–25

What We Fought For

WHEN ASKED to provide material for a history of World War II, President Franklin Roosevelt offered extracts from his public statements that he considered relevant to the topic, "What We Are Fighting For."[544] In his addresses to the nation he was always extremely effective in inspiring his fellow countrymen. More importantly, he was also able to capture the essence of their own motivation to sacrifice for a long and costly war.

(National Archives)

We are not a warlike people. We have never sought glory as a nation of warriors. We are not interested in aggression . . . Our vast effort, and the unity of purpose which inspires that effort are due solely to our recognition of the fact that our fundamental rights are threatened by Hitler's violent attempt to rule the world . . .

We are fighting today for security, for progress and for peace, not only for ourselves, but for all men, not only for one generation but for all generations. We are fighting to cleanse the world of ancient evils, ancient ills. We are fighting as our fathers have fought, to uphold the doctrine that all men are equal in the sight of God.

In this war of survival we must keep before our minds not only the evil things we fight against but the good things we are fighting for. We fight to retain a great past—and we fight to gain a greater future. The issue of this war is the basic issue between those who believe in mankind and those who do not—the ancient issue between those who put their faith in the people and those who put their faith in dictators and tyrants.[545]

President Roosevelt's words continue to inspire us and to remind us that we have duties and responsibilities to our nation and to God that go with the benefits of being an American.

Freely you have received, freely give. ~Matthew 10:8

Surrender

SUNDAY, SEPTEMBER 2, 1945, dawned gray and sullen over Tokyo Bay. The Japanese delegation considered the weather symbolic of their ancestors "weeping" as they climbed the ladder alongside the USS *Missouri* to formally surrender their nation. They were met by General Douglas MacArthur and representatives of China, the United Kingdom, the Soviet Union, Australia, Canada, France, the Netherlands, and New Zealand. Accompanying MacArthur were Generals Jonathan Wainright and Arthur Percival, both just liberated from Japanese prison camps. At nine o'clock General MacArthur stepped to the microphone to open the proceedings:

> *We are gathered here, representative of the major warring Powers, to conclude a solemn agreement whereby peace may be restored. The issues, involving divergent ideals and ideologies, have been determined on the battlefields of the world and hence are not for our discussion or debate. Nor is it for us here to meet, representing as we do a majority of the peoples of the earth, in a spirit of distrust, malice, or hatred. But rather it is for us, both victors and vanquished, to rise to that higher dignity which alone befits the sacred purposes we are about to serve.*[546]

Each representative was called to sign the peace accords, and General MacArthur then concluded the short ceremony reverently: *"Let us pray that peace be now restored to the world, and that God will preserve it always. These proceedings are closed."*[547] At that moment an armada of two hundred fifty aircraft flew over the *Missouri*, and the sun broke out from behind the clouds, shining on a world at peace. World War II was over.

> Righteousness will be his belt and faithfulness the sash around his waist. The wolf will live with the lamb, the leopard will lie down with the goat, the calf and the lion and the yearling together; and a little child will lead them . . . They will neither harm nor destroy on all my holy mountain, for the earth will be full of the knowledge of the LORD as the waters cover the sea. ~Isaiah 11:5–6, 9

Going Home

DENTON DABBS spent three years in military service and moved seventeen times. His assigned bases were often dull and drab places, as he put it, *"devoid of heart and soul."* Late in 1945, after the war was over, he was sent to Shreveport, Louisiana, to process out of the Army Air Corps. He finally boarded a train for his hometown, Chattanooga, Tennessee. As he got nearer to home, it was as if he were approaching the Promised Land:

> As the train came out of the tunnel through Lookout Mountain, I could see the city nestled there in the valley on the banks of the Tennessee River. Down below was the bend in the river, known as Moccasin Bend, and in the distance was Signal Mountain. I thought it was the most beautiful sight I had ever seen. It was familiar territory for my eyes and I was floating on air. The war was really over—I was heading home. It was not just a dream—there was the river and mountains and the city I knew so well. I grew up there and it was home.
>
> Going home—that was what it was all about. Going home to Ann—to mom and dad, my brothers...the people I loved and who loved me. The valley had never seemed so beautiful before, but on that day it was the most beautiful place in all the world.[548]

Denton Dabbs describes an almost heavenly picture: a place of scenic beauty, the presence of loved ones, and a time of blessed peace in the world. In Revelation, John describes his vision of heaven, and it includes some of these same qualities. There is one important difference, however, and that is the everlasting presence of God the Father. John's vision forms the basis of our hope for eternal peace in God's kingdom:

Now the dwelling of God is with men, and he will live with them. They will be his people, and God himself will be with them and be their God. He will wipe every tear from their eyes. There will be no more death or mourning or crying or pain, for the old order of things has passed away. ~Revelation 21:3–4

Bibliography

A Prayer Book for Soldiers and Sailors. New York: The Army and Navy Commission of The Protestant Episcopal Church, 1941.

Atkinson, Rick. *An Army at Dawn: The War in North Africa 1942–1943*. New York: Henry Holt and Company, LLC, 2002.

Astor, Gerald. *The Mighty Eighth*. New York: Dell Publishing, 1997.

Australians in the Pacific War: Royal Australian Air Force, 1941–1945. Canberra, Australia: Department of Veteran Affairs, 2005.

Avigdor, Isaac C. *From Prison to Pulpit: Sermons for All Holidays of the Year: Stories from the Holocaust*. Hartford, CT: Horav Publishing, 1975.

Bonhoeffer, Dietrich. *Ethics*. New York: The MacMillan Company, 1965.

Bradley, James. *Flyboys: A True Story of Courage*. New York and Boston: Back Bay Books, 2003.

Brandt, Edward A. *My Life as I Care to Remember It*. Unpublished manuscript, 2002.

Carroll, Andrew. *Grace under Fire: Letters of Faith in Times of War*. New York: Doubleday, 2007.

Churchill, Winston S. *The Hinge of Fate*. Boston: Houghton Mifflin Company, 1950.

Costello, Gerald M., ed. *Our Sunday Visitors Treasury of Catholic Stories*. Huntington, IN: Our Sunday Visitors Publishing, 1999.

Costello, John. *The Pacific War*. New York: Rawson, Wade Publishers, 1981.

Crosby, Donald F. *Battlefield Chaplains: Catholic Priests in World War II*. Lawrence, KS: University Press of Kansas, 1994.

Dabbs, Denton. *World War II Shared Memories*. Paducah, KY: Turner Publishing Company, 1999.

Davis, Burke. *Marine! The Life of Lt. Gen. Lewis B. (Chesty) Puller*. Boston: Little, Brown and Company, 1962.

Elson, Aaron. *9 Lives: An Oral History*. Langhorne, PA: Chi Chi Press, 1999.

Felber, Abraham, with Franklin S. Felber and William H. Bartsch. *The Old Breed of Marine: A World War II Diary*. Jefferson, NC: McFarland Company, 2002.

Ferguson, Howard E. *The Edge*. Cleveland, OH: Getting the Edge Company, 1990.

Fuchida, Mitsuo, and Masatake, Okumiya. *Midway: The Battle that Doomed Japan*. New York: Ballantine Books, 1955.

Gehring, Rev. Frederic P. with Martin Abramson. *Child of Miracles: The Story of Patsy Li*. Philadelphia: Jefferies and Manz, Inc., 1962.

Godefroy, Hugh Constant. *Lucky Thirteen*. Stittsville, Ontario, Canada: Canada's Wings, Inc., 1983.

Greene, Bob. *Once Upon a Town: The Miracle of the North Platte Canteen*. New York: Perennial, An imprint of HarperCollins Publishers, 2002.

Harris, John. *Dunkirk: 'The Storms of War.'* London: David & Charles, 1980.

Hersey, John. *Hiroshima*. New York: Random House, Vintage Books, 1946, 1989.

Hornfischer, James D. *The Last Stand of the Tin Can Sailors*. New York: Bantam Books, 2004.

Hoyt, Edwin P. *The GI's War: The Story of American Soldiers in Europe in World War II*. New York: McGraw-Hill Book Company, 1988.

Hughes, R. Kent. *1001 Great Stories and Quotes*. Carol Stream, IL: Tyndale House Publishers, 1998.

Jenkins, Roy. *Churchill: A Biography*. New York: Plume Books, 2002.

Langer, Howard J., ed. *World War II*. Westport, CT: Greenwood Publishing Inc., 1999.

Lewis, C. S. *The Screwtape Letters*. New York: Simon & Schuster, 1996.

Lewis, Jon E., ed. *The Mammoth Book of Eyewitness World War II*. New York: Running Press, 2002.

Lewis, Jon E. ed. *D-Day: As They Saw It*. New York: Running Press, 2004.

Litoff, Judy Barrett, and David C., Smith, ed. *Since You Went Away: World War II Letters from American Women on the Home Front*. New York, Oxford: Oxford University Press, 1991.

Lord, Walter. *The Miracle of Dunkirk*. Hertfordshire: Wordsworth Editions, 1998.

Mao Tse-Tung. *Quotations from Chairman Mao*. Peking: Foreign Language Press, 1966.

Mason, John T. Jr., ed. *The Pacific War Remembered: An Oral History Collection*. Annapolis, MD: Naval Institute Press, 1986.

Miller, Donald L., revised by Henry Steele Commanger. *The Story of World War II,* New York: Simon & Schuster, 1945, 2001.

Miller, Francis Trevelyan. *History of World War II*. Philadelphia: The John C. Winston Company, 1945.

Mohri, Tsuneyuki. *Rainbow over Hell: The Death-row Deliverance of a World War II Assassin*. Nampa, OH: Pacific Press Publishing Association, 2006.

Monsarrat, Nicholas. *The Cruel Sea*. New York: Alfred A. Knopf, 1951.

Morison, Samuel Eliot. *The Two-Ocean War: The Definitive Short History of the United States Navy in World War II*. New York: Ballantine Books, 1963.

North, Oliver. *War Stories III: The Heroes Who Defeated Hitler*. Washington, DC: Regnery Publishing, Inc. 2005.

O'Neill, Brian D. *Half a Wing, Three Engines and a Prayer: B-17s over Germany*. Blue Ridge Summit, PA: Aero, A Division of Tab Books, Inc., 1989.

O'Neill, William L. *The Oxford Essential Guide to World War II.* New York: Oxford University Press/ Berkley Books, 2002.

Potter, E. B., and Chester W. Nimitz, *Seapower: A Naval History.* Englewood Cliffs, NJ: Prentice-Hall, 1960.

Prange, Gordon W. *God's Samurai: Lead Pilot at Pearl Harbor.* Washington: Brassey's Inc., 1990.

Rickenbacker, Edward V. *Rickenbacker: An Autobiography.* Englewood Cliffs, NJ: Prentice-Hall, 1967.

Rose, Darlene Deibler. *Evidence Not Seen: A Woman's Miraculous Faith in the Jungles of World War II.* New York: Harper Collins Publishers, 1988.

Schultz, Duane. *The Last Battle Station: The Saga of the USS* Houston. New York: St. Martin's Press, 1985.

Skelly, Patrick G. *The Military Chaplaincy of the U. S. Army, Focusing on World War II Chaplains in Combat.* Masters Thesis, Norwich University, 2007.

Snaddon, Daniel C. *Through the Valley of the Shadow: A War Prisoner's Struggle for Survival.* Homosassa Spring, FL: Christian Missions Press, 1990.

Soldiers' and Sailors' Prayer Book. Compiled by Gerald Mygatt and Henry Darlington, New York: Alfred A. Knopf, Inc., 1944.

Spector, Ronald H. *The Eagle against the Sun: The American War with Japan.* New York: The Free Press, 1985.

Spellman, Francis J. *The Risen Soldier.* New York: The MacMillan Company, 1944.

Sperry, Willard L., ed. *Prayers for Private Devotions in War-Time.* New York and London: Harper & Brothers Publishers, 1943.

Stagg, J. M. *Forecast for Overlord: June 6, 1944.* New York: W. W. Norton & Co., 1971.

The Armed Forces Officer, Washington, DC: Department of Defense, 1950.

Tobin, James. *Ernie Pyle's War.* New York: Free Press, 1997.

Warren, Rick. *The Purpose Driven Life.* Grand Rapids, MI: Zondervan, 2002.

White, David F. *Bitter Ocean: Battle of the Atlantic.* New York: Simon & Schuster, 2007.

Winters, Harold A. *Battling the Elements: Weather and Terrain in the Conduct of War.* Baltimore and London: The Johns Hopkins University Press, 1998.

Zamperini, Louis, with David Rensin. *Devil at My Heels: A World War II Hero's Saga of Torment, Survival, and Forgiveness.* New York: HarperCollins Publishers, 2003.

Notes

1. *The Armed Forces Officer,* p. 6.

2. Lord, *The Miracle of Dunkirk,* 25.

3. Ibid., 272.

4. Mary Gardiner Brainard, American poet, 1860.

5. C. Horace Maycock, "The Darkest Hour," WW2 People's War, www.bbc.co.uk.

6. Matthew 6:34

7. King George VI Christmas Day broadcast, www.royal.gov.uk. The poem was written by Minnie Louise Haskins in 1908 and was a favorite of Queen Elizabeth.

8. Jenkins, *Churchill,* 592.

9. The Churchill Centre, www.winstonchurchill.org.

10. Ibid.

11. Lord, *The Miracle of Dunkirk,* 145.

12. Ibid., 167.

13. Ibid., 111.

14. Ibid., 72.

15. Ibid., 112.

16. Ibid., 272.

17. Winters, *Battling the Elements,* 23.

18. Suze Bond, "Leaving Dunkirk: My Father's Diary Account," www.bbc.co.uk

19. Bill Towey, "The Luck of the Draw," www.bbc.co.uk.

20. Ibid.

21. Ibid.

22. Lord, *The Miracle of Dunkirk,* 54.

23. T. J. Spiers, "Shot Down Over Dunkirk 28 May 1940," www.bbc.co.uk.

24. Paul Davey, "Falling Back to Dunkirk," www.bbc.co.uk.

25. The Churchill Centre, www.winstonchurchill.org.

26. Harris, *Dunkirk,* 151.

27. Ibid.

28. From a sermon by Rev. Ken Streitenberger, Epworth UMC., www.epworth.com

29. "The War of a Green Howard, Bill Cheall's Story," www.greenhowards.org.uk.

30. John Beard, quoted in the "The Battle of Britain, 1940," *Eyewitness to History*, www.eyewitnesstohistory.com.

31. Ibid.

32. Godefroy, *Lucky Thirteen*, 61.

33. Ibid., 132.

34. Kathleen Rainer, "Downed Pilots in Sussex," www.bbc.co.uk.

35. www.battleofbritain1940.net.

36. John Gillespie Magee, Jr., "High Flight." www.skygod.com.

37. Ronald Reagan, "Address to the Nation on the Challenger Disaster," January 28, 1986, www.reaganlibrry.com.

38. Sheila Delaney, "A Miraculous Escape," *Time Witnesses*. www.timewitnesses.org.

39. Dennis Robinson, "Shot Down in the Battle of Britain," www.bbc.co.uk.

40. Ibid.

41. Norman English, "A Child in the Battle of Britain," www.bbc.co.uk.

42. Sermon paraphrased by J. Brock in an article at www.sartma.com.

43. Ellen Batten, as told to Elizabeth Perez, "The Faith of a Child-Light in Darkness," WW2 People's War, www.bbc.co.uk.

44. The Churchill Centre, www.winstonchurchill.org

45. www.archives.gov.

46. www.fdrlibrary.marist.edu

47. *Time* magazine, Dec. 15, 1941, "What the People Said," www.time.com.

48. National Park Service Memorial to USS *Arizona*. www.nps.gov/usar.

49. Ibid.

50. *Starting Point Bible*, article on "Courage," 1567.

51. Article by Ken James at christiananswers.net

52. Roger Hare, "An Angel Sent By History," *Navy Anecdotes*, www.geocities.com/oralbio/harestory1.html.

53. From Henry Lauchenmayer's diary, quoted in *a New York Times* article of 6 December 1998, by Irvin Molotsky.

54. Article by Carl Zebrowski, *America in WWII Magazine*, December 2006. www.americainwwii.com

55. National Park Service Memorial, USS *Arizona,* www.nps.gov/usar.

56. Ibid.

57. www.eyewitnesstohistory.com

58. Oral history excerpt, www.history.navy.mil

59. William G. Farrow, 1st Lieutenant, U.S. Army Air Corps, www.arlingtoncemetery.net.

60. Ibid.

61. Ibid.

62. Jacob DeShazer, "I Was a Prisoner of Japan," www.georgiasouthern.edu.

63. Ibid.

64. Ibid.

65. Prange, *God's Samurai*, 187, 190.

66. Ibid., 200–204.

67. Ibid.

68. Fuchida, "From Pearl Harbor to Calvary," www.biblebelievers.com.

69. Mike McLaughlin, "The Miracle Before Midway," www.amvetsww2.org.

70. Oral History, Battle of Midway. Recollections of Commander John Ford, USNR. www.history.navy.mil.

71. www.history.navy.mil.

72. Ibid.

73. Alfred, Lord Tennyson. Written in 1854 memorializing the Battle of Balaclava during the Crimean War.

74. www.history.navy.mil

75. Ibid.

76. Oral History, Battle of Midway. www.history.navt.mil. Lt. Pollard later saw this man in the Naval Hospital, Pearl Harbor, on his way to recovery.

77. Actually the destroyer *Arashi*, detached from the carrier force earlier to prosecute a submarine contact.

78. Account of Lt. Cdr. Wade McClusky, Battle of Midway, www.cv6.org.

79. Ibid.

80. Fuchida and Okumiya, *Midway*, 7.

81. Morison, *The Two-Ocean War*, 24–25.

82. Potter and Nimitz, *Seapower*, 541. Quoting Churchill from *The Second World War*.

83. Morison, *The Two-Ocean War*, 204.

84. Lewis, *The Mammoth Book of Eyewitness World War II*, 129.

85. Frank Curry Diary, Veterans Affairs Canada, *Canada Remembers*, www.vac-acc.gc.ca.

86. *Eternal Father* is a hymn found in Protestant hymnals, written by Rev. William Whiting in 1861. In America, it is often called the *Navy Hymn,* and was played at the funerals of President Franklin Roosevelt and John F. Kennedy.

87. Frank Curry Diary, Veterans Affairs Canada, *Canada Remembers*, www.vac-acc.gc.ca.

88. Litoff and Smith, *Since You Went Away,* 17.

89. "Naval Armed Guard Service in WWII," www.history.navy.mil.

90. Report of Engagement, U.S. Atlantic Fleet, Patrol Wing 8, Squadron 82, 30 January 1942. (Postwar records failed to confirm this sinking. However, Mason did destroy U-503 on 15 March, for which he was promoted and awarded a second Distinguished Flying Cross.)

91. "Famous Navy Quotes," www.history.navy.mil

92. "Halcyon Class Minesweepers and Survey Ships of WW II." www.halcyon-class.co.uk.

93. Alexander Rothney, "To Murmansk and Back on the SS *Atlantic*," WW2 People's War, www.bbc.co.uk.

94. Bruce Felknor, "The Sinking of the Esso Tanker T. C. McCobb," www.usmm.org.

95. Lewis, *The Mammoth Book of Eyewitness World War II*, 118–20.

96. White, *Bitter Ocean*, and Glenn Tunney, "Four Chaplains' Sacrifice Should Inspire All Generations," http://freepages.history.rootsweb.com.

97. Carroll, *Grace under Fire*, 33–35.

98. "Attack on an Artic Convoy, 1942," EyeWitness to History, www.eyewitnesstohistory.com (2001)

99. "Whistles over the Water," by George Hirsch, in memory of his father, Paul Hirsch, www.armed-guard.com.

100. "Jottings," *Cougar Scream*, Vol. 1, No. 30, Jan. 1, 1942, a newsletter published weekly aboard the USS *Washington* "for the good of the ship and the service."

101. "Survival, The Arctic," by Ronald Healiss, quoted by Lewis, *The Mammoth Book of Eyewitness World War II*, 114. Healiss was one of thirty-nine who survived this tragedy (www.warship.org).

102. "One More Round," *Cougar Scream*, Vol. 2, No. 8, 4 July 1942, a newsletter published weekly aboard the USS *Washington* "for the good of the ship and the service."

103. "Attack on an Arctic Convoy, 1942," Eyewitness to History, http://www.eyewitnesstohistory.com

104. Marion Hunt, "Marion's Story, I Am Evacuated to America,"http://www.timewitnesses.org.

105. Written by John Ellerton. Details of the funeral from an article by Douglas Cornell in Lewis, *The Mammoth Book of Eyewitness World War II*, 452–53.

106. Nineteenth century hymn by Sarah Adams, Edward Bickersteth, and Lowell Mason.

107. "Dad's Advice," *Cougar Scream*, Vol. 1, No. 10, 2 August 1942, a newsletter published weekly aboard the USS *Washington* "for the good of the ship and the service."

108. A. H. Archer, "The Death of a Minesweeper," WW2 People's War, www.bbc.co.uk.

109. Sam Hakam, "Sinking of the SS *Lehigh*," American Merchant Marine at War, www.usmm.org.

110. Westminster Shorter Catechism, www.reformed.org.

111. *Cougar Scream*, Vol. 2, No. 7, 28 June 1942, a newsletter published weekly aboard the USS *Washington* 'for the good of the ship and the service.'

112. "Torpedoed in the Arctic," *The Mast Magazine*, February 1945, American Merchant Marine in World War 2, www.usmm.org.

113. Ibid.

114. Frank Curry Diary, Veterans Affairs Canada, *Canada Remembers*, www.vac-acc.gc.ca.

115. George X. Hurley, "Saga of the Murmansk Run," www.armed-guard.com. Used by permission.

116. Ibid. Used by permission.

117. "The Best Solvent," *Cougar Scream*, Vol. 2, No. 7, 28 June 1942, a newsletter published weekly aboard the USS *Washington* "for the good of the ship and the service."

118. Monsarrat, *The Cruel Sea*, 101.

119. Lewis, *The Mammoth Book of Eyewitness World War II*, 153–154. Quoting Alan Moorehead.

120. Ibid., 159.

121. Churchill, *Hinge of Fate*, 70.

122. Ibid., 69.

123. Churchill, *Hinge of Fate*, 404–5.

124. Lewis, *The Mammoth Book of Eyewitness World War II*, 174.

125. www.originofnations.org.

126. Lewis, *The Mammoth Book of Eyewitness World War II*, 193.

127. *Soldiers' and Sailors' Prayer Book*, "The President's Prayer," 7.

128. Quote from *An Army at Dawn* by Rick Atkinson, 59. Copyright © 2002 by Rick Atkinson. Reprinted by permission of Henry Holt and Company, LLC.

129. Ibid., 136.

130. Ibid., 138.

131. Ibid., 119. Reprinted by permission of Henry Holt and Company, LLC.

132. Ronald Reagan quote, March 30, 1981, *The American Experience*, www.pbs.org.

133. Atkinson, *An Army at Dawn*, 101–2.

134. Philip Massinger, *A Very Woman*, Act V, Sc. 4.

135. Quote from *An Army at Dawn* by Rick Atkinson, 159. Copyright © 2002 by Rick Atkinson. Reprinted by permission of Henry Holt and Company, LLC.

136. Peter Andrews, "A Place to Be Lousy In," *American Heritage Magazine*, www.americanheritage.com.

137. Atkinson, *An Army at Dawn*, 262.

138. Ibid., 335.

139. Sperry, *Prayers for Private Devotions in War-Time*, 25.

140. Skelly, *The Military Chaplaincy of the U.S. Army*, 6. Used by permission.

141. North, *War Stories III*, 88.

142. Atkinson, *An Army at Dawn*, 293.

143. Churchill, *The Hinge of Fate,* 688. June 30, 1943, remarks to the Guildhall.

144. "The War of a Green Howard, 1939–1945. Bill Cheall's Story," The Green Howards Regimental History, www.greenhowards.org.uk.

145. Hoyt, *The GI's War,* 182.

146. Atkinson, *An Army at Dawn,* 396–97.

147. *Time Magazine,* "A Matter of Days," August 9, 1943, www.time.com.

148. Atkinson, *An Army at Dawn,* 259.

149. Kenneth T. Downs, "Nothing Stopped the Timberwolves," *The Saturday Evening Post,* August 17, 1946.

150. Ibid.

151. *Soldiers' and Sailors' Prayer Book,* p. 91.2b

152. Lewis, *The Mammoth Book of Eyewitness World War II,* 162–67.

153. *O God, Our Help in Ages Past,* by Isaac Watts, 1719. Sung at the funeral of Winston Churchill, 1965.

154. Lewis, *The Mammoth Book of Eyewitness World War II,* 166.

155. Atkinson, *An Army at Dawn,* 411.

156. Lewis, *The Mammoth Book of Eyewitness World War II,* 152.

157. Chaplain A. M. Sherman, Jr., *Religion and Ethics Newsletter,* May 28, 2004, www.pbs.org. Excerpt from National Cathedral's exhibition, "Faith and Courage: U. S. Chaplains Service in World War II."

158. Hoyt, *The GI's War,* 202.

159. "Ernie Pyle," Indiana Historical Society, www.indianahistory.org.

160. Ibid.

161. Lewis, *The Mammoth Book of Eyewitness World War II,* 207–8.

162. Costello, *The Pacific War,* 382.

163. Rose, *Evidence Not Seen,* 41. Reprinted by permission of Harper-Collins Publishers.

164. Ibid.

165. Glenn Frazier, "Ex-POW Biography," American Ex-Prisoners of War, www.axpow.org.

166. Schultz, *The Last Battle Station,* 71.

167. www.rentz.navy.mil

168. Ibid.

169. poem by Lloyd Willey, www.rentz.navy.mil.

170. Adam Bernstein, *Washington Post,* June 2, 2004, www.washingtonpost.com.

171. Lewis, *The Mammoth Book of Eyewitness World War II,* 296–298.

172. Felber, *The Old Breed of Marine,* 3–4.

173. Mason, *The Pacific War Remembered,* 131.

174. Ibid., 138–39.

175. Ibid., 136.

176. Davis, *Marine!,* 121.

177. Ibid., 201.

178. Ibid.

179. www.arlingtoncemetery.net, search "Basilone."

180. *Soldiers' and Sailors' Prayer Book,* 85.

181. Medal of Honor citation, Douglas Albert Munro, www.uscg.mil/history.

182. James Quann, "A World War Hero from Cle Elum," *Columbia Magazine,* Fall 2000, Vol. 14, No. 3.

183. Gehring, *Child of Miracles,* 11–12.

184. Ibid.

185. Ibid., 10–11.

186. www.eyewitnesstohistory.com

187. Gehring, *Child of Miracles,* 3–5.

188. Miller, *The Story of World War II,* 156.

189. Ibid., 157, quoting Gen. Robert Eichelberger.

190. Ibid., 158.

191. Rear Adm. Robert G. Mills, USN (Ret.), "The Parson's Bible," U.S. Naval Academy Alumni Association, www.usna.com.

192. Ibid.

193. From *1001 Great Stories and Quotes* by R. Kent Hughes, ed., p. 234–235. Quoting Cmdr. Eric J. Berryman.

194. Ibid.

195. www.medalofhonor.com.

196. *Soldiers' and Sailors' Prayer Book,* 43.

197. Gehring, *Child of Miracles,* 156–57.

198. Snaddon, *Through the Valley of the Shadow.*

199. Ibid.

200. Ibid.

201. Ibid.

202. Mason, *The Pacific War Remembered,* 196.

203. Zamperini, *Devil at My Heels,* 84–85. Reprinted by permission of HarperCollins Publishers.

204. Ibid., 98.

205. Ibid., 123.

206. Ibid., 242–43.

207. Gehring, *Child of Miracles,* 15–32.

208. Ibid.

209. Ibid.

210. Ibid., 261.

211. Ibid.

212. Ibid., 298–99.

213. Napoleon, www.bartleby.com.

214. Mao Tse-Tung, *Quotations from Chairman Mao,* 139.

215. "Mosta Dome," Location Malta, www.locationmalta.com.

216. North, *War Stories III,* 102.

217. Ibid., 105.

218. Quotes from article by Stephen P. Weaver, NAS Sigonella Public Affairs, "Heroism During World War II Remembered at Ponte Dirillo," July 14, 2004, www.navy.mil.

219. North, *War Stories III,* 123.

220. Al Karr, "Exhibit Honors World War II's Chaplains," Episcopal Diocese of Washington, www.edow.org.

221. Ibid.

222. Ibid.

223. Carroll, *Grace under Fire,* 45–46.

224. Stan Scislowsiki, "Church Service at the Front," WW2 Peoples War, www.bbc.co.uk.

225. *Abide with Me,* Henry Lyte and William Monk, 1847. Five of eight stanzas. Written as Lyte was dying of tuberculosis.

226. Central Illinois World War II Stories, "Frank's Military Career WWII," by Frank C. Palilla, www.atlas.illinois.edu.

227. *A Prayer Book for Soldiers and Sailors.*

228. Robert G. Saxton, "Knocking a Bomb Out in the Italian Skies," Central Illinois World War II Stories, atlas.illinois.edu.

229. George Graves, "Somewhere in Italy," http://thedropzone.org.

230. Kathy Burd, "I've Been Blessed- A Legacy," Central Illinois World War II Stories, atlas.illinois.edu..

231. Ibid.

232. Lewis, *The Mammoth Book of Eyewitness World War II,* 438, quoting an article by Ernie Pyle.

233. Ibid.

234. Richard J. Ternyey, "My Mule and Me," Central Illinois World War II Stories, atlas.illinois.edu..

235. Ibid.

236. Carroll, *Grace Under Fire,* 43.

237. Ibid., 44–45.

238. Central Illinois World War II Stories, "From Coal Hole to Fox Hole to Easy Street," by Kathleen Filer, excerpted from James Coyle's atlas.illinois.edu..

239. Rudyard Kipling, "If . . ."

240. North, *War Stories III,* 124.

241. Robert Appel, "A Soldier's Last Days of Combat on the Anzio Beachhead," Central Illinois World War II Stories, atlas.illinois.edu.

242. Ibid.

243. "War Letters," American Experience, www.pbs.org. and "World War II Letters Home," *The Free Library*, www.thefreelibrary.com.

244. North, *War Stories III*, 128.

245. Steve Fry, "WWII Mystery Solved; Brother Finally Home," *Topeka Capital-Journal*, June 21, 2007.

246. Sperry, *Prayers for Private Devotions in War-Time*, 3.

247. Vaughn Gordy, "Shaken but Grateful," Central Illinois World War II Stories, atlas.illinois.edu.

248. Ibid.

249. Ibid.

250. C. Horace Maycock, "The Darkest Hour," WW2 People's War, www.bbc.co.uk.

251. Central Illinois World War II Stories, "The War for Me," by Albert Thomas, atlas.illinois.edu.

252. Skelly, *The Military Chaplaincy of the U.S. Army*, 12, quoting Rev. Parker Thompson, *Wallace Hale Eulogy*, March 11, 2007. Used by permission.

253. Wallace Hale, from the foreword to *Battle Rattle*, www.milhist.net.

254. Copyright 1939 by Irving Berlin, www.scoutsongs.com. Berlin dedicated royalties to the God Bless America fund for the Boy and Girl Scouts of the USA.

255. Ibid.

256. Charles M. Province, *The Unknown Patton*, CMP Productions (Electronic Version, 1998, "The Slapping Incident," www.pattonhq.com.

257. Miller, *The Story of World War II*, 216.

258. *Soldiers' and Sailors' Prayer Book*, p. 23.

259. 1 Chronicles 19:13 (KJV)

260. Ibid.

261. Inscription over the entrance to Summerall Chapel, The Citadel.

262. Astor, *The Mighty Eighth*, 20–21.

263. "Question Mark," *Journal of the Air Force Association*, March 2003, www.afa.org.

264. Astor, *The Mighty Eighth*, 415.

265. "Misery and Teamwork Over Misburg, 26 November 1944," by Frank Federici and Lt. Col. Vincent Mazza, ret., www.445thbomb-group.com.

266. O'Neill, *Half a Wing, Three Engines and a Prayer*, 57.

267. Ibid., 69.

268. Astor, *The Mighty Eighth*, 322–323.

269. O'Neill, *Half a Wing, Three Engines and a Prayer*, 70. Statement of Bud Klint.

270. Ibid., 101.

271. E. T. McMullen, "Aspects of Air Power in WWII, Including Bert Ramsey, E. L. McMullen, and Others," memorial and dedication service for Lt. Bert H.

Ramsey Jr., Nov. 25, 1945, author of poem unknown, http://personal.georgiasouthern.edu.

272. Ibid.

273. Astor, *The Mighty Eighth,* 361–62.

274. O'Neill, *Half a Wing, Three Engines and a Prayer,* 59–60.

275. Ibid.

276. North, *War Stories III,* 147.

277. Ibid., 148–49.

278. *Starting Point Study Bible,* "Commit," 1564.

279. Astor, *The Mighty Eighth,* 73.

280. Ibid., 103.

281. *Soldiers' and Sailors' Prayer Book,* 95.

282. Astor, *The Mighty Eighth,* 398.

283. John Frisbee, "Into the Mouth of Hell," *Journal of the Air Force Association,* September 1988, www.afa.org.

284. North, *War Stories III,* 157.

285. S. Clayton Moore quoting McGovern in "The Outspoken American," *Airport Journals,* May 2006.

286. Ibid.

287. George McGovern, "The Reason Why," *The Nation,* April 21, 2003, www.thenation.com.

288. Edward A. Brandt, *My Life as I Care to Remember It.* Used by permission.

289. Ruben G. Bork, *My Last Combat Mission,* Quentin C. Anderson, http://pages.prodigy.net/rebeljack/Bork.html.

290. *Art Kramer's WWII Stories,* "The Pilot Who Wouldn't Fly," www.coastcomp.com/artkramer.

291. "Hitting the Deck at Karlruhe, Germany," by Frank W. Federici, www.445thbomb-group.com.

292. Ibid.

293. Lewis, *The Mammoth Book of Eyewitness World War II,* 325–26.

294. Astor, *The Mighty Eighth,* 93–94.

295. *Australians in the Pacific War,* Pilot Officer Peter Gibbes, 6.

296. Ibid.

297. The "chaplain" of this story is Francis Spellman, the Archbishop of New York. He was elevated to the College of Cardinals in 1946. This story and the quotes are from his 1944 classic, *The Risen Soldier.*

298. Ibid.

299. Ibid.

300. Ibid.

301. Astor, *The Mighty Eighth,* 247.

302. Ibid., 502–3.

303. Ibid., 321–22.

304. Ibid.

305. Miller, *The Story of World War II*, 261.

306. Ibid.

307. www.nps.gov.

308. *"Liberty Ships: An Overview,"* www.fiu.edu.

309. From sermons by Bill Hayes (http://revbill.wordpess.com) and Norman Lao (http://jlrcm2008.wordpress.com).

310. Central Illinois World War II Stories, "On the Homefront," by Capri East, atlas.illinois.edu.

311. Lewis, *The Screwtape Letters*, 32.

312. North, *War Stories III*, 194–97.

313. Ibid.

314. Greene, *Once Upon a Town*, 33.

315. Tobin, *Ernie Pyle's War*, 100.

316. Ibid.

317. Carroll, *Grace under Fire*, 58–59.

318. Litoff and Smith, *Since You Went Away*, 157.

319. Ferguson, *The Edge*.

320. Ibid.

321. Carroll, *Grace under Fire*, 67–69.

322. Ibid., 70.

323. Chaplain (Capt.) William W. Edel, U.S. Navy, *Soldiers' and Sailors' Prayer Book*.

324. Litoff and Smith, *Since You Went Away*, 251–52.

325. Ibid., 115.

326. *A Prayer Book for Soldiers and Sailors*.

327. Carroll, *Grace under Fire*, 55–56.

328. Litoff and Smith, *Since You Went Away*, 84–85.

329. Lewis, *The Mammoth Book of Eyewitness World War II*, 332.

330. Lewis, *The Screwtape Letters*, 76–77.

331. Dabbs, *World War II Shared Memories*, 77–78.

332. Carroll, *Grace under Fire*, 57.

333. Robert Browning, *Prospice*, written in 1861, months after his wife's death.

334. Spellman, *The Risen Soldier*, 38–39.

335. Litoff and Smith, *Since You Went Away*, 97–98.

336. Franklin Roosevelt's D-Day Prayer, www.fdrlibrary.marist.edu.

337. Ibid.

338. Jerry Oncken, "Orange Juice Kiss," Central Illinois World War II Stories, atlas.illinois.edu.

339. Litoff and Smith, *Since You Went Away*, 237.

340. Ibid., 56.

341. Ibid.

342. Ibid., 138.

343. Popular song of WW I, written by Lena Ford and Ivor Novello.

344. Lifoff and Smith, *Since You Went Away,* 233–34. Letter from the MacArthur Memorial Archives and Library, Norfolk, VA. Record Group 3, SW Pac Area, CIC Correspondence. Reprinted by Litoff with permission.

345. H. Smith Shumway, Men of D-Day, www.6juin1944.com

346. Ibid.

347. Crosby, *Battlefield Chaplains,* 71, quoting Robert Sherrod, www.kansaspress.ku.edu. Used by permission of the publisher.

348. Skelly, *The Military Chaplaincy of the U.S. Army,* 19. Used by permission.

349. From "What Are We Fighting For?" by Samuel Shoemaker, quoted by Steven Gertz, "Christianity History Corner: Just War, Just Nation?" Oct. 1, 2002, www.christianitytoday.com.

350. Potter and Nimitz, *Seapower,* 772.

351. Remarks by Secretary of the Navy The Honorable Gordon R. England at the 1st Marine Division Annual Memorial, Washington, DC, 13 August 2004, www.navy.mil.

352. Ibid.

353. Rose, *Evidence Not Seen,* 57. Reprinted by permission of Harper-Collins Publishers.

354. Ibid.

355. Carroll, *Grace under Fire,* 41–42.

356. Richard Bruce Watkins, Capt. USMCR (ret), "Brothers in Battle," http://brothersinbattle.net.

357. Ibid.

358. Ibid.

359. Costello, *Our Sunday Visitor,* 354.

360. Ibid.

361. www.arlingtoncemetery.com, "Chaplains Hill and Three Monuments."

362. Crosby, *Battlefield Chaplains,* 201–2. www.kansaspress.ku.edu. Used by permission of the publisher.

363. Ibid.

364. U.S. Air Force Military Biographies, http://findarticles.com.

365. Hanson R. Boney, "Chaplain POWs in the Pacific Theater," US Army Chaplain Center and School, www.usachcs.army.mil.

366. Ibid.

367. Mohri, *Rainbow over Hell,* 128.

368. Ibid., 129.

369. Ibid.

370. Ibid.

371. Ibid.

372. Medal of Honor Citation, Fred Faulkner Lester, Medical Corpsman, 1st Battalion, 22nd Marines, http://22dmarines.org.

373. Richard Bruce Watkins, Capt. USMCR (ret), "Brothers in Battle," http://brothersinbattle.net.

374. Yazmin Lazcano, "Carlos Carrillo Quintana," U.S. Latino and Latina World War II History Project, www.lib.utexas.edu/ww2latinos.

375. Marine Corps History and Museums Division, Marines in World War II Commemorative Series, "Navy Chaplains," www.nps.gov.

376. Ibid.

377. Ibid.

378. "A Hero and His Everlasting Love," by James Adcock, as told to his daughter Nancy White, Central Illinois World War II Stories, atlas.illinois.edu. edu.

379. Ibid.

380. Ibid.

381. Medal of Honor citation, Major Gregory Boyington, USMCR, www.pappyboyingtonfield.com.

382. Congressional Medal of Honor Recipient, Major Gregory "Pappy" Boyington, www.medalofhonor.com.

383. Ibid., quoting from Boyington's book, *Baa Baa Black Sheep.*

384. Crosby, *Battlefield Chaplains,* 188–89. www.kansaspress.ku.edu. Used by permission of the publisher.

385. Eunice Kim, "WWII Vet Honored for his Service, Faith," *The Statesman Journal,* March 30, 2008, www.statesmanjournal.com.

386. Ibid.

387. Words and music by James Black, 1893.

388. Hornfischer, *The Last Stand of the Tin Can Sailors,* 22, 36–37.

389. Ibid., 150.

390. Ibid., 406.

391. Ibid., 269.

392. Ibid., 425.

393. Ibid., 426–27.

394. *Faith Magazine,* quoting Lewis L. Haynes article in *Saturday Evening Post,* August 6, 1955, www.catholicmil.org, search "conway."

395. Rickenbacker, *Rickenbacker,* 316

396. Ibid., 318. The group was rescued on November 13, 1942, after twenty-four days at sea. Seven of the eight survived.

397. Ibid., 243.

398. Ibid., 7–8.

399. From an article by Charles J. Hanley, Associated Press, "WWII Pilot Repaid Village That Saved His Life," *San Francisco Chronicle,* March 9, 2008, www.sfgate.com.

400. Ibid.

401. Ernie Pyle, www.ussconklin.org.

402. Timeline, 6/5/45, www.ussconklin.org., and "The Story of Frederick Morris and Clifford Farr of the USS *Conklin* in the Typhoon of June 1945," Destroyer Escort Sailors Association, www. desausa.org.

403. Potter and Nimitz, *Seapower*, 768.

404. Miller, *The Story of World War II*, 372.

405. "World War II Famous Quotes," from *J. D. Potter, Admiral of the Pacific*, http://members.aol.com/forcountry/ww2/quo.htm.

406. Snaddon, *Through the Valley of the Shadow*.

407. Ibid.

408. Ibid.

409. Directive for Operation Overlord, Potter and Nimitz, *Seapower*, 605.

410. Lewis, *D-Day*, 38–39, quoting Alan Moorehead.

411. Ibid.

412. www.army.mil.

413. Bob Benvenuto, "I Join the Navy—The Reality & the Realization," Http://members.aol.com/famjustin/LST7.html.

414. Lewis, *D-Day*, 60–61.

415. *Abide with Me*, Henry Lyte and William Monk, 1847. Four of eight stanzas. Written as Lyte was dying of tuberculosis.

416. Elson, *9 Lives*, 68. Used by permission.

417. Leslie Palmer Cruise, Jr., Men of D-Day, www.6juin1944.com

418. Ibid.

419. Lewis, *D-Day*, 66.

420. Ward Smith, "I Saw Them Jump to Destiny," BBC, "News of the World," www.6juin1944.com.

421. Malcolm Brennen, Men of D-Day, www.6juin1944.com.

422. Ibid. Excerpts from *Trees*, by Joyce Kilmer (1886–1918).

423. Marie-T Lavieille, Men of D-Day, www.6juin1944.com.

424. William E. Smith (the son of Lt. Smith), "D-Day on Omaha from the Eyes of a Forward Observer," Men of D-Day, www.6juin1944.com.

425. Ibid.

426. Langer, *World War II*, 211.

427. Elson, *9 Lives*, 72–74. Used by permission.

428. James H. Jordan, Men of D-Day, www.6juin1944.com.

429. Ibid.

430. Harley A. Reynolds, Men of D-Day, www.6juin1944.com.

431. Ibid.

432. Maltbie Davenport Babcock (1858–1901), "Be Strong."

433. Story of John Burkhalter, www.highrock.com/JohnGBurkhalter/d-day.html.

434. A nineteenth century hymn by George Duffield and George Webb.

435. Quoting an article by Ernie Pyle in the *Stars and Stripes* newspaper, June 1944.

436. Story of John Burkhalter, www.highrock.com/JohnGBurkhalter/d-day.html.

437. Distinguished Service Cross Citation, Capt. Joseph T. Dawson, www.homeofheroes.com.

438. Lewis, *D-Day,* 282.

439. Ibid., 284.

440. George A. Davison, Men of D-Day, www.6juin1944.com.

441. Ibid.

442. Albert J. Berard, Men of D-Day, www.6juin1944.com.

443. Carroll, *Grace under Fire,* 50–51.

444. "The Little Pocket Bible," by Dianne Smart, Central Illinois World War II Stories, atlas.illinois.edu. The Bible is now on display in the D-Day Museum on Utah Beach in France.

445. Carroll, *Grace under Fire,* 46–47.

446. Quentin C. Anderson, *A Fighter Pilot's Story, The Face of War,* http://prodigy.com/fighterpilot.

447. Ibid.

448. Myron Eberle, "World War II Stories: The Hand of God?" LeadershipU, www.leaderu.com.

449. Ibid.

450. Litoff and Smith, *Since You Went Away,* 45–46.

451. Ibid.

452. *Onward, Christian Soldiers,* 1865, selected verses, words by Sabine Baring-Gould, music by Arthur S. Sullivan.

453. Stagg, *Forecast for Overlord,* 15.

454. Potter and Nimitz, *Seapower,* 613.

455. www.archives.gov/education/lessons/d-day-message.

456. Ronald Reagan, "Remarks at the Ranger Monument," www.reaganfoundation.org.

457. German Surrender Documents, www.seattleu.edu.

458. Bonhoeffer, *Ethics,* 355–57.

459. Ibid., 15.

460. Ibid.

461. Ibid.

462. Ibid.

463. Ibid., 112, quoted by James Dobson, "A Day of Prayer that Changed History," May 2000, *www.focusonthefamily*.com.

464. Ibid.

465. Carroll, *Grace under Fire,* 62–63.

466. Lewis, *The Mammoth Book of Eyewitness World War II,* 448.

467. "The Story of the Prayer," by Msgr. James H. O'Neill, www.pattonhq.com

468. Ibid.

469. Ibid.

470. Patrick O'Donnell, "Night Raid," Central Illinois World War II Stories, atlas.illinois.edu.

471. Elson, *9 Lives,* 24–26. Used by permission.

472. Ibid., 29.

473. Letter written by Francis E. R. Ambler in May 1943, Peoples War, www.bbc.co.uk.

474. Abraham Lincoln's Second Inaugural Address, Mar. 4, 1865.

475. Lewis, *The Mammoth Book of Eyewitness World War II,* 420–24. Unfortunately, that relief would never come. By the 26th of September 1944, only 2,400 of 9,000 British paratroopers would make it back to friendly lines.

476. Prayer of St. Francis of Sales, Elson, *9 Lives,* 59. Used by permission. Corrected version from www.catholic.org.

477. "The Story of the Prayer," by Msgr. James H. O'Neill, www.pattonhq. com. Article includes these notes: "From the Review of the News 6 October 1971. This article appeared as a government document in 1950. At the time it appeared in the Review of the News, Msgr. O'Neill was a retired Brigadier General living in Pueblo, Colorado."

478. Crosby, *Battlefield Chaplains,* 149, www.kansaspress.ku.edu. Used by permission of the publisher.

479. Ibid.

480. Charles Ziers, "A Purple Heart," Central Illinois World War II Stories, atlas.illinois.edu. and "Memorial Day-Letter from WWII Soldier," www.blackfive.net.

481. Ibid.

482. Ibid.

483. Spellman, *The Risen Soldier,* 6–7, 10.

484. Skelly, *The Military Chaplaincy of the U.S. Army,* 16, quoting from Eichhorn, *The GI's Rabbi.*

485. Avigdor, *From Prison to Pulpit,* 230. Used by permission.

486. Patricia Moorhead, "An Irish Chaplain's Memories of D-Day Landings," WW2 People's War, www.bbc.co.uk.

487. Ibid.

488. Barrie Stephenson, "The Simple Faith of a Prisoner of War," WW2 People's War, www.bbc.co.uk.

489. Ibid.

490. North, *War Stories III,* 265.

491. Ibid.

492. Lewis, *The Mammoth Book of Eyewitness World War II*, 441, quoting Martha Gellhorn.

493. Ibid., 445.

494. Lewis, *D-Day*, 279.

495. Lawrence Donkin, "Two Wars," WW2 People's War, www.bbc.co.uk.

496. Ibid.

497. Carroll, *Grace under Fire*, 84–85.

498. Warren, *The Purpose Driven Life*, 194.

499. Spellman, *The Risen Soldier*, 33–35.

500. Greg Bradsher, "Nazi Gold: The Merkers Mine Treasure," The U.S. National Archives, www.archives.gov.

501. George VI, radio broadcast, VE Day, 8 May 1945, The British Monarchy, www.colinburns.com.

502. Abraham Lincoln, in response to a question during the Civil War, www.collegeboard.com and www.leaderu.com.

503. Potter and Nimitz, *Seapower*, 827.

504. "Fourth Inaugural Address of Franklin D. Roosevelt," The Avalon Project, www.yale.edu.

505. "Antwerp Ahoy," by an unknown author. Found in the ship's library of the SS *John W. Brown*, www.liberty-ship.com.

506. Congressional Medal of Honor citation, Capt. Joseph T. O'Callahan, www.medalofhonor.com.

507. Capt. Joseph T. O'Callahan, www.medalofhonor.com/worldwariio.htm.

508. "USS *Franklin*: Struck by a Japanese Dive Bomber During World War II," www.history.net.

509. Miller, *The Story of World War II*, 542.

510. Ibid., 541.

511. Ibid.

512. Ibid., 554.

513. Ibid., 552.

514. Ibid., 553.

515. O'Neill, *The Oxford Essential Guide to World War II*, 206.

516. Lewis, *The Mammoth Book of Eyewitness World War II*, 551–52.

517. *Soldiers' and Sailors' Prayer Book*, 75.

518. Carroll, *Grace under Fire*, 67–68.

519. *New York War Stories*, "Approaching the End of World War II Veterans," submitted by John Bezpa, WNET New York, www.thirteen.org.

520. Ibid.

521. Crosby, *Battlefield Chaplains*, 201, www.kansaspress.ku.edu. Used by permission of the publisher.

522. Ibid., 226.

523. *Religion and Ethics Newsletter*, May 28, 2004, www.pbs.org. Excerpt

from National Cathedral's exhibition, "Faith and Courage: U.S. Chaplains Service in World War II."

524. *Soldiers' and Sailors' Prayer Book,* 12.

525. Rose, *Evidence Not Seen,* 198. Reprinted by permission of Harper-Collins Publishers.

526. Ibid.

527. "Biography of Harry S. Truman," www.whitehouse.gov.

528. "Harry Truman Speaks," compiled by Raymond Geselbracht, Truman Library Archival Reference, www.trumanlibrary.org.

529. Ibid.

530. Ibid.

531. "Proclamation Defining Terms for Japanese Surrender, issued at Potsdam, July 26, 1945," National Diet Library, Government of Japan, www.ndl.go.jp/constitution.

532. Hersey, *Hiroshima,* 61.

533. Hymn 123, Lutheran Hymnal, selected verses. www.lutheran-hymnal.com.

534. Hersey, *Hiroshima,* 124–25.

535. The American Presidency Project, University of California at Santa Barbara, www.presidency.ucsb.edu.

536. Edward Andrusko, "Silent Night, Holy Night," *The Ukranian Weekly,* Dec. 22, 2002, No. 51, www.ukrweekly.com.

537. Ibid.

538. Litoff and Smith, *Since You Went Away,* 116–17.

539. Frank Curry Diary, Veterans Affairs Canada, *Canada Remembers,* www.vac-acc.gc.ca.

540. Excerpts from FDR's Christmas Address, The American Presidency Project, University of California at Santa Barbara, www.presidency.ucsb.edu.

541. Walter Kent and James Gannon, August 24, 1943.

542. Rose, *Evidence Not Seen,* 206–7. Reprinted by permission of Harper-Collins Publishers.

543. Miller, *History of World War II,* 34–35, radio address of General Douglas MacArthur, Sept. 2, 1945.

544. Ibid., preface. Official statements by Franklin D. Roosevelt selected by the White House from radio addresses and messages to Congress.

545. Ibid.

546. Ibid., 31–32.

547. Ibid., 33.

548. Dabbs, *World War II Shared Memories,* 138–39.

About the Author

L ARKIN SPIVEY is a decorated veteran of the Vietnam War and a retired Marine Corps officer. He commanded infantry and reconnaissance units in combat, and was trained in parachute, submarine, and Special Forces operations. He was with the blockade force during the Cuban Missile Crisis and served President Nixon in the White House. As a faculty member at The Citadel, he taught courses in U.S. military history, a subject of lifelong personal and professional interest. He now writes full-time and resides in Myrtle Beach, South Carolina, with his wife, Lani, and their four children. He is a lay eucharistic minister of the Episcopal Church and has been actively involved in the Cursillo Christian renewal movement and the Luis Palau Evangelistic Association. He has made numerous television and radio appearances nationwide and speaks frequently to church, veteran, and other groups with his patriotic and spiritual message.

For more information about the author, his other books, and speaking engagements, visit: www.larkinspivey.com.

Topical Index

Action: Feb. 2, Mar. 7, July 2, Nov. 3

Angels: Feb. 5, June 13, Nov. 12, 23, Oct. 26

Anger: July 8

Armor of God: June 19, Oct. 5, Oct. 14, Nov. 14

Bible: May 18, Oct. 6, 11, 22, Nov. 26

Casting Lots: Jan. 11

Chaplains: Apr. 16, Mar. 11,12, May 3, 10, 18, 21, 24, 28-30, June 6, 27, Aug. 29, 31, Sept. 7-9, 14, 17, 23,
Oct. 16, Nov. 16, 17, 20, 22, 28, 29, Dec. 4, 10, 11, 14

Children: Jan. 28, 30, Mar. 4, July 7, Aug. 23, Sept. 13, 25, Oct. 10

Christian Living/Service: Jan. 9, 13, Feb. 5, 9, 19, Mar. 7, 22, 27, Apr. 26, May 5-7, May 19, June 2, 14, July 4, 5, 13, 14, 24, Aug. 1, Sept. 6, Oct. 21, Nov. 3, 7, Dec. 28

Christmas: Mar. 27, Nov. 11, 17, Dec. 22-26

Church/ Body of Christ: Jan. 5, 23, 31, Mar. 7, 21, Apr. 28, May 6, 8, June 7, 8, 16, 21, 25, 27, 30, Oct. 3, 24, Nov. 1, 6, Dec. 22

Comforting/ Helping Others: Jan. 9, Feb. 9, Mar. 11, 14, Apr. 16, May 3, 28, June 26, Sept. 6, 7, 12, 14, 26, Nov. 13, 20, 22, Dec. 6, 7, 20

Corpsmen/Medics: Sep. 12, Dec. 7

Courage: Feb. 3, 21, 22, Mar. 2, 8, 16, 17, 26, May 12, 16, 23, June 4, 11, 21, July 11, 22, 27, Aug. 4, 17, Sept. 17, 20, 22, Oct. 11, 15, 18, Nov. 24, Dec. 4

Death: Jan. 24, Feb. 4, 12, Mar. 18, 29, Apr. 11, June 5, Nov. 5, 8, 22, 28, Nov. 11

Decisions: Mar. 10, Apr. 25, May 10, 17, July 5, Sept. 28, 29, Oct. 29

Discipline: Apr. 2, May 4, June 29, Nov. 2, 11

Duty: Feb. 21, 22, Mar. 13, 23, June 14, Sept. 20, 21

Ecumenism: May 14, Aug. 29, Dec. 11, 12

Evangelism: Feb. 13-17, Mar. 6, Apr. 16, May 22, 27, July 12, 27, Sept. 2, 9, 15, 28, Oct. 16, 28, Dec. 6, 25

Evil: Apr. 6, June 17, Dec. 5

Family: Feb. 11, 12, Mar. 9, June 9, July 28, 29, Aug. 6, 7, 9, 12, 18, 23, 25, Sept. 25, Dec. 7, 24

Fate: Jan. 22, 26, Mar. 18, 29, May 13, Oct. 29

Fear: Jan. 24, 27, Feb. 3, 25, Mar. 8, 18, June 20, July 11, 18, 27, Oct. 7, 8

Forgiveness: Feb. 13-17, Apr. 12, 15, 18, 22, June 24, July 19, 23

Friendship: Mar. 21, 24, Apr. 19, Sept. 22

God's Call: Feb. 18, May 8, June 6, June 11

God's Love: Feb. 8, Apr. 15, July 17, Sept. 13, 28

Good from Adversity: May 13, July 9, 29, Aug. 2, 9, Oct. 17, Nov. 4, 24, 27, Dec. 27

Grief/Suffering: Mar. 26, Apr. 19, Aug. 4, 8, 14, 24, 27, Oct. 1, Nov. 4, Dec. 20

Guilt: July 15, 19, Dec. 11

Hearing/Listening to God: Jan. 6, 11,

18, 20, 21, 25, Feb. 6, 7, Mar. 3, Apr. 1, 27, May 1, 15, June 15, 23, July 10, 20

Honesty: Jan. 14, Apr. 20

Hope: Jan. 10, 22, 24, 26, Feb. 12, Mar. 9, 14, 20, 29, Apr. 19, May 13, 25, June 5, 22, July 10, 16, 18, Aug. 11, 18, Sept. 3, 18, Oct. 7, 26, Nov. 5, 8, 24, 28, Dec. 13, 19, 23, 31

Humility: Apr. 8, 29, Aug. 5, 30, Sept. 16, 23, Oct. 18, Dec. 1

Humor: Feb. 10, Apr. 10, 20, Aug. 16, 25

Hymns/Songs: Jan. 5 (*Onward Christian Soldiers*), Mar. 2 (*Navy Hymn*), 20 (*Nearer My God to Thee*), Apr. 24 (*O God, Our Help in Ages Past*), June 8 (*Abide with Me*), 28 (*God Bless America*), Aug. 31 (*Pass the Ammunition*), Sept.18 (*When the Roll is Called*), Oct. 4 (*Abide with Me*), 28 (*Onward Christian Soldiers*), Dec. 19 (*O God, Our Help in Ages Past*), 22 (*Silent* Night), 26 (*White Christmas, I'll be Home for Christmas*)

Jesus Christ: Jan. 1, 4, 5, 12, 19, 21, 23, 28, Feb. 6, 17, 20, Mar. 9, 10, 15, 18, Apr 3-5, 17, 18, 22, 27, May 9, 21, 22, 24, June 27, July 1, 3, 10, 23, 25, 30, Aug. 1, 8, 12, 17, Sept. 11, 23, Nov. 7, 17, 19, 26, 29, Dec. 1, 7, 23

Leaders: Allen, Apr. 22, 23; Anderson, Apr. 13; Boyington, Sept. 16; Basilone, May 11; Bonhoeffer, Nov. 1-6; Cardinal Spellman, Nov. 19; Churchill, Jan. 3, 4, 15, 17; Eisenhower, Apr. 8, 14, 26, Oct. 2, 30; King George, Jan. 2, Nov. 30; MacArthur, Dec. 28, 30; McGovern, July 19, 20; Mitscher, Sept. 28; Montgomery, Apr. 5; Patton, Apr. 9,

12, Nov. 9, 10; Puller, May 8, 9; Reagan, Oct. 31; Rickenbacker, Sept. 24, 25, Dec. 15; Roosevelt, Feb. 1, Mar. 20, Aug. 21, 22, Dec. 2, 25, 29; Sanders, July 16; Schonland, May 20; Scott, Dec. 9; Spruance, Feb. 28; Truman, Dec. 17, 21

Leadership: Jan. 2, 3, 14, 15, 17, Feb. 20, Mar. 5, Apr. 8, 23, 26, May 9 10, July 14, Sept. 6, 19, 24, 28, Oct. 3

Lifeboat Survival: Mar. 9, 14, 22, 23, 25, 26, May 25–27, Sept. 24, Dec. 15

Loneliness: June 20

Mercy: Mar. 1, 15, Apr. 18, May 21, June 26, July 30, Nov. 13, 20, Dec. 1, 18, 30

Miracles/Providence: Jan. 7, 8, 16, 20, 29, Feb. 18, 26-28, Apr. 6, May 17, 26, June 1, 13, July 7, 21, Aug. 18, Sept. 24, 27, Oct. 22, 29, Nov. 12, 21, Dec. 21

Missionaries: May 1, Sept. 2, Dec. 16, 27

Overwhelming Odds: Jan. 15, Feb. 21, 22, Mar. 8, 16, May 16, Sept. 20, 21, Oct. 11, 13, 15

Peace: Jan. 19, Nov. 19, Dec. 2, 13, 18, 23, 28, 30, 31

Power of Faith: Jan. 22, Feb. 11, 12, Mar. 31, May 23, June 20, July 15, 16, 12, Aug. 6, 9, 11, 13, 20, 27, Sept. 8, Oct. 9, 19, Dec. 10, 16

Power of Prayer: Jan. 18, Mar. 14, 29, May 11, 14, 20, 26, June 23, July 11, Aug. 10, 14, 21, 22, Sept. 3, 4, 5, 21, 30, Oct. 2, 8, 21, 25, 27,Nov. 9, 10, 15, 16, 18, 25, Dec. 9, 15

Power of Scripture: Jan. 10, 21, Feb. 13, Feb. 14-17, Mar. 6, 12, May 2, 22, 30, July 18, Sept. 10, 11, 24, Oct. 5, 6, 22, 24, Nov.26

Prisoners of War: Feb. 13, 14, 16, Apr. 7-9, May 2, 22, 23, 27, July 6, Sept. 10, 11, Nov. 26

Proverbs/Advice for Living: Feb. 2, Mar. 21, 24, Apr. 30,June 16, 24, 29, July 2, 4, 6, 16, Aug. 3, 4, 16, Aug. 25, Sept. 22, Oct. 18, Nov. 20

Priorities: Jan. 12, 27, Feb. 4, Mar. 23, 25, May 31, July 3, 6

Quotes: Jan. 3 (blood, sweat, tears), 15 (never surrender), 25 (the face of God), 31 (the few), Mar. 6 (sighted sub), Aug. 31 (pass the ammunition), Sept. 7 (no atheists in a foxhole), 17 (definition of courage), Oct. 29 (OK, we'll go), Dec. Intro (uncommon valor)

Race Relations: Dec. 12

Responsibility: Apr. 3, May 19, Oct. 30

Rumors: Feb. 6, 7

Submission: Jan. 19, Apr. 1, 13

Suicide: Feb. 24, Sept. Intro, Nov. 15, Dec. Intro, Dec. 8

Thankfulness: Jan. 20, Mar. 28, May 14, 20, 28, July 15, 21, Aug. 3, 28, Sept. 26, Nov. 23, 30, Dec. 3, 23

Time/Eternity: Jan. 12, 22, Mar. 15, Apr. 24

Treasures in Heaven: Nov. 29, Dec. 27

Trusting God: Jan. 13, 18, 29, 30, 31, Feb. 1, 7, 8, 25, Mar. 3, 8, 23, 26, 31, Apr. 4, 13, May 5, 11, 29, June 15, 18, July 11, 13, 17, 18, 20, 25, 29, Aug. 1, 2, 8, 9, 11, 20, 27, Sept. 15, 17, 21, 29, Oct. 1, 2, 6, 19, 23, Nov. 15, 18, Dec. 10, 16

Understanding Others: June 12, 16, July 6, Oct. 20

Value of Life: Dec. 8

Vision: Sept. 2

War: Mar. 2, Apr. 21, July 31, Aug. 2, 3, Aug. 5, 15, 26, 30, Oct. 12, 13, Dec. 13

War and America: Feb. 2, 24, Apr. 7, 17, 30, June 3, July 2, Aug. 15, 19, 22, 26, 29, 30, Sept. 1, Oct. 13, 27, 31, Nov. 6, Dec.1, 2, 8, 12, 18, 21, 25, 27, 29

Worship: Apr. 28, May 18, 24, June 7, 25, Oct. 24, Nov. 11, 17, Dec. 22

Worry: Jan. 1, Mar. 30, Aug. 14, Oct. 1, 8